Credit, Consumers and the Law

Consumer law, particularly consumer credit law, is characterised by increasingly complex regulation in Western economies. Reacting to the Global Financial Crisis, governments in the UK, the EU, Australia, New Zealand and the United States have adopted new laws dealing with consumer credit, responsible lending, consumer guarantees and unfair contracts. Drawing together authors from all of these jurisdictions, this book analyses and evaluates these initiatives, and makes predictions as to their likely success and possible flaws.

Karen Fairweather is an Associate Lecturer at the TC Beirne School of Law, the University of Queensland. Prior to this she was a lecturer at Durham University in the UK. She has taught contract law, trusts, legal history and civil remedies. She has a particular interest in the history of consumer credit law and has published widely on historical aspects of consumer credit as well as on contemporary developments in the field.

Paul O'Shea was a Senior Lecturer at the TC Beirne School of Law at the University of Queensland and is now principal solicitor and director of O'Shea Lawyers. He is one of Australia's leading researchers in consumer law, particularly consumer credit law. He has taught consumer and commercial law at universities in Australia and throughout Asia and has published extensively in this field. His research has been cited in superior court decisions and by the Australian Commonwealth Treasury in support of legislation regulating consumer credit.

Ross Grantham is a Professor of Commercial Law at the TC Beirne School of Law, the University of Queensland, and the Director of the Australian Centre for Private Law. He is the author of a number of monographs, casebooks and numerous scholarly journal articles, and has co-edited four collections of essays. He is a member of the editorial boards of *The Company Lawyer* and the *Journal of Corporate Law Studies* and is the Australian editor of the *Journal of Business Law*. He was Dean of Law and Head of School at the TC Beirne School of Law between 2007 and 2012, having been Deputy Head of School 2005–2006, and Director of Research 2004–2005.

Markets and the Law

Edited by Geraint Howells
City University of Hong Kong

Markets and the Law is concerned with the way the law interacts with the market through regulation, self-regulation and the impact of private law regimes. It looks at the impact of regional and international organisations (e.g. EC and WTO) and many of the works adopt a comparative approach and/or appeal to an international audience. Examples of subjects covered include trade laws, intellectual property, sales law, insurance, consumer law, banking, financial markets, labour law, environmental law and social regulation affecting the market as well as competition law. The series includes texts covering a broad area, monographs on focused issues and collections of essays dealing with particular themes.

Other titles in the series:

Consumer Protection and Online Auction Platforms
Towards a Safer Legal Framework
Christine Riefa
ISBN 978-0-7546-7710-9

Consumer Debt and Social Exclusion in Europe
Edited by Hans-W. Micklitz and Irina Domurath
ISBN 978-1-4724-4903-0

Codifying Contract Law
International and Consumer Law Perspectives
Edited by Mary Keyes and Therese Wilson
ISBN 978-1-4724-1561-5

For more information on this series, visit www.routledge.com

Credit, Consumers and the Law

After the global storm

Edited by Karen Fairweather, Paul O'Shea and Ross Grantham

Routledge
Taylor & Francis Group
LONDON AND NEW YORK

First published 2017 by Routledge

2 Park Square, Milton Park, Abingdon, Oxfordshire OX14 4RN
711 Third AVenue, New York, NY 10017

Routledge is an imprint of the Taylor & Francis Group, an informa business

First issued in paperback 2018

British Library Cataloguing in Publication Data
A catalogue record for this book is available from the British Library

Library of Congress Cataloging in Publication Data
Names: Consumers, credit and the law symposium (2013 : University of Queensland) | O'Shea, Paul (Australian lawyer and law teacher), editor. | Fairweather, Karen, editor. | Grantham, Ross, editor. | Australian Centre for Private Law, sponsoring body.
Title: Credit, consumers and the law : after the global storm / edited by Paul O'Shea, Karen Fairweather, Ross Grantham.
Description: Abingdon, Oxon ; New York, NY : Routledge, 2016. | Series: Markets and the law | Includes index.
Identifiers: LCCN 2016016771 (print) | LCCN 2016018095 (ebook) | ISBN 9781472452344 (hbk) | ISBN 9781315574752 (e-book) | ISBN 9781317158080 (Web PDF) | ISBN 9781317158073 (ePub) | ISBN 9781317158066 (Mobipocket)
Subjects: LCSH: Consumer credit–Law and legislation–English-speaking countries–Congresses.
Classification: LCC K1096.A6 C655 2016 (print) | LCC K1096.A6 (ebook) | DDC 346.07/3–dc23
LC record available at https://lccn.loc.gov/2016016771

ISBN: 978-1-4724-5234-4 (hbk)
ISBN: 978-1-138-35895-9 (pbk)

Typeset in Baskerville
by Wearset Ltd, Boldon, Tyne and Wear

Contents

Contributors

James Devenney is McCann FitzGerald Chair in International Law and Business, University College Dublin, Ireland.

Kathleen C. Engel is a Professor of Law and Associate Dean for Intellectual Life at Suffolk University, Boston, USA.

Karen Fairweather is an Associate Lecturer at the TC Beirne School of Law at the University of Queensland and a fellow of the Australian Centre for Private Law.

Jodi Gardner is a Lecturer in Law and DPhil Candidate at Corpus Christi College, University of Oxford and Research Fellow at the Centre for Household Assets and Savings Management, University of Birmingham, UK.

Ross Grantham is a Professor of Commercial Law at the TC Beirne School of Law, the University of Queensland, and Director of the Australian Centre for Private Law.

Nicola J. Howell is a Senior Lecturer in Law at the Queensland University of Technology.

Mel Kenny is Rector, Riga Graduate School of Law, Latvia.

Paul O'Shea was a Senior Lecturer at the TC Beirne School of Law at the University of Queensland and is a fellow of the Australian Centre for Private Law. He is now a principal at O'Shea Lawyers.

Onyeka K. Osuji is a Senior Lecturer in Law at the University of Exeter, UK.

Gail Pearson is a Professor of Business Law at the University of Sydney and a member of the Fair Trading Advisory Council and a member of the consultative committee to the Consumer Trader and Tenancy Tribunal.

Kate Tokeley is a Senior Lecturer in Law at the Victoria University of Wellington, New Zealand.

Therese Wilson is an Associate Professor in Law at Griffith University, Brisbane, Australia, and is admitted as a solicitor of the Supreme Court of Queensland.

Acknowledgements

This book came about as the result of a symposium entitled 'Consumers, Credit and the Law' that was held in Brisbane, Australia, in July 2013. The aim of the symposium was to analyse the regulatory responses to the Global Financial Crisis and other developments in consumer law in a number of different jurisdictions.

We would like to express our gratitude to all those who inspired and participated in the very lively and productive day of discussion in Brisbane. For their assistance in staging the event, we would like to say a special thank you to Melissa Reynolds and Beth Williams. We would also like to thank Alison Kirk of Routledge for her enthusiasm for the project and to acknowledge the financial support accorded to the Australian Centre for Private Law by the University of Queensland, which made the event – and hence the book – possible.

Karen Fairweather, Paul O'Shea and Ross Grantham

Table of cases

Australia

European Union

United Kingdom

United States of America

Table of legislation

Australia

Secondary legislation

European Union

New Zealand

South Africa

United Kingdom

Secondary legislation

United States of America

Part I

Issues and themes

1 Consumer law

Paternalism, fragmentation and centralised enforcement

Karen Fairweather, Paul O'Shea and Ross Grantham

1 Introduction

The emergence over the last half-century of a body of law that had a sufficiently homogeneous core that it could be identified as 'consumer law' is one of the major developments in the law of most common law jurisdictions. Although consumer law necessarily rests on the underlying contract between the parties, the extent of legislative intervention and the aims of that legislation have increasingly carved consumer law out as a body of law distinct from the general law of contract. A law of consumer credit emerged as a distinct sub-species of this body of consumer law – distinct in the sense that granting of small loans, the financing of the purchase of consumer goods and residential mortgages were recognised as giving rise to similar issues. Consumer credit has also become more globalised. This was made plain by the Global Financial Crisis (GFC), in which the interconnectedness of the world's financial system was laid bare. It is also apparent in the regulatory responses of individual jurisdictions which demonstrate both remarkable similarities as well as clear divergence.

The chapters in this book seek to analyse the regulatory responses to the GFC and its impact on consumer law generally and consumer credit in particular in a number of different jurisdictions, primarily the United Kingdom, United States of America and Australia. In doing so, the aim is to encourage comparison and to stimulate analysis of the different approaches taken in the different jurisdictions, enabling more general conclusions to be drawn about the appropriate nature and form of regulation. In turn, these general conclusions may be used to inform policy and law making.

2 Themes and issues

As might be expected, the regulatory responses to the GFC and more recent legislative activities reflect the particular features of the jurisdiction in question. These features include the complexities of a federal as opposed to a unitary legislative system, demands of harmonisation within supra-national legal systems such as the European Union (EU), the different effects of the GFC on different jurisdictions, the different times those effects were felt and the changing ideology of those holding political power. Nevertheless, the chapters also reveal a number of important common themes and issues. Of these, three in particular are worth highlighting as representing fundamental changes in the approach to the regulation of consumer credit: the rise of an overtly paternalistic approach, whereby consumers are seen to need to be protected from themselves; moves to address the fragmentation in consumer law and consumer finance regulatory regimes through enhanced convergence; and the increasing centralisation of the enforcement of consumer law through the establishment of powerful national regulators with extensive administrative powers to ensure compliance.

2.1 The rise of paternalism

Classical liberal theory, which underpins the common law of contract[1] and, therefore, consumer law, both justifies and limits what should be done to address unfairness and inequality. John Stuart Mill famously said that 'the only purpose for which power can be rightfully exercised over any member of a civilised community, against his will, is to prevent harm to others. His own good, either physical or moral, is not a sufficient warrant'.[2] In the context of contracts, this may be interpreted as allowing people, in particular consumers, to make bad bargains. It is clearly against paternalism, which favours using regulatory power over consumers 'for their own good'.

While Mill's classical liberalism is usually referred to in discussions of civil society as a whole, he did touch on questions of contracts and trade which he described as 'a social act'.[3] He argued against the control by governments of prices and the quality of goods but he did so for the mostly utilitarian reason that, in his view, it did not work to 'produce the results which it is desired to produce by them'.[4] Mill seemed somewhat conflicted on the 'doctrine of free trade' as he called it. On the one hand he considered that 'restrictions on trade, or on production for the purposes of trade, are indeed restraints and all restraint *qua* restraint is an evil'. On the other, he did identify certain questions, arising out of the potential for harm to others, which may be resolved by the imposition by government of laws to prevent, for instance, frauds, maintenance of public health and the protection of workers in dangerous occupations. Ultimately, these matters should be resolved by the principle that 'leaving people to themselves is always better *ceteris paribus* than controlling them, but that they may be legitimately controlled for these ends is in principle undeniable'. Interestingly, Mill may have been an unconscious philosopher of consumer law since he took most exception to those 'interferences' which are 'objectionable not as infringements on the liberty of the producer or seller but on that of the buyer'.[5]

The intrinsic value of the liberty of buyers or consumers to make choices, even bad ones, in a free market was championed in the 1960s and 1970s by economists such as Milton Freidman,[6] and political scientists such as Robert Nozick.[7] It found legal expression in the work of the so-called 'Chicago School', in particular Richard Posner, which combined law and economics to argue that the proper goal of any legal system regulating contracts, and therefore consumer transactions, was the

1 Patrick S Atiyah, *The Rise and Fall of Freedom of Contract* (Oxford University Press 1979).
2 John Stuart Mill, *On Liberty* (Penguin 1974) 69.
3 Ibid 164.
4 Ibid.
5 Ibid.
6 Milton Friedman, *Capitalism and Freedom* (University of Chicago Press 1962).
7 Robert Nozick, *Anarchy, State and Utopia* (Basic Books 1974).

efficient operation of markets. To the proponents of the law and economics approach even breaches of contracts may be tolerated if they are efficient and economic.[8] Overall, both parties, consumers and suppliers, benefit from participation in economic transactions. If there is a resultant inefficient and uneconomic allocation of resources, for instance a rise in consumer bankruptcies or property repossessions, this indicates a market failure which may justify regulatory intervention. Milton Friedman acknowledged the importance of these market failures when he said that 'the possibility of coordination through voluntary cooperation rests on the elementary – yet frequently denied – proposition that both parties to an economic transaction benefit from it, provided the transaction is bilaterally voluntary and informed'.[9] Consumers should, therefore, if fully informed about their choices, be left to make them.

Thus, properly informing consumers became the principal function of consumer law. The premise was that a properly informed consumer would act in his or her own interests and, therefore, interact with similarly self-interested suppliers to produce a perfectly operating consumer market which maximised benefits for society as a whole. The influence of this thinking in consumer credit law resulted in rafts of legislation mandating comprehensive and detailed disclosure regimes for consumer credit transactions in Australia,[10] the United Kingdom[11] and, even earlier, in the United States.[12] Disclosure and its enforcement dominated consumer law and consumers were perceived as *homo economicus*. 'Truth in lending' became the catch-cry of consumer advocates, legislators and regulators.

In the early 1990s, however, the work of behavioural economists challenged the primal role of disclosure in consumer law. Behavioural economics questions the incentives for real-world consumers to either absorb or act on information supplied to them about their transactions. In 1991, Richard Thaler published *The Winner's Curse: Paradoxes and Anomalies of Economic Life*.[13] Thaler challenged the received economic wisdom by revealing many of the paradoxes that abound even in the most painstakingly constructed transactions. He demonstrated, often with telling practical examples, that markets do not always operate with the trap-like efficiency we impute to them. In 2000, Cass Sunstein, a colleague and collaborator of Thaler, published *Behavioural Law and Economics*.[14] It audaciously challenged the assumptions underlying traditional law and economics (and, therefore, the Posnerian Chicago School of law and economics), saying that they were based on a crude understanding of human behaviour. Sunstein presented new findings in cognitive psychology and behavioural economics which showed that people are frequently both unselfish and over-optimistic; that people have limited willpower and limited

8 R Posner, *Economic Analysis of Law* (4th edn, Little Brown 1992) 131.

9 M Friedman, *Capitalism and Freedom* (University of Chicago Press 1962) 13.

10 Consumer Credit (Queensland) Act 1994 and by the other states 'adopting' the template: Consumer Credit (New South Wales) Act 1995, Consumer Credit (Victoria) Act 1995, Consumer Credit (South Australia) Act 1995, Consumer Credit (Northern Territory) Act 1995 and the Consumer Credit (Australian Capital Territory) Act 1995, Consumer Credit (Western Australia) Act 1995, Consumer Credit (Tasmania) Act 1996.

11 Consumer Credit Act 1974 (UK).

12 Consumer Credit Protection Act 1968 (US) Pub L 90-321.

13 R Thaler, *The Winner's Curse: Paradoxes and Anomalies of Economic Life* (Princeton University Press 1993).

14 C Sunstein, *Behavioral Law and Economics* (Cambridge University Press 2000).

self-control; and that people are 'boundedly' rational in the sense that they have limited information-processing powers and frequently rely on mental short-cuts and rules of thumb.[15]

Taking this research on board, consumer lawyers such as Michael Trebilcock reasoned that if the value consumers put on information in terms of 'making a better choice about what goods or services to buy and on what terms' is not high then 'in a world of information overload, consumer protection instruments that actually generate information that is costly for consumers to interpret or access may be counterproductive'. He suggested that this may be particularly so for statutes 'that mandate detailed disclosure of contents or ingredients, complex details of the price, terms and conditions of a transaction or very specific caveats about the use of the product'.[16] Empirical research in the United States[17] and Australia[18] supported his conclusion. In other words, mandated disclosure in consumer transactions will, by itself, fail to prevent market failures.

Paternalism, formerly derided, became more respectable among scholars seeking to justify more intervention in consumer markets. Sunstein and Thaler argued that 'libertarian paternalism is not an oxymoron',[19] and Colin Camerer and co-authors made the case for 'asymmetric paternalism'.[20] Consumer credit was a prime target for such arguments. As Iain Ramsay wrote in 2005, regulation of consumer credit was moving from 'truth in lending to responsible lending'.[21]

15 Bounded rationality was first propounded as a concept by Herbert Simon in 1972 in 'Theories of Bounded Rationality' in CB McGuire and R Radner (eds), *Decision and Organization* (North-Holland Publishing Company 1972) ch. 8, but in relation to bureaucracy not consumers.

16 M Trebilcock, 'Rethinking Consumer Protection Policy' in C Rickett and T Telfer (eds) *International Perspectives on Consumers' Access to Justice* (Cambridge University Press 2003) 70–75.

17 L Mandell, 'Consumer Perception of Incurred Interest Rates: An Empirical Test of the Efficacy of the Truth-In-Lending Law' (1971) 26 The Journal of Finance 1143; GS Day and WK Brandt, 'Consumer Research and the Evaluation of Information Disclosure Requirements: The Case of Truth in Lending' (1974) 1 The Journal of Consumer Research 21; W Whitford, 'The Functions of Disclosure Regulation in Consumer Transactions' (1973) Wisconsin Law Review 400; WK Brandt, GS Day and T Deutscher, 'Information Disclosure and Consumer Credit Knowledge: A Longitudinal Analysis' (1975) 9 Journal of Consumer Affairs 15; J Davis, 'Protecting Consumers from Overdisclosure and Gobbledygook: An Empirical Look at the Simplification of Consumer-Credit Contracts' (1977) 63 Virginia Law Review 841.

18 Justin Malbon, 'Taking Credit, Report for the Consumer Credit Code Post-Implementation Review' (Tasmania, Department of Justice and Industrial Relations, September 1999) www.creditcode.gov.au which was the basis for Justin Malbon, 'Shopping for Credit: Empirical Study of Consumer Decision-making' (2001) 29 Australian Business Law Review 44. The NCP report itself is *KPMG Consulting NCP Review of the Consumer Credit Code Final Report December 2000*; Justin Malbon 'Predatory Lending' (2005) 33 Australian Business Law Review 224, 236; Paul O'Shea and Carmel Finn, 'Consumer Credit Code Disclosure: Does It Work' (2005) 16 Journal of Banking and Finance Law and Practice 5; Paul O'Shea, Ministerial Council for Consumer Affairs, *Simplification of Pre-Contractual Disclosure in Consumer Credit: Experimental Research and Redesign* (March 2010) 2–4.

19 C Sunstein and R Thaler, 'Libertarian Paternalism is not an Oxymoron' (Working Paper No. 43, Public Law and Legal Theory Workshop, University of Chicago Law School, May 2003) www.law.uchicago.edu/publications/papers/publiclaw.

20 C Camerer, S Issacharoff, G Loewenstein, T O'Donoghue and M Rabin, 'Regulation for Conservatives and the Case for "Asymmetric Paternalism"' (2003) 151 University of Pennsylvania Law Review 1211. For a larger sample of the voluminous literature on this topic see Chapter 2.

21 Iain Ramsay, 'From Truth in Lending to Responsible Lending' in Geraint Howells, Andre Janssen and Reiner Schulze (eds), *Information Rights and Obligations* (Ashgate 2005).

In consumer credit there has always been an apprehension about predatory lending and flawed markets which allow loans to consumers who lack the capacity to repay them without hardship.[22] The Australian *Uniform Consumer Credit Code* of 1996 included, for the first time, as one of the factors which courts may address when considering an unjust contract, whether or not the (consumer) could meet their obligations under the credit contract or at least without substantial hardship.[23] This may have served to discourage irresponsible lending, but such reactive measures were largely ineffective.[24] They were a far cry from a more paternalistic approach which mandated responsible lending so that credit providers would be prohibited from lending in such circumstances. This latter approach leads to a reduction in consumer choice in order to prevent potential consumer harm. It is 'illiberal' in the classical sense. It is paternalistic consumer protection. It may, of course, be necessary particularly for vulnerable consumers.

The intellectual ground work for the paradigm shift towards greater paternalism in consumer credit was well and truly laid by the middle of the first decade of the twenty-first century. Elsewhere in this book is an explication of the gradual adoption of more paternalistic approaches to consumer credit in the UK and European Union around this time. It was not until after the GFC, however, that the United States (at a federal level), New Zealand and Australia mandated pro-active responsible lending regimes.[25] One of the themes of this book, therefore, is how different jurisdictions with different experiences of the GFC produced remarkably similar regulatory responses, all of them more paternalistic than what had gone before. Some of the common features of these responses include: price and product controls; the mandating of responsible lending; and increased powers for newly centralised regulators. Previously fragmented consumer protection regimes became consolidated with greater and more paternalistic powers.

2.2 Curing fragmentation

Fragmentation has been a conspicuous problem in many of the consumer law regimes considered in this book. Fragmentation of mortgage regulation and supervision coupled with the doctrine of 'federal pre-emption'[26] paved the way for 'charter shopping' in the United States in the run-up to the subprime mortgage crisis.[27] 'Charter shopping' was the practice of converting to a different type of charter (for example, national banks converting to national thrift[28] charters or vice versa, or state banks or non-bank lenders converting to national bank or thrift charters) with a view to ensuring that the institution was regulated by the laxest laws and regulators. In particular, the objective was to avoid the application of state anti-predatory

22 Such concerns were evident in the United Kingdom as early as the 1880s in the parliamentary debates on the Bills of Sale Act (1878) Amendment Act 1882.

23 s 70 (2)(l).

24 See Chapter 10.

25 Ibid.

26 That is the doctrine that when state and federal law conflict, federal law prevails as a consequence of the supremacy clause of article 6, s 2 of the Constitution.

27 See Kathleen C Engel and Patricia A McCoy, *The Subprime Virus: Reckless Credit, Regulatory Failure, and Next Steps* (Oxford University Press 2011) ch. 8.

28 A 'thrift' is a savings bank or a savings and loan association.

lending laws which began to proliferate in the first decade of the millennium in response to the increasing concerns about predatory and unsafe lending practices. As Matasar and Pavelka have observed, this wreaked havoc with federal regulators' ability and willingness to keep a tight rein on their regulatees.[29] The result was the practice of 'competition in laxity' among regulators and a race to the bottom in terms of lending practices and underwriting standards among mortgage lenders. The rest is history.

The Dodd–Frank Wall Street Reform and Consumer Protection Act addressed the problem of fragmentation by making the new Consumer Financial Protection Bureau (CFPB) consumer protection regulator of *all* institutions that engage 'in offering or providing a consumer financial product or service'.[30] The CFPB has supervisory, enforcement and rule-making powers. The Act does not, however, prevent states from imposing *higher* levels of consumer protection and has restricted the power of federal pre-emption.[31] State attorneys general are given the power to enforce the provisions of the Consumer Protection Act (that is Title X of the Dodd–Frank Act) in the courts of their states against all persons to which they apply other than national banks and thrifts. They are also empowered to bring such enforcement actions, including against national banks and thrifts, in respect of regulations made by the CFPB.[32]

In the Australian context, the National Consumer Credit Protection Act 2009 (Cth) (NCCPA) was intended to remedy the fragmentation resulting from the vesting of legislative competence for credit in the States and Territories as opposed to the Commonwealth. While the uniform national legislative scheme created in 1996 by the Uniform Consumer Credit Code (UCCC)[33] had gone some way towards reducing this fragmentation, a number of areas, including crucial matters such as licensing, interest rate ceilings and assessments of consumers' capacity to repay, remained matters for the States and Territories. The rationale for Commonwealth regulation was 'the existence of a national market consisting of consumers with uniform characteristics and needs. In such cases Commonwealth regulation under a single regime is efficient and serves the needs of consumers'.[34] In introducing a national scheme, including a national licensing regime, applicable to *both* brokers[35] and credit providers, overseen and operated by a single regulator, the Australian Securities and Investments Commission (ASIC), the NCCPA was a quantum leap in terms of convergence and coherence.

The problem of fragmentation has manifested itself rather differently in the UK. The need to bring conduct of business regulation for *all* financial services under a single regulator with a view to 'ending confusion for consumers, duplication for

29 Ann B Matasar and Debrah D Pavelka, 'Federal Banking Regulators' Competition in Laxity: Evidence from CRA Audits' (1998) 4 International Advances in Economic Research 56, 57.

30 Dodd–Frank Act, s 1002(6). The CFPB does not have supervisory and enforcement authority in respect of banks, thrifts or credit unions with total assets of $10 billion or less: Dodd–Frank Act, s 1025. The Federal Trade Commission will continue to play an enforcement role in respect of non-depositary institutions.

31 Dodd–Frank Act, ss 1044 (for banks) and 1046 (for thrifts).

32 Dodd–Frank Act, s 1042.

33 Through Queensland template legislation: see (n 10).

34 Australian Government, The Treasury, *Financial Services and Credit Reform: Improving, Simplifying and Standardising Financial Services and Credit Regulation* (Green Paper, June 2008) 13.

35 There was no national regime for finance brokers: ibid 9–10.

many firms, and ensuring a single strategic regulatory view across retail financial services'[36] emerged as a priority in the wake of the GFC. With the decision made to transfer responsibility for consumer credit, which was governed by the Consumer Credit Act 1974 (CCA) and included second-charge mortgage lending, from the Office of Fair Trading (OFT) to the newly created Financial Conduct Authority (FCA)[37] by 1 April 2014, the exact design of the regulatory framework that was to apply became a pressing problem. Ultimately, the Government settled on a 'hybrid model', which blends the Financial Services and Market Act 2000 (FSMA) regime with elements of the CCA that have been retained. The result is a complex patchwork of primary legislation contained in two Acts and associated secondary legislation, as well as high-level standards, rules and guidance made by the FCA. Pursuant to its rule-making powers under the FSMA, the FCA has added a specialist Consumer Credit Sourcebook (CONC) to its Handbook. Most of the conduct-related provisions of the CCA and its secondary legislation remained in place after the transfer, but those conduct-related provisions that were repealed were carried across into CONC in the form of rules. A large body of OFT guidance was also carried across into CONC in the form of guidance and, more controversially, rules. The FCA has until 2019 to review the CCA conduct-related provisions with a view to deciding whether to develop FSMA rule-based alternatives.

First-charge mortgage lending is governed by the FSMA regime via the Mortgage Conduct of Business (MCOB) rules and, since 1 April 2013, has been regulated by the FCA. Further changes in the regulation of mortgage lending are imminent, with the transposition of the EU Mortgage Credit Directive (MCD)[38] due in March 2016. Significantly, the Government saw transposition as the occasion for abolishing the awkward regulatory split between first- and second-charge lending that has plagued this area for so long.[39] Second-charge mortgages would be brought within the definition of a 'regulated mortgage contract' so as to bring them within the MCOB rules with the addition of some specifically targeted rules.

Within the EU consumer law landscape the problem of fragmentation appears more intractable. Three facets of fragmentation are evident: the fragmentation created by divergent transposition of minimum harmonisation directives in the different Member States; that which results from diverse national interpretations of the *acquis*' legal concepts (and is exacerbated when national courts refuse to make reference to the CJEU in appropriate cases);[40] and that caused by a '"patchwork" of individual measures that are not "joined up"'.[41] The result is a consumer contract

36 Her Majesty's Treasury and Department for Business Innovation and Skills, *A New Approach to Financial Regulation: Transferring Consumer Credit Regulation to the Financial Conduct Authority* (March 2013) 3.

37 The FCA took over the Financial Services Authority's functions as a conduct of business regulator on 1 April 2013.

38 Directive 2014/17/EU of the European Parliament and of the Council of 4 February 2014 on credit agreements for consumers relating to immovable property and amending Directives 2008/48/EC and 2013/36/EU and Regulation (EU No 1093/2010).

39 Financial Services Authority, *Mortgage Market Review* (Discussion Paper 09/3, October 2009) paras 9.10–9.15.

40 As in the *Abbey National* litigation discussed by Kenny and Devenney in Chapter 11.

41 See Stephen Weatherill, 'The Consumer Rights Directive: How and Why a Quest for "Coherence" has (Largely) Failed' (2012) 49 Common Market Law Review 1279, 1283.

acquis that has been described as 'wildly unsystematic'[42] and lacking in coherence.[43] Unsurprisingly, one of the EU's proposed remedies, a move from a minimum to maximum harmonisation approach, has been met with strong political resistance as is evident from the fate of the (maximum harmonisation) 2008 Proposal for a Directive on Consumer Rights.[44] Consumer contract law inevitably involves contested political questions. The suggestion that the high level of protection provided by some Member States should be watered down in the name of the better functioning of the internal market was bound to be met with hostility. Ultimately, as Weatherill has observed, 'maximum harmonization involves sufficiently radical re-distribution of regulatory competence to call into question the very legitimacy of the EU's law-making pretensions'.[45]

2.3 Centralised enforcement

The third trend evident in the chapters in this book relates to the enforcement of consumer law, and consumer credit in particular. Historically, enforcement in the consumer law context was largely a matter of enforcement of the contract between the parties to the transaction in the ordinary courts.[46] On the market failure rationale of consumer law, the principal regulatory intervention was mandated disclosure and a range of implied terms as to quality and fitness. These obligations were designed to address the informational asymmetries between the consumer and the presumptively more powerful and better informed commercial party.[47] The mandated disclosure and implied terms allowed consumers to make informed and rational decisions about their own preferences and to reduce the transaction costs of the parties. However, once the market failure had been corrected, the parties to the consumer transaction were largely left to their private law rights and remedies. If a consumer decided it was not worth his or her while to seek to enforce the contractual rights in the ordinary courts, then the matter lay where it fell.

However, over the last few decades a very different approach to enforcement has emerged. What we have seen to one degree or another in all of the jurisdictions touched on in this book is a move away from private rights and private enforcement through the ordinary courts to a regime where consumer law is enforced by a central regulator by means of administratively imposed rules, licensing requirements, and financial sanctions, and where individual transaction disputes are dealt with outside of the normal legal process by special-purpose dispute resolution schemes on the basis not of private law rights and duties but on what each party can live with as a practical outcome. This trend was particularly marked in the immediate post-GFC era and, if anything, has accelerated in the last few years as legislatures seek to bolt the stable door.

42 Ibid.
43 See European Commission, *Action Plan on a More Coherent European Contract Law*, COM(2003)68.
44 See Chapter 11.
45 Weatherill (n 41) 1316.
46 Generally, see Jack Beatson and Daniel Friedman, 'Introduction: From "Classical" to Modern Contract Law' in Jack Beatson and Daniel Friedman (eds), *Good Faith and Fault in Contract Law* (Oxford University Press 1997) 8–9.
47 See text following n 11 above.

Although prior to the GFC there were state agencies with considerable powers of enforcement in relation to consumer credit, there was a perception, largely borne of the GFC itself, that these regulators were ineffective and their powers inadequate. The result was legislative reforms designed to create new, powerful and more active central regulators. In Australia, one of the major changes brought about by the NCCPA was the federalisation of consumer regulation and the establishment of the Australian Securities and Investments Commission (ASIC) as the national regulator of consumer credit.[48] ASIC's powers as consumer regulator include not only most of the powers previously held by state-based regulators, but also new additional administrative and regulatory powers,[49] such as the power to issue infringement notices[50] and impose civil penalties, that have turned the enforcement pyramid into an 'enforcement obelisk'.[51] Similarly, in the UK the disestablishment of the OFT and FSA in favour of a new national conduct of business regulator with enhanced powers,[52] the FCA, seemed to reflect a perception of the inadequacies of these agencies. The FCA would, it was announced, adopt a more pro-active and interventionist approach towards supervision and enforcement, with less appetite for risk and a particular focus on intervening earlier in the financial product's life cycle.[53] In the United States, as mentioned, where the presence of a central regulator has been a feature of the general regulatory approach in a wide range of areas since the 1930s,[54] the Dodd–Frank Act established a new federal consumer law regulator, the CFPB with supervisory, enforcement and rule-making powers in respect of institutions offering or providing consumer financial products or services.

The fundamental change that has been brought about in the immediate post-GFC and post-post-GFC periods in the basis and means of enforcement of consumer law appears to be driven by three factors. First, when it comes to the enforcement by consumers of their contractual rights and rights afforded by consumer law generally, there is a structural inequality between consumers and suppliers in that consumers may be practically unable to enforce their rights in the ordinary courts. This inequality arises principally because of two aspects of the ordinary civil justice system. The system is expensive, both relative to the value of the consumer's claims and in absolute terms. The costs of seeking redress in the courts may far exceed the value of the goods or services being purchased by the consumer. It may, therefore, be uneconomic for the consumer to prosecute the claim. The costs of litigation are also significant in absolute terms. As compared with a large, commercial supplier, a consumer may simply be unable to fund litigation. The other factor is delay. The civil justice system is, at best, slow and can be made even slower by tactics adopted by well-advised commercial parties. Although the burden of the delay is slightly different as between claims in respect of consumer goods and consumer credit, the

48 NCCPA, ss 47–53. See also, Paul O'Shea, 'Regulatory Consistency and Powers' in Justin Malbon and Luke Nottage (eds), *Consumer Law and Policy in Australia and New Zealand* (Federation Press 2013) 383.

49 See generally, Gail Pearson, *Understanding Australian Consumer Credit Law: A Practical Guide to the National Consumer Credit Reforms* (CCH Australia 2010).

50 NCCPA, s 331.

51 Paul O'Shea, (n 48) 383.

52 For example, the power to ban financial products.

53 HM Treasury, *A New Approach to Financial Regulation* (Cm 8012, 2011) paras 4.49–4.51.

54 For example, the Securities and Exchange Commission established following the Wall Street Crash.

burden of delay generally falls more heavily on the consumer. The somewhat belated recognition of the obstacles consumers face in enforcing consumer law through litigation has been addressed in some jurisdictions by establishing specialised consumer dispute resolution mechanisms. In the UK, the Financial Ombudsman Service was given statutory powers in 2001 to settle disputes between consumers and UK-based providers of financial services; in Australia, consumer credit matters are now dealt with by one of two alternative dispute resolution schemes: the Financial Ombudsman Service and the Credit and Investments Ombudsman (formerly the Credit Ombudsman Service Limited). The availability of these schemes to consumers is provided for by requirements in the NCCPA that anyone holding a credit licence must be a member of one of these alternative dispute resolution (ADR) schemes.

Second, the new enforcement regime is arguably a necessary consequence of the greater paternalism evident in many of the legislative reforms analysed in this book. As discussed above, the post-GFC regimes in the United Kingdom, United States and Australia all take a much more interventionist approach and seek in many cases to directly regulate who may sell consumer financial products, the content or features of the product being sold and how that product should be sold.[55] In a regime that is premised on the inability of consumers to make rational choices or to protect themselves from abuse and thus the need to protect consumers from themselves, it follows, on the one hand, that it is inappropriate to then expect consumers to have the capacity, let alone resources, to enforce the protective provisions and, on the other hand, that there needs to be a powerful central regulator to watch over and protect consumers.

From one perspective, the changes in the nature and basis of enforcement complete the transition of the essential nature of consumer law. Where historically it could be viewed as a sub-species of the general law of contract law, consumer law now has more in common with administrative law. The contractual rights of the parties to consumer transactions are much less relevant to the content and operation of consumer law than the policy goals and regulatory strategies of the central regulator. However, looking forward, the most important question posed by the centralised, public enforcement of consumer credit rules is whether this regime makes for better consumer law than the preceding, private law regime. This is, of course, a large question and the answers must wait to be informed by empirical evidence. However, there are reasons to approach this question with a degree of scepticism and concern.

First, the paternalism apparent in the enforcement regimes reflects an underlying assumption that the central regulator is better able to know what is best than individual consumers. In support of this assumption, one can point to the potentially greater expertise of the regulator and its greater ability to assimilate information from a wide range of sources and experiences. However, there are also reasons to doubt the appropriateness of this assumption. As mentioned above, recent work in the field of behavioural economics suggests that regulators suffer from the same limitations that ordinary consumers do.[56] Regulators suffer equally from bounded

55 For example, the suitability requirements of the responsible lending obligations.

56 James Cooper and William E Kovacic, 'Behavioral Economics: Implications for Regulatory Behavior' (2012) 41 Journal of Regulatory Economics 41. See also Thaler (n 13) and Trebilcock (n 16).

rationality and flawed heuristics.[57] They are also affected by capture by their stakeholders. Thus, on the one hand, regulators must seek to please (or appease) their political pay masters if they are to survive and, on the other hand, regulators need the cooperation of those they are regulating. As the GFC has shown, and as ASIC has found out to its cost, the large financial institutions and corporations of the world are both too big to fail and too big to gaol.

Second, one may question the use of a centralised enforcement regime in terms of the efficiency of the outcomes. In terms of resource allocation, one of the benefits of private enforcement is that the individual has a strong incentive to pursue only those claims that are worth the candle. Where, however, the enforcement is undertaken by a central regulator expending public funds, it is not clear that the decision to enforce will represent the most efficient allocation of resources. Because the criteria for success of regulatory agencies tend to be more about 'outputs' rather than 'outcomes', a central regulator may take enforcement actions that might not do much for consumers as a whole or may pursue easy targets in preference to more complex, but more serious matters. In Australia, as a result of criticism of its performance,[58] there is some suggestion that ASIC may look to improve its enforcement record by going after 'low hanging fruit'.[59]

Finally, there is a sense that the reforms in the United States, the United Kingdom and Australia were a reaction to the GFC. This is clearly true of the Frank–Dodd Act, but equally the UK reforms were a response to the problems identified by the FSA's *Mortgage Market Review*,[60] and although Australia escaped the immediate effect, the NCCPA was a pre-emptive strike against GFC-type issues arising in the future. While there were undoubtedly serious issues arising out of the way institutions were providing consumer credit, the life cycle of capitalist economies has always been one of boom, bust, scandal and knee-jerk regulation.[61] Regulation is always one step behind the reality of the market and is always a response to the last scandal, not the next.

3 The chapters

The remaining chapters in this book have been organised into three groups. The chapters in Part II are concerned with broad questions about the function of consumer law and who consumer credit is seeking to protect and from what harms. In Chapter 2, Kate Tokeley takes the bull by the horns and suggests that the legal regimes now regulating consumer credit are characterised by a high degree of legal paternalism. That is, the purpose or function of consumer credit regimes is not merely to facilitate choice, but rather to protect consumers from themselves. The chapter goes on to identify weaknesses in current academic theories as to the

57 For example, a regulator, like an ordinary consumer, may suffer from excessive optimism, the benefits of hindsight and a myopic view of the issues.

58 In 2014, the Senate of the Australian Federal Parliament held an inquiry into the performance of ASIC. The Senate's report was not complimentary: Senate Economics References Committee, Parliament of Australia, *Performance of the Australian Securities and Investments Commission* (June 2014).

59 Michael Pascoe, 'Interest-Only-Loans Crackdown: ASIC Protecting Consumers or Feeding the Nanny State?' *Sydney Morning Herald*, 20 August 2015.

60 Financial Services Authority, Mortgage Market Review (n 39).

61 See generally, JK Galbraith, *A Short History of Financial Euphoria* (Penguin 1998).

legitimacy of such a paternalistic approach and to suggest a new multi-factorial approach for determining when paternalism in consumer credit law is justified. This framework for decision making is applied to the problem of consumer over-indebtedness and the proposal to introduce responsible lending legislation in New Zealand.

Chapters 3 and 4 are concerned with the tension now manifest in consumer law and consumer credit law, in particular between the goals of protecting the wider financial system and the goal of ensuring the protection of the individual consumers. In Chapter 3, Gail Pearson develops a typology of the functions of consumer law that distinguishes, on the one hand, the suitability of a product for particular consumers and, on the other hand, the safety of the product for all members of society. Thus, while all consumers should be protected from products that are unsafe, the suitability of the product is necessarily determined by the needs of the particular consumer. The chapter concludes that by preserving a distinction between safety for all and suitability for a particular individual or group, the regulatory regime in Australia is better able to achieve a balance between the preservation of the autonomy of the individual consumer and the need for consumers to be protected. In Chapter 4, Onyeka Osuji explores a similar theme in the context of the responsible lending obligation in the UK. Here, the tension is one between the need to protect the individual consumer from unsuitable financial products and the need for prudential regulation of the financial system as a whole. As Dr Osuji notes, not only do these goals potentially pull in different directions, but they lead to considerable complexity and regulatory overlap. In the UK, as in Australia, although consumer protection and the prudential regulation of the financial system may share similar regulatory techniques, they are undertaken by different regulators and the goals of the two systems of regulation may diverge.

In Chapter 5, Kathleen Engel addresses the problem of complexity in consumer credit products, something certainly not unique to the United States. She argues that complexity enables lenders of credit to extract rents from consumers who do not have sufficient financial literacy to protect themselves. Examining a wide range of common law and legislative attempts in the United States to better regulate the consumer credit market to protect consumers, she concludes that the law is an inherently poor tool to curtail complexity and that law and policy makers should be looking towards extra-legal means to assist consumers to cut through the complexity of consumer credit products. From this perspective, Professor Engel speculates that the internet may provide opportunities for 'choice agent' software to empower consumers by sifting through the complexities of complex products for them, thus clarifying the salient features of those products in terms which consumers can understand and which assist in valid comparisons.

The chapters in Part III are all concerned with the issue of responsible lending, an issue which came to the fore in the aftermath of the GFC and which now forms the cornerstone of consumer credit regulation. In Chapter 6, Nicola Howell examines the issue of the so-called payday loan in Australia. Although very small loans have historically been associated with financial distress and particularly vulnerable consumers, in Australia they only attracted specific regulatory attention in the recent consumer credit reform process. The new regime, which includes the outright banning of very short loans, manifests a departure from traditional disclosure-based regulation in favour of a very much more interventionist and paternalistic approach. In so doing, the new regime highlights the policy tensions in the law between the need for increased accountability for lending practices and the minimising of the potential for the exclusion of some consumers from access to credit altogether.

Picking up on the themes of paternalism and short-term, high-cost loans, Jodi Gardner, in Chapter 7, explores the philosophical bases for legislative intervention in the otherwise private contractual relation between consumer and lender. Identifying 'danger' and 'harm' as exceptions to the libertarian approach to 'freedom of contract', she argues that high-cost credit is a 'dangerous product' that therefore justifies higher levels of state intervention. Free market principles lack application to high-cost credit because the market for these products lacks transparency and fair competition. Moreover, the characteristics of the borrowers, such as their particular vulnerability and the arguably aggressive and potentially abusive conduct of the lenders in this area, attracts the attention of those principles which have historically mitigated strict freedom of contract based on equity. These features not only justify additional regulatory intervention in this market, but also justify restricting the activities of high-cost lenders, such as by interest-rate capping and financial hardship provisions for all credit providers, including utilities.

One of the perceived causes of the GFC and the failure of banks and financial institutions was that too many institutions had lent to borrowers who had little or no hope of ever repaying the loans. Thus, one of the principal objectives of legislative reforms in both the UK and Australia has been to ensure that borrowers are protected from themselves and that lenders act responsibly and refuse to lend where borrowers are likely to be unable to repay the loan. In Chapter 8, Karen Fairweather explores and compares (in the particular context of mortgage lending) the recent reforms in Australia and the UK to the obligation imposed on lenders to adopt responsible lending practices. Although the regimes adopt broadly similar goals and mechanisms, the varying levels of protection, prescription and complexity, and the different enforcement and remedial options, may potentially produce very different outcomes.

An important consequence of the recent legislative reforms, including the responsible lending and suitability requirements and the banning of small loans, has been the effective exclusion of some borrowers, typically the most needy and vulnerable, from access to credit altogether. In Chapter 9, Therese Wilson explores one strategy to address the problems faced by the financially excluded, the funding by government of Community Development Finance Institutions (CDFIs). While these institutions exist to address financial exclusion, a central issue is in how to identify those bodies that are indeed performing the desirable public service and to distinguish other 'fringe' credit providers. This requires criteria to define the boundaries that exist between all forms of social enterprise and conventional for-profit enterprises and, in the consumer sector, the boundaries between genuine CDFIs, for-profit lenders and fringe credit providers. Dr Wilson suggests that an articulated social purpose or mission is an appropriate and practical criterion. This would involve evidence of the social purpose or mission being operationalised by the organisation, guiding its activities, and this would in turn involve some profit sacrifice.

Part IV contains chapters that address the issue of unfair contract terms. In Chapter 10, Paul O'Shea examines the unfair contract terms legislation adopted in the Australian Consumer Law (ACL) in the wake of the GFC. Standard term contracts challenge effective freedom of contract for consumers as they are not the subjects of negotiation or competition, are frequently non-transparent and are almost never read by consumers. Historically, attempts by the courts and previous legislation to remedy 'unjust contracts' or 'unconscionable conduct' failed because they were situationally specific and did not address the structural nature of consumer transactions. The unfair contract terms provisions in the ACL, however, are now focused on the issue of structural inequality. The increased variety of remedies available to both regulators and consumers allow for the almost a priori prohibition of unfair terms in consumer contracts. Yet, the ACL also achieves a balance between consumer paternalism and consumer autonomy by excluding from the scope of the unfair contract 'core terms' such as price and description of goods. In Chapter 11, Mel Kenny and James Devenney explore unfair contract terms in the UK in light of the momentous decision of the Supreme Court in *OFT v Abbey National plc*,[62] in which it was held that terms on bank charges were exempted from the unfairness test. This decision has left the demarcation of the unfairness assessment, as between exempted 'core' or 'price' terms and assessable 'peripheral' and/or contingent terms, under the Unfair Terms Directive (UTD), as implemented in the Unfair Terms in Consumer Contracts Regulations (UTCCR), in a state of disarray. Professors Kenny and Devenney evaluate the fragility of the distinctions drawn in *Abbey National*, placing the unfairness exemption in its disjointed context, which includes the Supreme Court's failure to refer the UTD interpretation to the Court of Justice of the European Union and the attempt to correct the law in the Consumer Rights Act 2015. The chapter concludes that the fragility of the tentative demarcation between core and peripheral terms and the inadequacy of the approach taken in the recent Consumer Rights Act 2015 will inevitably lead to a complex re-litigation of *Abbey National* and the issues of what constitutes an unfair contract term in the UK.

The final chapter returns to the issue of the fragmentation in consumer law, this time in the context of surety agreements and the maze that is EU law. Professors Devenney and Kenny observe that the European project to harmonise consumer law, however worthwhile and sound the policy reasons for which it has been undertaken, has in fact led to the horizontal fragmentation of the private law of individual Member States. Contracts of surety or guarantees by their atypical poly-contextual nature present challenges for the harmonisation of EU private consumer law. These challenges have to date proven too great, with the result that the law in EU Member States is now confused and complex. Professors Devenney and Kenny argue that a dual-track strategy which uses both legislative and non-legislative harmonisation to respond to such poly-contextuality may be the only answer.

62 [2009] UKSC 6, [2010] 1 AC 696.

Part II

Functional perspectives

2 It's for your own good

Legal paternalism and New Zealand consumer credit laws

Kate Tokeley

1 Introduction

New Zealand consumers make choices every day about what services and goods to purchase. Some of these choices are arguably *poor* choices that appear to decrease our welfare. Many of us choose to buy unhealthy foods, not save enough for our retirement, spend money on gambling, purchase large quantities of alcohol, engage in dangerous sporting activities, smoke cigarettes and tan ourselves under sunbeds. The seemingly *poor* consumer choices that this chapter will focus on are those that relate to credit. Research published in late 2008 showed that many New Zealand consumers make seemingly *poor* choices about how much to borrow and on what terms.[1]

This chapter examines the issue of whether the law should intervene to protect consumers from themselves.[2] Often a debate about this kind of law reverts to an exchange of broad, unexamined assertions. Those opposing the proposed law might brush it aside as too paternalistic or an example of the nanny state; those in favour make vague assertions about the need for consumer protection. The recent introduction of responsible lending obligations into New Zealand credit law has generated discussion about the legitimacy of paternalism.[3] When submissions were called for on the initial proposal to impose responsible lending obligations, the opinions were varied. The majority of submissions supported adding responsible lending

1 Jaimie Legge and Anne Heynes, *Beyond Reasonable Debt Part 1: A Background Report on the Indebtedness of New Zealand Families* (Research Report 8/08, Families Commission and Retirement Commission 2008) www.familiescommission.org.nz/web/beyond-reasonable-debt/part-one.html accessed 12 December 2014; New Zealand Ministry of Consumer Affairs, *Review of the Operation of the Credit Contracts and Consumer Finance Act 2003* (Discussion Paper, September 2009) www.consumeraffairs.govt.nz/legislation-policy/policy-reports-and-papers/discussion-papers/review-of-the-operation-of-the-credit-contracts-and-consumer-finance-act-2003 accessed 12 December 2014.

2 This chapter is based in part on some of the ideas previously published by the author in two essays. See Kate Tokeley, 'Consumer Law and Paternalism: A Framework for Decision-making' in Susy Frankel (ed), *Learning from the Past, Adapting for the Future: Regulatory Reform in New Zealand* (LexisNexis 2011) 267 and 'Consumer Law and Paternalism: A Framework for Decision-making' in Susy Frankel and Deborah Ryder (eds), *Recalibrating Behavior: Smarter Regulation in a Global World* (LexisNexis 2013) 265.

3 The responsible lending obligations were added to the Credit Contracts and Consumer Finance Act 2003 (NZ) on 27 May 2014. Section 2(5) of the Credit Contracts and Consumer Finance Amendment Act 2014 (NZ) specifies that all amendments will be in force no later than a year after the Act received royal assent, which was on 6 June 2014.

provisions to the Credit Contracts and Consumer Finance Act 2003 (NZ) (CCCFA).[4] There were, however, some concerns expressed about the paternalistic nature of the proposal. For example, the Auckland Law Society was of the view that the majority of consumers would consider the proposal 'paternalistic and invasive'.[5] The Bank of New Zealand submission argued that ultimately it should be the borrowers' prerogative when to borrow, not the banks'.[6] On the other side of the debate, the Regulatory Impact Statement on the proposed New Zealand legislation primarily justified the proposal by claiming it to be necessary for 'consumer protection'.[7]

The aim of this chapter is to use the example of consumer credit law to develop a useful framework for decision making about the legitimacy of paternalism.[8] Without such a framework there is a danger that serious debate about paternalism is neglected. It is not the goal of this chapter to argue for an exact point at which to draw the line between individual liberty and paternalistic legal intervention. The goal is to identify the kinds of factors that should be addressed in any debate on the topic and in doing so to identify the reasons as to why in some cases it might be legitimate to protect consumers from themselves.

2 New Zealand consumer credit law and reform

The regulation of consumer credit in New Zealand has recently undergone a substantial review. After considerable consultation, Parliament passed major amendments, including the introduction of responsible lending obligations to the CCCFA on 27 May 2014. Section 2(5) of the Credit Contracts and Consumer Finance (CCCF) Amendment Act 2014 (NZ) specifies that all amendments will be in force no later than a year after the Act received royal assent, which was on 6 June 2014. The CCCFA regulates all consumer credit contracts in New Zealand.[9] Prior to the recent amendments, the prevailing approach was to require adequate levels of

4 See New Zealand Ministry of Consumer Affairs, *Credit Contracts & Consumer Finance Amendment Bill (Consultation Draft)* (Submission Summary, June 2013) 16 www.consumeraffairs.govt.nz/pdf-library/legislation-policy-pdfs/CCCF-Amendment-Bill-Consultation-Draft-Submissions-Summary-June-2013.pdf accessed 12 December 2014.

5 See submission by Auckland District Law Society Inc., 'Credit Contracts and Consumer Finance Amendment Bill Exposure Draft' (Submissions to the Ministry of Consumer Affairs, 24 May 2012) 5 www.consumeraffairs.govt.nz/legislation-policy/policy-reports-and-papers/summary-submissions/credit-review-2013-submissions-on-cccf-amendment-bill-exposure-draft accessed 12 December 2014.

6 See submission by Bank of New Zealand, 'Credit Contracts and Consumer Finance Amendment Bill (Exposure Draft)' (Submissions to the Ministry of Consumer Affairs, 25 May 2012) www.consumeraffairs.govt.nz/legislation-policy/policy-reports-and-papers/summary-submissions/credit-review-2013-submissions-on-cccf-amendment-bill-exposure-draft accessed 12 December 2014.

7 See generally, *Responsible Lending Requirements for Consumer Credit Providers* (Regulatory Impact Statement, October 2011) www.consumeraffairs.govt.nz/pdf-library/CCCFA-RIS-Responsible-Lending-Requirements-for-Consumer-Credit-Providers.pdf accessed 12 December 2014.

8 The Organisation for Economic Co-operation and Development has produced several papers that examine the issue of regulatory reform in general terms. The report most relevant to issues of paternalism is Peter Lunn, *Regulatory Policy and Behavioural Economics* (OECD Publishing 2014) www.oecd.org/regreform/regulatory-policy/behavioural-economics.htm accessed 12 December 2014. The report provides examples of how behavioural economics is influencing policy making but does not develop any kind of framework for decision making about the legitimacy of paternalism.

9 'Consumer credit contracts' are defined as those that are 'primarily for personal, domestic or household purposes': CCCFA, s 11.

information disclosure in order to allow consumers to make the best decision for themselves.[10] The Act aimed to protect consumers by providing meaningful disclosure of key information before the consumer became irrevocably committed to the contract. The imposition of disclosure requirements remains central. In addition, the Act imposes some limits on the conduct of lenders. For example, there is a prohibition on oppressive credit contracts and unreasonable fees and there is some protection for consumers in cases of unforeseen hardship.[11] Prior to the recent reform there was, however, no requirement that lenders behave responsibly when loaning money to consumers.

In 2011 a New Zealand Financial Summit brought together people from community groups, budgeting services, non-government organisations, banks, financial regulators and credit providers to consider appropriate responses to consumer credit problems. The participants concluded that the CCCFA 2003 was, at that time, not providing sufficient consumer protection from unscrupulous lenders. They supported the idea of following Australia's lead by introducing legislation to require responsible lending.[12]

The recommendations at the Summit were finally brought to fruition in the CCCF Amendment Act 2014.[13] When section 9 of the CCCF Amendment Act 2014 came into force, a new Part 1A was added into the principal Act which places a statutory obligation for lenders when entering consumer credit contracts to be responsible lenders. Lenders of credit to consumers are expected to exercise reasonable care and skill in the provision of credit.[14] Not only do they have to provide consumers with adequate information expressed in a clear, concise and intelligible manner, they also have to ensure that the terms of the credit contract are appropriate for the consumer.[15] Specifically, the lender is required to make reasonable inquiries as to the consumer's financial position and their credit requirements so as to be satisfied that the credit contract will meet the consumer's objectives and that the consumer can be expected to make payments under the agreement without suffering substantial hardship.[16]

Unlike the Australian credit law reform, the New Zealand reform does not include a cap on interest rates.[17] New Zealand policy makers are counting on the amendments that require responsible lending to adequately encourage lenders to

10 Ibid sch 1.

11 Ibid ss 41–44 (unreasonable fees), ss 55–59 (unforeseen hardship) and ss 117–131 (oppressive credit contracts).

12 The Australian responsible lending obligations can be found in the National Consumer Credit Protection Act 2009 (Cth), ch. 3.

13 A breach of the responsible lending principles will not necessarily prohibit the enforcement of the credit contract. Instead, the court can ban the lender from acting as a creditor if they have breached the responsible lending obligations more than once. In addition, the Commerce Commission can take civil proceedings for breach of the principles.

14 See s 9C(2)(a).

15 See s 9C(3)(a), (b) and (c).

16 See s 9C(3)(a). The Consumer Affairs Minister is to develop a Responsible Lending Code to provide detailed guidance to lenders on how to meet their responsibilities: ss 9E and 9F.

17 The Australian National Consumer Credit Protection Amendment (Enhancements) Act 2012 (Cth) imposes a cap of 48 per cent on the cost of credit for all regulated loans.

behave more responsibly and thus drive interest rates down without the need for specific bright line caps.[18]

3 What is legal paternalism and how paternalistic are various consumer credit laws?

For the purposes of this chapter, legal paternalism will be viewed in broad terms as any law that has the goal of re-shaping consumer behaviour in order to increase consumer welfare.[19] These laws operate by limiting the consumer's liberty so as to coerce or nudge consumers into making what the government considers to be a *better* choice. The restriction of liberty can range from minor to extreme.

At the minor end of the spectrum are interventions that encourage, rather than coerce, the consumer to make *better* choices.[20] These interventions are sometimes called soft paternalism. Examples include taxes on tobacco, plain packaging on tobacco, opt-out retirement savings schemes and restrictions on alcohol advertising. Although advocates of soft paternalism argue that such policies completely preserve freedom of choice, this is not entirely accurate.[21] Soft paternalistic interventions work by deliberately imposing an obstacle to the consumer choosing the *detrimental behaviour*. They can cause a product to have a higher price or be less easily available, or they might make it harder to receive information about the product or require the consumer to take the time and effort to opt out of the government's preferred option. Unlike hard paternalism, however, these interventions do not attempt to completely remove consumers' ability to make the *poor* choice. In the area of credit law, a law requiring warnings about a risky credit product would be an example of soft paternalism. The law discourages, but does not force, the consumer to avoid purchasing a particular credit product.

At the more extreme end of the spectrum the law attempts to coerce the consumer into making the *better* choice. This form of paternalism, where a consumer's liberty is severely restricted, is sometimes called hard paternalism.[22] Examples of hard paternalism include bans on the sale of products such as flammable nightwear, unsafe toys, untested medicines and recreational drugs. In the area of credit law, interest rate caps are an example of hard paternalism because they ban a category

18 See Chris Tremain, 'Tougher Laws for Loan Sharks' (2 April 2012) www.beehive.govt.nz/release/tougher-laws-loan-sharks accessed 14 June 2016.

19 Several scholars have grappled with the question of how to define paternalism and have arrived at different conclusions. See, for example, Thaddeus Pope, 'Counting the Dragon's Teeth and Claws: The Definition of Hard Paternalism' (2004) 20 Georgia State University Law Review 659; Gerald Dworkin, 'Paternalism' in Robert Ausi (ed), *The Cambridge Dictionary of Philosophy* (2nd edn, Cambridge University Press 1995); Peter Suber 'Paternalism' in Christopher B Gray (ed), *Philosophy of Law: An Encyclopaedia* (Garland Publishing Co. 1999).

20 Richard Thaler and Cass Sunstein, *Nudge: Improving Decisions about Health, Wealth, and Happiness* (Penguin Books 2009). Thaler and Sunstein argue that soft paternalism is a legitimate form of government intervention.

21 Ibid 5: 'we strive to design policies that maintain or increase freedom of choice'.

22 Some scholars also use the term 'hard paternalism' to refer to interventions that override voluntary decisions and 'soft paternalism' to mean interventions that restrict behaviour that is not substantially voluntary. See, for example, Thaddeus Pope, 'Is Public Health Paternalism Really Never Justified? A Response to Joel Feinberg' (2005) 30 Oklahoma City University Law Review 121, 122. This is not how the terms are used in this chapter.

of products from the market. The consumer no longer has the freedom to choose these products, as they will no longer be available. The introduction of responsible lending obligations into New Zealand credit law is also an example of hard paternalism. If the lender considers that the repayment of the credit is likely to cause substantial hardship to the consumer, the result will be that the consumer is unable to purchase that credit product. The consumer does not have the freedom to say: 'I know the risks and I still choose to enter this credit agreement.' It is not a mere nudge or discouragement. Responsible lending laws coerce the consumer to make the decision that is considered, by the government, to be the *better* choice. The New Zealand Regulatory Impact Statement on responsible lending suggests that the restrictions on lending are analogous to the 'fitness for purpose' guarantee under the Consumer Guarantees Act 1993 (NZ).[23] This comparison, however, is not entirely accurate. The fitness for purpose guarantee means, for example, that a supplier cannot supply a consumer with a lawn mower that is incapable of mowing lawns. The responsible lending obligations are more analogous to not allowing a supplier to sell a lawn mower to a person who has a bad back and is likely to suffer back pain if they use a lawn mower.

In assessing whether a particular intervention is paternalistic, it is crucial to assess the goal of the intervention. Some consumer laws do not have the goal of re-shaping consumer behaviour in order to protect consumers from themselves. These laws are not paternalistic. For example, laws that aim to ensure consumers make voluntary and fully informed purchasing decisions should not be categorised as paternalistic. The New Zealand credit disclosure laws are an example of non-paternalistic consumer laws. The goal is to improve consumer information in order to allow consumers to more effectively choose in line with their own preferences. The disclosure requirements also aim to make it easier for consumers to compare alternative credit options so they can effectively choose which one they prefer. The intention is not to guide or force consumers to make choices that the government perceives as being in consumers' best interests. Thus, the New Zealand approach to consumer credit laws prior to the current reforms was a non-paternalistic one.

The issue of assessing whether a particular law is paternalistic can be complicated by the fact that some laws have both paternalistic goals (protecting consumers from themselves) and non-paternalistic goals (protecting other people from being harmed by the consumer's behaviour). For example, tobacco regulation might be said to have both the paternalistic goal of reducing consumer harm and the non-paternalistic goal of reducing the costs imposed on the health system by smoking-related illnesses. The existence of additional non-paternalistic goals might strengthen the justifications for the regulation; it should not, however, mask the reality of the paternalistic component of the regulation. In the area of credit law it might be argued that responsible lending laws have the non-paternalistic goal of protecting the rest of society and the economy as a whole from the negative effects of reckless borrowing. However, this is not the stated goal of the proposed New Zealand responsible lending laws. The Credit Contracts and Financial Services Law Reform Bill and credit reform policy documents refer to the purpose of the law being to protect vulnerable consumers of credit.[24]

23 See *Responsible Lending Requirements for Consumer Credit Providers* (n 7) 10.

24 See Credit Contracts and Financial Services Law Reform Bill (Explanatory Note). See also ibid 7.

4 Current academic theories on the legitimacy of paternalism

Whether a paternalistic legal intervention can ever be justifiable has been the subject of much legal, philosophical and economic debate for hundreds of years. Plato, Aristotle and Thomas Aquinas all accepted that people should be protected not only from others but also from themselves.[25] In the 1960s and 1970s, several scholars argued in favour of some legal paternalism. For example, John Locke and John Rawls maintained that paternalism is acceptable due to the social contract, in which human beings hand over some of their rights to the state in order to attain social order and receive protection.[26] Gerald Dworkin argued that paternalism is justified for decisions that are far-reaching, potentially dangerous and have irreversible consequences.[27]

Scholars on the other side of the debate have argued against legal paternalism. As far back as the mid-1800s, John Stuart Mill argued against legal paternalism. He claimed that the law was only justified in exercising power over people if its aim was to prevent harm to others.[28] He was against any legal intervention that limited a person's freedom in order to make that person happier.[29] Paternalistic consumer laws, such as responsible lending obligations, do just this; they prevent or discourage certain consumer behaviour for the consumer's own good.

Anti-paternalism is closely aligned with classical contract theory, which is based on principles of freedom of contract and sanctity of contract.[30] Paternalistic interventions, such as responsible lending obligations, interfere with these principles. They attempt to influence the types of contract that credit consumers enter into. In addition, they allow consumers to escape contractual obligations and impose obligations on credit suppliers beyond those that would be voluntarily assumed in a free market.

Neoclassical economic theory also firmly rejects paternalism as a goal of consumer regulation. This theory is rooted in the view that in most situations a free market will produce a better result than government regulation. It is based on the assumption that fully informed consumers and suppliers in a free market will make rational choices that are in line with their preferences and have the best chance of improving their welfare.[31] This is the polar opposite of the assumption

25 Alan Ebenstein and William Ebenstein, *Introduction to Political Thinkers* (Wadsworth Group 2002).

26 Pete Laslett, 'Introduction' in John Locke, *Two Treatises of Government: A Critical Edition with an Introduction and Apparatus Criticus* (Cambridge University Press 1960); John Rawls, *A Theory of Justice* (Harvard University Press 1971).

27 Gerald Dworkin, 'Paternalism' (1972) 56 The Monist 64.

28 John Stuart Mill, *On Liberty* (JW Parker 1859) ch. 1.

29 Ibid.

30 See *Printing and Numerical Registering Co v Sampson* (1875) LR 19 Eq 462, 465 (CA). See also Patrick S Atiyah, *The Rise and Fall of Freedom of Contract* (Oxford University Press 1979); Jack Beatson and Daniel Friedmann, 'From Classical to Modern Contract Law' in Jack Beatson and Daniel Friedmann (eds), *Good Faith and Fault in Contract Law* (Oxford University Press 1995).

31 Richard Posner, *Economic Analysis of Law* (7th edn, Aspen Publishers 2007) 17. He states that 'rationality means little more to an economist than a disposition to choose, consciously or unconsciously an apt means to whatever ends the chooser happens to have'. See Richard Epstein, 'The Neoclassical Economics of Consumer Contracts' (2007–2008) 92 Minnesota Law Review 803. See also Ministry of Consumer Affairs, *The Economic Context of the Ministry of Consumer Affairs* (1999). This policy paper emphasises the role of the law in removing impediments to voluntary and informed exchanges, especially by reducing transaction costs. Transactional costs include, for example, the costs to consumers of obtaining relevant information and the compliance costs to businesses of labelling laws.

behind paternalistic intervention that there are times when consumers make choices that decrease their welfare.

The assumption of consumer rationality has been challenged by recent developments in the area of behavioural economics. Research has shown that consumers in a free market do not always act rationally by entering transactions that will maximise their self-interests. They make mistakes because they suffer from irrational thinking, information-processing limitations, self-control problems, status quo bias, susceptibility to framing effects and misperceptions about the costs and benefits of certain products.[32] For example, studies have shown that consumers with a higher default risk may irrationally choose a credit card with a lower interest rate and a higher late payment fee than one with a higher interest rate and a lower late payment fee.[33] The findings of behavioural economics raise important questions for consumer regulators. The various responses given by anti-paternalists to these findings are discussed in Section 5.

It has been found that many consumers make *poor* credit decisions for the following types of reason:

- They may struggle with the complexity of financial information about concepts such as interest rates and default fees.
- They can be susceptible to framing. For example, one study found recipients of junk mail advertising short-term loans were more likely to take up the offer when a photograph of a woman's face was included in the advertisement.
- Many consumers of credit suffer from overconfidence. They may be overly optimistic about both their ability to control future spending and their future income and overestimate their ability to pay back a loan.
- Many consumers suffer from poor self-control around spending and saving.
- Consumers often misperceive costs and benefits. They are liable to overspend because they overestimate the beneficial impact of a purchased item.[34]

32 Peter Diamond and Hannu Vartiainan (eds), *Behavioural Economics and its Applications* (Princeton University Press 2007); Melvin Aron Eisenberg, 'The Limits of Cognition and the Limits of Contract' (1995) 47 Stanford Law Review 211 (describing how limits of cognition provide a rationale for the non-enforcement of certain kinds of contract); Christine Jolls, Cass Sunstein and Richard Thaler, 'A Behavioural Approach to Law and Economics' (1998) 50 Stanford Law Review 1471, 1545; Russell B Korobkin and Thomas S Ulen, 'Law and Behavioural Science: Removing the Rationality Assumption from Law and Economics' (2000) 88 California Law Review 1051; William Samuelson and Richard Zeckhauser, 'Status Quo Bias in Decision Making' (1988) 1 Journal of Risk and Uncertainty 7. See also New Zealand Ministry of Economic Development, *Behavioural Analysis for Policy: New Lessons from Economics, Philosophy, Psychology, Cognitive Science and Sociology* (New Zealand Ministry of Economic Development 2006).

33 Oren Bar-Gill, 'Seduction by Plastic' (2004) 98 Northwestern University Law Review 1373; Oren Bar-Gill, 'The Behavioral Economics of Consumer Contracts' (2008) 92 Minnesota Law Review 749. See also Richard Epstein, 'Behavioral Economics: Human Errors and Market Correction' (2006) 73 University of Chicago Law Review 111. Epstein argues that the findings of behavioural economics do not warrant legal intervention. Oren Bar-Gill responds to Epstein's arguments by arguing that the findings of behavioural economics show that consumers make systemic mistakes in certain markets, and that sellers' strategic responses to take advantage of these mistakes can reduce welfare and potentially justify legal intervention.

34 See generally, Richard Tooth, *Behavioural Economics and the Regulation of Consumer Credit* (New Zealand Law Foundation 2012). See also Iain Ramsay, 'From Truth in Lending to Responsible Lending' in Geraint Howells, Andre Janssen and Reiner Schuls (eds), *Information Rights and Obligations* (Ashgate 2005) ch. 4.

Scholars such as Richard Thaler and Cass Sunstein argue that the new insights into consumer behaviour justify soft paternalism, where a consumer is nudged rather than coerced into making better choices. This approach is described as 'libertarian paternalism'.[35] Thaler and Sunstein maintain that it is permissible for the government to intervene in ways that retain freedom of choice but help consumers to act according to their 'real' or 'deep' preferences.[36]

Advocates of libertarian paternalism do not support hard paternalism. They would therefore not be in favour of responsible lending laws. These laws do not simply nudge consumers into making better decisions. They remove consumer choice in respect of what are considered high-risk, dangerous credit products. In contrast, Sarah Conley makes the case for hard forms of paternalism in her 2013 book *Against Autonomy*.[37] Like Thaler and Sunstein, her concern is to help consumers to achieve their 'real' goals; however, she advocates using hard paternalism. Conley argues that consumers are often irrational and thwart the achievement of their own goals. Therefore consumers' goals would, in many situations, be achieved more efficiently if government were simply to prevent them from behaving according to their own decisions. She claims that soft paternalism 'fails to give us the results we want, because people can still have options to pursue bad courses of action'.[38] Her theory supports adopting responsible lending laws.

Another branch of paternalism that has developed in response to the findings of behavioural economics is asymmetric paternalism.[39] Under this theory, a paternalistic regulation is legitimate if it creates larger benefits for those who make errors while inflicting little or no harm on those who are fully rational. In the case of responsible lending laws, the idea of asymmetric paternalism might suggest caution. The relevant question would be to what extent the responsible lending law might harm low-income consumers who happen to also be rational and capable of managing their finances effectively. Responsible lending laws might result in these consumers being prohibited from accessing credit that might only be a problem for a less capable and rational consumer.

5 Anti-paternalist responses to the findings of behavioural economics

The findings of behavioural economics undermine the neoclassical, anti-paternalist conception of a market populated by rational welfare-enhancing consumers, thus weakening the foundation of one of the main lines of reasoning used against paternalism. Nevertheless, many anti-paternalist scholars remain opposed to legal

35 Richard H Thaler and Cass R Sunstein, 'Libertarian Paternalism' (2003) 93 American Economic Review 175; Thaler and Sunstein, *Nudge* (n 20).

36 See, for example, Thaler and Sunstein, 'Libertarian Paternalism' (n 35); Cass R Sunstein and Richard H Thaler 'Libertarian Paternalism is not an Oxymoron' (2003) 70 University of Chicago Law Review 1159; Thaler and Sunstein, *Nudge* (n 20); Daniel Ariely, *Predictably Irrational: The Hidden Forces that Shape our Decisions* (Harper Collins 2010).

37 Sarah Conley, *Against Autonomy* (Cambridge University Press 2013). Conley favours hard paternalism over soft paternalism.

38 Ibid 8.

39 See Colin Camerer and others, 'Regulation for Conservatives: Behavioral Economics and the Case for "Asymmetric Paternalism"' (2002–2003) 151 University of Pennsylvania Law Review 1211.

paternalism.[40] Indeed, it is difficult to argue that the findings of behavioural economics, in and of themselves, justify the government stepping in and manipulating or coercing consumers into choosing differently whenever it thinks consumers are making any kind of mistake. If that were the case, there should be laws against purchasing uncomfortably tight clothing. There are two objections to paternalistic consumer laws that are not inconsistent with an acceptance of the findings in behavioural economics that consumers in a free market appear to act irrationally at times. Both objections are based on ideas about freedom.

The first objection is about the relationship between freedom and welfare. It says that although behavioural economics might show that consumers seem to behave irrationally, allowing consumers to retain freedom of choice remains the most reliable, albeit less than perfect, way of enhancing consumer welfare.[41] Paternalistic laws are said to be objectionable because they make the mistake of assuming that the government is better equipped than consumers to determine what is in consumers' best interests. This, it is argued, is particularly worrying when it is accepted that the government decision makers themselves have cognitive limitations and are prone to error.[42] In the case of responsible lending legislation, not only is the government making decisions on behalf of consumers, it is also handing over decision making responsibility to lenders. Presumably lenders, like borrowers, can make irrational decisions.

It is difficult for governments to deduce consumers' true preferences by assessing what the consumer would have done if he or she had the ability to process all information, no self-control problems and no cognitive biases. Decisions about credit are not straightforward. One writer asks questions such as whether it is worse to let the lighting bill go 60 days behind or borrow for the fourth pay period in a row from a payday lender.[43] He concludes that the likely answer may well be not paying the lighting bill, because the utility company might turn off the electricity. Many consumer decisions are complicated by the fact that consumers themselves often have to choose between sets of conflicting preferences. Their short-term preference might be to eat unhealthily, save little, extend their credit or smoke cigarettes, whereas if asked what their long-term preferences are, they may say that they want to lose weight, save more, have less debt and stop smoking. Moreover, consumers are not a homogenous group with identical preferences. One consumer may prefer to take the risk of borrowing and be happy to suffer a subsequent level of financial hardship in order to access money immediately; another consumer may wish they had more self-control about spending and borrowing. These differences in

40 See, for example, Mario J Rizzo and Douglas Glen Whitman, 'The Knowledge Problem of New Paternalism' (2009) BYU Law Review 905. See also Mario J Rizzo and Douglas G Whitman, 'Little Brother is Watching You: New Paternalism on the Slippery Slopes' (2009) 51 Arizona Law Review 685; Gregory Mitchell, 'Why Law and Economics' Perfect Rationality Should not be Traded for Behavioral Law and Economics' Equal Incompetence' (2002) 91 Georgetown Law Review 67; J Wright and D Ginsburg, 'Behavioural Law and Economics: Its Origins, Fatal Flaws, and Implications for Liberty' (2012) 106(3) Northern University School of Law Review 1033.

41 See, for example, Rizzo and Whitman, 'The Knowledge Problem of New Paternalism' (n 40); Epstein, 'The Neoclassical Economics of Consumer Contracts' (n 31).

42 Edward Glaeser, 'Paternalism and Psychology' (2006) 73 University of Chicago Law Review 133.

43 See Ronald J Mann, 'After the Great Recession: Regulating Financial Services for Low- and Middle-Income Communities' (2012) 69 Washington and Lee Law Review 729, 746.

consumer preferences between individuals and across time make policy decisions about welfare complex and problematic.[44]

Scholars such as Rizzo and Whitman argue that the paternalists believe that they are implementing policies that improve consumer welfare according to consumers' 'true' preferences, but are in fact implementing policies based on what the paternalists think are the 'right' preferences.[45] Robert Sugden argues that in situations where consumer preferences are unstable, there is inherent value in consumers having the opportunity to make their own choices, even if these choices sometimes appear irrational.[46]

Anti-paternalists are likely to be concerned that responsible lending laws ask one party to a contract (in this case the lender) to determine the suitability of a product for the other party (the consumer). They might argue that it is more appropriate to limit the lender's obligation to clearly explaining the nature and risks of the product and that the consumer should have the final decision as to whether to proceed with the credit contract. Suppliers of many other questionable products are not under an obligation to determine consumer suitability. For example, a supplier of extremely high-heeled shoes is not obliged to refuse to sell these shoes to a consumer who has bunions and foot problems.

The second remaining objection to legal paternalism is also based on the idea of freedom. It says that even if consumers are making irrational decisions, a paternalistic law is still unjustifiable because it violates consumers' fundamental right to freedom of choice – even the freedom to make mistakes that harm themselves.[47] This argument is about the importance of liberty itself, not about how good consumers are at using their freedom to make good decisions. It says that consumer freedom of choice has intrinsic worth. Making choices is what makes us human; it provides us with dignity and the ability to be self-reliant.

This emphasis on the importance of freedom is also tied in with ideas about personal responsibility and the sanctity of contract. In an unregulated market, consumers also have the opportunity to learn from their mistakes or to pay for professional consumer advice.[48] A consumer making a *poor* credit decision might suffer because of excessive debt. However, this experience might make that consumer reluctant to make the same mistake again, it might incentivise him or her to find a better income and it might bring a greater appreciation of a later stage in life when debt is no longer a problem.

The value of consumer freedom of choice and the potential costs associated with removing this freedom are never articulated in the New Zealand Regulatory Impact

44 See Mitchell (n 40) arguing that the assumption of uniformly imperfect rationality found in behavioural law and economics is no more plausible than the assumption of uniformly perfect rationality found in law and economics.

45 Rizzo and Whitman, 'The Knowledge Problem of New Paternalism' (n 40). See also Rizzo and Whitman, 'Little Brother is Watching You' (n 40).

46 See Robert Sugden, 'The Value of Opportunities Over Time when Preferences are Unstable' (2007) 29(4) Social Choice and Welfare 665.

47 The philosophies of Milton Friedman, Robert Nozick and Joel Feinberg are all based on the idea that the freedom to make choices has an intrinsic value. See Milton Friedman, *Capitalism and Freedom* (University of Chicago Press 1962); Robert Nozick, *Anarchy, State and Utopia* (Basic Books 1974); Joel Feinberg, *The Moral Limits of the Criminal Law. Vol 3: Harm to Self* (Oxford University Press 1986).

48 Epstein, 'Behavioral Economics' (n 33); Jonathan Klick and Gregory Mitchell, 'Government Regulation of Irrationality: Moral and Cognitive Hazards' (2006) 90 Minnesota Law Review 1620.

Statement on the proposal to introduce a responsible lending law. When discussing the costs of introducing the law, the Impact Statement focuses on implementation costs to business.[49] It is assumed that there are no costs to consumers (beyond minimal increases in loan charges to cover the implementation costs that lenders may incur).[50] When discussing the status quo, the discussion refers only to consumer detriment.[51] There is no mention of any potential value to consumers in retaining freedom of choice and there is no reference to the legitimacy of excluding that freedom. There may well be many very good reasons for overriding this freedom in the case of consumer credit; however, there is something wrong with the quality of the debate if that freedom is not even mentioned.

6 Do the existing theories help policy makers decide which way to go?

Uncompromising anti-paternalism is unhelpful. New Zealand, along with many other countries in the developed world, already has a range of widely accepted paternalistic laws. We do not have heroin on supermarket shelves, tobacco is not available to children and there is no option for consumers to negotiate a cheaper price for goods that have no quality guarantees. Complete anti-paternalism offers little help to those policy makers who are open to the idea that paternalism might be appropriate in some situations. On the other hand, modern democratic societies such as New Zealand value individual liberty too highly for uncritical paternalism to be acceptable. Restrictions on liberty should proceed with caution. In the case of responsible lending laws, the intention is to prevent a voluntary informed agreement between two parties. This kind of legal intervention needs a fully developed justification. Neither of the extreme positions on paternalism provides guidance for policy makers seeking to assess the legitimacy of paternalism in any given situation.

Libertarian paternalism and asymmetric paternalism accept a level of paternalism but do not provide policy makers with a detailed account of the various factors that might be relevant to making a decision in respect of any given consumer problem. Libertarian paternalism advocates nudges and not coercion. It cannot therefore adequately account for hard paternalistic measures such as responsible lending laws. Yet the proponents of the concept of libertarian paternalism admit in the penultimate chapter of their book, *Nudge*, that a product ban might be justified in some circumstances.[52] The book gives little analysis of what factors might be relevant to establishing a rationale for coercion. This is understandable given that the central thesis of libertarian paternalism rests on the premise that only soft forms of paternalism are legitimate because these measures respect individual liberty. Neither does the book provide any guidance on how to filter out the types of *poor* consumer decision making where even soft paternalism is inappropriate. For example, there is no mechanism in the theory for excluding government intervention to correct

49 *Responsible Lending Requirements for Consumer Credit Providers* (n 7) 11.

50 Ibid 10.

51 Ibid 8, 9 and 10.

52 Thaler and Sunstein, *Nudge* (n 20) 250–252. Thaler and Sunstein refer to asymmetric paternalism as an appropriate strategy for cautiously proceeding down the slippery slope away from nudges to coercion.

consumer errors, such as buying an elaborate kitchen renovation that does not bring an anticipated increase in wellbeing.

Asymmetric paternalism also has limitations in its ability to assist the policy maker. Unlike libertarian paternalism, it provides a rationale for some instances of hard paternalism by arguing that an intervention is justifiable where benefits to the irrational consumer are large and there is little cost to the rational consumer. However, there is no scope in the theory for taking into account the degree to which consumers are in favour of having their liberty reduced.

So how are policy makers to distinguish between arguably legitimate interventions and those interventions that are illegitimate? It is unconvincing to argue that behavioural economics somehow allows the government to legitimately intervene whenever it thinks consumers are making a mistake.

7 A multi-factorial approach to the legitimacy of paternalism (stage 1)

Any debate about the legitimacy of paternalism should begin with the assumption that consumer freedom is generally a good thing. A paternalistic intervention ought therefore to proceed with caution. This chapter recommends moving away from a single-premise approach to determining legitimacy and instead adopting a multi-factorial approach which better recognises the complexity of the problem. It argues that various factors should be assessed in order to determine if a paternalistic intervention to protect consumers might be legitimate.

The first stage requires policy makers to define the consumer behaviour that they are proposing to alter by way of legal paternalism. Then they should consider the following factors when determining whether a paternalistic intervention might be legitimate:

- the magnitude of potential consumer harm;
- the probability of consumer harm;
- the irreversibility of potential consumer harm;
- the degree to which addiction is affecting consumer choice;
- the degree to which consumers want to be protected;
- the degree to which consumers are dealing with complex, large quantities of information they are unable to easily process;
- the degree to which the problem is affecting children, young adults or other potentially disadvantaged groups;
- the degree to which there are additional, non-paternalistic reasons for enacting the law; and
- the probability of non-legal responses, such as education or support programmes, failing to provide solutions to the problem within an acceptable time frame.

Each of these factors requires policy makers to make a detailed assessment of the extent and nature of the consumer problem. Consideration of each factor will produce results on a spectrum ranging from high to low. All the factors are relevant to mounting a challenge to the two objections to paternalism based on ideas of freedom (discussed in Section 4).

Where a particular consumer problem gives results at the higher end of some or all of the spectra, there is a more compelling argument for paternalistic intervention than if the answers are at the lower end of the spectrum. So, for example, where the magnitude of potential consumer harm appears extreme, there is a stronger case for intervention than where it is minor. Likewise, in situations where there is a high level of consumer desire to be protected, it is easier to argue that freedom is expendable and that paternalism might be justified. For example, consumers in an unregulated airline market would have the freedom to choose the combination of price and safety that they prefer. However, most consumers in this case are likely to be happy to be relieved of the burden of freedom of choice and are likely to be in favour of airline safety regulation.

Other consumer *mistakes* are likely to score at low levels on most of the factors. For example, consumers often make hasty, irrational purchasing decisions to buy items such as gadgets they never use, unaffordable holidays or bad haircuts. Most people would agree that these are not problems for which it is legitimate to introduce a paternalistic regulation to alter consumer behaviour. These examples show that any call to view behavioural economics as some kind of all-round justification for paternalistic interventions in free markets is misguided.

In other situations where consumers appear to be making decisions that are not in their best interests, an assessment of the factors will produce more ambiguous results. Perhaps some factors point to a possible justification for intervention and other factors do not, or perhaps the factors are all assessed at moderate levels. Results are often mixed where consumers are making trade-off decisions between short-term benefits and long-term costs. For example, a consumer might be choosing between the short-term pleasures of smoking, gambling or unhealthy eating and the potential long-term costs of these behaviours. Making *poor* decisions about borrowing also falls into this category. These areas involve problems of self-control and a tendency to overvalue the present in comparison to the future.[53] The problem with intervening in these areas is that there is likely to be a huge variation in the degree of support that consumers would give to restrictions on their freedom. There may also be disparity among consumers as to whether they even see themselves as making a mistake. Many who are engaged in seemingly self-defeating behaviours will want to be left alone to make their own decisions about their welfare. It may be impossible for the policy maker to know that consumers would change their behaviour if they had complete information, unlimited cognitive abilities and no lack of self-control.[54] Consequently, anti-paternalists will claim it is safer to leave consumers to make their own decisions about their own welfare. Other scholars insist that when harm reaches a certain level it is facile to deny the welfare implications. For example, O'Donoghue and Rabin argue that:

> Economists will and should be ignored if we continue to insist that it is axiomatic that constantly trading stocks or accumulating consumer debt or

53 See Shane Frederick, George Loewenstein and Ted O'Donoghue, 'Time Discounting and Time Preference: A Critical Review' (2002) 40 Journal of Economic Literature 351, 393–394; David Laibson, 'Golden Eggs and Hyperbolic Discounting' (1997) 112 Quarterly Journal of Economics 443.

54 See Rizzo and Whitman, 'The Knowledge Problem of New Paternalism' (n 40); Gregory Mitchell, 'Libertarian Paternalism is an Oxymoron' (2005) 99 Northwestern University Law Review 1245.

becoming a heroin addict must be optimal for the people doing these things merely because they have chosen to do it.[55]

The policy debate in this area must explicitly address the question of whether there are some situations where we can safely assume that consumers do make inferior decisions about their own welfare. The factors listed above are crucial to this debate.

8 Applying the multi-factorial approach to responsible lending laws

The following is an attempt to apply the multi-factorial approach described above to the issue of *poor* consumer choices about credit. The goal is to identify the factors that strengthen a case for endeavouring to change this consumer behaviour by way of a paternalistic intervention such as a responsible lending law.

8.1 Magnitude of potential consumer harm

Where it can be shown that consumer behaviour is leading to potentially devastating consumer harm, there is a weakening of the argument that consumer freedom of choice is the best method of maximising consumer welfare. It also becomes questionable whether freedom of choice has intrinsic value if that freedom can lead to severe suffering. So, for example, the potential for heroin to cause extreme consumer harm means that there is a stronger argument for paternalistic intervention than in a case such as ear piercing, where the harm is minor and temporary.

Poor credit decisions do not lead to direct bodily harm. Consumers do not die from over indebtedness in the same way as a consumer who uses a sunbed might die from melanoma. Nevertheless, the financial difficulties that can arise from *poor* credit decisions can be devastating. In many cases the borrower will not be able to repay the loan and might agree to roll over the loan or borrow more to repay the original loan. This can lead to a spiral of out-of-control debt. If the loan is secured on the borrower's assets, the borrower can lose these assets if they are unable to repay the loan. These accumulating financial difficulties can cause consumers to suffer significant declines in both mental and physical wellbeing.[56]

8.2 Probability of consumer harm

It is difficult to predict the likelihood of a *poor* credit decision resulting in consumer harm. To a large extent it depends on the way in which a *poor* credit decision is defined. The New Zealand responsible lending laws are intended to eliminate *poor* credit decisions by requiring lenders to be satisfied that 'it is likely' that the credit provided will meet the consumer's requirements and objectives and that the consumer will make the payments under the credit agreement without suffering

55 Ted O'Donohue and Matthew Rabin, 'Studying Optimal Paternalism: Illustrated by a Model of Sin Taxes' (2003) 93 American Economic Review 186, 186.

56 See Families Commission, *Escaping the Debt Trap: Experiences of New Zealand Families Accessing Budgeting Services* (Research Report 6/09, Families Commission 2009). See also research documents on consumer credit listed on the New Zealand Ministry of Consumer Affairs website at www.consumeraffairs.govt.nz/legislation-policy/policy-development/credit-review accessed 14 June 2016.

'substantial hardship'.[57] The scope of the consumer behaviour that the new law will eliminate is very much dependent on the interpretation of the phrases 'is likely to' and 'substantial hardship'.[58] If these terms are interpreted narrowly then the consumer behaviour that is eradicated might be only the type of high-risk lending that is highly likely to lead to consumer harm. If a broader or more cautious interpretation is used, then the rules could also result in the wiping out of moderately high-risk loans.

Assessing the probability of consumer harm is made more complicated by the different money habits of each individual consumer. One consumer may be overly optimistic about his or her ability to repay the loan. Repayment of the loan might be very likely to cause this consumer a substantial level of hardship. Another consumer in the same situation might have a realistic plan in terms of budgeting and future earning that will allow repayment to not become a problem. Perhaps the repayments will involve some degree of financial hardship, but will still be doable for that consumer.

8.3 The irreversibility of potential consumer harm

Where consumer harm is reversible there is greater opportunity for consumers to learn from their mistakes.[59] If the harm is irreversible then it is too late for learning. Any market feedback mechanism comes too late to undo the harm caused by the *poor* choice. Leaving matters such as the safety of medicines or airlines to be optimised by the free market risks some consumers suffering death or injury. Financial hardship is not irreversible in the same way that permanent bodily injury or death is. There is always the possibility that a consumer can reverse a situation of excessive debt. Nevertheless, this can be extremely difficult. Mistakes in the area of consumer credit are more difficult to reverse than other more minor mistakes such as buying the wrong sized cardigan. Where consumer behaviour is causing irreversible harm, the arguments about the importance of preserving consumer liberty are weakened. So, too, are arguments that consumers are in the best position to maximise their own welfare.

57 See CCCF Amendment Act 2014, s 9C(3)(a).

58 The CCCF Amendment Act 2014 anticipates the publication of a Responsible Lending Code which will elaborate on the lender responsibility principles and offer guidance on how to implement these principles, see ss 9E to 9I. This Code is to be published not later than two years after the responsible lending obligations come into force. The Code could, theoretically, give guidance on how to interpret 'can be expected' and 'substantial hardship'.

59 See Timothy Irwin, *Implications of Behavioural Economics for Regulatory Reform in New Zealand* (Sapere Research Group 2010) 61 www.srgexpert.com accessed 12 December 2014, navigate to title *Behavioural Economics Provides New Insights for Policy Reform.* Irwin proposes regulators should ask whether a proposed paternalistic regulation covers a domain where people have good opportunities to learn from their mistakes as opposed to a domain where feedback will come too late. See also the following articles where the importance of giving the consumer the opportunity to learn from their mistakes is discussed: Epstein, 'The Neoclassical Economics of Consumer Contracts' (n 31); Klick and Mitchell (n 48).

8.4 The degree to which addiction is affecting consumer choice

Addiction explains, at least in part, why in some situations consumers cause themselves severe harm.[60] It is relevant to consumer decisions in respect of activities such as smoking, drinking excessive alcohol and gambling. Addiction can cause consumers to lose the ability to think rationally or to choose freely.[61] In cases of strong addiction, it becomes harder to argue that freedom of choice has intrinsic value and is the best way of maximising consumer welfare.

Although addiction is not a direct factor in consumer credit problems, it might play a part in some *poor* credit decisions. Consumers who suffer from addictions such as smoking and gambling may be more likely to make *poor* credit choices in an attempt to finance their addiction.

8.5 The degree to which consumers want to be protected

The more likely it is that consumers want to be protected, the harder it is to maintain that freedom of choice has intrinsic value or that freedom is the best way of maximising consumer welfare. Determining the degree of support for a paternalistic intervention will sometimes be challenging and may involve a degree of hypothesising. Moreover, using the *degree of support* as a relevant factor implies a rejection of a revealed preference model where consumer choices made in the marketplace are considered the most accurate way to gauge what consumers really want and what is in their best interests.

In some situations, even if consumers know what actions are in their best interests, they understand that they are either unable or unwilling to take these actions without the state's assistance. If there is a domain in which it can be shown, either by direct evidence or reasonable supposition, that most consumers would support having their freedom restricted in some way, this will strengthen arguments that some kind of paternalistic regulation might be legitimate.

It is difficult to assess the degree to which consumers of credit want to be protected from making seemingly *poor* decisions about credit. A paternalistic intervention in this area is likely to be resisted less strongly than smokers resist their habit being regulated. On the other hand, it is probably more controversial (from a consumer point of view) than a paternalistic law that protects consumers from entering into standard form contracts with unfair terms or a law that prevents consumers from entering a door-to-door sales contract without a cooling-off period.

It is unlikely that consumers of credit will all feel the same way with regard to laws that aim to protect them by removing their ability to choose certain credit products.

60 Addiction can be defined as physical and/or psychological dependence on mood-altering substances or behaviours which temporarily alter the chemical profile of the brain; see Daniel H Angres and Kathy Bettinardi-Angres, 'The Disease of Addiction: Origins, Treatment, and Recovery' (2008) 54 Disease-a-Month 696.

61 See Ole Rogeberg, 'Taking Absurd Theories Seriously: Economics and the Case of Rational Addiction Theories' (2004) 71 Philosophy of Science 263; Jon Elster, 'More than Enough: Review of *Accounting for Tastes*' (1997) 64 University of Chicago Law Review 749; Jon Elster, *Alchemies of the Mind: Rationality and the Emotions* (Cambridge University Press 1999); George Loewenstein, 'Out of Control: Visceral Influences on Behaviour' (1996) 65 Organizational Behaviour and Human Decision Processes 272. See also Jonathan Gruber and Botond Köszegi, 'Is Addiction "Rational"? Theory and Evidence' (2001) 116 Quarterly Journal of Economics 1261.

Some consumers may be desperate to borrow money on any terms. Others may welcome a legal intrusion that puts the hand brakes on certain high-risk loans. The degree to which consumers will want to be protected may well depend on whether alternative, lower-risk credit is available or whether, for some consumers, the alternative to high-risk loans is in fact no loan at all. This issue is discussed further in Section 9.

8.6 The degree to which consumers are dealing with complex or large quantities of information they are unable to easily process

Consumers do not have the cognitive powers to quickly process large amounts of complex information.[62] It can sometimes be difficult for consumers to make meaningful comparisons with alternative products in a realistic time frame. Some consumer problems are therefore unable to be effectively addressed by simply requiring more information to be presented to consumers. In these cases a paternalistic approach might be appropriate. The government (or another delegated party) might have the potential to devote more time and resources to processing the relevant information, calculating risks and determining acceptable minimum standards.

Clearly the complexity and quantity of information can be an issue with some credit contracts. Research has shown that even if provided with full and transparent disclosure, many consumers (particularly those who have a low level of financial literacy) will continue to make *poor* credit choices.[63] The consumer's cognitive limitations in respect of information mean that in the case of a credit decision, it is not clear that freedom of choice will result in a rational, fully informed and welfare-enhancing decision. Lenders are arguably in a better position than consumers to make a rational choice on behalf of consumers. They have more experience with the relevant financial information and they are less likely to suffer from overconfidence in respect of the borrower's financial situation.

8.7 The degree to which the problem is affecting children, young adults or other potentially disadvantaged groups

As has been discussed above, the latest findings in behavioural economics suggest that consumers consistently suffer from cognitive biases and weaknesses that appear to reduce their ability to make welfare-enhancing decisions. Cognitive weaknesses might also be more prevalent in certain groups of particularly vulnerable or disadvantaged consumers, such as the young, the elderly, illiterate, mentally impaired or sick.[64]

62 See Amos Tversky and Daniel Kahneman, 'Judgment Under Uncertainty: Heuristics and Biases' in Daniel Kahneman, Paul Slovic and Amos Tversky (eds), *Judgment Under Uncertainty* (Cambridge University Press 1982) 3; Robert E Goodin, 'Democracy, Preferences and Paternalism' (1993) 26 Policy Sciences 229; Dan Ariely (n 36).

63 Lauren E Willis, 'Decisionmaking and the Limits of Disclosure: The Problem of Predatory Lending: Price' (2006) 65(3) Maryland Law Review 707. See also Ramsay (n 34) ch. 4; Kathleen C Engel and Patricia A McCoy, 'A Tale of Three Markets: The Law and Economics of Predatory Lending' (2002) 80(6) Texas Law Review 1255, 1309.

64 See, for example, Lynda Sharp Paine, 'Children as Consumers: An Ethical Evaluation of Children's Television Advertising' (1984) 3 Business and Professional Ethics Journal 119. Sharp argues that there are significant differences between child consumers and adult consumers that justify them being treated differently by the law.

If a paternalistic intervention is targeted at vulnerable types of consumer, then the anti-paternalistic argument that consumers should be left alone because they are rational welfare-maximising beings is less persuasive.

Problems with consumer credit are more likely to affect vulnerable low-income consumers.[65] Those with low education levels or who are illiterate are even more vulnerable to making *poor* credit decisions. Responsible lending laws are targeted at protecting these vulnerable consumers.[66]

8.8 The degree to which there are additional, non-paternalistic reasons for enacting the law

Some forms of self-defeating consumer behaviour have a negative effect on not just the consumer, but also the rest of society. For example, the consumption of alcohol has the potential to cause direct harm to others, including violence to innocent people, damage to property, car crashes and health and social service costs. A government might be attempting to both reduce consumer harm (paternalism) and protect other people from being harmed by the consumer behaviour (non-paternalism). Having additional non-paternalistic goals can strengthen the case for an intervention that also has paternalistic goals.

The problem of over-indebtedness can cause harm to people other than the individual consumer making the *poor* decision. There is concern that excessive borrowing can weaken the economy as a whole. In his most recent book, Richard Posner analyses the Global Financial Crises. He argues that although people make decisions that are individually rational, they can make collectively irrational financial decisions and this is what led to the collapse of the entire economy.[67] Over-indebtedness also puts stress on the borrower's relationships with family and friends.[68] In addition, it can create social costs by putting a strain on community services, such as budgetary advice and food banks.

The New Zealand move to introduce responsible lending laws does not appear to be based on the non-paternalistic goal of preventing harm to the rest of society. The focus is very much on the paternalistic goal of protecting vulnerable consumers.[69] Moreover, unlike the Australian responsible lending laws, the New Zealand responsible lending obligations do not cover mortgages on residential investment properties.[70] The law will therefore be more limited in its ability to curtail subprime mortgages, which have been identified as part of the cause of the 2009 Global Financial Crisis.[71]

65 See Credit Contracts and Financial Services Law Reform Bill (Explanatory Note). See also Regulatory Impact Statement: Responsible Lending Requirements for Consumer Credit Providers (n 7) para 21.

66 Ibid.

67 See Richard Posner, *A Failure of Capitalism: The Crisis of '08 and the Descent into Depression* (Harvard University Press 2009). See also Therese Wilson, 'The Responsible Lending Response' in Therese Wilson (ed), *International Responses to Issues of Credit and Over-indebtedness in the Wake of Crisis* (Ashgate 2013) 109.

68 See Families Commission (n 56) 13.1.3.

69 See Credit Contracts and Financial Services Law Reform Bill (Explanatory Note). See also *Responsible Lending Requirements for Consumer Credit Providers* (n 7) paras 1, 2 and 3.

70 The responsible lending obligations apply to 'consumer credit contracts' which are contracts predominantly for personal credit. This includes mortgages but will not include mortgages on investment properties. See CCCF Amendment Act 2014, s 10.

71 Kathleen Engel and Patricia McCoy, *The Subprime Virus: Reckless Lending, Regulatory Failure and Next Steps* (Oxford University Press 2011).

8.9 The probability of non-legal responses, such as education or support programmes, failing to provide solutions to the problem within an acceptable time frame

One key question that policy makers should ask themselves when determining the legitimacy of legal paternalism is how likely it is that non-legal responses, such as education or support programmes, will solve the consumer problem in an acceptable time frame. The amount of time that is considered acceptable will depend on matters such as the seriousness and irreversibility of the consumer harm.

In some cases, government engagement in an education campaign or support programme might be enough to guide consumers in the right direction and thus render regulation unnecessary. Unfortunately, in the case of consumer credit, research suggests that education programmes to increase financial literacy are often ineffective and do not change consumer behaviour.[72]

Approaches that acknowledge that credit problems are exacerbated by social factors, such as unemployment, poverty and ill health, are likely to be more successful. Investigating the deep-rooted social and cultural factors that underpin *poor* decision making in respect of credit should be a part of finding appropriate policy and legislative solutions. Indeed, policy makers need to be wary of avoiding more direct responses to these underlying problems. As one academic writes:

> Indeed, the seductive power of the behavioralist strategy is its promise of activist regulators, intervening aggressively to solve important problems. But in truth, I suggest, the main effect of that strategy is to divert attention from real solutions to the real problems that plague [the] finances [of low- and middle-income communities]. What we need to do is help them with the difficulties of being poor, not pretend that their poverty is irrelevant to their financial choices.[73]

Broader measures to reduce poverty or government schemes to offer safe, affordable short-term loans might provide alternative or additional solutions. These ideas are discussed further in Section 9.

9 Effectiveness and unintended consequences (stage 2)

If an examination of a consumer problem suggests that there are sufficient factors present to indicate that a paternalistic goal is legitimate, the second step should be to consider issues of effectiveness and unintended consequences. The question at this second stage moves beyond the philosophical one of whether or not it is legitimate to interfere with consumer liberty to a more practical question of whether the proposed regulation is likely to achieve its goals and whether there is a possibility of negative unintended consequences. There is no point considering issues of effectiveness and unintended consequences if the question of legitimacy has not been answered in the affirmative. Of course, it would be perfectly possible, for example, to design a very effective regulation to eradicate *poor* decision making in respect of

72 JA Smith Jr, 'Financial Literacy, Regulation and Consumer Welfare' (2004) 8 North Carolina Banking Institute Journal 77, 86; see also Lauren E Willis, 'Against Financial Literacy Education' (2008) 94 Iowa Law Review 197.

73 See Mann (n 43) 745.

high-heeled shoes. However, if a paternalistic approach is unjustifiable then it is irrelevant that it is likely to be effective.

It is not possible in this chapter to examine these issues in detail. Instead, the example of responsible lending laws is used to present some introductory ideas about the importance of effectiveness and unintended consequences.

9.1 Effectiveness

In a sense, ineffectiveness can be seen as the most obvious type of unintended consequence. Effectiveness will be determined by the responsiveness of consumers to the paternalistic regulation.[74] Regulators need to assess the likelihood of consumers altering their behaviour in the anticipated way.

A hard paternalistic measure, such as the proposed responsible lending obligations, is likely to be effective because it essentially bans the behaviour it is endeavouring to eradicate. The responsible lending obligations prohibit consumers from entering agreements for high-risk, unsuitable levels of debt. Nevertheless, it is possible that even such a coercive approach might not eradicate the unwanted behaviour. There remains the possibility that a black market for credit will develop, allowing those consumers who want to access credit, whatever the terms, to continue to do so.

9.2 Unintended consequences

> [O]ur ability to predict the full effects of governmental actions – much less the synergetic effects of hundreds of thousands of simultaneous government actions – is very limited. Far too often there are unanticipated results and costs, despite the most careful efforts of government officials.[75]

It is vital that policy makers assess whether a paternalistic intervention might have unintended negative consequences that outweigh any beneficial effects. In some cases, while the regulation might effectively reduce the targeted consumer behaviour, it might also unintentionally promote other harmful consumer behaviour. For example, one US study has shown that a tax increase on beer was followed by a rise in the teenage consumption of cannabis.[76] Another study showed that while cigarette taxes reduce smoking, they are also associated with higher rates of obesity.[77]

74 Note that, even if a proposed intervention is likely to be effective in achieving the desired outcome, ideally it should be compared to other potentially effective legal interventions to determine the option that will maximise the outcome for a given budget. This type of economic analysis is called 'cost-effectiveness analysis'. It attempts to show which of alternative proposed regulatory measures is the least costly. It measures effectiveness in non-monetary terms, such as the number of lives saved, or the number of smokers to quit and so on. See Jeremy D Fraiberg and Michael J Trebilcock, 'Risk Regulation: Technocratic and Democratic Tools for Regulatory Reform' (1998) 43 McGill Law Journal 835, 867–869.

75 Alex Kozinksi, 'The Dark Lessons of Utopia' (1991) 58 University of Chicago Law Review 575, 592–593.

76 John DiNardo and Thomas Lemieux, 'Alcohol, Marijuana, and American Youth: The Unintended Consequences of Government Regulation' (2001) 20 Journal of Health Economics 991.

77 Shin-Yi Chou, Michael Grossman and Henry Saffer, 'An Economic Analysis of Adult Obesity: Results from the Behavioural Risk Factor Surveillance System' (2004) 23 Journal of Health Economics 565.

Responsible lending laws are intended to prevent consumers from taking on high-risk debt and to ensure that loan sharks offer more affordable credit. The ultimate aim is to enhance consumer welfare.[78] There may, however, be some unintended negative consequences.

The cost to businesses of implementing the responsible lending obligations might be high and this might lead to an increase in the cost of lending to all consumers of credit. The New Zealand proposed responsible lending law extends to a wide range of lenders, not just third-tier loan sharks.

It is possible that responsible lending obligations might cause low-income consumers to be excluded from any affordable credit provision either because their loan applications are refused or lenders who would have offered them credit exit the market.[79] Some commentators have argued that short-term credit is an 'essential service' comparable to electricity, water and telecommunications.[80] It is the only way for some people to cover emergencies and smooth out the costs of large purchases.

The overall welfare of vulnerable consumers might decrease. Some consumers might suffer consequences even more detrimental than financial turmoil. They may be unable to buy essentials such as food and medicine. Alternatively, they might access black market credit operators with even worse terms and conditions and end up in more financial strife than under the current system.

The vague concepts of 'make reasonable inquiries' and 'substantial financial hardship' might result in lenders being overly cautious and significantly reducing credit to a wide group of borrowers, including those making reasonable choices. Some consumers may be conservatively judged by lenders as not suitable to lend to when in fact they would have been responsible and able to repay. These consumers could be denied the choice to take the risk and obtain the loan. The New Zealand Regulatory Impact Statement acknowledges that of the over 130,000 New Zealanders who have borrowed from a third-tier lender in the past two years, not all have suffered detriment.[81] But after the enactment of responsible lending laws, some of these consumers may suffer the detriment of not having access to credit.

It is not the intention of this chapter to determine the likelihood of these potential negative consequences. The important point is that these are the kinds of issues that the framework for decision making recommended by this chapter requires policy makers to consider.

New Zealand policy documents on the responsible lending proposal fail to examine these issues. Consequently, the policy debate overlooks ways in which the government could mitigate negative consequences. For example, consideration could be given to the government establishing an affordable low-income loan scheme. The government could contribute some funding and work in partnership

78 See Credit Contracts and Financial Services Law Reform Bill (Explanatory Note), cl. 4.

79 See Mann (n 43) 747–748, who argues that regulators should move beyond the 'flaming toaster' model of regulation: 'Fixing the product will not help anybody if "fixing" is functionally the same as banning, and if the product is the best alternative available to consumers.' See also 'Access to Affordable Credit/ Social and Community Lending Break out Group' (notes from the New Zealand Financial Summit 2011, Auckland, August 2011) www.consumeraffairs.govt.nz/pdf-library/Access-to-Affordable-Credit-Social-and-Community-Lending-Breakout-Group.pdf accessed 12 December 2014.

80 Nicola Howell and Terese Wilson, 'Access to Consumer Credit: The Problem of Financial Exclusion in Australia and the Current Regulatory Framework' (2005) 5 Macquarie Law Journal 127, 130.

81 See *Responsible Lending Requirements for Consumer Credit Providers* (n 7) 5.

with financial organisations and charities.[82] Australia has accepted that there is a role for government to support the establishment of affordable lending schemes and has partnered with the private sector to promote affordable credit to low-income consumers.[83]

The New Zealand government indicated in its 2013 Budget an intention to investigate the option of the government working with charity and financial organisations to offer micro-financing.[84] Ideally these options would have formed part of the policy debate about responsible lending rather than arising months after the drafting of the responsible lending legislation and in an unrelated forum. A further option for addressing the possible negative consequences of responsible lending legislation would be to require lenders to inform low-income consumers about the availability of any alternative affordable lending schemes and any applicable social welfare assistance that might be available to the consumer.[85]

It may be impossible to guarantee that there will be no unintended negative consequences from a paternalistic intervention such as the responsible lending legislation. Faced with uncertainty, the regulator will need to decide whether the reasons for intervention are strong enough to justify experimental regulation. This decision needs to take into account that status quo bias, a key insight from behavioural economics, applies to government officials as much as consumers. In other words, once a regulation has been introduced it might be difficult to remove or change it. If experimental regulation, such as responsible lending legislation, is introduced, it is crucial that a process is established for monitoring and reviewing the regulation in order to assess whether it has achieved the desired effects and whether there have been any unexpected negative outcomes. The Regulatory Impact Statement indicates that there is an intention to monitor and review the responsible lending legislation to assess whether it achieves the desired outcomes.[86]

82 Social lending is a concept recommended by the New Zealand Expert Advisory Group on Solutions to child poverty. See Expert Advisory Group on Solutions to Child Poverty, *Solutions to Child Poverty In New Zealand* (Issues and Options Paper for Consultation, 28 August 2012) www.nzdoctor.co.nz/media/1972883/issues_and_options_paper_for_consultation.pdf accessed 12 December 2014. See also Laura Benedict, *Social Lending: A Tool for Grant Makers, an Opportunity for Communities* (Fulbright New Zealand 2010) www.fulbright.org.nz/wp-content/uploads/2011/12/axford2010_benedict.pdf accessed 12 December 2014.

83 The Australian Government established the Community Development Financial Institutions (CDFI) pilot in 2009 as part of a package to assist those most at risk of financial and social exclusion. The CDFI pilot project aims to attract investment and inject funds into community finance organisations that offer financial services and products to those individuals who would otherwise not be able to access mainstream sources. For more information visit www.fahcsia.gov.au/our-responsibilities/communities-and-vulnerable-people/programs-services/financial-management-program/community-development-financial-institutions-cdfi-pilot-project.

84 See press release: Paula Bennett, 'Microfinance Support for People on Low Incomes' (16 May 2013) www.beehive.govt.nz/release/microfinance-support-people-low-incomes accessed 12 December 2014.

85 Currently there is a New Zealand Government 'Special Needs Grant' available for those on a very low income who have an urgent and necessary need that they cannot pay for in any other way. See www.workandincome.govt.nz/individuals/a-z-benefits/special-needs-grant.html#Formoreinformation3.

86 See *Responsible Lending Requirements for Consumer Credit Providers* (n 7) para 44.

10 Conclusion

This chapter has used the examples of consumer credit laws, in particular responsible lending laws, to outline an analytical framework for deciding when paternalistic interventions in the marketplace might be appropriate. The decision-making framework suggested in this chapter is not intended to easily produce definitive answers since quantification of the factors is difficult and, ultimately, a value judgement about importance of liberty is required. Paternalistic interventions are inherently controversial and good policy making requires that they are debated in full and supported by robust justifications.

This chapter has recommended the consideration of multiple factors when determining the legitimacy of a paternalistic intervention in respect of any given consumer problem. This approach acknowledges the complexity of the problem and targets the main objections to paternalism which are based around ideas about the value of freedom. Applying this approach to consumer credit problems highlights many reasons why it might be a good idea to curtail consumer freedom when it comes to decisions about credit.

The second stage of the decision-making framework recommended by this chapter requires policy makers to determine the likelihood of the proposed regulation effectively achieving its goal and the possibility of unintended negative consequences. The main danger in enacting responsible lending obligations is that it will result in a group of low-income, vulnerable consumers being unable to access any credit. The paternalistic response to consumer harm might inadvertently lead to different and potentially greater consumer harm. It is vital that the government address the issue of consumer credit with a strategy that not only eradicates high-risk debt, but also replaces it with affordable and safe credit for low-income consumers. If this strategy is not part of the policy response to risky debt, then the responsible lending laws might cause more consumer harm than they prevent. In many ways the problems that responsible lending laws are attempting to address are problems of poverty. Policies aimed at reducing poverty are likely to be an important part of resolving the problem of consumer over-indebtedness.

3 Credit

Suitable for one or safe for everyone?

Gail Pearson

1 Flannelette

In 1910 there was a Committee of Inquiry into flannelette. The concern was that too many were dying because their clothes caught fire. It was not clear if the cause was open fires or flannelette clothes. The Committee considered remedial legislation. It said:

> Prohibition being out of the question, the most that can be done by enactment would be to provide for due notice being given to intending purchasers of the true character of the material offered to them by dealers in flannelette. People who buy flannelette may do so in ignorance of the risk which they are running; or, knowing generally the character of the material, they may take the risk, putting cheapness before safety; or again, they may be misled by the specious description under which the article is sold.[1]

The Committee decided it could not ban flannelette. It decided to amend existing legislation to provide for the above.[2] It declined to institute a compulsory system of product labelling, as singling out one of many common dangerous products would be unfair. Flannelette of different types stayed in the market in the hope that a process to reduce flammability would establish itself in the market at a reasonably low cost.

Credit is not flannelette, but there are some striking parallels in considering how to deal with a new product that could have a negative and dangerous impact on consumers. To list these: the characteristics of the product may not be properly described; there should be disclosure so individuals receive information about the true character of the product; individuals may not understand the risks; individuals may understand the risks but may go ahead anyway, based on price rather than safety. Can certain products be banned as unsafe? As many products may be dangerous or unsafe, is it fair to single-out particular products?

1.1 Credit and flannelette

Credit is not flannelette and we have addressed many of these concerns in consumer credit regulation. Nevertheless, the tension remains between regulating for

1 *Coroners' Committee of Inquiry into the Question of the Danger Arising from the Use of Flannelette for Articles of Clothing* (1910), [Cd 5376], 5.

2 Merchandise Marks Act 1887 (UK).

the individual and regulating for the community as a whole. A suitable product or service is one that meets the needs of a particular individual. A safe product or service is one that is safe for anyone to acquire. Suitability looks to the purpose of the individual. Safety looks to protection from harm. Suitability is judged objectively against the individual's requirements and capacity. Safety is judged against community expectations.

There should be no dichotomy between suitability and safety for an individual. If it is suitable, it should be safe. The question arises when we expand beyond a standard for a particular individual to a community, public or generalised standard. What is suitable for one person's circumstances may not be suitable for another person. Hence we have the requirement of communication of those purposes from an acquirer to a supplier in order to found liability on the supplier.[3]

There are circumstances when products will not be suitable for any person's circumstances. In this case they should not be in the market; they should not be saleable.[4] We moved from saleability to safety through the course of regulating the characteristics of items.[5] Unless they met certain prescribed standards, they might not otherwise be safe for the community at large. We have not done this for all products.

But to return to the flannelette analogy, children's nightshirts are among products where there are safety standards and warnings.[6] Such a product cannot be in the market unless it meets the standards. Unless it meets the standards, no one can buy such a product. Further, there are some products for which there are no standards. They are regarded as not safe for anyone. They are banned.[7] Further, if there is any product on the market that fails to meet a general community expectation of safety and that product, in defined circumstances, causes injury, there is a right of recovery.[8] If goods or services are associated with death, serious injury or illness, this must be reported.[9] In this account, notions of saleability, quality, suitability, purpose and safety jostle with each other.

There is widespread agreement that consumer credit should be safe, that risks should be mitigated, that individuals should not die or be damaged because they borrow money.[10] This is the point of the analogy between credit and goods; between flannelette and innovative credit products. Despite new credit legislation in

3 This is the requirement that an acquirer communicate a particular purpose for the 'fit for purpose' standard in sale of goods.

4 This is the old merchantable quality standard in sale of goods.

5 In Australia, this evolution can be traced through Sale of Goods legislation, the now repealed Trade Practices Act 1974 (Cth) and into the consumer guarantee of acceptable quality in the Competition and Consumer Act 2010 (Cth), sch 2, Australian Consumer Law, s 54.

6 Trade Practices (Consumer Product Safety Standards) (Children's Nightwear and Paper Patterns for Children's Nightwear) Regulations 2007. This is based on Australian and New Zealand Standard, AS/NZS 1249:2003. The standard includes fire warning labels. On safety standards, see Competition and Consumer Act 2010 (Cth), sch 2, Australian Consumer Law, pt 3.3, div 1.

7 On banned products, see Competition and Consumer Act 2010 (Cth), sch 2, The Australian Consumer Law, pt 3.3, div 2. See also Product Safety Australia www.productsafety.gov.au/content/index.phtml/itemId/970715#toc3 accessed 10 December 2014.

8 Competition and Consumer Act 2010 (Cth), sch 2, Australian Consumer Law, pt 3–5, div 1.

9 Ibid ss 131 and 132.

10 Oren Bar-Gill and Elizabeth Warren, 'Making Credit Safer' (2008) 157 University of Pennsylvania Law Review 1; Lauren Willis, 'Will the Mortgage Market Correct? How Household and Communities Would Fare if Risk were Priced Well' (2009) 41 Connecticut Law Review 1177.

Australia, enhanced legislation and a further phase to legislation, there is ongoing debate about how best to ensure this. This chapter looks at the differences between ensuring suitability for one person and hence safety for that person, and measures that aim to ensure safety in credit for all or for particular community groups. I argue that the standard of *not unsuitable* in the Australian responsible lending regime can be roughly assimilated to the old requirement that a product should be fit for the purpose if that purpose was communicated by the acquirer to the provider.[11] The responsible lending provisions mandate this communication as they require the lender to ascertain the objectives and purpose of the borrower.[12] In this, they go further than what is required to imply a term in a goods contract, which does not require a supplier to ask a particular consumer about the purpose of goods. Nottage and Kozuka argue that responsible lending is more akin to merchantability.[13] Their notion of merchantability is derived not from the old implied concept of saleability, but from the modern iteration that requires the product to be satisfactory or acceptable according to some objective standard. Further, drawing on product liability or regulation, they argue there should be a General Safety Provision for credit with the aim that the only products sold are safe products.

These questions raise the issue of whether any particular form of regulation is to protect the interests of the particular acquirer or the interests of everyone in general, irrespective of their individual circumstances. Of course, the interests of the individual articulate with protection for all and the issue here is not how protection of the individual ultimately protects the community. The question is whether regulation should mandate a standard that protects the whole community irrespective of individual circumstances. Some regulation does this. Some products are banned and some products are subject to mandatory safety standards and warnings. This was not the case for flannelette in the 1910s – and now flannelette is not perceived as a product that kills. It is safe.

Australian regulation of consumer credit balances the interests of different individuals in accessing varieties of products with the interests of the community in designating certain product features unsafe for anyone. It is trite to say credit is not flannelette, but regulation continues to puzzle through the differences between tangible goods with a physical presence and intangibles such as credit. It is not difficult to regulate physical characteristics for tangibles whose performance is intrinsically linked to those characteristics. The one uncertainty is the difference in the way a person may use physical goods. Regulation protects expected use, not totally idiosyncratic use. I am not protected if I choose to use a toaster as a foot warmer for a child.

Apart from idiosyncratic use, it is easy to assess the performance characteristics of tangibles. The performance characteristics and use of credit is much harder to predict. Will interest rates go up or down? Will the reverse mortgage see me out?

11 Gail Pearson, 'Reading Suitability Against Fitness for Purpose: The Evolution of a Rule' (2010) Sydney Law Review 17; Gail Pearson, 'Suitable for an Individual or Acceptable for All? A Response to Nottage and Kozuka' (2012) 22(8) Australian Product Liability Reporter 266.

12 Both the credit assistant (broker) and credit provider (lender) must make enquiries about the consumer's requirements and objectives regarding the credit: National Consumer Credit Protection Act 2009 (Cth) (NCCP Act), ss 117(1)(a) and 130(1)(a).

13 Luke Nottage and Souichirou Kozuka, 'Lessons from Product Safety Regulation for Reforming Consumer Credit Markets in Japan and Beyond' (2012) 34 Sydney Law Review 129.

And with irrational optimism, I'm sure I'll never lose my job, become ill, fall pregnant or have a large unexpected expenditure, so I'll certainly be able to continue to make payments towards my loans. Suitability and safety measures are meant to guard against our cognitive biases.[14]

1.2 The meaning of suitability and safety in this context

How do we judge suitability and safety? We test whether a product suits the requirements of a particular individual through an objective test. We might say that it should be up to the individual rather than the broker or lender to judge if the product is suitable for his or her needs. We do not do this for goods, where there has long been a statutory objective test. The suitability of a particular credit product for a particular person is judged objectively at a particular point in time. It takes into account two matters. The first is the requirements and objectives of the individual. The second is the ability of the individual to pay for the product, that is to meet the obligations under the particular product, the credit contract.[15] Explicitly calculating an individual's ability to repay mitigates individual risk of harm. The danger in credit products is that individuals will not be able to meet their repayments or may do so at great personal cost. Failure to meet repayments has a flow-on effect and may lead to loss of that for which the credit was acquired, such as a house or a car.

A safe product is one that is not dangerous to anyone. It is safe for any person in the community – it will do no one harm. Financial harm is financial distress, bankruptcy, mortgage foreclosure, economic instability which causes job losses and distress in neighbourhoods, and paying more than expected on loans.[16] Implicit designation of a product or its features as unsafe for all involves a value judgement that no one should take on the risk of harm from this product. Some products are potentially dangerous to certain groups within the community. They may be suitable for some categories of persons but unsafe for others.

2 Recap of credit regulation

The National Consumer Credit Protection Act 2009 (Cth) (NCCPA) preserved the former Uniform Consumer Credit Code as the National Credit Code. This contains the pre-contractual and contractual disclosure obligations relating to the credit contract. These are directed towards what the credit contract is – that is, describing what the product is. Other preserved provisions are those dealing with whether the transaction or contract is unjust.[17] Those concerned with the changed circumstances of one of the parties to the contract, the borrower, the substantial hardship

14 The classic work on social psychology and behavioural economics is Daniel Kahneman, *Thinking Fast and Slow* (Farrar, Straus and Giroux 2011). See also Susan Bloch-Lieb and Edward Janger, 'The Myth of the Rational Borrower Rationality, Behavioralism and the Misguided "Reform" of Bankruptcy Law' (2006) 84 Texas Law Review 1481.

15 NCCP Act, ss 118(2)(a), 119(2)(a) and 131(2)(a).

16 Bar-Gill and Warren (n 10) 3, 56–58.

17 NCCP Act, sch 1, s 76.

provisions, were subsequently amended.[18] A further provision deals indirectly with the changed circumstances of the lender.[19]

The 2009 Act introduced the unsuitability or responsible lending provisions. These obligations fall on the 'credit assistant' or broker, and on the 'credit provider' or lender. In brief, both must undertake enquiries and make an assessment as to whether proposed or offered credit products are 'not unsuitable' for the potential acquirer.[20]

There are amendments subsequent to the 2009 National Consumer Credit Protection Act. The background to this was the July 2010 Green Paper *National Credit Reform Enhancing Confidence and Fairness in Australia's Credit Law,* which spoke of regulatory gaps and consumer detriment and safeguards.[21] It dealt with the regulation of credit cards, reverse mortgages, regulation of investment lending and regulation of short-term, small-amount lending.

2.1 Home loan key fact sheets and credit cards

In July 2011 the National Consumer Credit Protection Amendment (Home Loans and Credit Cards) Act 2011 (Cth) passed. This introduced Key Fact Sheets for standard home loans and credit cards,[22] regulated credit card offers, fees and payments[23] and prohibited mortgage exit fees on residential property.[24] This amending Act also prohibits offers and invitations to apply for credit card limit increases.[25] It prohibits charging fees on use of a credit card over the credit limit unless the consumer has given express consent.[26] The final provisions regulate the ordering of payments made under a credit card particularly to first pay off higher interest rate debts.[27] In concert, the regulations provided for a minimum repayment warning for credit card statements[28] and notification to the debtor if the credit card is over the limit.[29]

2.2 Stillborn bills

In June 2011, an independent Senator (Xenophon) introduced the Consumer Credit Protection Amendment (Fees) Bill to provide that credit fees and charges must be reasonable and, if not, the regulator could apply for them to be annulled.

18 NCCP Act, sch 1, s 72.
19 NCCP Act, sch 1, s 66. Provided it is not a fixed-rate contract, this sets out the communication required if a lender unilaterally varies interest rates.
20 NCCP Act, ss 115 and 128.
21 The Treasury, Australian Government, *National Credit Reform: Enhancing Confidence and Fairness in Australia's Credit Law* (Green Paper, July 2010).
22 NCCP Act, ss 133AC and 133AD; National Consumer Credit Protection Regulations 2010 (NCCP Regulations), sch 5, reg 28LB; NCCP Act, ss 133BC and 133BD; NCCP Regulations, sch 6, reg 28LFA.
23 NCCP Act, ss 133BE, 133BI, 133BO, 133BP, 133BQ and 133BH; NCCP Regulations, regs 79B and 28LJ(1).
24 NCCP Regulations, reg 79A.
25 NCCP Act, s 133BE.
26 Ibid s 133BI.
27 Ibid ss 133BO, 133BP and 133BQ.
28 NCCP Regulations, reg 79B.
29 NCCP Act, s 133BH; NCCP Regulations, reg 28LJ(1).

This proceeded to the Senate's Economic Legislation Committee[30] which reported but did not proceed.

The Banking Consumer Credit Protection Amendment (Mobility and Flexibility) Bill 2011, which was introduced by a single member of the House of Representatives (Bandt) in August of that year, went to a second reading but did not proceed. It would have facilitated bank switching by allowing the new Authorised Deposit-Taking Institution (ADI) to arrange for the transfer of direct debits, the termination of mortgage indemnity insurance with termination of the contract, disclosure to borrowers of the existence of legislation regarding unjust transactions and unconscionable charges and timely disclosure of when a term deposit was about to end.

The Consumer Credit Legislation Amendment (Enhancements) Act 2012 (Cth), which amended the NCCPA, provides for: short-term and small-amount credit contracts; price regulation via interest rate caps for non-ADI loans; reverse mortgages; unconditional representations about a consumer's eligibility for credit without a suitability assessment; and enhanced hardship provisions. It also has restrictions on the use of words such as *financial counsellor* and *independent*. It had taken nearly a year from the initial bill, two subsequent Parliamentary Committees and a Treasury discussion paper, concerned with risk and financial inclusion.[31]

2.2.1 Payday lending: suitability and cost caps

To protect borrowers who depend on amounts that are relatively small, credit has been categorised as short term, small amount and medium amount. These are non-credit card contracts with a non-ADI lender. Short term and small amount are for $2,000 or less.[32] Short-term contracts are for 15 days or fewer. Small-amount contracts are for at least 16 days, no longer than a year, and must be unsecured.[33] Medium-amount credit contracts are for more than $2,001, and not more than $5,000 and for between 16 days and two years.[34]

Brokers and lenders cannot offer short-term credit by making a suggestion, assisting an individual to apply for such a contract or to increase the credit limit of a short-term contract, or by entering into such a contract.[35] They may negotiate small-amount credit provided they observe certain restrictions and meet particular requirements.[36] The small-amount credit rules must be reviewed after July 2015.[37] There is less restriction on medium-amount credit contracts.[38]

30 Senate Economics Legislation Committee, *Consumer Protection Amendment (Fees) Bill Report* (September 2011).

31 Parliamentary Joint Committee on Corporations and Financial Services, *Inquiry Into Consumer Credit and Corporations Legislation Amendment (Enhancements) Bill 2011* (2011); Senate Economics Legislation Committee, *Consumer Credit and Corporations Legislation Amendment (Enhancements) Bill 2011 (Provisions)* (2011); The Treasury, *Strategies for Reducing Reliance on High-Cost, Short-term Small Amount Lending* (Discussion Paper, April 2012).

32 NCCP Act, s 5(1).

33 Ibid s 5(1).

34 NCCPA sch 1, s 204(1).

35 NCCP Act, ss 124A and 133CA.

36 Ibid ss 124B, 133CB, 130(1A), 131(3A), 133(3A) and 133CC; NCCP Regulations, reg 28S.

37 NCCP Act, s 335A.

38 NCCP Act sch 1, s 32B(1).

2.2.2 *Reverse mortgages*

Reverse mortgages have been regulated by information requirements, enhanced suitability requirements, provisions about occupation rights, curtailing the lender's enforcement rights, and in a limited situation protecting the debtor from owing more money than the value of the house.[39]

2.2.3 *Hardship*

The Enhancements legislation changed the requirements for reopening a contract on grounds of hardship.[40] A request for a variation to a contract on grounds of hardship is no longer limited to illness, unemployment or other reasonable cause. If a debtor gives a 'hardship notice', the debtor receives the benefit of a legislated process.[41]

2.2.4 *Conduct and words*

The new legislation introduced provisions similar to statutory unconscionability factors designed to protect those within a group from being unfairly targeted by intermediaries, with the result that individuals entered loans they would not otherwise contemplate.[42] It provided that neither brokers nor lenders can make statements about eligibility for a loan without doing a suitability assessment.[43] It also prohibited the use of certain words; independent, impartial, unbiased, financial counsellor.[44]

2.3 Further changes

There are further proposals. In March 2013 the National Consumer Credit Protection Amendment (Credit Reform Phase 2) Bill 2012 was released as draft legislation for consultation. This includes provisions on small business credit, credit for investment purposes and private lending.

In April 2013, the Treasury released a discussion paper, *Changes to Disclosure Requirements under the National Consumer Protection Act 2009*,[45] which canvassed whether there should be better pre-contractual disclosure of commissions by credit providers, whether there should be better alignment of the Financial Summary Table and the Home Loans Key Fact Sheet, whether there should be an Information Sheet for Lenders Mortgage Insurance, the form of disclosure for store cards, credit cards and car loans, and the form of disclosure for reverse mortgages, including

39 NCCP Act ss 133DC, 133DD, 133DB and 133DE; sch 1, ss 17(15A), 18B, 18A, 86A, 86B, 26(6) and 86D.

40 For a comparison of new and old law, see Consumer Credit Legislation Amendment (Enhancements) Bill 2012, Revised Explanatory Memorandum Table, 15.

41 NCCP Act, sch 1, s 72.

42 NCCP Act s 180A.

43 Ibid s 128.

44 Ibid ss 160B and 160C.

45 The Treasury, Australian Government, *Changes to Disclosure Requirements under the National Consumer Protection Act 2009* (Discussion Paper, April 2013).

whether this should include break fees for fixed-rate loans. This was based on experimental work undertaken by Paul O'Shea.[46]

3 Suitable or safe?

My categorisation of a measure as going towards suitability for one person, or towards safety for all, rests on a distinction between whether the measure is designed to give individuals choice or mandate an assessment of the individual, compared with measures which establish a standard for all products. The first includes information to facilitate choice of products and suitability assessments. The second involves measures which restrict access to products and prescribe the characteristics of products or ways to alter the characteristics or use of products. I have included a category to capture those forms of regulation that are not directed towards the community as a whole but to special sections within it.

The balance between measures to support and protect individuals and measures that focus on the community at large has not changed appreciably over time. The introduction of the 'not unsuitable' standard to complement information for individual choice is an intensification of measures designed specifically for individuals. However, this is counter-balanced by measures to ban or regulate certain products more closely. Specific regulation of the characteristics of a product is a shift from regulating the access to a product. Regulating or restricting access to a product implies that the product is safe for some people but that it is not safe for all to receive unfettered opportunity to acquire the product or service.

Table 3.1 represents current credit regulation and attributes to it a function of regulation for suitability for the individual or safety for all.

4 Safety for all

This section explores the strategies and purposes of measures taken to protect all within the community or within a special section of the community from financial harm.

4.1 Banning: short-term credit

Short-term credit of $2,000 or less for 15 days or fewer provided by a non-ADI lender (that is not a credit card debt) is banned.[47] The Explanatory Memorandum suggests this is 'very short term credit'.[48] It can be neither suggested nor provided. It is not safe for anyone to acquire this product from a non-ADI lender, but logically, safe from an ADI lender if they are prepared to lend. The reason given for banning this product is the risk in having to repay within a very short time frame rather than capacity to repay. Those most exposed to this risk are said to be on low incomes and have to pay a disproportionate amount of their income to meet the short repayment

46 P O'Shea, *Simplifying Disclosure in Consumer Credit; Empirical Research and Redesign* (Ministerial Council for Consumer Affairs 2010).

47 NCCP Act, ss 5(1), 124(A) and 133CA.

48 Consumer Credit Legislation Amendment (Enhancements) Bill 2012, Revised Explanatory Memorandum, para 4.14.

Table 3.1 Credit regulation by suitable for one or safe for everyone

Regulation	*One/individual*	*Community/everyone*	*Special groups*
Pre-NCCPA			
UCC disclosure	x		
No unsolicited credit cards		x (unsafe for anyone to receive)	
Variation for substantial hardship (pre-amendment)	x		x
Interest rate caps (now extended to all states)		x (unsafe for everyone if above)	
NCCPA			
National licensing: providers and brokers		x (market participant regulation)	
Responsible lending – credit	x		
Responsible lending – margin loans	x		
Responsible lending – leases	x		
Post-NCCPA			
NCCPA Amendment (Home Loans and Credit Cards)			
Key Fact Sheets (for products – home loans; credit cards)	x (individual chooses)		
Ban on residential mortgage exit fees (product characteristic regulation) (Reg 79A)		x	
No unsolicited invitations to increase credit limit on credit card	x (exception: subject to consent)	x (unsafe for anyone to receive)	
Notify use of credit card above credit limit (Reg 28LJ(1)		x (generally unsafe for all not to know)	

Limitation on imposing additional fees for use of credit card above credit limit	x (exception: subject to the consent of the debtor)	x	
Minimum credit card repayment warning (Reg 79B)		x	
Allocation of payment hierarchy – pay amount in last statement of account with highest rate of interest first	x (exception: pay an amount as requested by consumer)	x	
Enhancements			
Ban on short-term credit (non-ADI lenders)		x	
Small-amount credit (non-ADI lenders) enhanced suitability, presumption of substantial hardship	x		
Ban on small amount credit (non-ADI lenders) to certain social security recipients			x
Reverse mortgages – information sheet	x		
Reverse mortgages – equity projection prior to suitability assessment	x		
Reverse mortgage product regulation – occupation; curtailed enforcement for certain debtor faults		x	
Reverse mortgage product regulation – termination to ensure no negative equity		x	
Hardship	x		
Unfair or dishonest conduct			x (class with special disadvantage)
Unconditional representations of eligibility for credit	x		
Representation of independent, etc.; of financial counsellor	x		

period and are likely to have to repeatedly borrow or face financial hardship.[49] This measure is directed towards protecting a special group within the community, but the effect is to impose a ban applicable to all in the interests of overall safety.

4.2 Banning for some: small-amount credit

The situation is different with small-amount credit. These loans are also for $2,000 or less from a non-ADI lender and not credit card debt.[50] The difference is that small-amount credit must be for 16 days or more but not longer than a year and must be unsecured credit.[51] Small-amount credit is not banned outright but the effect is to ban it depending on the circumstances of the individual as a member of a group. In this way it is a safety provision but restricted to a defined or special group within the community.

Small-amount loans cannot be made to certain social security recipients. If the potential acquirer of small-amount credit is a social security recipient, there is a ban on lending to those who receive more than 50 per cent of their gross income from social security and the repayments amount to more than 20 per cent of their gross income.[52] Small-amount credit is deemed unsafe for this group as a class of people.

Further provisions which result in small-amount credit being deemed unsuitable and therefore unable to be provided depend less on the attributes of the individual and more on their borrowing and repayment history. For this reason they are categorised with regulation directed towards assessing whether the small-amount credit is suitable for the individual and are dealt with below.

Ali, McCrae and Ramsay argue that placing payday loans into categories was a response to the payday loan industry and has complicated regulation.[53] They are critical of changes made to the original Enhancements Bill. In particular, they single-out significant increases to allowable levels of the caps on fees and charges which increase the rate of return and cost of borrowing, allowing capped fees in addition to the 48 per cent interest rate cap and removing prohibitions on concurrent loans and refinancing. Their conclusion is that the Enhancement Bill requirements will not protect the vulnerable from the harm of payday lending.[54]

4.3 Restricting access and modifying use: credit cards

Australia has long restricted sending unsolicited credit cards to individuals.[55] Now, subject to consent, Australians cannot receive unsolicited offers to alter the terms of an existing debt product. Unsolicited invitations to increase the credit limit on a credit card are generally banned. There is an exception if an individual has consented to receiving such invitations to increase the credit card limit.

49 Ibid paras 4.19 and 4.20.

50 NCCP Act, s 5(1).

51 Ibid s 5(1).

52 Ibid s 133CC; NCCP Regulations, reg 28S.

53 Paul Ali, Cosima McCrae and Ian Ramsay, 'The Politics of Pay Day Lending Regulation in Australia' (2013) 39(2) Monash University Law Review 411.

54 Ibid 451.

55 Trade Practices Act 1974 (Cth), s 63A (Act repealed); Competition and Consumer Act 2010 (Cth), sch 2, Australian Consumer Law, s 39.

A further measure does not restrict access per se, but it aims to inhibit access. This is the measure that requires a lender to notify a credit card holder if they use the card above the credit limit of the product.[56] Here, we have decided that it is generally unsafe for all not to know that they have gone over their credit limit. In an associated provision, the credit provider cannot impose additional fees or a higher interest rate because the debtor has gone over the credit limit, unless the credit provider obtains express consent.[57]

The mandatory warning that paying off only the stipulated minimum amount on a credit card will lead to increased debt via increased interest charges and take a longer time for the debtor to repay is also a safety provision. It is required on all card statements and does not discriminate between those who regularly pay off the entirety of their cards and those who habitually accrue debt through paying off the minimum. It is designed to protect all from escalating debt.

The measures on the allocation of payments of credit card debt do not restrict access. They modify the use of the product by all who acquire it, thus enhancing its safety. The provisions set out the order of payments. First, any payment is to be applied to the amount outstanding from the last statement which has the highest interest.[58] The payments must then cascade downwards in turn from amounts with the highest interest to those with the lowest interest. If the balance from the previous statement has been fully paid out then the payment is allocated according to the credit contract.[59] There is an exception to this if the debtor asks the credit provider to apply a payment to a particular amount.[60] The Explanatory Memorandum suggests this could be if the consumer wants an 'interest free' purchase paid off.[61]

The three exceptions to the safety provisions for credit cards – allowing consumers to choose if they wish to receive invitations to increase a credit card limit; the consumer consenting to higher fees or interest rates because they are over the credit limit; and allowing consumers to direct repayments to specific amounts – fall outside a measure designed to ensure safety for all. They are directed at what suits the purpose of the particular individual who makes those choices.

4.4 Banning attributes of a product: mortgage exit fees

Exit fees on mortgages over residential property are banned.[62] This is to promote flexibility in changing from one lender to another. The prohibition does not apply to break fees, discharge fees or fees for a contract terminated before the supply of any credit.[63] Break fees are when there is a charge for early repayment of a fixed rate contract attributable to the loss to the credit provider when there are differences in interest rates, namely when the fixed rate is higher than prevailing

56 NCCP Act, s 133BH.
57 Ibid s 133BI.
58 Ibid s 133BQ.
59 Ibid s 133BR.
60 Ibid s 133BP.
61 National Consumer Credit Protection Amendment (Home Loans and Credit Cards) Bill 2011, Explanatory Memorandum, para 3.66.
62 NCCP Regulations, reg 79A.
63 Ibid reg 79A(2).

rates.[64] A discharge fee is the provider's reasonable administrative costs for terminating the loan early.[65] Promoting greater flexibility in the residential mortgage market is linked to competition in the economy. Preventing inflexibility is a safety measure to ensure no one is locked into a product due to its fee structure. It is for all.

4.5 Product regulation: reverse mortgages

Reverse mortgages have been characterised as potentially dangerous products that require specific regulation. A reverse mortgage is an arrangement which involves a credit contract and associated mortgage over 'a dwelling or land'. The following conditions must be met. The debtor's total liability may exceed the maximum amount of credit without the debtor being obliged to reduce the liability below that maximum amount. The second is meeting any prescribed prerequisites for the arrangement.[66] A bridging finance contract is not a reverse mortgage.[67]

Reverse mortgages do not have to allow anyone else other than the debtor to occupy the premises. If the mortgage does allow others to occupy the house, the contract must allow the debtor to nominate or revoke the nomination of that other person or persons.[68] If the reverse mortgage does not permit a person other than the debtor to occupy the premises, the debtor must be clearly informed of this.[69] These measures safeguard the ability of debtors to control who may live with them. The Explanatory Memorandum refers to residency rights after the borrower has died.[70] A product that without a debtor's knowledge denies the residency rights of others is not safe for debtors who may wish to protect a non-title-holding spouse or others.

Certain provisions curtail the enforcement rights of the credit provider in a reverse mortgage. The lender can neither enter into nor change a reverse mortgage credit contract to allow enforcement in some circumstances involving a failure by the debtor. These are: not giving information to the lender regarding another person occupying the place; leaving the place unoccupied; not paying a third party, for example council rates, for three years; not complying with the contract if it does not clearly set out how to do so; breaching another credit contract with the lender.[71] The policy is to ensure reverse mortgage debtors are not in default for 'minor' matters.[72] All these measures protect the continued residency of the debtor and on that account make a reverse mortgage a safer product.

The new reverse mortgage rules are said to ensure 'a statutory "no negative equity" guarantee' so that borrowers will never have to pay back more than the market value of the property.[73] If the debtor's liability is more than the adjusted

64 Ibid reg 79A(3).
65 Ibid reg 79A(3).
66 NCCP Act, sch 1, s 13A.
67 Ibid sch1, s 13A; see also s 204(1).
68 Ibid s 17(15A).
69 Ibid s 18B.
70 Consumer Credit Legislation Amendment (Enhancements) Bill 2012, Revised Explanatory Memorandum, para 3.59.
71 NCCP Act, sch 1, s 18A.
72 Consumer Credit Legislation Amendment (Enhancements) Bill 2012, Revised Explanatory Memorandum, para 3.64.
73 Ibid para 3.80.

market value of the property and the lender receives an amount equal to this adjusted market value, either as payment from the debtor or as proceeds from the sale of the property by the credit provider, the debtor's obligations under the contract are discharged and the reverse mortgage contract comes to an end.[74] If the borrower has engaged in fraud or made a misrepresentation before or after entering the reverse mortgage, the contract will not come to an end.[75]

The lender cannot demand or accept further payments from the debtor to make up the difference between the adjusted market value and the debt.[76] While the no negative equity provision protects a person who has entered into a reverse mortgage from further debt, it does not protect their occupation of what was once their house. This is a safety provision, but we can query the extent of this safety. While the reverse mortgage provisions are not restricted to any particular group, they have a special function in ensuring a measure of safety for those with equity in their home. This is likely to be the elderly with limited income streams. Burns argues that characterisation of the family home of the elderly as a 'risk object' asset will require additional regulation for safety. She suggests consideration of the age at which a person can take out a reverse mortgage, the rate of equity depletion and what released monies can be spent on.[77]

4.6 Redressing unfair broker conduct: for those within a class of special disadvantage

The new credit-specific prohibition on unfair or dishonest conduct is partly directed towards protecting the vulnerable. It is limited to conduct in providing a credit service but does not include conduct by a credit provider.[78] The conduct in connection with the credit service must result in entry into a credit contract the debtor would not otherwise have entered, or entry into a credit contract on different terms than the debtor would otherwise have entered or payments to the broker or someone else.[79] The conduct can occur before or after the credit service is provided.[80]

In deciding if the conduct is unfair or dishonest, the court must take into account a list of factors and the more those circumstances exist, the more likely the conduct is unfair or dishonest.[81] One of the factors is that the plaintiff is a member of a class whose members were more likely than people who were not members of the class to be at a special disadvantage.[82] The special disadvantage must be in dealing with the defendant in regard to a transaction which involves the conduct, a credit contract

74 NCCP Act, sch 1, ss 86A and 86B. A reverse mortgage credit contract cannot contain a term that prohibits an early payment in these circumstances: sch 1, s 26(6).

75 Ibid s 86E.

76 Ibid s 86D. If the credit provider receives more than the adjusted market value, this must be paid to the debtor: s 86C.

77 Fiona Burns, 'The Evolving Statutory Regulation of Reverse Mortgages in Australia's "Risk Society"' (2013) 39(3) Monash University Law Review 611.

78 NCCP Act, ss 180A(1)(a)(b) and 180A(8).

79 Ibid s 189A(1)(c).

80 Consumer Credit Legislation Amendment (Enhancements) Bill 2012, Revised Explanatory Memorandum, para 2.31.

81 NCCP Act, s 180A(3).

82 Ibid s 180A(4)(b).

and another payment contract for which the plaintiff entered the credit contract.[83] Another factor is that a reasonable person must consider that the conduct was directed towards that class whose members were more likely than others not of that class to be at a disadvantage.[84] A further factor is that the plaintiff was unable, or considered herself unable, to enter into a credit contract with anyone else.[85] There are further factors which are similar to those found in statutory unconscionability regimes.[86]

In general, the enquiry regarding unconscionable, unjust or unfair transactions is directed towards the characteristics of the individual and the particular transaction. Few statutory factors look to comparisons with like transactions. The Explanatory Memorandum says:

> The purpose of this provision is to address practices where a credit service provider will target a class of persons (for example, elderly or commercially unsophisticated persons) on the basis the perceived characteristics of the class mean that individuals within it are more likely to succumb to unfair or dishonest conduct (irrespective of whether the credit service provider is aware that any particular individual under the class was under a special disability).[87]

This conduct provision is aimed at ensuring that particular groups of people are safe from unscrupulous practices by those providing credit services, potentially brokers and debt aggregators.

4.7 Price and product regulation: the cost of debt for all

For intangibles such as credit, the price of the product is inbuilt as a characteristic of the product. Fees, charges and interest rates are the terms of the contract. This is a fundamental distinction between tangibles and intangibles. There is a long human history of prohibiting and regulating a price for debt. Human societies at different times have decided that it is not safe for individuals to pay any price or have set the bar at what is an unacceptable price. In other words, they have regulated the characteristics of the product.

In Australia today, no consumer credit product can have an annual cost rate greater than 48 per cent.[88] Neither brokers nor credit providers can advise on or enter into credit contracts where the annual cost rate is greater than 48 per cent.[89] The annual cost rate of a medium-amount credit contract must not exceed 48 per cent.[90] A medium-amount credit contract is one provided by a non-ADI and is not a

83 Ibid s 180A(4)(a).
84 Ibid s 180A(4)(c).
85 Ibid s 180A(4)(d).
86 Ibid s 180A(4)(e), (f) and (g) – against conscience; the defendant determining or significantly influencing the terms; the terms less favourable to the plaintiff than terms of comparable contracts.
87 Consumer Credit Legislation Amendment (Enhancements) Bill 2012, Revised Explanatory Memorandum, para 2.44.
88 The calculation of the annual cost rate is set out in the legislation in NCCP Act, sch 1, s 32B.
89 NCCP Act, sch 1, s 32A. This cap was already in force in the Australian Capital Territory, New South Wales and Queensland.
90 Ibid s 32B(1).

continuing credit contract. It is for more than $2,001 and less than $5,000 and for between 16 days and two years.[91]

There are special provisions for small-amount contracts. These restrict interest, fees and charges on small-amount contracts.[92] The only permissible fees are establishment fees, monthly fees, default fees and government fees and charges.[93] No establishment fee can be charged to refinance another small-amount contract.[94] There are limits on the amounts that can be charged as an establishment fee or as a monthly fee.[95] There is a prohibition on subsequently varying a small-amount contract if the effect is to exceed the 48 per cent annual cost rate.[96]

Not only do the small-amount provisions restrict cost, they also restrict use. No amount of small-amount credit can be used to pay the lender.[97] This is in part to prevent credit providers from increasing the amounts debtors must pay by also requiring them to purchase goods and services from the credit provider, sometimes at inflated prices.[98] There are exceptions for the permitted fees and charges.[99] Small-amount credit can also be used to refinance other small-amount credit provided by that credit provider.[100] Small-amount borrowers are protected by a limitation on the amount that can be recovered by the lender if the debtor is in default.[101] The limit is twice the adjusted credit amount.[102] Any term in the contract that provides otherwise is void.[103]

These measures which circumscribe the cost and use of small-amount credit are designed to make small-amount credit safer. Many small-amount debtors are people on very low incomes.[104] The threat to borrowers is that, as suggested in the Explanatory Memorandum, a combination of circumstances may very quickly lead to a debtor being unable to repay.[105] These are set out as the lower the income the greater the reduction in income to meet repayments; the shorter the term the less the borrower is likely to receive from other income sources to repay; the more credit contracts entered into in a short period, the more income is used for repayments

91 Ibid s 204(1).
92 These provisions commenced on 1 July 2013. See NCCP Act, sch 1 (Enhancements legislation sch 4). For details, see Nicola Howell, 'Interest Rate Caps and Price Regulation in Consumer Credit' in J Malbon and N Nottage (eds), *Consumer Law and Policy in Australia and New Zealand* (The Federation Press 2013) table 2, 317–318.
93 NCCP Act, sch 1, ss 31A and 31B.
94 NCCP Act, sch1, s 31A(1A).
95 NCCP Act, sch 1, ss 31A(2) and 31A(3). These are, respectively, 20 per cent of the adjusted credit amount and 4 per cent of the adjusted credit amount.
96 NCCP Act, sch 1, s 32AA.
97 NCCP Act, sch 1, s 39A.
98 Consumer Credit Legislation Amendment (Enhancements) Bill 2012, Revised Explanatory Memorandum, para 5.63.
99 NCCP Act, sch 1, s 39A(2).
100 NCCP Act, sch 1, s 39A(2)(ba).
101 NCCP Act, sch 1, s 39B.
102 NCCP Act, sch 1, s 39B(1).
103 NCCP Act, sch 1, s 39B(2).
104 Consumer Credit Legislation Amendment (Enhancements) Bill 2012, Revised Explanatory Memorandum, para 5.7.
105 Ibid para 5.8.

than for ongoing expenses; different credit providers have had different costs and some borrowers have need to borrow irrespective of the cost.[106]

5 Suitable for one

The disclosure model of credit regulation presupposes that individuals will make rational choices, that they will choose a service or product that is suitable for them. We know this does not always happen.[107] Nevertheless, information obligations are directed towards enabling that choice.

We have seen above that some products, small-amount or payday loans and reverse equity or reverse mortgages, are cast as so dangerous that they are not safe for anyone without specific regulation. Most consumer credit products are not regarded as so dangerous and are available to be chosen by anyone. The purpose of information requirements is to ensure that there is information available about the product from which individuals might choose what is suitable or even best for them.

5.1 Mandatory information and banned statements: for comparison and choice

To encourage individuals to compare products and choose something suitable for them, there are Key Fact Sheets for home loans and credit cards.[108] If a lender's website has the capacity for consumers to enquire or apply for a loan, the website must have the ability to generate a Key Fact Sheet.[109] Similarly, there are information sheets for reverse mortgages. Potential borrowers under a reverse mortgage must receive information about the nature of reverse mortgages. If a broker or a lender has a website to provide information about reverse mortgages, they must have a reverse mortgage information sheet on the website.[110] This information statement must also be given to a consumer if she asks for one.[111]

Three new information requirements acknowledge that notwithstanding the information that must be given to consumers to compare and choose, certain representations can muddy the waters. The impact of certain statements, if not wholly true, may encourage consumers to choose to deal with persons who may not be suitable for them.

Credit licensees cannot use the words independent, impartial, unbiased or financial counsellor.[112] There are defences for the use of these words. For the first three – independent, impartial, unbiased – the defence in essence sets out what would be required to ensure the use of the words is accurate. It is a defence if the licensee or licensee's employer does not receive any commissions (unless they are fully rebated to the client) or receive gifts or benefits that might influence the licensee; if a broker is free from any restrictions regarding with whom he may arrange credit

106 Ibid para 5.7.
107 On the shortcomings of mandatory disclosure, see Omri Ben-Shahar and Carl Schneider, *More Than You Wanted to Know: The Failure of Mandated Disclosure* (Princeton University Press 2014).
108 NCCP Act, ss 133AC and 133AD; NCCP Regulations, sch 5, reg 28LB; NCCP Act, ss 133BC and 133BD; NCCP Regulations, sch 6, reg 28LFA.
109 NCCP Act, s 133AC.
110 Ibid s 133DC.
111 Ibid s 133DD.
112 Ibid ss 160B and 160C.

contracts; if the broker is free from conflicts of interest with lenders which might influence the broker in providing the service.[113] A credit provider cannot use the term reverse mortgage when negotiating or entering into a credit contract unless the product truly has the characteristics of a reverse mortgage.[114] Use of the words financial counsellor or financial counselling may be defended if the licensee is a non-remunerated financial counsellor or if the term is used in association with a negative to indicate a person is not a financial counsellor.[115]

Neither credit providers nor credit assistants can unconditionally represent that a consumer is eligible to enter a credit contract or increase a credit limit unless they have undertaken a suitability assessment.[116] This is designed to prevent representations about the availability of credit irrespective of 'personal circumstances or credit history'.[117] While not directed towards protecting the vulnerable, it should also offer protection by fettering inducements to deal with brokers or lenders.

A further information requirement is to persuade individuals to consider choosing not to acquire specific products. Brokers and lenders may represent that they are able to assist or provide small-amount credit, provided they display prescribed information.[118] This information at offices and websites is a mandatory display of a warning. The office warning asks: 'Do you really need a loan today?'[119] The website warning includes: 'It can be expensive to borrow small amounts of money and borrowing may not solve your money problems.'[120]

5.2 Suitability to protect against irrational choice and information deficits

The 2009 legislation introduced a regime under which brokers and lenders must assess whether credit is 'not unsuitable' for a prospective debtor and make it an offence to propose or provide credit that is not suitable. The suitability provisions require a credit assistant or broker to make a preliminary assessment as to whether proposed credit at a particular point in time is 'not unsuitable' for an individual.[121] If it is unsuitable, it cannot be recommended.[122] Similarly, a prospective lender must also make a suitability assessment and cannot provide credit if the product is not 'not unsuitable'.[123]

One of the criteria for judging lack of suitability of the product for that particular individual is that the prospective debtor will only be able to comply with the repayment obligations with substantial hardship.[124] The standard of 'not unsuitable' does not require either the broker or lender to propose or provide a product that is best for the borrower.

113 Ibid s 160B(2).
114 Ibid s 133DE.
115 Ibid s 160C(2); NCCP Regulations, reg 20(5).
116 NCCP Act, s 128.
117 Consumer Credit Legislation Amendment (Enhancements) Bill 2012, Revised Explanatory Memorandum, para 2.61.
118 NCCP Act, ss 124B and 133CB.
119 NCCP Regulations, reg 28XXA.
120 Ibid reg 28XXB.
121 NCCP Act, s 116.
122 Ibid s 115.
123 Ibid ss 128 and 129.
124 Ibid ss 123(2)(a) and 132(2)(a).

The 2012 legislation enhances the approach to suitability for two products. These are the same products for which there is safety regulation via prescriptive product characteristics: small-amount loans and reverse mortgages. Prior to making the suitability assessment, both brokers and lenders must provide the person considering a reverse mortgage with a projection of his or her equity over time in the proposed property if he or she were to enter into a reverse mortgage.[125] These projections are to be made using an Australian Securities Investments Commission approved website and the consumer must be given a printed copy of the projections.[126] These projections are expected to show the impact over time of a reverse mortgage on the equity a person holds in their house.[127] The Explanatory Memorandum foreshadows Regulations that prescribe further information that must be given to the consumer, including that the consumer should consider alternatives to the reverse mortgage such as selling their house; and that a reverse mortgage may affect their entitlement to government benefits.[128] These matters do not go directly to suitability but they are addressed to the personal circumstances of the potential reverse mortgage debtor and directed not towards the suitability of a product but towards the lack of suitability of the class of products for that individual.

The small-amount credit provision is also about lack of suitability. When either the broker or lender undertakes the suitability assessment, they must consider the potential borrower's ADI account statements (if there are any) for the preceding 90 days.[129] For small-amount credit there is a presumption that in certain circumstances a prospective debtor will be able to comply with repayment obligations with substantial hardship.[130] Thus the proposed product will be unsuitable for the individual. The presumption arises if at the time of the preliminary assessment, the consumer has another small-amount contract and is in default under that contract or if in a 90-day period before the preliminary assessment the consumer has been a debtor under more than two other small-amount contracts.[131] This provision is concerned with the individual circumstances of the individual and whether a particular small-amount credit contract is suitable for that person.

6 No longer suitable, is it still safe?

The suitability assessment judges the suitability of particular products for a particular individual at a particular point in time. We have mentioned the potential for the performance characteristics of financial products to change over time. This is less likely for credit than for some other products. Nevertheless, the terms of a product such as the interest rate in a variable-rate product can change. The circumstances of an individual may change. What was once suitable may no longer be suitable for that individual due to a change of circumstances.

125 Ibid s 133DB.
126 Ibid ss 133DB(1)(a)(ii) and 133DB(1)(b).
127 Consumer Credit Legislation Amendment (Enhancements) Bill 2012, Revised Explanatory Memorandum, para 3.27.
128 Ibid para 3.28.
129 NCCP Act, s 130(1A).
130 Ibid s 118(3A).
131 Ibid s 118(3A)(a)(b).

There has long been provision to reopen a contract on grounds of substantial hardship.[132] The limitation of the grounds on which an application could be made limited this provision to potential safety only for certain classes of people. The potential safe harbour of the new hardship provisions apply to all. They link diminished suitability to safety.

Now, on any grounds, if debtors consider they will be unable to meet their obligations they can give the lender notice of this.[133] On receipt of the hardship notice, the lender may choose to send the debtor a request for further information (with which the debtor must comply) to enable it to assess whether the debtor is unable to meet those obligations and how to change the contract if this is the case.[134] In any case, after a set period, the credit provider must notify the debtor either that the lender and debtor have agreed to change the contract or that they have not agreed.[135] In the latter case, the lender must give reasons and notification of the lender's External Dispute Resolution scheme.[136] The option for a debtor to ask the court to reopen is still available if the credit provider declines to vary the contract.[137]

The open grounds for asking for a hardship variation will benefit some debtors. The hardship notice will also have an impact on enforcement proceedings. If before or after the credit provider gives the required default notice as a prelude to enforcement, the debtor gives a hardship notice (provided one had not been given in the last four months or, if given, was not materially different), the credit provider cannot commence enforcement until 14 days after responding to the hardship notice.[138]

7 Back to flannelette

Flannelette is now regarded as an old-fashioned comforting product. There is no longer danger from the surrounding circumstances of open fires. It is regarded as both suitable and safe. It may not be suitable for the objectives and requirements of some individuals, but these may be idiosyncratic purposes. Many may require flannelette for pyjamas but few would want to fashion a ball gown from flannelette. Yet it would be safe for both. There is no report or discussion paper considering banning flannelette. A product that was once unsuitable and unsafe for many has become safe for all. Judgments about the acceptability and safety of a product will reflect the purposes to which members of the community will put a product. Few will want to deliberately create financial distress for themselves and risk bankruptcy and loss of a house. The regulatory measures to guard freedom from financial harm for all or for special groups protect the community at large. By preserving a distinction between safety for all, specific safety measures for some groups and suitability for a particular individual, the regulatory design permits individuals a latitude of choice within generally safe parameters. The question for ongoing debate will be: how safe is safe?

132 For a comparison of new and old law, see Consumer Credit Legislation Amendment (Enhancements) Bill 2012, Revised Explanatory Memorandum, table 15.
133 NCCP Act, sch 1, s 72(1). This can be given orally or in writing.
134 NCCP Act, sch, s 72(2).
135 NCCP Act, sch 1, s 72(4).
136 NCCP Act, sch 1, s 72(4)(b)(ii), (iii) and (iv).
137 NCCP Act, sch 1, s 74.
138 NCCP Act, sch 1, s 89A.

4 Responsible lending

Consumer protection and prudential regulation perspectives

Onyeka K. Osuji

1 Introduction

Recent amendments to the UK Financial Services and Markets Act 2000 (FSMA) by the Financial Services Act 2012 reflect the growing orthodoxy of duality of financial (prudential) regulation and consumer protection, a path also followed in sections 129 to 131 of Australia's National Consumer Credit Protection Act 2009 and in the establishment of the US Consumer Financial Protection Bureau. The duality of regulation model has led to the creation of two separate bodies for regulating the activities of banks and financial institutions. One regulator is typically responsible for prudential regulation while consumer protection broadly defined is the second regulator's responsibility. Although the assumption is that prudential regulation and consumer protection operate in different coherent spheres, their dividing line is often nebulous in practice.

One area where both financial regulation and consumer protection concerns overlap is consumer indebtedness. In August 2014, the aggregate personal debt in the UK was £1.455 trillion; the average household debt was £55,088; the average individual adult debt was £28,813, which was about 116 per cent of earnings; estimated interest repayments were £162 million per day and £59.2 billion over a 12-month period; average household annual interest repayments were £2,242, while individuals paid £1,173 constituting about 4.7 per cent of earnings in annual interest repayments. The total outstanding mortgage debt relating to about 11.1 million households was £1.29 trillion. Households owed on average £115,940 in mortgage debt and paid average annual interest of £3,733. In relation to consumer credit, the outstanding lending was £162.2 billion, while the average individual adult and household consumer credit debts were £3,220 and £6,155, respectively. In relation to credit cards, the average household debt was £2,180. Interest payments for the total debt of £57.6 billion would cost the average credit card holder £54 per month to clear the debt in five years or £38 per month to clear in ten years.

The size of consumer debt in the UK renders it a significant phenomenon. Size alone does not turn a phenomenon into a problem, but there is also evidence of market failure. For example, recent consumer indebtedness statistics in the UK suggest a huge and growing problem despite widespread public concern and varying degrees of regulatory intervention.[1] The Citizens Advice Bureaux in England and

1 The Money Charity, *The Money Statistics October 2014* http://themoneycharity.org.uk/money-statistics accessed 13 October 2014.

Wales report 6,405 new consumer indebtedness cases every working day. On average, in the UK, one person every five minutes and 297 every day are declared bankrupt. There are 118 mortgage possession claims, 87 mortgage possession orders and 71 repossessions of mortgaged properties every day in the UK.

It is largely because of the consequences of consumer indebtedness that *responsible lending* is attracting increased attention. Responsible lending involves evaluating contextual factors that impact on a borrower's ability to repay loans. The factors include existing indebtedness, employment situation, caring responsibilities, psychological, physical and emotional health situations, personal habits and consumption. As a result, Charlie McCreevy, the European Union Internal Market Commissioner, described responsible lending and responsible borrowing respectively as '[w]here the credit products sold are appropriate for consumers' needs and are tailored to their ability to repay' and 'where consumers provide relevant, complete and accurate information on their financial conditions'.[2] The Internal Market Commissioner, therefore, regarded both responsible lending and responsible borrowing as 'vital components in ensuring a stable and effective market'.[3]

At its most extreme, irresponsible lending is when a lender lends money without the slightest interest in assessing the borrower's ability to repay. A clear case of irresponsible lending recounted by Gary Rivlin was in relation to a store manager of a large US payday lender who was sacked for not complying with the management's instruction to the effect that 'if a body walks in the door, you loan 'em money'.[4]

There are at the least two dimensions of irresponsible lending on a cause-and-effect analysis. On the one hand, consumer protection concerns arising from irresponsible lending include regulatory avoidance and unfair practices by lenders and associated suppliers of consumer goods and services, consumer debt traps and debt spirals, and high administrative costs of obtaining, maintaining and repaying consumer loans such as excessive interest rates and fees and charges for the establishment and maintenance of facilities and defaults. On the other hand, irresponsible lending can have serious consequences for the banking and financial sector and affect national and global financial stability. The recent Global Financial Crisis (GFC) is, for instance, regarded as a failure of banking regulation, including the failure to deal with irresponsible consumer lending.[5] This is easily illustrated by the case of Hibernian Bank of Scotland (HBOS) in the UK. The Parliamentary Commission on Banking Standards described the collapse of HBOS during the GFC as a product of 'a failure of regulation' by the Financial Services Authority (FSA), of

2 Charlie McCreevy, Financial Services: Commission Launches Consultation on How to Ensure Responsible Lending and Borrowing in the EU (press release IP/09/922, 15 June 2009) http://europa.eu/rapid/press-release_IP-09–922_en.htm?locale=en accessed 10 August 2014.

3 Ibid.

4 Gary Rivlin, *Broke USA: From Pawnshops to Poverty Inc – How the Working Poor Became Big Business* (Harper Collins 2011) 189.

5 Emilios Avgouleas, 'The Global Financial Crisis, Behavioural Finance and Financial Regulation: In Search of a New Orthodoxy' (2009) 9 Journal of Corporate Law Studies 121; Emilios Avgouleas, 'The Global Financial Crisis and the Disclosure Paradigm in European Financial regulation: The Case for Reform' (2009) 6 European Company and Financial Law Review 440.

'colossal failure of management' and of 'reckless lending'.[6] The Commission observed that 'regulatory failure played a major role in permitting standards to slip in the banks [and this] in turn added to the severity of the crisis'.[7]

This chapter examines the implications of segregating or diffusing the consumer protection and financial regulation functions in different regulators. There are three key questions relevant to the analysis of this dual regulatory structure. The first is whether there are considerable differences in the mandates and consequences of prudential regulation and consumer protection. The second is whether the consumer protection and financial regulation approaches can exist efficiently and effectively side by side. The third is whether the techniques, tools and effects of the consumer protection and financial regulation approaches to responsible lending coincide or are distinctive. At the core of these questions is the need for proper regulation, allocation of regulatory resources and clarity of regulatory goals and powers. A clash of regulatory powers and goals between competing regulators who may not see their roles as complementary promotes neither consumer protection nor financial stability. In fact, Principle One of the Basel Committee's Core principles for effective banking supervision states that 'an effective system of banking supervision has clear responsibilities and objectives for each authority involved in the supervision of banks and banking groups'.[8]

The rest of this chapter proceeds as follows. First, there is an analysis of the consumer finance market which is followed by an outline of the UK approaches to prudential regulation and consumer protection. The two approaches are then applied to responsible lending, an issue of common concern for both consumer protection and prudential regulation. It is found that although the goals of prudential regulation and consumer regulation may differ, the two approaches can and often do use similar regulatory techniques and tools. The third segment looks at the new dual-regulator system in the UK. It concludes that its complexities are problematic and make it heavily reliant on the personalities of individual officers of the regulatory bodies to achieve a coordinated and efficient regulatory system. This may not be good enough in the long term.

2 Regulating the consumer finance market

The dual regulator orthodoxy can be understood as a response to the special intermediation roles that banks and other financial institutions play in the consumer finance market and the economy generally. Banks provide financial services that are typically regarded as 'credence goods' because of consumer inexperience and

6 Parliamentary Commission on Banking Standards, *'An Accident Waiting to Happen': The Failure of HBOS* (Fourth Report of Session 2012–13, HL Paper 144, HC 705, April 2013) www.publications.parliament.uk/pa/jt201213/jtselect/jtpcbs/144/144.pdf accessed 10 August 2014; Parliamentary Commission on Banking Standards, *Changing Banking for Good* (First Report of Session 2013–14, HL Paper 27-1, HC 175-1, June 2013) 130–131, 396–397 www.parliament.uk/documents/banking-commission/banking-final-report-volume-i.pdf accessed 10 August 2014.

7 Parliamentary Commission on Banking Standards, *Changing Banking for Good* (n 6) 473–477 [1055].

8 Basel Committee on Banking Supervision, *Core Principles for Effective Banking Supervision* (Bank for International Settlements 2012) www.bis.org/publ/bcbs230.pdf accessed 12 September 2014.

incomprehension of the processes and consequences of such transactions.[9] Consequently, article 9 of the Unfair Commercial Practices Directive (UCPD) acknowledges that 'financial services ... by reason of their complexity and inherent serious risks, necessitate detailed requirements, including positive obligations on traders'.[10]

Prudential regulation and consumer protection constitute interventionist approaches to the failures of the market and aim to provide schemes for appropriate conduct by market participants. Both regulatory approaches may relate to the same market and target a similar class of market participants and issues. However, as outlined below, the objectives and consequences of prudential regulation and consumer protection can arguably differ.

2.1 Prudential regulation

Prudential regulation targets the risk exposure of banks in order to prevent systemic problems and ensure the stability of the financial system. At the macro-level, prudential regulation is designed to ensure the stability of the entire financial system, while at the micro-level it may involve the supervision of individual financial institutions. Micro-prudential regulation ensures financial system stability through the control of risky loans and excessive exposures, prevention of non-performing loans, capital adequacy requirements, improved corporate governance, prevention of market abuse and other measures. The Basel Committee's core principles for effective banking supervision contain detailed provisions on corrective and sanctioning powers (principle 11), corporate governance (principle 14), risk management process (principle 15), credit risk (principle 17), problem assets, provisions and reserves (principle 18), risk concentration and exposure (principle 19), market risks (principle twenty-two), interest rate risk (principle 23), liquidity risk (principle 24), operational risk (principle 25), internal control and audit (principle 26) and abuse of financial services (principle 29). These provisions essentially confirm that prudential regulation is risk management and prevention of market abuse.[11]

Therefore, prudential regulation provides institutional frameworks for capital adequacy, liquidity and solvency, as well as the control and reduction of risks. Particularly significant is the recognition of the credit risk arising from borrowers' default and the liquidity risk arising from the maturity discrepancies between the customers' short-term deposits that can be withdrawn on demand, and long-term and illiquid loans that are critical to the business of banking. This is why a key goal of risk management in banking supervision is the control, reduction and monitoring of credit risks and liquidity risks.[12]

9 Peter Rott, 'Consumer Credit' in Norbert Reich and others, *European Consumer Law* (2nd edn, Intersentia 2014) 200.

10 Directive 2005/29 on unfair business-to-consumer commercial practices in the internal market [2005] OJ L149/22 implemented in the UK by the Consumer Protection from Unfair Trading Regulations 2008 SI 1999/2083.

11 Basel Committee on Banking Supervision (n 8).

12 Panagiotis K Staikouras, 'A Novel Reasoning of the UK Supreme Court Decision in *Lehman Brothers*: The MiFID Segregation Rule from the Angle of Financial Intermediation and Regulation Theory' (2014) 2 Journal of Business Law 97, 104.

2.2 Consumer protection

Consumer protection focuses on party autonomy and other issues of private law. It plays a critical regulatory function that is different from private law protection techniques such as the contractual concepts of undue influence and misrepresentation.[13] In the business to consumer situations, consumer protection regulations typically treat 'consumers as presumptively weaker parties and therefore fit for protection from abuses by the stronger contracting parties'.[14] There are at the least three dimensions of consumer protection including the 'informed consumer', 'vulnerable consumer' and 'weaker' (party) standards.[15] This chapter, however, uses consumer protection as an umbrella term for, and interchangeably with, a number of concepts such as consumer welfare and consumer interest which share the goals of protecting weak and vulnerable consumers, shielding consumers from being victims of unfairness, empowering consumers through information, and promoting consumer alertness and confidence.

Thus, consumer protection involves substantive and procedural elements – redress mechanisms and other provisions that enshrine 'rules to protect consumers from inappropriate behaviour of traders'.[16] Areas of intervention include procedural formalities, information access and quality, cancellation and withdrawal rights, and enforcement rights. A major technique of consumer protection is consumer education and information, although this has limited success.[17] The quality and quantity of information have to be right: while proliferation of information imposes time and other constraints on the consumer's ability to read the materials provided, overly complex and poor-quality information hinders the consumer's ability to understand the information purportedly provided. This is why the effectiveness of information disclosure in consumer credit is particularly challenging.[18]

The consumer protection approach is an exception to the principle of *pacta sunt servanda* – that is *agreements must be kept* – an almost self-evident value for any just and efficient system of private law. Apart from the procedural formalities it may require, the approach may allow the courts to examine the substantive fairness of business to consumer transactions. For example, the courts may reopen consumer credit

13 See *Royal Bank of Scotland v Etridge (No 2)* [2001] UKHL 44; *Hewett v First Plus Financial Group plc* [2010] EWCA Civ 312.

14 *Director General of Fair Trading v First National Bank plc* [2001] UKHL 52, [2002] 1 AC 481 [31] (Lord Steyn).

15 See Nobert Reich and Hans-Wolfgang Micklitz, 'Economic Law, Consumer Interests, and EU Integration' in Norbert Reich and others, *European Consumer Law* (2nd edn, Intersentia 2014) 45–52.

16 Louise Sylvan, 'Activating Competition: The Consumer–Competition Interface' (2004) 12 Competition and Consumer Law Journal 191, 194.

17 Better Regulation Executive and National Consumer Council, *Warning: Too Much Information Can Harm* (Department for Business, Enterprise and Regulatory Reform 2007); Marianne Bertrand and Adair Morse, 'Information Disclosure, Cognitive Biases, and Payday Borrowing' (2011) 66 Journal of Finance 1865; P Dolan, M Hallworth, D Halpern, D King, R Metcalfe and I Lvaev, 'Influencing Behaviour: The Mindspace Way' (2012) 33 Journal of Economic Psychology 264; Geraint Howells, 'The Potential and Limits of Consumer Empowerment by Information' (2005) 32 Journal of Law and Society 349; Rossella Incardona and Cristina Poncibó, 'The Average Consumer, the Unfair Commercial Practices Directive, and the Cognitive Revolution' (2007) 30(1) Journal of Consumer Policy 2; Lauren E Willis, 'Decisionmaking and the Limits of Disclosure: The Problem of Predatory Lending – Price' (2006) 65 Maryland Law Review 707.

18 Willis (n 17).

contracts and impugn contractual terms on grounds such as excessive interest, charges and exploitation of consumers.[19] The consumer protection approach often adopts a general scheme that applies to consumers, in particular business-to-consumer transactions. For instance, the reflective opportunity and other protective measures contained in the right to cancel contracts concluded away from the business premises apply consistently to all consumers and do not distinguish the consumers' ability to negotiate.[20]

The consumer protection approach, exemplified by the Consumer Credit Directive 2008/48/EC,[21] articles 4, 5, 6, 8, 10, 12 and 18, contains provisions on the nature and content of credit advertisements and pre-contractual information including the rate, total cost, total amount, annual percentage rate of charge and duration of the credit and required ancillary services; the amount, frequency and allocation of repayments; charges and consequences of payment and other defaults; pre-contractual advice by the lender or an intermediary to enable the consumer to make an informed decision on the suitability of a loan; the lender's assessment of the consumer's creditworthiness; the form and content of consumer credit agreements; and the amount and conditions of overdraft and overrunning facilities. Articles 13 and 14 contain the consumer's rights to terminate and withdraw from credit agreements and opt for early repayment of loans, while article 23 contemplates sanctions against lenders for violating consumer protection rules. There are further provisions in articles 15 and 21 for protecting consumers in linked agreements and in transactions involving intermediaries.

3 Regulatory perspectives on responsible lending

We can see from the brief outlines above that the consumer protection and prudential regulation approaches to responsible lending reflect different goals and therefore suggest separate regulatory terrains. However, while consumer protection arises in business-to-consumer transactions, prudential regulation can apply to both business-to-business and business-to-consumer transactions. For example, a relevant factor for managing credit risks is ensuring the borrower's ability to repay. This is equally an issue in business-to-business lending and underwriting transactions involving financial institutions and other firms, and in a business-to-consumer context where consumers are borrowers. An example is consumer credit, defined as:

> [T]he provision of credit to a natural person where the credit is provided wholly or predominantly for personal, household, or domestic purposes, where a charge is made for providing the credit and where the credit is provided in the course of a business providing credit or as part of or incidental to any other business of the credit provider.[22]

19 Eva Lomnicka, 'Unfair Credit Relationships: Five Years On' (2012) 8 Journal of Business Law 713.

20 *Swift v Robertson* [2014] UKSC 50 [26] (Lord Kerr, JSC).

21 Directive 2008/48/EC of the European Parliament and of the Council of 23 April 2008 on credit agreements for consumers and repealing Council Directive 87/102/EEC OJ L133/66. See the analysis by Rott (n 9) 207–234.

22 Therese Wilson, Nicola Howell and Genevieve Sheehan, 'Protecting the Most Vulnerable in Consumer Credit Transactions' (2009) 32 Journal of Consumer Policy 117, 118.

Consumer credit has been a battleground for rules against irresponsible lending. The driving force behind irresponsible lending is the urge to obtain the borrower's *agreement* to a credit facility at any cost and careless indifference as to the affordability and manageability of the loan for the borrower and its recoverability for the lender. From the prudential regulation perspective, it is irresponsible lending when a lender deliberately shuts its eyes to facts or neglects to evaluate facts that suggest that borrowers cannot afford loans and have no reasonable means of making repayments. It is irresponsible lending when the staff or other agents of the lender are mainly motivated by the prospect of a bonus, meeting targets or other rewards to promote short-termism by, for example, not conducting proper due diligence and credit checks and ignoring facts relevant to a long-term and sustainable view of loan facilities and borrowers. For instance, a prospective borrower who is already heavily indebted to the lender or other lenders and is struggling to service these loans is not a good candidate for fresh loans. Similarly, a responsible lender will be wary of proceeding if the lender knows or has reasons to believe that a prospective borrower will use the borrowed funds for unworthy or wasteful projects that the borrower does not really need. Examples include when the borrowing is to be used to fund a gambling habit and to organise an expensive birthday party. Since having full knowledge of the terms and conditions of the loan is critical to a borrower's informed decision, a lender is irresponsible if it proceeds with a facility despite knowing or having reason to believe that the borrower is unaware of or mistaken as to the loan's exact terms and conditions.

Irresponsible lending from the consumer protection perspective occurs, for example, when a lender deliberately misleads the borrower about the extent of a loan facility and obligations arising under it, fails or neglects to make the exact terms and conditions of a loan facility available to the borrower, or conceals information that may enable the borrower to make an informed decision on the loan's affordability. It is similarly irresponsible lending when the lender applies harassment or oppressive tactics to attract borrowers since such actions adversely affect the borrower's ability to make an informed decision. If borrowers subsequently have difficulties in repaying loans and fulfilling their obligations under the loan agreements, it may be irresponsible lending if harassment or aggressive and oppressive methods are applied by lenders and debt collectors contracted to enforce loan agreements. Such actions can cause serious emotional or psychological distress for the consumer. It is for this reason that using threats of legal actions to compel consumers to make repayments of loans that fail to comply with formal and procedural requirements of consumer credit law is regarded as an unfair commercial practice.[23]

There are, therefore, procedural steps relating to information gathering and dissemination and decision-making for the lender and borrower that lenders need to take to avoid the irresponsible lending tag. A lender can conduct appropriate due diligence and credit checks, investigate the borrower's circumstances from the borrower and other sources to ascertain the borrower's overall level of indebtedness and ability to repay any further loans. A responsible lender refrains from misleading advertising and fully explains the terms and conditions of loans to borrowers to enable them make an informed decision on whether to borrow or not to borrow. Responsible lenders treat borrowers fairly before and throughout the loan

23 See *In Re London Scottish Finance Ltd, Jack v Craig* [2013] EWHC 4047 (Ch), [2013] WLR (D) 498.

agreement and avoid harassing, aggressive and oppressive actions that can cause distress to borrowers and cause them to make decisions that are not in their interest. Responsible lenders monitor the loan and repayments, investigate borrowers' repayment difficulties and offer assistance to borrowers to ensure that loan repayments continue in a healthy way and avoid writing off loans as non-performing. These steps are necessary to comply with the demands of both prudential regulation and consumer protection for assessing the borrower's suitability for the loan facility, the loan's affordability for the borrower and the viability of the loan agreement for the lender. This suggests that the two approaches can make similar regulatory demands and use similar techniques, although their goals may be distinct. A number of these demands and techniques in relation to responsible lending are outlined below.

3.1 Paternalism

Consumer protection and prudential regulation can share paternalistic goals of constraining freedom of contract for the benefit of either party or both parties to a transaction. Consumer protection's paternalistic[24] slant challenges libertarian arguments that insist on freedom of contract for consumer lending in contrast to legal interventions.[25] It is a paternalistic approach arising from the belief that individual consumers may be unable to choose an instrumentally or intrinsically good or desirable decision or outcome for themselves and society.[26]

The main difference between consumer protection and prudential regulation is the subject of paternalism. While prudential regulation focuses on the lender as an institution or component of the financial system, the consumer is the protected subject of consumer protection. Consumer protection often proceeds on the basis that the lender owes the consumer a duty of care. For example, section 1C(2)(e) and (f) of the FSMA requires the Financial Conduct Authority (FCA) to consider:

> [T]he general principle that those providing regulated financial services should be expected to provide consumers with a level of care that is appropriate having regard to the degree of risk involved in relation to the investment or other transaction and the capabilities of the consumers in question [and] the differing expectations that consumers may have in relation to different kinds of investment or other transaction.

3.2 Fairness

Although it may not be necessary for prudential regulation, fairness to consumers is a major objective in consumer protection. For example, the consumer's right to

24 Robert Mayer, 'When and Why Usury Should Be Prohibited' (2003) 116 Journal of Business Ethics 513, 524.

25 For such libertarian arguments, see David Baker and MacKenzie Breitenstein, 'History Repeats Itself: Why Interest Rate Caps Pave the Way for the Return of the Loan Sharks' (2010) 127 Banking Law Journal 581; Alyssa Labat and Walter E Block, 'Money Does Not Grow on Trees: An Argument for Usury' (2012) 106 Journal of Business Ethics 383.

26 Riccardo Rebonato, 'A Critical Assessment of Libertarian Paternalism' (2014) 37 Journal of Consumer Policy 357, 358.

withdraw from contracts in the Consumer Rights Directive[27] protects consumers from exploitation by commercial parties and enhances their ability to avoid irrational decisions.[28] The central role of fairness in the consumer protection perspective to responsible lending can be seen from the UCPD. While article 3(1) incorporates pre- and post-contract conduct, article 2(d) defines a commercial practice as 'any act, omission, course of conduct or representation, commercial communication including advertising and marketing, by a trader, directly connected with the promotion, sale or supply of a product to consumers'. The European Court of Justice (ECJ) considered this 'a particularly wide definition of the concept of commercial practices'[29] and, for instance, confirmed that loans from commercial lenders to consumers are commercial practices that can be examined under the unfairness provisions of the UCPD.[30] The unfair terms provisions of directive 93/13 also apply to consumer loans.[31] These provisions apply similar 'significant imbalance' tests which are:

> [M]et if a term is so weighted in favour of the supplier as to tilt the parties' rights and obligations under the contract significantly in his favour. This may be by the ... imposing on the consumer of a disadvantageous burden or risk or duty ... whether a given term is or is not to be so regarded depends on whether it causes a significant imbalance in the parties' rights and obligations under the contract.[32]

It is significant that the major cases in the UK concerning the unfairness provisions of directive 93/13[33] and the UCPD and their implementing UK legislations (the Unfair Terms in Consumer Contracts Regulations 1999 and Consumer Protection from Unfair Trading Regulations 2008 (CPUTR))[34] involve banks.[35] Therefore, the concept of fairness has several ramifications for banks and other lenders. Unfairness is particularly prominent in discussions regarding interest rates, charges, non-payment, late payment, honour, dishonour, over-limit and other service fees,

27 Directive 2011/83/EU of the European Parliament and of the Council of 25 October 2011 on consumer rights, OJ L304, 22.11.2011, 0064-0088, preamble 39.

28 JA Luzak, 'To Withdraw or not to Withdraw? Evaluation of the Mandatory Right of Withdrawal in Consumer Distance Selling Contracts Taking into Account Its Behavioural Effects on Consumers' (2014) 37 Journal of Consumer Policy 91; Christian Twigg-Flesner and Reiner Schulze, 'Protecting Rational Choice: Information and the Right of Withdrawal' in Geraint G Howells, I Ramsay and Thomas Wilhelmsson (eds), *Handbook of Research on International Consumer Law* (Edward Elgar Publishing 2010).

29 *Zentrale zur Bekämpfung unlauteren Wettbewerbs eV v Plus Warenhandelsgesellschaft mbH* (C-304/08), 14 January 2010 [36].

30 C-453/10 *Perenicova v SOS Financ Spol sro* [2002] 2 All ER (Comm) 907 (ECJ (1st Chamber)).

31 C-26/13 *Kásler v OTP Jelzálogbank Zrt* [2014] WLR (D) 180.

32 *Director General of Fair Trading v First National Bank plc* (n 14) [17] (Lord Bingham).

33 Directive 93/13 on unfair terms in consumer contracts [1993] OJ L095/29 implemented in the UK by the Unfair Terms in Consumer Contracts Regulations 1999 (UTCCR) SI 2008/1277.

34 The Consumer Protection from Unfair Trading Regulations 2008 (SI 2008/1277) implementing Directive 2005/29/EC concerning unfair business–consumer commercial practices in the internal market [2005] L149/22, SI 2008/1277 in force on 26 May 2008.

35 See *Director General of Fair Trading v First National Bank plc* (n 14); *Office of Fair Trading v Abbey National plc* [2009] UKSC 6; *Office of Fair Trading v Lloyds TSB Bank plc* [2007] UKHL 48, [2008] 1 AC 316. For charges see *MBNA Europe Bank Ltd v Thorius* [2010] ECC 8.

penalties and costs of credit which are often seen as exploitative of consumers and directly linked to over-indebtedness.[36] Unfairness provisions have been used when, for example, the annual percentage rate for borrowings is mis-stated or inflated.[37] In *Director General of Fair Trading v First National Bank plc* it was explained that 'fair dealing requires that [lenders] should not, whether, deliberately or unconsciously, take advantage of the consumer's necessity, indigence, lack of experience, unfamiliarity with the subject matter of the contract, and weak bargaining position'.[38] Consumers equally need to be treated fairly. This may require 'forbearance and consideration towards borrowers experiencing difficulty [and] providing them with reasonable time and opportunity to meet repayments'.[39] It may also relate to 'proportionality in dealings between creditors and borrowers [which may require that] [a]ctions taken in respect of arrears or default should give proper consideration to available options with repossession of a borrower's home only being used as a last resort'.[40]

3.3 Consumer responsibility

Despite the differences in the paternalistic approaches of consumer protection and prudential regulation, the need for consumers' responsibility for their decisions and actions is normally acknowledged in both approaches. It is in the interest of the financial system and consumers generally for the legal system to support, facilitate and enforce credit agreements in order to incentivise lenders and provide a competitive market that ensures the availability of credit. This is why the information paradigm focuses on consumer *responsibilisation* by ensuring that 'individuals become responsible consumers through the use of information, the development of financial capability, and financial literacy programmes'.[41] Consequently, the FCA is required to recognise 'the general principle that consumers should take responsibility for their decisions' (section 1C(2)(d) of the FSMA). This may involve the consideration of 'the differing degrees of risk involved in different kinds of investment or other transaction [and] the differing degrees of experience and expertise that different consumers may have' (section 1C(2)(a) and (b)).

3.4 Market competition and financial inclusion

A competitive consumer market is desired by both consumer protection and prudential regulation approaches. Prudential regulation ensures that financial institutions continue to play their intermediation roles which are critical to the financial

36 European Economic and Social Committee, *Opinion on 'Credit and Social Exclusion in an Affluent Society'* 2008/C44/19 [4.1]; S Brown, 'Using the Law as a Usury Law: Definitions of Usury and Recent Developments in the Regulation of Unfair Charges in Consumer Credit Transactions' (2011) 1 Journal of Business Law 91, 94–96.

37 DM Collins, 'Misleading APRs in Consumer Credit Agreements: A New Influence?' (2012) 7 Journal of Business Law 629.

38 *Director General of Fair Trading v First National Bank plc* (n 14) [17] (Lord Bingham).

39 Office of Fair Trading, *Irresponsible Lending: OFT Guidance for Creditors* (March 2010, updated February 2011) [2.3] http://webarchive.nationalarchives.gov.uk/20140402142426/http://www.oft.gov.uk/shared_oft/business_leaflets/general/oft1107.pdf accessed 1 November 2014.

40 Ibid.

41 Iain Ramsay, 'Consumer Law, Regulatory Capitalism and the "New Learning" in Regulation' (2006) 28 Sydney Law Review 9, 13.

system and the economy. On the other hand, one of the goals of consumer protection is to create and improve options for consumers and ensure 'that notions of consumer choice [do not] lose meaning'.[42] It is also for this reason that a regulatory regime facilitates schemes that allow comparisons of financial products and services.

Both prudential regulation and consumer protection can consider issues of credit access and financial inclusion. Thus, avoiding financial exclusion sits alongside over-indebtedness concerns and incorporates both the need for credit access and its affordability.[43] From the financial regulation perspective is the increasing acknowledgement of the role of banks in providing, improving and expanding access to credit for the financially excluded and disadvantaged.[44] Consumer protection similarly recognises the need to provide and promote access to credit and financial services for poor and vulnerable consumers.[45] Thus, financial exclusion is 'the lack of access by certain consumers to appropriate low cost, fair and safe financial products and services from mainstream providers'.[46] Consumer protection's competition and financial inclusion goals are probably the reason why, as part of its competition objective, the FCA may consider:

> [T]he ease with which consumers who may wish to use those services, including consumers in areas affected by social or economic deprivation, can access them, the ease with which consumers who obtain those services can change the person from whom they obtain them, the ease with which new entrants can enter the market, and how far competition is encouraging innovation.[47]

42 Marcus Banks and others, *Caught Short: Exploring the Role of Small, Short-Term Loans in the lives of Australians* (Final Report, Social Policy Unit, the University of Queensland, Brisbane, August 2012) www.uq.edu.au/swahs/news/CaughtShortFinalReport.pdf accessed 12 August 2014.

43 Wilson, Howell and Sheehan (n 22) 118.

44 Emilios Avgouleas, 'Access to Finance, Microfinance, and International Banking Regulation: A New Approach to Development' (2007) 4 Manchester Journal of International Economic Law 3; Thorsten Beck, Asli Demirguc-Kunt and Maria Soledad Martinez-Peria, 'Reaching Out: Access to and Use of Banking Services across Countries' (2007) 85 Journal of Financial Economics 234; Tzu-Kuan Chiu, 'Putting Responsible Finance to Work for Citi Microfinance' (2014) 119 Journal of Business Ethics 219; Marek Hudon, 'Should Access to Credit Be a Right?' (2009) 84(1) Journal of Business Ethics 17; Dean Karlan and Jonathan Zinman, 'Expanding Credit Access: Using Randomized Supply Decisions to Estimate the Impacts' (2010) 23(1) Review of Financial Studies 433.

45 See European Economic and Social Committee (n 36); Department for Business, Innovation and Skills, *A Better Deal for Consumers: Delivering Real Help Now and Change for the Future* (White Paper, Cm 7669, 2009) [2.1] www.gov.uk/government/uploads/system/uploads/attachment_data/file/238580/7669.pdf accessed 11 September 2014; Department for Trade and Industry, *Fair, Clear and Competitive: A Consumer Credit Market for the 21st Century* (White Paper, Cm 6040, 2003) [5.1], [5.46] www.gov.uk/government/uploads/system/uploads/attachment_data/file/273325/6040.pdf accessed 11 September 2014; Treasury Committee, *Financial Inclusion: Credit Savings Advice and Insurance* (Twelfth Report of Session 2005–2006, HC 848-1, 7 November 2006) www.publications.parliament.uk/pa/cm200506/cmselect/cmtreasy/848/848i.pdf accessed 11 September 2014; Brown (n 36) 96–97, 115.

46 Chant Link and Associates, *A Report on Financial Exclusion in Australia* (Australian and New Zealand Banking Group 2004) 58.

47 Section 1E(2) of the Financial Services and Markets Act 2000 as amended by the Financial Services Act 2012.

3.5 Affordability

Affordability is central to the responsible lending and financial inclusion goals of both consumer protection and prudential regulation. Affordability is the calculation of consumers' ability to repay loans without substantial difficulties and hardship to them or their families. This calculation involves, for example, the borrower's present and future net income and individual and household expenditure in relation to repayments for the principal sum and present and future increased interest rates.[48]

3.6 Credit ratings

Credit ratings are relevant to the determination of affordability and can therefore be targeted by both prudential regulation and consumer protection. Their effect on the financial system makes credit rating and reference agencies a candidate for prudential regulation. For instance, the quality, objectivity, reliability and credibility of credit ratings have been linked to recent national banking scandals and financial crises, and this has inspired increasing attention to their regulation.[49] Similarly, article 8 of the Consumer Credit Directive 2008 indicates that the need for assessment of consumer creditworthiness and responsible lending based on information from a suitable consumer information database is equally an appropriate consumer protection issue.[50] Regulation of credit ratings from the consumer protection perspective also prevents financial exclusion through incorrect credit rankings.

3.7 Adequacy of collateral

Another relevant factor for affordability is the value of collateral for secured loans. Prudential regulation would require that property and other security for a loan should be valued properly. This is in the interest of the lender. Where property is, for example, negligently overvalued, the lender may not be able to recover the value of the loan in case of the borrower's default.[51] A consumer protection view may be interested in a valuation process that does not, for example, hinder the consumer's access to credit through undervaluation.

3.8 Borrower verification

Affordability concerns from both consumer protection and prudential regulation perspectives demand that lenders should verify prospective borrowers' circumstances. This requires investigation of the consumer's financial situation, living and

48 Financial Services Authority, *Mortgage Market Review: Feedback on CP11/31 and Final Rules* (Policy Statement 12/16, October 2012) 7 www.fca.org.uk/static/documents/policy-statements/fsa-ps12-16.pdf accessed 12 September 2014.

49 Peter Yeoh, 'Self-Regulation, Regulation, Co-Regulation: The Credit Rating Industry Case' (2013) 2 Journal of Business Law 186.

50 Directive 2008/48/EC of the European Parliament and of the Council of 23 April 2008 on credit agreements for consumers and repealing Council Directive 87/102/EEC.

51 See *Kenny & Good Pty Ltd v MGICA* (1992) Ltd (1999) 199 CLR 413; *St George Bank Ltd v Quinerts Pty Ltd* (2009) 25 VR 666.

household expenses, the purpose of the loan and other circumstances that can impact on the ability to repay the loan; and verification of the information supplied by the consumer in that regard. Both consumer protection and prudential regulation may require the consumer and the lender to investigate the suitability of a facility through a demands, needs and suitability assessment. Lenders may be required to put questions to prospective borrowers to enable the lender to assess the suitability and appropriateness of a loan facility for a particular lender. The know-your-customer requirement serves an additional purpose in prudential regulation in helping to prevent and reduce fraudulent wastages of funds in the financial system. For instance, verifying the identity and signature of prospective borrowers is necessary to prevent lending to fraudulent people who are ultimately unable to repay loans.[52]

3.9 Databases and data sharing

The requirements of affordability checks, borrower verification and assessment of borrowers' creditworthiness make the maintenance of creditors' access to public and private databases and information sharing systems an important component of both prudential regulation[53] and consumer protection.[54] The correctness of information in databases is also a consumer protection issue that has prompted data protection rules that grant consumers access to and opportunity to challenge database information.[55]

3.10 Information disclosure

Although prudential regulation may contain information requirements to enable informed decisions on affordability, tackling the asymmetric information problem between lenders and consumers is a central consumer protection issue. In *Director General of Fair Trading v First National Bank plc* it was observed that lender-generated information must be given 'fully, clearly and legibly, containing no concealed pitfalls or traps [and] appropriate prominence should be given to terms which might operate disadvantageously to the customer'.[56] The information paradigm for consumer credit regulation exemplified in the US Truth in Lending Act 1968 is based on 'informed consumer choice in the credit market place'.[57] Similarly, the UK Consumer Credit Acts 1974 and 2006 require lenders to provide certain information to prospective borrowers to enable them to make an informed decision as to the need for and affordability of loans. The Consumer Credit (Total Charge for Credit)

52 See the facts of *Hunt & Hunt Lawyers v Mitchell Morgan Nominees Pty Ltd* [2013] HCA 10 [2], [3].

53 See *Consultation on the Removal of Barriers to the Sharing of Non-consensual Credit Data* (DTI URN 06/1357); European Commission, *Consultation Document on Report of the Expert Group on Credit Histories* (15 June 2009) http://ec.europa.eu/internal_market/consultations/docs/2009/credit_histories/consultation_en.pdf accessed 10 July 2014.

54 See Consumer Credit Directive 2008, preamble 28 and article 9.

55 See Consumer Credit Directive 2008, article 9(4); Directive 95/46/EC of the European Parliament and of the Council of 24 October 1995 on the protection of individuals with regard to the processing of personal data and on the free movement of such data.

56 *Director General of Fair Trading v First National Bank plc* (n 14) [17] (Lord Bingham).

57 Ndiva Kofele-Kale, 'The Impact of Truth-in-Lending Disclosures on Consumer Market Behaviour: A Critique of the Critics of Truth-in-Lending Law' (1984) 9 Oklahoma City University Law Review 117, 117.

Regulations 2010[58] require that lenders state all the components of a credit facility and specify the *credit* and *total charge for credit* so that borrowers will be in a better position to make their own decisions as to affordability.

Fairness is another reason for these information requirements. Consequently, the UK Office for Fair Trading (OFT) advised that responsible lending includes:

> Transparency in dealings between creditors and borrowers, with information and documentation directed at – or provided to – borrowers being compliant with relevant legislative requirements and not in any way misleading [and] disclosure of key contract terms and conditions (including rates and charges), ensuring terms and conditions are fair (including ensuring that they are not unfairly balanced in favour of the creditor), clear and intelligible, so as to be understandable by borrowers.[59]

Under the FSMA, the FCA must consider 'the needs that consumers may have for the timely provision of information and advice that is accurate and fit for purpose' as part of its consumer protection objective and in its competition objective (section 1C(2)(c)) and may consider 'the needs of different consumers who use or may use those services, including their need for information that enables them to make informed choices' (section 1E(2)(a)).

3.11 Consumer education

Consumer education is increasingly recognised for helping to sustain the notion of consumer responsibility. Consumer credit providers may be required to verbally warn prospective borrowers of the need, expense and suitability of loans or by putting up relevant notices in correspondence, business premises and on websites. Regulators may also be required to undertake consumer education. For example, section 1C(2)(g) of the FSMA provides that the FCA must consider 'any information which the consumer financial education body has provided to the FCA in the exercise of the consumer financial education function'. Under section 3S, the 'consumer financial education body' has the 'consumer financial education function' which is, 'to enhance – (a) the understanding and knowledge of members of the public of financial matters (including the UK financial system); and (b) the ability of members of the public to manage their own financial affairs'. According to section 3S(4), the function includes:

> (a) promoting awareness of the benefits of financial planning; (b) promoting awareness of the financial advantages and disadvantages in relation to particular decisions relating to different kinds of goods or services; (c) promoting awareness of the benefits and risks associated with different kinds of financial dealing (which includes informing the FCA and other bodies of those benefits and risks); (d) the publication of educational materials or the carrying out of other educational activities; [and] (e) the provision of information and advice to members of the public.

58 Consumer Credit (Total Charge for Credit) Regulations 2010 SI 2010/1014 issued under the Consumer Credit Acts 1974 and 2006.

59 Office of Fair Trading, *Irresponsible Lending: OFT Guidance for Creditors* (n 39).

Debt management is a prominent component of consumer education that can be facilitated by public consumer protection bodies or private persons with the support of public bodies. This explains why the 'consumer financial education function' also includes:

> Assisting members of the public with the management of debt [and] working with other organisations which provide debt services, with a view to improving – (i) the availability to the public of those services, (ii) the quality of the services provided, (iii) consistency in the services available, in the way in which they are provided and in the advice given (section 3S(f) and (g) FSMA).

3.12 Credit advertising

In the UK, the increasingly 'vigorous advertising'[60] of consumer credit services has led to affordability concerns from both the prudential regulation and consumer protection perspectives. Advertising can create undue and excessive demand for consumer credit which may have adverse consequences for individual consumers and the financial system. Therefore, both prudential regulation and consumer protection may regulate credit advertising. An example is article 4 of the Consumer Credit Directive 2008, which provides for standard information requirements in credit advertising that will facilitate decisions on affordability.

Fairness, suitability and vulnerability are additional reasons for consumer protection interest in credit advertising. As the OFT advised:

> Borrowers should not be targeted with credit products that are clearly unsuitable for them, subjected to high pressure selling, aggressive or oppressive behaviour or inappropriate coercion, or conduct which is deceitful, oppressive, unfair or improper, whether unlawful or not. Borrowers who may be particularly vulnerable by virtue of their current indebtedness, poor credit history, or by reason of age or health, or disability, or for any other reason, should, in particular, not be targeted or exploited.[61]

3.13 Licensing

To ensure that lenders are *suitable* persons, prudential regulation and consumer protection often include licensing and registration requirements and sanctions for *illegal* lending that contravenes regulations. The importance of licensing to prudential regulation is recognised by principle 4 of the Basel Committee's core principles for effective banking supervision.[62] Sections 19, 20, 22 and 23 of the FSMA similarly allow only authorised and exempt persons to carry out regulated activities. The consumer protection approach is apparent in sections 26A, 27, 28 and 28A of the FSMA, which declare that credit agreements by or through unlicensed lenders are unenforceable and give debtors the right to recover any money or property transferred under such agreements and to seek compensation for losses.

60 Margaret Griffiths, 'Consumer Credit Advertising: Transparent at Last?' (2006) 11(3) Communications Law 75, 75.

61 Office of Fair Trading, *Irresponsible Lending: OFT Guidance for Creditors* (n 39).

62 Basel Committee on Banking Supervision (n 8).

3.14 Creditor fitness test

Licensing is sometimes supported by creditor fitness tests carried out during and after the business of lending. The FSMA demonstrates that such tests may be used for both consumer protection and prudential regulation. Section 56 gives both the Prudential Regulation Authority (PRA) and the FCA the power to issue a 'prohibition order' against an individual who is not 'a fit and proper person' to carry out functions related to a regulated activity. Section 63 allows the regulators to withdraw approvals given to persons who are subsequently not fit and proper.

3.15 Creditor officer responsibility

Both prudential regulation and consumer protection may provide for the responsibility and liability of individual credit officers for violating relevant rules. There may be provisions for sanctions, including withdrawal and reduction of pay, bonuses and compensation packages. A regulatory regime may require employers and licensed persons to report disciplinary actions taken against employees and other persons holding credit-related roles. For instance, section 64C requires authorised persons to report to either the PRA or the FCA '(a) the issuing of a formal written warning; (b) the suspension or dismissal of the person; (c) the reduction or recovery of any of the person's remuneration to any person for contravening any rules made by the relevant regulator'.

3.16 Intermediaries

Both consumer protection and prudential regulation may require the lender to ensure that brokers, agents, representatives and other intermediaries acting for or on its behalf are suitable persons and comply with relevant legal rules and industry codes of conduct. For example, in addition to the sound and proper needs, demands and suitability assessment requirement in section 6, section 5 of the 2004 Lending Code of the Finance and Leasing Association (FLA) require its members to deal with 'responsible' credit brokers only and avoid dishonest and incompetent brokers and those that disregard the code. Section 5 also requires members to monitor the activities of credit brokers who act on their behalf and demand their compliance with both the FLA code and the code of the Finance Industry Standards Association.[63]

The relationship with intermediaries is also a fairness issue for consumer protection. For example, non-disclosure of payment of commissions to brokers or related third parties may be considered unfair.[64] Lenders may be affected by the unfair trading practices of suppliers when they provide the financing for consumers' purchase of goods and services even if such lenders have not been blameworthy, or acted unlawfully or contrary to regulatory obligations. This is because of the concept of related debtor–creditor–supplier agreements recognised in consumer credit law

63 See *Plevin v Paragon Personal Finance Ltd, Conlon v Black Horse Ltd* [2013] EWCA Civ 1658, [2013] WLR (D) 500 [70]–[73] (Briggs LJ).

64 *Harrison v Black Horse* [2010] EWHC 3152; *Plevin v Paragon Personal Finance Ltd, Conlon v Black Horse Ltd* (n 63).

of some jurisdictions, including in the UK.[65] The UK cases on mis-selling of payment protection insurance (PPI) provide an example.[66] The PPI cases also demonstrate that the liability for third-party actions from the consumer protection approach may not necessarily require proof of unlawful or blameworthy conduct on the part of the lender.[67]

3.17 Public enforcement

Public enforcement is often provided for in prudential regulation and consumer protection. Designating a public agency to bring claims on behalf of consumers may be necessary because the monetary value of claims may be too insignificant to incentivise individual consumers whose numbers, dispersal and lack of organisation in any case can hinder their ability to bring claims before the court. For example, regulation 19 of the CPUTR designated some public enforcement authorities for the UCPD,[68] although some observers note that such bodies have undertaken little civil and criminal enforcement.[69]

3.18 Formal requirements and enforceability

Formal requirements for credit agreements are one of the techniques used to ensure consumer protection. Formalities may include a 'prescribed form' for consumer credit agreements, for instance under section 61 of the Consumer Credit Act 1974.[70] Credit agreements may be unenforceable if certain formalities are not followed by the lender, marking out unenforceability of loans as one of the policing tools of the consumer protection approach. For example, the Consumer Credit (Information Requirements and Duration of Licences and Charges) Regulations 2007[71] require lenders to provide periodic statements containing certain information to borrowers. Failure to comply fully with the requirements can render a loan facility unenforceable by the lender.[72]

65 *Forthright Finance Ltd v Ingate (Carlyle Finance Ltd, Third Party)* [1997] 4 All ER 99; *Plevin v Paragon Personal Finance Ltd, Conlon v Black Horse Ltd* (n 63).

66 See *Harrison v Black Horse Ltd* (n 62); *Plevin v Paragon Personal Finance Ltd, Conlon v Black Horse Ltd* (n 63); *Scotland v British Credit Trust Ltd* [2014] EWCA Civ 790, [2014] WLR (D) 252.

67 See *Harrison v Black Horse Ltd* (n 62); *Plevin v Paragon Personal Finance Ltd, Conlon v Black Horse Ltd* (n 63).

68 Office of Fair Trading/Department for Business Enterprise & Regulatory Reform, *Guidance on the Consumer Protection from Unfair Trading Regulations* (Office of Fair Trading/Department for Business Enterprise & Regulatory Reform 2008).

69 Office of Fair Trading, *Home Maintenance Tops List of Consumer Protection Cases One Year On* (Office of Fair Trading 2009); Jane Williams and Caroline Hare, 'Early Experiences of the Enforcement of the Unfair Commercial Practices Directive in Scotland' (2010) 33 Journal of Consumer Policy 377, 387, 396–397.

70 See *Bassano v Toft* [2014] EWHC 377 (QB).

71 Consumer Credit (Information Requirements and Duration of Licences and Charges) Regulations 2007 (SI 2007/1167) issued under the Consumer Credit Acts 1974 and 2006.

72 *JP Morgan Chase Bank NA v Northern Rock (Asset Management) plc* [2014] EWHC 291 (Ch).

3.19 Debt collection

Although formal court and debt collection proceedings may be open to creditors, the relative size of consumer debts and the expense and slow speed of formal procedures make them unattractive for creditors.[73] Creditors often refer consumer debtors to debt collection agencies that sometimes purchase consumer debts at a discount. However, the conduct of creditors and debt collection agencies sometimes raise consumer protection concerns. For example, the provisions of the UCPD[74] and the CPUTR[75] can be applied against aggressive debt recovery practices. In the case of the Protection from Harassment Act 1997, the fact of the consumer's indebtedness to the creditor or that the debt is actually due or that the lender is entitled to commence recovery proceedings is immaterial to harassment claims.[76] Although it did not refer to the Protection from Harassment Act 1997, the CPUTR and the UCPD, a court in one case prevented a lender from recovering a debt owed by a consumer on the ground that the lender's frequent and untraceable telephone calls to the consumer constituted harassment.[77]

3.20 Consumer claims

A consumer protection regime can provide for the right of individual consumers to initiate legal proceedings against lenders for non-compliance with prescribed pre-contract and post-lending procedures. For example, section 150 of the FSMA permits borrowers to claim against banks that have acted in violation of the Conduct of Business Rules of the FCA.[78] The prevalence of statutory enforcement rights in consumer credit has led to an explosion of consumer-related litigation in the area.[79]

3.21 Alternative dispute resolution

A consumer protection regime can provide for an ombudsman scheme for the resolution of disputes between lenders and borrowers. An example is the Financial Ombudsman Scheme established under section 226A of the FSMA and section 59 of the Consumer Credit Act 2006 for 'fair and reasonable' determination of business–consumer disputes.[80] Section 1C(2)(h) of the FSMA accordingly requires the FCA to consider 'any information which the scheme operator of the ombudsman scheme has provided to the FCA'.

73 Giuseppe Bertola, Richard Disney and Charles Grant, 'The Economics of Consumer Credit Demand and Supply' in Giuseppe Bertola, Richard Disney and Charles Benedict Grant (eds), *The Economics of Consumer Credit* (MIT Press 2006); Onyeka K Osuji, 'Business-to-Consumer Harassment, Unfair Commercial Practices Directive and the UK – A Distorted Picture of Uniform Harmonization?' (2011) 34 Journal of Consumer Policy 437, 441.

74 Articles 8, 9, Annex 1.

75 Reg 7, Sch 1, items 24–31.

76 Osuji (n 73) 448.

77 *Harrison v Link Financial Ltd* [2011] EWHC B3 (Mercantile) (28 February 2011) [52]–[53], [56], [78], [83] (Judge Chambers QC).

78 See *Green v Royal Bank of Scotland plc (Financial Conduct Authority intervening)* [2013] EWCA Civ 1197.

79 Geraint Howells, 'The Consumer Credit Litigation Explosion' (2010) 126 Law Quarterly Review 617.

80 See *R (on the application of Heather Moor & Edgecomb Ltd) v FOS* [2008] EWCA Civ 642; *R (on the application of the BBA) v FSA and FOS* [2011] EWHC 999 (Admin).

4 The UK's dual regulators

Having shown that prudential regulation and consumer protection can involve both different and similar regulatory techniques, the new regime introduced by the Financial Services Act 2012 in the UK presents an opportunity to examine whether the coincidence of techniques has any practical and significant consequences. Prior to the new system, the FSA[81] and the OFT[82] provided guidance and other measures on irresponsible lending for mortgage lending and consumer credit respectively.[83] Therefore, in the previous regime there were 'parallel developments' from the FSA and the OFT in the area of protection of bank customers, particularly requirements for consumer information and fair treatment.[84] Regulatory measures by the two regulators often covered similar fields and sometimes were undertaken fairly simultaneously. For example, various reports, measures and pronouncements of the FSA around the year 2008 recognised 'treating customers fairly' as a key principle in the relationships between financial institutions and their customers.[85] Meanwhile, the OFT investigated the fairness of operating personal current accounts around the same period and identified as consumer protection concerns a lack of transparency

81 See Financial Services Authority, *Mortgage Market Review: Responsible Lending* (Consultation Paper 10/16, July 2010) www.fsa.gov.uk/pubs/cp/cp10_16.pdf accessed 10 August 2014; Financial Services Authority, *Mortgage Market Review: Proposed Package of Reforms* (Consultation Paper 11/31, December 2011) www.fca.org.uk/static/documents/consultation-papers/fsa-cp11-31.pdf accessed 10 August 2014; Financial Services Authority, *Mortgage Market Review: Feedback on CP11/31 and Final Rules* (n 48); Financial Services Authority, *Mortgage Market Review (Conduct of Business) Instrument 2012* http://media.fshandbook.info/Legislation/2012/2012_46.pdf accessed 10 August 2014; Financial Services Authority, *Prudential Requirements for Non-Deposit Taking Lenders Instrument 2012* http://media.fshandbook.info/Legislation/2012/2012_47.pdf accessed 10 August 2014.

82 See Office of Fair Trading, *Irresponsible Lending: OFT Guidance for Creditors* (n 39); Office of Fair Trading, *Irresponsible Lending: Summary of Responses to the OFT's Consultation on the Scope of the Irresponsible Lending Project* (December 2008) http://webarchive.nationalarchives.gov.uk/20140402142426/http://www.oft.gov.uk/shared_oft/business_leaflets/consumer_credit/oft1012resp.pdf accessed 5 September 2014; Office of Fair Trading, *Irresponsible Lending: A Scoping Paper* (August 2008) http://webarchive.nationalarchives.gov.uk/20140402142426/http://www.oft.gov.uk/shared_oft/business_leaflets/consumer_credit/oft1012.pdf accessed 5 September 2014.

83 See Financial Services Authority, *Mortgages: Conduct of Business FSA Handbook Release 064* (April 2007) www.fsa.gov.uk/pubs/hb-releases/rel64/rel64mcob.pdf accessed 10 October 2014; Office of Fair Trading, *Irresponsible Lending: OFT Guidance for Creditors* (n 39).

84 Anu Arora, 'Unfair Contract Terms and Unauthorised Bank Charges: A Banking Lawyer's Perspective' (2012) 1 Journal of Business Law 44, 45, 52–55, 69–70.

85 See Financial Services Authority, *Fairness of Terms in Consumer Contracts: Firms' Awareness of and Compliance with the Unfair Terms in Consumer Contracts Regulations 1999* (Consumer Research, GfK NOP, June 2008) www.fca.org.uk/static/fca/documents/fsa-consumer-contracts-report.pdf accessed 6 September 2014; Financial Services Authority, *Update on the Treating Customers Fairly Initiative and the December Deadline* www.fsa.gov.uk/pubs/other/tcf_deadline.pdf accessed 6 September 2014; Financial Services Authority, *Unfair Contract Terms: Improving Standards in Consumer Contracts* (January 2012) www.fca.org.uk/static/pubs/guidance/fg12_02.pdf accessed 6 September 2014; Financial Services Authority, *Consumer Perceptions of Fairness Within Financial Services* (June 2010) www.fs-cp.org.uk/publications/pdf/fsa_fairness_report.pdf accessed 6 September 2014.

and complexity of information relating to fees and charges for unarranged or unauthorised overdrafts, as well as difficulty in switching accounts.[86]

The UK has recently adopted the dual regulator model for the financial services sector through part 1A of the FSMA inserted by the Financial Services Act 2012, which came into force on 1 April 2014. Although the legislation concentrates prudential regulation in the Bank of England, it separates macro-prudential regulation and micro-prudential regulation. While a subcommittee of the Bank of England known as the Financial Policy Committee is responsible for macro-prudential regulation, which is mainly tackling systemic risks to financial stability, the existing sole micro-prudential regulator, the FSA, was replaced with a dual system of regulation composed of the PRA and the FCA.[87] The PRA is a subsidiary of the Bank of England and is responsible for the supervision (micro-prudential regulation) of banks, insurance companies and major investment companies. The FCA regulates the *conduct* of financial institutions regulated by the PRA in addition to the prudential regulation of firms that are not within the regulatory remit of the PRA. It is within this *conduct regulation* that the FCA is regarded as the main protective body for financial consumers.

The PRA is established under section 2A of the FSMA with the general micro-prudential objective of 'promoting the safety and soundness of PRA-authorised persons' to avoid any adverse effect on the stability of the UK financial system' and 'minimise the adverse effect that the failure of a PRA-authorised person could be expected to have on the stability of the UK financial system' (section 2B(2)(3)). The PRA is required to consult the directors of the Bank of England in designing its regulatory strategy (section 2E(2)). The general functions of the PRA are to make rules and issue codes, general policies and principles (section 2J(1)). The establishment of the PRA and its integration within the Bank of England is designed to put prudential regulation under the single authority of the central bank (Bank of England) unlike the previous unsatisfactory regime of monetary policy and banking supervision roles for the bank and the FSA respectively.[88]

Created under section 1A of the FSMA, the FCA is mainly designed to replace the defunct FSA and the OFT. Unlike the PRA, the FCA is distinct from the Bank of England and is not a subsidiary of the latter. Section 6 provides that the functions of the FCA are rule making, issuance of codes and general guidance, policies and principles. According to section 1B(1), the FCA is required to act in ways that are compatible with its 'strategic objective' and advance its 'operational objectives'. While the strategic objective is to ensure the proper functioning of the market (section 1B(2)), the operational objectives are consumer protection, integrity and

86 Timothy Edmonds, *Retail Banking: Overdraft and Credit Card Charges & the OFT Review into the Current Account Market* (Standard Note BT/3947, 3 June 2014) www.parliament.uk/briefing-papers/SN03941.pdf accessed 11 September 2014; Office of Fair Trading, *Investigation under the Unfair Terms in Consumer Contracts Regulations into the Fairness of Personal Current Account Contract Terms Providing for Unarranged Overdraft Charges* (April 2007) http://webarchive.nationalarchives.gov.uk/20140402142426/http://www.oft.gov.uk/OFTwork/markets-work/personal; Office of Fair Trading, *Personal Current Accounts in the UK* (Market Survey, January 2013) http://webarchive.nationalarchives.gov.uk/20140402142426/http://www.oft.gov.uk/shared_oft/reports/financial_products/OFT1005rev accessed 11 September 2014.

87 Financial Services Authority, *The Financial Conduct Authority: Approach to Regulation* (June 2011) www.fsa.gov.uk/pubs/events/fca_approach.pdf accessed 12 September 2014; Parliamentary Commission on Banking Standards, *Changing Banking for Good* (n 6) [1055].

88 Parliamentary Commission on Banking Standards, *Changing Banking for Good* (n 6) [1057].

competition, with protecting 'the interests of consumers' as an overarching goal (section 1B(3)(4)). Section 1C(1) defines the consumer protection objective as 'securing an appropriate degree of protection for consumers' while the competition objective is defined by section 1E(1) as 'promoting effective competition in the interests of [financial] consumers in the markets'.

It has been argued that the new regime offers 'a clearer articulation of both prudential and conduct cases in areas where the two naturally come together and can (again, naturally) lead to different preferences for outcomes'.[89] However, this claim seems unsupported by the provisions of the FSMA. For example, the 'integrity objective' of the FCA is similar to the objective of the PRA. Under section 1D(1), the integrity objective of the FCA is 'protecting and enhancing the integrity of the UK financial system' while section 1D(2) defines this 'integrity' to include:

> (a) its soundness, stability and resilience; (b) its not being used for a purpose connected with financial crime; (c) its not being affected by behaviour that amounts to market abuse; (d) the orderly operation of the financial markets; and (e) the transparency of the price formation process in those markets.

Second, section 2H(1) provides that the PRA has a secondary objective of facilitating 'effective competition in the markets for services provided by PRA-authorised persons in carrying on regulated activities'. This is very similar to the competition objective of the FCA.

Some provisions allow either regulator to act unilaterally or override the other in certain cases where the regulators may share regulatory remit. For instance, section 64A provides that the PRA and the FCA can each issue 'rules of conduct' for practically the same persons or class of persons. Another example is section 3I, which permits the PRA to give directions to the FCA if it thinks that a proposed action by the FCA may '(a) threaten the stability of the UK financial system, or (b) result in the failure of a PRA-authorised person in a way that would adversely affect the UK financial system'. However, the FCA may not 'comply with a direction under this section if or to the extent that in the opinion of the FCA compliance would be incompatible with any EU obligation or any other international obligation of the United Kingdom' (section 3I(8)).

There are provisions that require the PRA and the FCA to work together. For example, the PRA must consult the FCA when it issues or alters its guidance (section 2I(2)) and before it gives the FCA directions under sections 3I and 3J and under section 60(7). Each regulator is required to consult the other if it intends to vary or revoke a prohibition order it issued against unfit persons (section 56(7)–(7C)). The PRA and the FCA are both required by section 3Q:

> [T]o cooperate with the Bank of England in connection with – (a) the pursuit by the Bank of its Financial Stability Objective, and (b) the Bank's compliance with its duties under sections 58 and 59 of the Financial Services Act 2012 (duty to notify Treasury of possible need for public funds and of subsequent changes).

89 Ibid.

Section 3D(1) similarly imposes a duty on both the FCA and the PRA to ensure a coordinated exercise of their functions. In the words of the section:

> (1) The regulators must co-ordinate the exercise of their respective functions conferred by or under this Act with a view to ensuring, (a) that each regulator consults the other regulator (where not otherwise required to do so) in connection with any proposed exercise of a function in a way that may have a material adverse effect on the advancement by the other regulator of any of its objectives; (b) that where appropriate each regulator obtains information and advice from the other regulator in connection with the exercise of its functions in relation to matters of common regulatory interest in cases where the other regulator may be expected to have relevant information or relevant expertise; [and] (c) that where either regulator exercises functions in relation to matters of common regulatory interest, both regulators comply with their respective duties under section 1B(5)(a) or 2H(1)(a), so far as relating to the regulatory principles in section 3B(1)(a) and (b).

According to section 3D(3), 'matters of common regulatory interest' to both the PRA and the FCA are when:

> (a) the other regulator exercises similar or related functions in relation to the same persons; (b) the other regulator exercises functions which relate to different persons but relate to similar subject matter; or (c) its exercise could affect the advancement by the other regulator of any of its objectives.

A regulatory turf war between the PRA and the FCA is therefore a distinct possibility. This has apparently been acknowledged in the enabling legislation. For example, sections 3G and 3H allow the Treasury, with parliamentary approval, to designate either the PRA or the FCA with certain regulatory responsibility and to require either regulator to carry out or refrain from carrying out any regulatory function or to consult the other. Section 3B(1) requires both the PRA and the FCA to apply the following principles:

> (a) the need to use the resources of each regulator in the most efficient and economical way; (b) the principle that a burden or restriction which is imposed on a person, or on the carrying on of an activity, should be proportionate to the benefits, considered in general terms, which are expected to result from the imposition of that burden or restriction; (c) the desirability of sustainable growth in the economy of the United Kingdom in the medium or long term; (d) the general principle that consumers should take responsibility for their decisions; (e) the responsibilities of the senior management of persons subject to requirements imposed by or under this Act, including those affecting consumers, in relation to compliance with those requirements; (f) the desirability where appropriate of each regulator exercising its functions in a way that recognises differences in the nature of, and objectives of, businesses carried on by different persons subject to requirements imposed by or under this Act; (g) the desirability in appropriate cases of each regulator publishing information relating to persons on whom requirements are imposed by or under this Act, or

> requiring such persons to publish information, as a means of contributing to the advancement by each regulator of its objectives; [and] (h) the principle that the regulators should exercise their functions as transparently as possible.

Section 3E(1) requires the PRA and the FCA to agree on a memorandum of understanding (MOU) describing:

> in general terms (a) the role of each regulator in relation to the exercise of functions conferred by or under this Act which relate to matters of common regulatory interest, and (b) how the regulators intend to comply with section 3D in relation to the exercise of such functions.

The MOU may contain specific provisions on a range of activities and functions undertaken by both regulators and must describe the coordination of their roles in their membership of and relations with European and other external regulatory bodies (section 3E(2)(3)). In addition to several non-statutory MOUs between the regulators, there are now six inter-locking statutory MOUs on issues such as financial crisis management, relationship with international organisations, markets supervision and infrastructure and the Financial Services Compensation Scheme.[90] These attempts at coordination of regulatory functions are laudable and reflect principle 3 of the Basel Committee's core principles for effective banking supervision which provides that '[l]aws, regulations or other arrangements provide a framework for cooperation and collaboration with relevant domestic authorities and foreign supervisors'.[91]

However, it is doubtful whether the MOUs and statutory provisions can resolve 'difficulties of coordination and communication'[92] in the new regulatory arrangements. Although the Parliamentary Commission on Banking Standards claimed that '[t]he new regulatory structure aims to address conflicts that arose from a single regulatory body being responsible for both prudential and conduct regulation',[93] it is unclear how far this goal can be achieved. After all, at the end of the day it is human actors who implement the rules. Personalities can affect the regulatory space, particularly where the applicable rules have created gaps and ambiguity that can be exploited. One of the criticisms of the previous regime is of:

> [C]onduct of business and prudential people in the same building arguing like cat and dog because they had never been together before and whether it was mortgage endowments or whatever the issue was, there was a prudential aspect and a conduct of business aspect.[94]

It is doubtful that this kind of argument will cease when people working in different *buildings* meet over issues that are equally within their regulatory powers. The Parliamentary Commission on Banking Standards rightly admitted: '[i]t will be a matter

90 Ibid [1061].
91 Basel Committee on Banking Supervision (n 8).
92 Parliamentary Commission on Banking Standards, *Changing Banking for Good* (n 6) [1058].
93 Ibid [1056].
94 Ibid [1057].

of time to see how well the new structure works'.[95] Nonetheless, what is indisputable is that the new regulatory system relies heavily 'on the coordinating ability of key individuals, and their ability to cooperate and work as a team, [and] carries risks, particularly in a crisis [since] effective management of a crisis should not depend entirely on the personalities in post'.[96]

5 Conclusion

The Parliamentary Commission on Banking Standards observed that the new UK financial regulatory regime has replaced 'regulatory underlap' (of insufficient powers) with 'overlap' of membership of regulatory bodies, functions and roles.[97] The 'complexity of the new arrangements'[98] has a lot to do with the blurred boundaries of prudential regulation and consumer protection. The two regulatory approaches may reflect different goals. While prudential regulation in both its macro and micro components is largely designed to promote the stability of the financial system, consumer protection focuses on protecting the (vulnerable) consumer against exploitation and often acts contrary to the notion that the law should not intervene to destroy bargains properly agreed. However, prudential regulation and consumer regulation can share identical regulatory territory. The fact that prudential regulation can operate in both the business-to-business and business-to-consumer contexts creates an overlap with consumer protection which operates in the latter field.

This chapter has used responsible lending to illustrate that the diffusion of regulatory authority for financial institutions can lead to regulatory overlap and complexity rather than the simplified regulatory structure and distinctly defined goals the dual regulator model seems to assume. It demonstrates that although prudential regulation and consumer protection show differences in their focus and approach to paternalism, they can also share similar goals such as responsible lending, affordability, competition and financial inclusion. The similarity of regulatory goals and domains makes the similarity of regulatory tools possible. Consequently, both consumer protection and prudential regulation can contain rules on credit advertising, procedural formalities for credit agreements, third-party relationships, pre-contract disclosures, consumer education, credit officer responsibility, assessment of credit worthiness, public enforcement, information database and sharing and creditor suitability via licensing and fitness tests. A more simplified regulatory structure would make these similar goals and techniques available exclusively for a single regulator rather than two or more regulators. This avoids too much dependence on individual relationships between regulatory officers and the personalities of those officers for a coordinated and efficient system.

95 Ibid.
96 Ibid [1060].
97 Ibid [1058].
98 Ibid [1061].

5 Can consumer law solve the problem of complexity in US consumer credit products?

Kathleen C. Engel[1]

1 Introduction

People like to know and understand the total cost of credit products they are considering. They also like to know and understand products' terms and features. Given these preferences, issuers of credit should market products with transparent features and simple pricing. That is not the case. In fact, over the last few decades we have seen a plethora of complex terms in products such as mortgage loans, credit cards and prepaid debit cards.

As credit products have become ever more complex, consumers have more choices and can select products that satisfy their particular needs and preferences. No longer are borrowers limited to a 30-year, fixed-rate mortgage. If they know they will be moving in a few years, a three-year fixed-rate mortgage with a low interest rate that coverts to a 27-year adjustable-rate mortgage based on the London Interbank Offered Rate (LIBOR)[2] might be the right product for them. However, for borrowers who do not understand the complexities of a '3–27' mortgage loan, the low, initial interest rate could be a costly lure. Confusion is commonplace. In one study giving consumers a choice between two credit cards that varied only in terms of the annual fee and the interest rate, 40 per cent of the participants chose the more expensive card.[3]

One would expect that consumers, who cannot decipher terms and calculate the cost of complex products, would turn to those with easy-to-understand terms. There are some simple products on the market. Instead, consumers often misperceive that the more complex products are less expensive than the simple ones. Thus, they shun the products that would be in their best interest.

In this chapter I explain why borrowers make sub-optimal choices when selecting credit products. I then analyse whether extant laws could be used to address obfuscating complexity. I ultimately conclude that policy makers should look to extra legal remedies to protect consumers against exploitative complexity.

1 With thanks to Joseph Singer and Jim Rebitzer for talking though my ideas for the proposed 'choice agent' and to Molly Goodman and Ulrich Binne for their excellent research assistance.

2 The London Interbank Offered Rate, which is the average rate at which major London banks loan money to one another.

3 Sumit Agarwal, Souphala Chomsisengphet, Chunlin Liu and Nicholas S Souleles, 'Do Consumers Choose the Right Credit Contracts?' (2006) 4 and 11 http://ssrn.com/abstract=843826 accessed 18 November 2014.

2 Borrower decision-making

Research on behavioural anomalies sheds some light on why consumers opt for complex credit products that are more expensive than straightforward options. Complexity, almost by definition, means that a credit product has multiple moving parts. For example, credit cards often have variable fees, shifting interest rates and multiple timing requirements and trigger events. In what Scott Adams of Dilbert fame coined a *confusopoly*,[4] and what behavioural economists call 'information overload', people often cannot determine the actual cost of different credit offers or the consequences of non-payment.

Confusion is most acute for people with low levels of literacy, both financial and general. A federal literacy study found that only 20 per cent of adults have been educated beyond the twelfth grade and the average American has a ninth-grade reading level. The average credit card agreement is written at a 12.37 grade level.[5] Financial literacy is lowest among women, those who have low incomes, the young and the less educated.[6] As a result, people in these groups are less likely to make optimal decisions and more likely to suffer more dire consequences for their bad decisions than their older, more privileged counterparts.

There is also the problem of misplaced trust. During the subprime lending fury, borrowers trusted brokers, who they often knew through social circles or were recommended by friends or colleagues.[7] There were also brokers who targeted people with shared cultural or racial backgrounds, hoping to induce trust through common heritage. What borrowers did not know was that the brokers were paid larger commissions if they brokered loans that generated a return that exceeded the minimum a lender would accept.[8] In a variant on this phenomenon, we see celebrities marketing products to appeal to specific groups of borrowers. The Boy Scouts, Magic Johnson and Justin Bieber all hawk reloadable prepaid cards. Bieber's campaign, targeted at teenagers, appears to be about smart spending: 'you know when I was a kid, we didn't have a lot of money, so me and my family had to watch the money that we spent.... Managing your money is important', yet his card charges cardholders if they check their balances at an Automatic Teller Machine. There is even a charge to consumers if they do not use their cards for 30 days.[9]

Magic Johnson describes his card as magic mojo.[10] The cost of the mojo includes having to pay $5.95 for a paper statement and $2.00 per call to customer service if you call more than once in a month. On the *scoutsarethrifty* website, the Boy Scouts

4 Scott Adams, *The Dilbert Future: Thriving on Business Stupidity in the 21st Century* (HarperBusiness 1997) 159–163.

5 Connie Prater, 'U.S. Credit Card Agreements Unreadable to 4 out of 5 Adults' (CreditCards.com, 22 July 2010) www.creditcards.com/credit-card-news/credit-card-agreement-readability-1282.php accessed 18 November 2014.

6 Sebastian Bauhoff Katherine Carman and Amelie Wuppermann, 'Evidence from Low-Income Populations in the United States: Financial Literacy and Consumer Choice of Health' (2013) 12–13 http://papers.ssrn.com/sol3/papers.cfm?abstract_id=2326756 accessed 18 November 2014.

7 Kathleen Engel and Patricia McCoy, *The Subprime Virus: Reckless Credit, Regulatory Failure and Next Steps* (Oxford University Press 2011) 23.

8 Ibid 32.

9 Andrew A Newman, 'Bieber Backs a Debit Card for Teenagers, From Parents' *New York Times* (11 April 2013) B2.

10 'Magic by Magic Johnson' (*OneWest Bank*) www.onlymagiccard.com accessed 26 April 2013.

tout that their card 'not only answers the needs of parents, but also the needs of Scouts'.[11] To reload the Scouts card from a checking account, the fee is $4.95. If you want to close the account, the fee is $10.00.

Teaser pricing, where the initial cost is low and then rises over time, lures borrowers who are not savvy. An example from mortgage markets is pay-option adjustable-rate mortgages, which have low initial monthly payments that rise dramatically when the loan is recast.[12] Economists Gabaix and Laibson use the example of printers, which can be very inexpensive to purchase, but require expensive cartridges. If borrowers do not look beyond the initial purchase price, they wrongly believe they are getting the best deal if they buy the least expensive printer. In contrast, products with simple pricing structures, for example, one price for a given set of features, or a base price with a clear list of the costs for any additional features, can appear more expensive than goods and services with teaser rates and expensive, obfuscated add-ons. Unsophisticated consumers will steer clear of the more transparent products because, on the surface, they look to be more expensive.

3 Rationales for remedying complexity

The primary normative rationale for restricting or prohibiting *obfuscatory* credit contracts is the exploitation of unsophisticated consumers. Practices that favour sophisticated consumers to the detriment of less sophisticated shoppers smack of unfairness, particularly given that it is difficult for people to educate themselves about credit products.

Another rationale is based on the goal of having competitive markets. Where credit issuers are able to extract rents that dramatically exceed the marginal cost of providing credit, the market is not competitive and intervention is needed to benefit consumers. Markets should not be purposefully confusing; the goal should be to make it possible for people to make rational choices with full information.

Lastly, the subprime lending crisis demonstrated that uninformed consumer decision making can have consequences for the economic stability of the country and the world. When consumers naively enter credit transactions that could impact their economic wellbeing, the consequences can extend beyond their households.

4 The role of the law

Given that complexity will persist and borrowers can be exploited by complexity, do extant laws provide any protection? Consumer protection laws fall into three general

11 'Prepared. For Life' (*Discover*) www.scoutsarethrifty.com accessed 26 April 2013.

12 Pay-option loans give borrowers three different payment options. They can pay the full principal and interest just as they would be required to do on a fully amortising loan. They can pay just the interest or they can pay an amount that is less than the interest payment due, in which case the unpaid interest is tacked onto the principal, causing the principal amount to increase each month until the principal reaches a certain percentage of the original loan amount, typically 120 per cent. Once borrowers hit the cap on the principal, the loan is recast for the remaining period of the loan to take into account the larger principal balance. Engel and McCoy (n 7) 34; see also Allen J Fishbein and Patrick Woodall, 'Exotic or Toxic? An Examination of the Non-Traditional Mortgage Market for Consumers and Lenders' (Consumer Federation of America 2006) www.consumerfed.org/pdfs/Exotic_Toxic_Mortgage_Report0506.pdf accessed 18 November 2014.

categories: broad standards, specific restrictions on loan terms and disclosure requirements, all of which are imperfect. In this section of the chapter, I describe and critique those approaches and then briefly discuss alternative methods for addressing complexity in credit markets.

4.1 Broad standards

4.1.1 Unconscionability

Unconscionability is the 'absence of meaningful choice on the part of one of the parties together with contract terms which are unreasonably favourable to the other party'.[13] Unconscionability defies a straightforward application. Most, although not all, courts require that consumers prove both procedural and substantive unconscionability.[14] Procedural unconscionability in consumer credit transactions is the easier prong to prove because it is satisfied if the consumer lacks meaningful choice, usually because the issuer of credit has superior bargaining power or has hidden key terms in a lengthy or complex contract.[15] Courts have also taken into account contracting parties' education, sophistication and wealth (or lack of) in determining whether a contract is procedurally unconscionable.[16]

Substantive unconscionability presents a higher hurdle for consumers, in part because it is hard to know exactly what the term means. Generally, for a court to deem a contract substantively unconscionable, it must contain terms that are oppressive or one-sided.[17] The analysis requires looking at the entire transaction. One overly harsh term does not an unconscionable contract make. Rather, courts consider the combined effect of all the terms, including the impact of terms that favour the consumer over the provider of credit.[18]

If a complex credit product costs significantly more than a comparable straightforward product and the higher cost does not reflect any additional benefits to the consumer, courts may be more likely to find the contract unconscionable.[19] In other

13 *Williams v Walker-Thomas Furniture Co* 350 F2d 445, 449 (DC Cir 1965). The Uniform Commercial Code codified the principle of unconscionability in UCC s 2–302(1) (1998). For a historical discussion of 2–302, see Jean Braucher, 'Form and Substance in Consumer Financial Protection' (2012) 7 Brooklyn Journal of Corporate, Financial and Commercial Law 107, 112–116.

14 Kathleen C Engel and Thomas J Fitzpatrick IV, 'Complexity, Complicity, and Liability up the Securitization Food Chain: Investor and Arranger Exposure to Consumer Claims' (2012) 2 Harvard Business Law Review 345, 354–355.

15 Engel and McCoy (n 7) 355.

16 Russell Korobkin, 'Bounded Rationality, Standard Form Contracts and Unconscionability' (2003) 70 University of Chicago Law Review 1203, 1266; see also *Denlinger, Inc v Dendler,* 415 Pa Super 164, 608 A 2d 1061, 1066 (1992) (refusing to find procedural unconscionability where buyer was sophisticated).

17 See, for example, *Walker-Thomas Furniture* (n 13) 449 (finding substantive unconscionability when a contract unreasonably favoured the seller).

18 Korobkin (n 16) 1273; see also Steven W Bender, 'Rate Regulation at the Crossroads of Usury and Unconscionability: The Case for Regulating Abusive Commercial and Consumer Interest Rates under the Unconscionability Standard' [1994] 31 Houston Law Review 721, 725–732, 746–753 (discussing the various approaches courts have taken in deciding unconscionability claims based on interest rates).

19 Bender (n 18) 754 (discussing unconscionability claims based on the difference in the price the seller paid for goods and the price it charged the buyer or the net profit to the seller after taking into account operational costs).

words, it is plausible that a court could find that credit contracts in which issuers exploit consumers' inability to disentangle complex terms to extract rents are substantively unconscionable.

Although it is possible to frame an unconscionability claim to challenge complex credit products, consumers have not had much success bringing unconscionability claims based on the terms in credit contracts. This is, in part, because courts resist rendering rulings based on price terms and because they often believe that unconscionability claims interfere with the right to contract.

Unconscionability claims are also expensive to litigate and hard to prove.[20] As a result, the threat of unconscionability claims does not create an incentive for lenders to reform their contracts to make them more understandable and unconscionability does not provide borrowers with hope for relief.

4.1.2 UDAP and UDAAP

Since 1938, the United States has had laws protecting consumers against unfair and deceptive acts and practices. The oldest federal law, the Federal Trade Commission Act (FTC Act), makes unlawful 'unfair or deceptive acts or practices in or affecting commerce'.[21] The most recent federal legislation in the field is the Dodd–Frank Wall Street Reform and Consumer Protection Act[22] (the Dodd–Frank Act or Dodd–Frank), which empowered the newly created Consumer Financial Protection Bureau (CFPB) to enforce a new law prohibiting unfair, deceptive and abusive acts and practices (UDAAP) 'in connection with any transaction with a consumer for a consumer financial product or service, or the offering of a consumer financial product or service'.[23] On the state level, all 50 states have statutes prohibiting unfair and deceptive acts and practices (UDAP).[24]

4.1.3 State UDAP laws

The various state statutes vary widely in terms of who is subject to the laws, who can enforce the laws, and what remedies are available. For example, some exclude credit transactions or cover deceptive, but not unfair, acts.[25] Not all states grant a private right of action to consumers.[26] Others ban or restrict consumers' right to recover attorneys' fees; in these jurisdictions it is difficult for private attorneys to afford to

20 See Sinai Deutch, *Unfair Contracts: The Doctrine of Unconscionability* (Lexington Books 1977) 243 (discussing the cost and risk of litigating unconscionability claims based on price); Arthur Allen Leff, 'Unconscionability and the Crowd: Consumers and the Common Law Tradition' (1969) 31 University of Pittsburgh Law Review 349, 354–357.

21 15 USC s 45(a)(1).

22 Pub L No 111-203, 124 Stat. 1376.

23 15 USC s 1031(d).

24 Jonathan Sheldon and Carolyn Carter, *Unfair and Deceptive Acts and Practices* (National Consumer Law Center 2004) s 1.1.

25 Ibid ss 2.1–2.2.1.4 and 2.3.1; see also Carolyn L Carter, 'Consumer Protection in the States: A 50-State Report on Unfair and Deceptive Acts and Practices Statutes' (National Consumer Law Center 2009) www.nclc.org/images/pdf/car_sales/UDAP_Report_Feb09.pdf accessed 16 November 2014.

26 Prentiss Cox, 'Goliath Has the Slingshot: Public Benefit and Private Enforcement of Minnesota Consumer Protection Laws' (2006) 33 William Mitchell Law Review 163, 167 (noting that Iowa does not allow for a private right of action in its UDAP statute).

take UDAP cases.[27] In all the states, attorneys general can bring enforcement actions.

Despite the broad language in state UDAP statutes and the potential for both private and public actions in many states, UDAP claims against credit issuers are infrequent. There are several explanations for this. One is the Class Action Fairness Act, which restricts the rights of class action plaintiffs to have their claims heard in state courts, where judges and juries have historically been more sympathetic.[28] A second impediment is arbitration clauses that preclude consumers from seeking relief in the courts.[29] Lastly, the incentives to bring UDAP claims against issuers of credit are low because the cases require a nuanced understanding of financial services products and markets, and require expenditure of significant resources for often small recoveries.

4.1.4 FTC Act and UDAAP

The FTC Act prohibits unfair and deceptive acts and practices.[30] The Dodd–Frank Act gave the CFPB the power to take action against unfair, deceptive or abusive practices. Of these, abusive is the least understood claim and is subject to ongoing concern and scrutiny.

The FTC can enforce the UDAP provisions in the FTC Act against non-depository institutions. The CFPB can enforce the UDAAP prohibitions against lenders, including depository institutions, mortgage brokers and servicers, and other entities involved directly or peripherally in the extension of credit with the exception of auto dealers, over whom the CFPB has more limited jurisdiction.[31] There is no private right of action under the FTC Act for UDAP violations nor does the Dodd–Frank Act allow for private UDAAP claims.

4.1.4.1 UNFAIRNESS

Under the FTC Act, the FTC cannot declare an act or practice unfair:

> [U]nless the act or practice causes or is likely to cause substantial injury to consumers which is not reasonably avoidable by consumers themselves and not outweighed by countervailing benefits to consumers or to competition. In determining whether an act or practice is unfair, the Commission may consider established public policies as evidence to be considered with all other evidence. Such public policy considerations may not serve as a primary basis for such determination.[32]

27 Sheldon and Carter (n 24) ss 8.8.2.1–8.8.6.2. In some states, courts have ordered unsuccessful consumers to pay their opponents' attorneys' fees: Carter (n 25).

28 Pub L 109-2 (18 February 2005) 119 s 4 (codified in scattered sections of 28 USC).

29 Consumer Financial Protection Bureau, 'Arbitration Study Preliminary Results' (12 December 2013) http://files.consumerfinance.gov/f/201312_cfpb_arbitration-study-preliminary-results.pdf accessed 14 November 2014.

30 State laws typically parallel the prohibitions in the FTC Act.

31 12 USC ss 5331(a) and (b).

32 15 USC s 45(n).

The Dodd–Frank Act is patterned on the FTC Act with just a slight variation. The law states that an act or practice involving a consumer financial service or product is not unfair unless the Bureau has a reasonable basis[33] to conclude that:

> (A) the act or practice causes or is likely to cause substantial injury[34] to consumers which is not reasonably avoidable by consumers; and
> (B) such substantial injury is not outweighed by countervailing benefits to consumers or to competition.[35]

Like the FTC Act, Dodd–Frank allows the CFPB to consider public policy, but public policy goals cannot be the primary basis for determining that an act or practice is unfair.[36]

At first glance, the 'reasonably avoidable' condition would seem to dramatically curtail consumers' rights to redress for contracts with confusing and complex terms. Issuers could argue that consumers always have the choice not to enter a contract and thus avoid any terms that are so complex they cannot understand them. This construction would undermine virtually all unfairness claims. That may be why the FTC in its Unfairness Policy Statement further elucidated the term 'reasonably avoidable' to say:

> It has long been recognized that certain types of sales techniques may prevent consumers from effectively making their own decisions.... Most of the Commission's unfairness matters are brought under these circumstances. They are brought, not to second guess the wisdom of particular consumer decisions, but rather to halt some form of seller behaviour that unreasonably creates or takes advantage of an obstacle to the free exercise of consumer decision making.
>
> Sellers may adopt a number of practices that unjustifiably hinder such free market decisions. Some may withhold or fail to generate critical price or performance data, for example, leaving buyers with insufficient information for informed comparisons. Some may engage in overt coercion, such as by dismantling a home appliance for inspection and refusing to reassemble it until a service contract is signed. And some may exercise undue influence over highly susceptible classes of purchasers as by promoting fraudulent 'cures' to seriously ill cancer patients. Each of these practices undermines an essential precondition to

33 The standard of proof for unfairness that applies to the CFPB under Dodd–Frank is less stringent than the FTC standard.

34 The requirement that the injury be substantial is a significant hurdle. The FTC has interpreted substantial injury to include economic harms that 'consist of small harm to a large number of consumers, or significant harm to each affected individual': J Howard Beales, 'The FTC's Use of Unfairness Authority: Its Rise, Fall and Resurrection', (Federal Trade Commission 2003) www.ftc.gov/public-statements/2003/05/ftcs-use-unfairness-authority-its-rise-fall-and-resurrection accessed 19 November 2014. The CFPB recently made clear that consumers' injuries for unfairness violations are not limited to financial harms. Rather, emotional distress can contribute to or, standing alone, constitute a substantial injury: Consumer Financial Protection Bureau, 'Prohibition of Unfair, Deceptive, or Abusive Acts or Practices in the Collection of Consumer Debts' (10 July 2013) 2 http://files.consumerfinance.gov/f/201307_cfpb_bulletin_unfair-deceptive-abusive-practices.pdf accessed 17 November 2014.

35 12 USC s 5331(c)(1).

36 12 USC s 5331(c)(2). Although Congress cribbed from the FTC Act's UDAP provisions when setting out the CFPB's UDAAP authority, the CFPB is not bound to follow the FTC's interpretation of these provisions: 15 USC ss 41–58 (as amended).

a free and informed consumer transaction, and, in turn, to a well-functioning market. Each of them is therefore properly banned as an unfair practice under the FTC Act.[37]

For several reasons, there are few reported cases applying the unfairness doctrine and none of them involve credit transactions. First, the FTC's statement takes a narrow view of the kinds of behaviour that can form the basis for cognisable unfairness claims. None of the listed behaviours encompasses complexity per se.[38] In addition, for political reasons that are beyond the scope of this chapter, the FTC has been extremely reluctant to pursue claims based on unfairness.[39] Another problem for consumers is that most issuers of credit are now very careful to disclose all the contractual terms. Their disclosures may well insulate them from liability for unfairness.

The CFPB has brought several unfairness enforcement actions, but none have involved allegations that a substantive term in a contract was unfair. Rather, they have addressed unfair and deceptive debt collection and billing practices.[40] With the CFPB still a new agency, it is uncertain whether it will be more aggressive in its pursuit of unfairness claims or follow the cautious path set by the FTC.

4.1.4.2 DECEPTIVE

The FTC set forth its deception standard in a 1983 letter from former FTC Chairman Miller to former Senator Dingell:

1. there must be a representation, omission or practice that is likely to mislead the consumer ...
2. [the FTC must examine] the practice from the perspective of a consumer acting reasonably in the circumstances. If the representation or practice affects or is directed primarily to a particular group, the Commission examines reasonableness from the perspective of that group.
3. the representation, omission, or practice must be a 'material' one. The basic question is whether the act or practice is likely to affect the consumer's conduct or decision with regard to a product or service. If so, the practice is material, and consumer injury is likely, because consumers are likely to have chosen differently but for the deception.[41]

37 Letter from the FTC to Hon Wendell Ford and Hon Jack Danforth, Committee on Commerce, Science and Transportation, United States Senate, Commission Statement of Policy on the Scope of Consumer Unfairness Jurisdiction (17 December 1980), reprinted in *International Harvester Co*, 104 FTC 949, 1070 and 1073 (1984).

38 It is important to note that the FTC wrote the Unfairness Policy Statement in 1980, when loan products were simple and most Americans did not yet have credit cards. At the time, the FTC was focused on acts and practices associated with the purchase of consumer goods, not financial products.

39 Federal Trade Commission, 'Advertising to Kids and the FTC: A Regulatory Retrospective that Advises the Present' 5–8 www.ftc.gov/sites/default/files/documents/public_statements/advertising-kids-and-ftc-regulatory-retrospective-advises-present/040802adstokids.pdf accessed 19 November 2014 (chronicling the history of a law restricting the FTC's ability to use the unfairness doctrine to limit advertisements directed at children); 15 USC s 57a(i).

40 Consumer Financial Protection Bureau, 'Newsroom' www.consumerfinance.gov/newsroom/?topic=enforcement accessed 18 November 2014.

41 James C Miller III, 'FTC Policy Statement on Deception' (Federal Trade Commission 1983) www.ftc.gov/public-statements/1983/10/ftc-policy-statement-deception accessed 18 November 2014.

The Dodd–Frank Act does not define deception, but in its Supervision and Examination Manual, the CFPB provides a definition that resembles the FTC's:

> A representation,[42] omission, act or practice is deceptive when:
>
> (1) the representation, omission, act, or practice misleads or is likely to mislead the consumer;
> (2) the consumer's interpretation of the representation, omission, act, or practice is reasonable under the circumstances; and
> (3) the misleading representation, omission, act, or practice is material.[43]

Like the FTC, when looking at a practice, the CFPB must do so from the perspective of a reasonable consumer. The CFPB also takes into account whether the representations were aimed at a specific group. The CFPB's examples of such groups include senior citizens and 'financially distressed consumers'.[44] Where particular groups are targeted, communications are

> considered from the perspective of a reasonable member of the target audience. A statement or information can be misleading even if not all consumers, or not all consumers in the targeted group, would be misled, so long as a significant minority would be misled.[45]

When confusing contracts have the effect of deceiving consumers about the terms to which they have agreed, consumers are not getting what they want or thought they were getting in the transaction.[46] And, when issuers of credit target complex products to less educated consumers and there is evidence that the complexity in the terms misled a significant percentage of those targeted, the practice could be deemed deceptive.

42 The CFPB

> looks at implied representations, including any implications that statements about the consumer's debt can be supported. Ensuring that claims are supported before they are made will minimize the risk of omitting material information and/or making false statements that could mislead consumers

Consumer Financial Protection Bureau, 'Prohibition of Unfair, Deceptive, or Abusive Acts or Practices in the Collection of Consumer Debts' (n 34) 3.

43 Consumer Financial Protection Bureau, 'Supervision and Examination Manual: Version 2.0' (October 2012) 178–179 www.consumerfinance.gov/guidance/supervision/manual/ accessed 18 November 2014. The CFPB has defined material information as 'information that is likely to affect a consumer's choice of, or conduct regarding, the product or service. Information that is likely important to consumers is material': Consumer Financial Protection Bureau, 'Prohibition of Unfair, Deceptive, or Abusive Acts or Practices in the Collection of Consumer Debts' (n 34) 4.

44 Consumer Financial Protection Bureau, 'Prohibition of Unfair, Deceptive, or Abusive Acts or Practices in the Collection of Consumer Debts' (n 34) 3.

45 Ibid 4.

46 Joseph Singer, 'Foreclosure and the Failures of Formality, or Subprime Mortgage Conundrums and How to Fix Them' (2013) 46 Connecticut Law Review 497, 535.

4.1.4.3 ABUSIVE

'Abusive' is defined by Dodd–Frank, as an act or practice that:

(1) materially interferes with the ability of a consumer to understand a term or condition of a consumer financial product or service; or
(2) takes unreasonable advantage of:

  (A) Lack of understanding on the part of the consumer of the material risks, costs or conditions of the product or service;
  (B) The inability of the consumer to protect the interests of the consumer in selecting or using a consumer financial product or service; or
  (C) The reasonable reliance by the consumer on [any person that engages in offering or providing a consumer product or service] to act in the interests of the consumer.[47]

Arguably, abusive encompasses complicated contract terms that impede consumers' ability to understand the terms or conditions of a credit product. In the same vein, if issuers of credit deliberately obfuscate key terms, knowing that consumers cannot appreciate terms that are complicated, they could be found to have taken unreasonable advantage of consumers' lack of understanding of 'the material risks, costs or conditions of the product or service'.[48] The meaning of the term 'unreasonable advantage' has generated a great deal of debate. If, as some have said, the inquiry focuses on a reasonable consumer, the analysis will not take into account variations in consumers' financial literacy.[49] Others have asked whether a product can be abusive if many consumers find the product beneficial.[50] Still others have criticised the term 'abusive' as vague and overbroad.[51]

The CFPB has provided scant guidance on the abusiveness standard. As of the fall of 2014, the Bureau had filed (and settled) only three complaints alleging that defendants engaged in abusive acts.[52] All three claims involved activities related to debt collection and the CFPB had extremely strong evidence in support of each of the claims. From this, it is fair to conclude that the CFPB is acting with great caution when exploring the abusiveness terrain. It will likely be years, if ever, before the

47 12 USC s 5531(d); 12 USC s 5481(6).

48 Ibid.

49 Tiffany S Lee, 'No More Abuse: The Dodd–Frank Consumer Financial Protection Act's "Abusive Standard"' (2011) 14 Journal Consumer and Commercial Law 118, 122.

50 Ibid 121.

51 Ibid 121.

52 Consumer Financial Protection Bureau, 'CFPB Takes Action to Stop Florida Company from Engaging in Illegal Debt-Relief Practices' (30 May 2013) www.consumerfinance.gov/newsroom/cfpb-takes-action-to-stop-florida-company-from-engaging-in-illegal-debt-relief-practices/ accessed 7 November 2014 (debt relief company); Consumer Financial Protection Bureau, 'CFPB Sues CashCall for Illegal Online Loan Servicing' (16 December 2013) www.consumerfinance.gov/newsroom/cfpb-sues-cashcall-for-illegal-online-loan-servicing/www.consumerfinance.gov/newsroom/cfpb-sues-for-profit-college-chain-itt-for-predatory-lending accessed 7 November 2013 (payday loan servicing and collection); Consumer Financial Protection Bureau, 'CFPB Takes Action Against ACE Cash Express for Pushing Payday Borrowers into Cycle of Debt' (10 July 2014) www.consumerfinance.gov/newsroom/cfpb-takes-action-against-ace-cash-express-for-pushing-payday-borrowers-into-cycle-of-debt accessed 7 November 2014 (debt collection).

Bureau takes the bold step of challenging complexity as an abusive feature of credit products.

4.1.5 Broad standards: summary

Although complex contracts can be unconscionable, unfair, deceptive and abusive, courts and agencies are unlikely to find that complex contracts violate any of these standards. Obfuscating complexity is in the eye of the beholder. The same complex contract may be understandable to one person and befuddle the next. Similarly, if borrowers differ in the extent to which their own actions can trigger or avoid the difficult to understand parts of a contract, the contract can be more or less complex. For example, if an interest rate adjustment is confusing, someone who refinances before the time of the first interest rate adjustment will not have to worry about the confusing term.

4.2 Specific restrictions on loan terms

There are numerous state and federal laws that ban or restrict particular terms in consumer credit contracts. These include usury limits, state anti-predatory lending laws (APLs),[53] the Dodd–Frank Act's mortgage loan prohibitions and the Credit Card Accountability Responsibility and Disclosure Act of 2009 (CARD Act).[54]

4.2.1 Usury laws

Interest caps have gone in and out of favour since their first adoption in England in the 1500s.[55] In the United States, Congress pre-empted state usury caps on first lien loans on homes and mobile homes under the Depository Institutions Deregulatory and Monetary Control Act (DIDMCA).[56] States can still set their own usury ceilings for other types of consumer credit. Usury laws cannot solve the problem of complexity. Loans can have costly and complex features that borrowers cannot decipher, but the interest rates on the loans can still fall below the caps.[57]

4.2.2 State anti-predatory lending laws

State APLs vary by jurisdiction. Examples of the different provisions are restrictions on balloon payments and prepayment penalties, limits on broker compensation, requirements that loans be affordable given a borrower's financial situation, and provisions aimed at ending the practice of repeated refinancings that have no value to borrowers.

53 See generally, Raphael Bostic, Kathleen C Engel, Patricia A McCoy, Anthony Pennington-Cross and Susan M Wachter, 'State and Local Anti-Predatory Lending Laws: The Effects of Assignee Liability and Legal Remedies' (2008) 60 Journal of Economics and Business 47.
54 Pub L No 111-24, 123 Stat. 1734 (codified in scattered sections of 15 USC s 1637).
55 Bender (n 18) 725–732.
56 Pub L No 96-221, 94 Stat 164 (1980); see also Kathleen Engel and Patricia McCoy, 'A Tale of Three Markets: The Law and Economics of Predatory Lending' (2002) 80 Texas Law Review 1255, 1275 (discussing the rationales for DIDMCA).
57 Engel and McCoy, 'A Tale of Three Markets' (n 56) 1349.

4.2.3 Dodd–Frank Act and CARD Act

With the Dodd–Frank Act,[58] Congress amended the Truth in Lending Act (TILA) to impose prohibitions and limitations on the terms in mortgage loans.[59] These included prohibiting creditors from making loans unless they have made 'a reasonable and good faith determination based on verified and documented information that, at the time the loan [was] consummated, the consumer [had] a reasonable ability to repay the loan'.[60] The Act also limited the situations in which loans could have balloon payments and prepayment penalties, and prohibited yield spread premiums.[61] Lastly, Dodd–Frank created incentives for loan purchasers to police the behaviour of lenders and brokers.[62] Like Dodd–Frank, the CARD Act amended TILA to add substantive rules governing credit cards, for example limitations on increases in interest rates, certain billing practices and various types of penalties and fees.[63]

4.2.4 Specific restrictions on loan terms: summary

Usury laws, APLs and TILA, as amended by Dodd–Frank and the CARD Act, do not prohibit complexity, and so, on their face, do not protect consumers against contracts that they cannot parse. Just the same, the laws may have reduced complexity. This is because all the laws, except usury limits, ban certain terms that used to be commonplace in contracts, the impact of which has been to reduce the number of terms in credit card contracts and mortgage loans. I suspect this is a temporary phenomenon. There is every reason to believe that credit issuers will add new terms to credit contracts because they are able to grab excess profits when consumers misunderstand contracts for credit.

4.3 Disclosure

Until the CARD Act and Dodd–Frank, most federal laws governing credit transactions were based on the idea that with adequate disclosures, consumers would make optimal decisions.[64] During the mortgage lending boom, consumer advocates and academics, who were trying to get policy makers to understand that lenders were putting borrowers in loans that they could not understand or afford, ran into the disclosure wall. The problem for consumers, according to disclosure aficionados, was lack of information: if sellers disclosed the terms governing their products, consumers could make rational choices given their resources and desires. Congress and federal regulators deferred to this view.

58 This description of Dodd–Frank does not include all of the Act's mortgage-related provisions. For a fuller description, see Dee Pridgen, 'See Changes in Consumer Financial Protection: Stronger Agency and Stronger Laws' (2013) 13 Wyoming Law Review 405, 420–425.

59 TILA also contains special restrictions on loan terms in higher-cost and high-cost loans that are defined in an amendment to TILA known as Home Ownership and Equity Protection Act (HOEPA). HOEPA is akin to a federal APL: Engel and McCoy, *The Subprime Virus* (n 7) 194–198.

60 15 USC s 1639c(a)(3).

61 Engel and McCoy, *The Subprime Virus* (n 7) 228–232.

62 Ibid 234–236.

63 Pridgen (n 58) 425–430.

64 HOEPA is an exception; see (n 59).

Although disclosure is important, it is not a stand-alone solution to the problems of confusion and exploitation. From an efficient market perspective, disclosures that do not effectively inform consumers fail at their essential purpose. They actually promote inefficient markets by making it difficult or impossible for many consumers to understand the cost and terms of credit options, thus preventing consumers from effectively comparison shopping.

There is a second problem with disclosures. If issuers of credit can evade liability by simply disclosing credit terms – even if in small font, buried in contracts that are dozens of pages long, and using terms like 'annual percentage rate' that the average consumer will not understand – there is an incentive to use obfuscating disclosures.

Simple and bold disclosures have an obvious appeal, but they do not guarantee that consumers will be able to calculate the costs and the risks they are undertaking.[65] Many factors make it difficult for consumers to absorb multiple terms, even if disclosures are straightforward. Most people can only focus on a few terms. As a result, consumers run the risk of overlooking the most salient terms in a consumer contract. This is particularly true if the products contain multiple moving parts, like variable interest rates and different triggers. As Jean Braucher has written: 'Trickery need not involve nondisclosure or even buried disclosure; it can be based on exploiting another's lack of understanding of what has been clearly disclosed as well as consumer errors such as underestimation of future credit use.'[66]

Another set of challenges arises from the difficulty people have assessing probabilistic events. To understand whether they can afford a credit product, consumers often have to take into account future events, ranging from their future employment prospects to the movement of the yield on US Treasury bonds. Any uncertainties about the future make such assessments impossible and disclosures are of no help.

The Dodd–Frank Act has a provision that addresses the quality of disclosures; the CFPB can write rules mandating that disclosures be complete, accurate and effective 'in a manner that permits consumers to understand the costs, benefits, and risks associated with the product or service'.[67] While the effort to make contracts more clear is laudable, it is possible, and perhaps even likely, that no amount of careful drafting will result in effective disclosures if products have multiple terms, especially if the costs and risks shift in response to changes in consumer behaviour, interest rates and other events.[68]

65 A number of recent articles chronicle the many ways in which disclosure has been a failed strategy. See generally, Tom Baker and Peter Siegelman, 'You Want Insurance With That? Using Behavioral Economics to Protect Consumers from Add-on Insurance Products' (2013) 20 Connecticut Insurance Law Journal 1; Omri Ben-Shahar and Carl Schneider, 'The Failure of Mandated Disclosure' (2011) 159 University of Pennsylvania Law Review 101; Lauren Willis, 'Decisionmaking and the Limits of Disclosure: The Problem of Predatory Lending – Price' (2006) 65 Maryland Law Review 707.

66 Jean Braucher, 'Form and Substance in Consumer Financial Protection' (2012) 7 Brooklyn Law Review 107, 114.

67 12 USC s 5532(a).

68 Pridgen (n 58) 420.

5 Filling the gap when law fails

Given that the law cannot solve the problem of complex contracts that result in borrowers making ill-advised decisions, we should look at other mechanisms for assisting consumers. One proposal that was considered and rejected when Congress was drafting the Dodd–Frank Act was to require that lenders offer all consumers standard, low-risk loans (called 'plain vanilla' loans).[69] Although Congress refused to include the plain vanilla loan requirement in the Dodd–Frank Act, Congress did adopt provisions that create incentives for lenders to offer simpler products. For example, the Act's 'ability to pay rule'[70] creates a presumption of compliance[71] with the rule if mortgages do not contain features like negative amortisation and balloon payments that are known to be risky.[72]

A step that is bolder than the plain vanilla proposal is to standardise credit products such that there are only a few moving parts. For example, the only variation in the terms of mortgage loans could be the interest rate and points.[73] This approach would eliminate complexity, but it would also have the effect of limiting people's options. For low- and moderate-income borrowers, eliminating options like adjustable-rate mortgage loans and purchase money loans with no or low down payments would prevent them from owning homes.

Another approach would be to harness social media. Online rating systems like Zagat or Yelp could be designed to rate credit providers and their individual products. If successful, a system like this would obviate the need for consumers to disentangle complexity. Instead, they could select the product that was the most highly rated. This, of course, would only work if there were mechanisms to ensure the integrity of the rating system.[74]

A completely different tack would be to tax complexity. If providers of credit wanted to offer products that consumers could not easily understand, the creditors would have to pay a tax. The creditors would pass the tax on to consumers in the price of their products, which would hopefully encourage consumers to purchase less expensive and therefore less complex products. A blunter tool would be a very large, very bright warning that creditors would be required to place on particularly complex credit products.

Pre- and post-sale testing could have the effect of limiting obfuscating contracts on the market. With pre-sale testing, credit products would have to go through something akin to the Food and Drug Administration (FDA) approval process

69 Joe Adler, 'How Bank-Defeated "Plain Vanilla" Requirements Live On' (*National Mortgage News*, 4 November 2013) www.nationalmortgagenews.com/features/How-Bank-Defeated-Plain-Vanilla-Mortgage-Requirements-Live-On-1039717-1.html accessed 18 November 2014.

70 15 USC s 1639c(a).

71 Loans that are qualified, but higher-priced, as defined in the statute, are entitled to a rebuttable presumption of compliance: Consumer Financial Protection Bureau, 'Ability to Repay and Qualified Mortgage Standards under the Truth in Lending Act' 78 Fed. Reg. 6407, 6408 (30 January 2013) (amending 12 CFR Part 1026).

72 15 USC s 1639c(b)(2)(A).

73 Points are paid at closing in exchange for a lower interest rate. One point equals 1 per cent of the loan amount.

74 See Michael Luca, *Reviews, Reputation, and Revenue: The Case of Yelp.com* (Harvard Business School Working Paper 2011) www.hbs.edu/faculty/Publication%20Files/12-016_0464f20e-35b2-492e-a328-fb14a325f718.pdf accessed 18 November 2014 (discussing the reliability of YELP reviews).

before they could go on the market. Testing would involve not only review of the products, but also consumer testing in lab settings to determine how well consumers understand the terms of particular products and whether the complexity of the products outweighs their benefits. There are many problems with this approach. First, most people would agree that the FDA approval process is too slow and costly. Second, if every product had to go through this process, there would be less innovation and development of both good and potentially 'bad' products.

Post-sale monitoring is a bit less concerning. One form of post-sale monitoring already exists. Federal agencies like the CFPB have online complaint forms that enable them to investigate entities and products that generate a significant volume of complaints. Such monitoring could extend beyond collecting complaints to include CFPB-run focus groups, consumer testing and analyses of default data to see if defaults are clustered among specific issuers or products. Like pre-sale monitoring, the goal of post-sale monitoring would be to determine whether products are so complex that, on the whole, they should not be on the market.

The approach I find most appealing is to use digital technology to help consumers make decisions. A software programme would act like an agent, helping consumers determine what they could afford, what product would best meet their needs and, lastly, would generate bids from providers of the product. Several goals motivate this idea: (1) the approach is preventative; (2) it does not require the courts to interpret vague standards; (3) it is less costly than litigation; (4) it protects unsophisticated consumers without requiring them to become sophisticated; and (5) it permits consumers to 'pull' the information they need to select a product, rather than having issuers 'push' hundreds of pages of information to them on multiple products.

My proposal is a two-step process using a software programme that would help consumers determine the most suitable features of the credit product they are considering, taking into account their income, employment, debts, credit score, spending and bill-paying habits, etc.[75]

With this information, the software would determine which features best suit the consumer. As an example, say a consumer has a marginal credit history and wants to try to rebuild her credit score. Most credit card issuers would charge a high interest rate to compensate for the risk the consumer presented. The choice agent I am proposing might suggest that the consumer seek a secured credit card with no application fee or annual fee.[76]

The second stage in the process would be for the consumer to solicit bids from issuers of secured credit cards. The consumer would use the same software to enter her financial information, and the amount of the initial deposit she would be willing to make. The issuers would then bid to offer the consumer the card. The bids would be for the price terms like the interest rate and penalty fees. To make the bidding

75 Ideally, this information could be uploaded from data warehouses.

76 A secured credit card requires a consumer to post a set amount with the card issuer. The deposit serves as security for the credit card and the consumer cannot have a balance that exceeds the collateral. Typically, if the consumer pays the credit card bill on time for a year, the collateral is returned to them and they receive a modest increase in their maximum balance. In this way secured credit cards can help consumers build or improve their credit histories: Pat Curry, '10 Questions Before Getting Secured Credit Cards' (*Bankrate.Com*, 23 August 1999) www.bankrate.com/finance/credit-cards/10-questions-before-getting-a-secured-credit-card-1.aspx accessed 18 November 2014.

truly competitive, it could take place as a reverse auction, where issuers could underprice each other's bids.[77]

6 Conclusion

Complexity persists and enables issuers of credit to extract rents from consumers who do not have sufficient financial literacy to protect themselves. The law is a poor tool to curtail complexity and it may be impossible to craft a law that protects vulnerable consumers without overreaching. Given the limitations of the law, we should look to technology to help consumers make choices that are in their best interests.

77 This is a very spare description of the choice agent I propose. I realise there are many details to work out, including the need for issuers to make their offers contingent on verifying borrowers' creditworthiness. I intend to more fully develop my proposal in subsequent work.

Part III

Responsible lending and financial exclusion

6 Making payday loans safer

The Australian approach to regulating small and medium sized loans

Nicola J. Howell

1 Introduction

In mid-2013, national price regulation for consumer credit came into effect in Australia, driven largely by concerns about payday loans and other small, short-term loans. As explained by the Australian Government at the time of law's passing, the reforms had been introduced 'to reduce the financial harm caused by lenders who ruthlessly impose excessive fees and charges simply because vulnerable consumers cannot obtain alternative access to credit'.[1] These changes have brought some finality to a long and heated debate about the need or otherwise for 'bright-line' price regulation[2] and/or other forms of regulation to respond to concerns about payday loans.

Under the former state and territory-based regime in Australia, interest rate caps existed in some states and territories, but there was no nationally consistent approach. The staged transfer of consumer credit regulation to the Commonwealth Government from 2009 provided a platform for further discussion and debate on the need for price caps or other regulation. The discussion was often framed in the context of a need to address financial exclusion, which has shown a general increase over seven years of collecting data (although with a slight decrease in 2013).[3] Financial exclusion is said to exist 'where individuals lack access to appropriate and affordable financial services and products – the key services and products are a transaction account, general insurance and a *moderate amount of credit*'.[4] In consumer credit, the focus is on access to mainstream credit, rather than the 'informal financial sector or the fringe market, such as payday lenders'.[5] If fringe credit and payday

1 Bill Shorten (Minister for Financial Services and Superannuation), 'Payday Borrowers Better Protected as Bill Passes Parliament' (media release No 051, 20 August 2012).

2 The concept of 'bright-line' price regulation is used to distinguish regulation that sets an explicit maximum price from regulation that merely prohibits prices that are 'unconscionable' or 'unjust'. For example, the National Credit Code (NCC) includes a prohibition against unconscionable interest rates and certain fees: NCC, s 78. The difficulty with these types of prohibitions is that it is not always clear whether a particular rate or fee is unconscionable without resort to litigation.

3 Chris Connolly, 'Measuring Financial Exclusion in Australia' (Centre for Social Impact for National Australia Bank 2014) 5. In 2013, around 17 per cent of the adult population in Australia were either fully or severely excluded from financial services, compared to around 17.7 per cent in 2011. Note also, that in the first year of this survey (2007), only 16 per cent of the population were fully or severely excluded: 11.

4 Ibid 5 (emphasis added).

5 Ibid 6.

loans are not considered to be appropriate or affordable, then addressing financial exclusion can involve reducing the use of these products and/or making them safer and more affordable. Imposing a maximum price for small loans can then been seen as part of the broader project to reduce financial exclusion.

In Australia, price regulation has been imposed through the National Consumer Credit Protection Act 2009 (Cth) and the National Credit Code. The approach taken in Australia does not replicate the previous interest rate cap regimes in some Australian jurisdictions, where the same price cap applied to all consumer credit products. Instead, the national price cap imposes a differentiated price cap, with different requirements for 'short-term credit contracts', 'small-amount credit contracts', 'medium-amount credit contracts' and other credit contracts.

The changes are still relatively new and, at the time of writing (January 2015), there has been no comprehensive assessment of their impact released. However, some preliminary observations on the impact of the new laws are made in this chapter. This chapter provides a brief background to the recent changes in Australia, and then sets out the key price regulation and other provisions that have been introduced to respond to concerns about high-cost small loans. The chapter then examines the preliminary information on the impact of the changes, particularly on the industry and on consumers, and considers some remaining issues for this market, including avoidance activities and disclosure of comparative price information. The chapter then locates these new laws in the context of a changing approach to consumer credit regulation, from a traditional focus on *truth in lending* to a greater focus on *fairness in lending* through (among other things) regulation of product features, and suggests that a similar change in approach is also beginning to be seen in the broader consumer financial services market. The chapter concludes with a call for more effort on the broader financial inclusion product and for a commitment to empirical research on the impact of the changes in light of the independent review of some of the changes that is required 'as soon as practicable' after 1 July 2015.[6]

2 Short history and background to the Australian changes

Payday lending first entered the Australian consumer credit market in the late 1990s. Since then, the sector has grown rapidly, although reliable figures of the size of the market are hard to come by.[7] In 2011, an Australian Government Regulation Impact Statement reported that there were at least 567 branches of short-term loan providers, based on details published from eight major lenders. A review of branch and outlet numbers as published on the same lender websites in 2014[8] suggests that there are at least 456 branches and outlets. However, it is also clear that there has been an expansion into online lending, such that branch numbers are unlikely to

6 National Consumer Credit Protection Act 2009 (Cth) (NCCPA), s 335A(1). The review is to consider the operation of the specific responsible lending provisions applicable to small-amount credit contracts, the need for a national database of small-amount credit contracts and whether any additional provisions relating to small-amount credit contracts are needed.

7 See, for example, Australian Government, 'The Regulation of Short Term, Small Amount Finance' (Regulation Impact Statement, June 2011) 22.

8 The lenders were Cash Converters, City Finance, Nimble (formerly Cash Doctors), Cash Stop, Fast Access Finance, Cash Loan Money Centre and Money3. Another lender referred to in the Regulation Impact Statement in 2011, The Cash Store, went into liquidation in 2013.

accurately represent the size of the industry.[9] Reports from some lenders also show increasing business in recent years.[10]

Prior to 2009, consumer credit was regulated in Australia by the states and territories under a cooperative scheme, with the Uniform Consumer Credit Code[11] being the primary regulatory instrument. Although the cooperative scheme had national uniformity as its focus, the scheme did permit non-uniformity in interest rate caps. By 2009, three jurisdictions (New South Wales, Queensland and the Australian Capital Territory) had imposed an all-inclusive interest rate cap of 48 per cent on consumer credit products, while another, Victoria, had imposed an interest rate cap of 48 per cent on unsecured consumer loans and 30 per cent on secured consumer loans. There was no interest rate cap imposed in the remaining jurisdictions: South Australia, Tasmania, Western Australia and the Northern Territory.[12]

In 2008, following a recommendation by the Productivity Commission,[13] the Commonwealth Government announced that an agreement had been reached for the state and territory-based regime to be transferred to a national credit regime in two main phases. The first phase resulted in the introduction of the National Consumer Credit Protection Act 2009 (Cth) and National Credit Code, which included new licensing and responsible lending obligations. In the second phase, various new proposals for reform were considered, including price regulation.

As in many other jurisdictions, the Australian debate about the merits of imposing bright-line price regulation in consumer credit was a heated one, with strongly held views expressed by the short-term loan industry, consumer advocates and others. In contrast to the debate in some other jurisdictions, there was only limited empirical work available to guide decision making. The major academic piece of work on the industry and its customers involved customer surveys and interviews with customers, lenders and policy makers in 2010 and 2011.[14] This report (the *Caught Short* report) found, among other things, that having a lack of sufficient income to meet regular living expenses was one of the major reasons reported by respondents for taking out loans, that different types of repeat borrowing was

9 For example, Cash Doctors was reported in the Regulation Impact Statement as having branches in 79 towns: Australian Government (n 7) 22. Cash Doctors (renamed Nimble) now operates entirely online, see www.nimble.com.au.

10 See discussion below.

11 The Uniform Consumer Credit Code (UCCC) was the Appendix to the Consumer Credit (Queensland) Act 1994 (Qld). Other jurisdictions applied the UCCC locally through local consumer credit legislation – for example, the Consumer Credit (Victoria) Act 1995 (Vic).

12 For a discussion of the applicable legislation before 2009, see Zac Gillam and Consumer Action Law Centre, *Payday Loans: Helping Hand or Quicksand* (Consumer Action Law Centre 2010) 165–181.

13 Productivity Commission, *Review of Australia's Consumer Policy Framework* (Inquiry Report 107, 30 April 2008) 107 (recommendation 5.2).

14 Marcus Banks, Greg Marston, Howard Karger and Roslyn Russell, 'Caught Short: Exploring the Role of Small, Short-term Loans in the Lives of Australians' (Social Policy Unit, University of Queensland, August 2012). Note that in this research less than 20 per cent of the borrowers interviewed were recruited through financial counselling services: 4.

common, and that while many borrowers reported that they did not like needing to take out loans, they felt they had few options.[15]

The Government determined that there was a case for introducing price regulation, arguing that caps on credit contracts were needed to 'address specific risks of financial detriment or harm to consumers, through the use of relatively high cost credit'.[16] However, the Government was also concerned to ensure industry viability. There was significant opposition from industry members to the original proposals, as well as concerns raised by two Parliamentary Committees.[17] In response to these concerns, changes were made and the final form of the legislation included a higher price cap than was originally proposed, as well as different responsible lending obligations to those originally proposed.[18] The price regulation provisions came into effect on 1 July 2013, while some of the additional responsible lending obligations on providers of small loans came into effect on 1 March 2013.

3 The new Australian laws

3.1 Categories of credit contracts

The new price regulation and other provisions apply only to credit regulated by the National Consumer Credit Protection Act 2009 (Cth) and National Credit Code. This will only occur when credit is provided to individual debtors and strata corporations, and where the credit is provided wholly or predominantly for personal, domestic or household purposes, or for investment in residential property.[19] Consequently, the protections do not apply to business loans, including small business loans.

The new laws do not take a one-size-fits-all approach; instead, different obligations are imposed on different types of consumer credit contracts. Three categories of credit contract are specifically identified in the legislation: small-amount credit contracts, short-term credit contracts and medium-amount credit contracts.[20] Table 6.1 details the key features of these different contracts. There is also effectively a fourth category of consumer credit contracts: contracts that are not short-term credit contracts, small-amount credit contracts or medium-amount credit contracts.

15 Ibid vii. Other relevant studies include Gillam and Consumer Action Law Centre (n 12); Anna Ellison and Robert Foster, 'Payday in Australia: A Research Study of the Use and Impact of Payday Lending in the Domestic Australian Market' (Policis) http://policis.com/pdf/International/Payday%20borrowers%20FINAL.pdf accessed 12 December 2014. See discussion of some of these studies and their findings on the characteristics of payday borrowing in Nicola Howell, 'Interest Rate Caps and Price Regulation in Consumer Credit' in Justin Malbon and Luke Nottage (eds), *Consumer Law and Policy in Australia and New Zealand* (The Federation Press 2013) 325.

16 Parliament of the Commonwealth of Australia, Senate, 'Revised Explanatory Memorandum, Consumer Credit and Corporations Legislation Amendment (Enhancements) Bill 2012 (Cth)' 62.

17 Parliamentary Joint Committee on Corporations and Financial Services, *Inquiry into Consumer Credit and Corporations Legislation Amendment (Enhancements) Bill 2011* (2011); Senate Economics Legislation Committee, *Consumer Credit and Corporations Legislation Amendment (Enhancements) Bill 2011 (Provisions)* (2011).

18 The amending legislation is the Consumer Credit Legislation Amendment (Enhancements) Act 2012 (Cth).

19 NCC, s 5(1).

20 Note that the medium-term credit contract is only relevant to the NCC; the NCCPA does not include this concept, referring only to small-amount credit contracts and short-term credit contracts.

Table 6.1 Categories of consumer credit contracts

Loan type	*Term*	*Credit limit*	*Secured or unsecured*	*Common features*
Short-term credit contract[a]	15 days or fewer	$2,000 or less	Not prescribed	• The lender is not an Authorised Deposit-Taking Institution • The contract is not a continuing credit contract • The contract meets any other requirements prescribed by the regulations[b]
Small-amount credit contract[c]	16 days to 1 year	$2,000 or less (actual funds received by the borrower)[d]	Unsecured	
Medium-amount credit contract[e]	16 days to 2 years	$2,001 to $5,000	Not prescribed	

Notes

a NCCPA, §5(1).

b Definitions of small-amount credit contract and short-term credit contract in NCCPA, §5(1); see also NCC, §204(1). Definition of medium-amount credit contract in NCC, §204(1).

c NCCPA, §5(1).

d The prescribed limit of $2,000 effectively refers to the maximum funds that the borrower receives 'in their hands'. The regulations were amended in mid-2014 to provide that the credit limit is increased by the amount of the fees and charges imposed under the contract: National Consumer Credit Protection Regulations 2010 (Cth) (NCCPR), reg 4D.

e NCC, §204(1).

3.2 Price regulation

The changes introduced in Australia impose a differentiated price cap on consumer credit loans, where the size and form of the cap varies for these different categories of credit contracts.[21]

For small-amount credit contracts (SACCs) there are price caps on specific fees, and a prohibition on charging interest or any other fees. The maximum costs that can be charged for a SACC are an establishment fee of 20 per cent of the 'adjusted credit amount'[22] and a monthly fee of 4 per cent of the adjusted credit amount,[23] where the adjusted credit amount is the first amount of credit to be provided under the contract.[24] Lenders are permitted to pass on a direct debit processing fee or charge[25] and any relevant government fees and charges.[26] Also, and importantly, the total amount that can be recovered in the event of a default is capped at 200 per cent of the adjusted credit amount.[27] Except for those fees mentioned, no other fee, charge or interest can be imposed on a SACC.[28]

For medium-amount credit contracts (MACCs) and other credit contracts, there is a price cap imposed on the total cost of credit expressed as an annual cost rate.

21 However, the price regulation does not apply to credit products offered by Authorised Deposit-Taking Institutions (banks, building societies and credit unions) – see definitions of small-amount and medium-amount credit contracts in NCCPA, s 5(1) and NCC, s 204(1); also NCC, s 32A(4).

22 NCC, s 31A(2). The establishment fee does not have to reflect actual establishment costs.

23 Ibid s 31A(3).

24 Ibid s 204(1).

25 Australian Securities and Investments Commission Class Order [CO 13/818].

26 NCC, s 31A(1)(d).

27 Ibid s 39B; however, the calculation excludes enforcement expenses.

28 Ibid ss 23A(1)(a) and 31A(1); see also s 31B.

The annual cost rate is inclusive of credit fees and charges and fees payable by the debtor to third parties (for example, a broker).[29] For both 'other' credit contracts and MACCs, the maximum annual cost rate is 48 per cent; however, in the case of medium-amount contracts, an additional $400 establishment fee is also permitted.[30]

Credit providers are prohibited from imposing a monetary obligation that is inconsistent with these cost restrictions.[31]

Short-term credit contracts (STCCs) are effectively prohibited outright as a result of concerns about the high risk associated with these contracts for borrowers on low incomes.[32] There is therefore no price regulation for STCCs.

3.3 Additional responsible lending obligations

In addition to the imposition of price regulation for all consumer credit contracts, a range of additional responsible lending and other obligations have been imposed where the credit product being offered is a SACC. The general rationale for imposing these additional obligations was 'to improve lending and broking processes standards and therefore, the outcomes for consumers'.[33] More specifically, the obligations were designed to reduce the risk of debtors entering into a debt spiral.[34] The key responsible lending obligations are set out below.

First, the changes have introduced a presumption that a credit contract will cause substantial hardship if the loan applicant is in default under a SACC, or has, in the previous 90 days, been the debtor under two or more SACCs.[35] If a loan causes substantial hardship it is unsuitable, and therefore cannot be issued to that borrower.[36]

29 See the calculation formula in NCC, s 32B. The formula used is similar to that used in the New South Wales legislation: Parliament of the Commonwealth of Australia, 'Revised Explanatory Memorandum' (n 16) 72 [5.54].

30 NCC, s 32B(2), where the formula used for calculating the annual cost rate includes an allowance of $400 (or other amount prescribed by the regulations) in the case of medium-amount credit contracts. This is designed to provide for a bridging cap on costs for medium-amount credit contracts: Parliament of the Commonwealth of Australia, House of Representatives, 'Supplementary Explanatory Memorandum, Consumer Credit and Corporations Legislation Amendment (Enhancements) Bill 2011 (Cth)' 18 [1.84].

31 Such a provision is void and any amount prohibited can be recovered from the credit provider: NCC, ss 23 and 23A. It is also an offence for a credit provider to enter into a credit contract imposing a prohibited monetary obligation, or to require or accept payment in respect of a monetary obligation that cannot be imposed consistently with the National Credit Code: NCC, s 24(1A). In addition, providers of credit assistance are prohibited from suggesting, or assisting with, an application to a particular small-amount credit contract and credit provider if the person knows (or is reckless as to whether) the contract will contain prohibited monetary obligations: NCC, s 24A.

32 NCCPA, ss 124A and 133CA. The Supplementary Explanatory Memorandum explains that 'the short period of the loan means that the repayment will consume a disproportionate amount of the borrower's income, resulting in risk of repeat use or financial hardship': Parliament of the Commonwealth of Australia, 'Supplementary Explanatory Memorandum' (n 30) 13 [1.48] and [1.49].

33 Parliament of the Commonwealth of Australia, 'Supplementary Explanatory Memorandum' (n 30) 14 [1.57]. Reference was made to the findings of 'inconsistent standards' in Australian Securities and Investments Commission, 'Review of Micro Lenders' Responsible Lending Conduct and Disclosure Obligations' (Report No 264, November 2011) 16.

34 See Parliament of the Commonwealth of Australia, 'Revised Explanatory Memorandum' (n 16) 6.

35 NCCPA, s 118(3A).

36 Ibid s 133.

Note that this is only a presumption; it can be rebutted by the lender showing that the loan would not cause substantial hardship.[37]

Second, credit providers issuing SACCs are required to obtain and review the last 90 days of statements if the borrower has an account with an Authorised Deposit-Taking Institution.[38]

Third, a protected income amount regime has been imposed, where for borrowers who receive 50 per cent or more of their gross income as payments under the Social Security Act 1991 (Cth), only a maximum of 20 per cent of their gross income can be allocated to repayments under small-amount credit contracts.[39]

Fourth, providers of SACCs must include prescribed warnings, including information about other options, on their website and premises.[40] Credit providers and credit assistance providers must also give verbal warnings when offering to provide credit assistance or to provide small-amount credit contracts by telephone.[41]

Fifth, where there have been two failed attempts under a direct debit authority (direct debit authorities are a common way of repaying SACCs),[42] SACC providers must contact, or make a reasonable attempt to contact, the borrower.[43]

This combination of price regulation and additional responsible lending obligations demonstrates a multi-faceted approach to dealing with concerns about the safety and affordability of high-cost small loans – one that seeks to minimise the upfront and ongoing cost of such loans, as well as address concerns about irresponsible lending and consumer awareness. This approach reflects an acceptance of the importance of regulating product features (and not just disclosing the relevant features) and of there being a role for governments in addressing unfairness and financial exclusion. The next section discusses some initial indicators of the impact of the new laws.

4 Assessing the impact of the new laws

4.1 Overview

The obligations described above represent a significant change in the regulation of small consumer loans in Australia. The introduction of the new laws was accompanied by statements of purpose from the Government and predictions of impact from different stakeholder groups. In terms of the overall purpose and objective of the laws, the Government expressed the view that the changes affecting small loans

37 Ibid s 118(3A). A similar obligation is imposed on credit assistance providers: s 123(3A).

38 Authorised Deposit-Taking Institutions are banks, building societies and credit unions.

39 NCCPA, s 133CC; NCCPR, reg 28S. Payments under the Social Security Act include unemployment benefits and sole parent, disability, aged and carer's pensions.

40 NCCPA, ss 133CB (creditor providers) and 124B (credit assistance providers). Non-compliance is an offence (ss 124B(2) and 133CB(2)), and a civil penalty can also be sought (ss 124B(1) and 133CB(1)). For the prescribed text for the warnings, see NCCPR, schs 7 (warning on premises) and 9 (warning on websites). For a review of the presentation and content of website warnings of some credit providers, see Consumer Action Law Centre, 'What Warning: Observations About Mandated Warnings on Payday Lender Websites' (August 2013).

41 NCCPA, ss 133CBA (credit providers) and 124BA (credit assistance providers). For the information to be included in the warning, see NCCPR, regs 124BA and 133CBA.

42 Paul Ali, Cosima McRae and Ian Ramsay, 'The Politics of Payday Lending Regulation in Australia' (2013) 39 Monash University Law Review 411, 423–424.

43 NCCPA, s 39C; NCCPR, reg 79C.

were designed to 'strike the right balance between allowing a viable and regulated credit industry to provide credit to consumers in need and at the same time providing safeguards to protect the interests of those consumers'.[44]

Predictions of the impact of the new laws from the industry were largely negative; the major concern was that price regulation would have a significant impact on their ability to stay in business.[45] These concerns were partially addressed by an increase in the size of the cap during the consultation period on the legislation; however, concerns were expressed that the new cap would still not permit a sustainable industry.[46] In turn, industry members argued, this would lead to financial exclusion and consumer hardship, as the alternatives to payday loans were not available in sufficient quantity to meet the existing demand.[47] It had also been suggested that price caps would increase the risk of creating the conditions for unlicensed lenders to enter the market, to the detriment of consumers.[48] In terms of industry viability, it is interesting to note that the Government had previously estimated that perhaps 25 per cent of small loan providers would leave the industry if a cap of $30 per $100 were introduced.[49] The price regulation that was ultimately introduced was less generous to credit providers than this model, so the impact may have been greater.

In contrast to industry members, consumer advocates had argued for a different (and more restrictive) price cap and were 'cautiously hopeful' that the original proposals would lead to 'a reduction in harm caused by high cost short-term loans, including a reduction in fees and effective interest charged'.[50] Subsequently, when the price cap was raised during the consultation period, concerns were expressed that the price regulation that was ultimately settled on represented 'a win' for payday lenders.[51] On the issue of repeat borrowing, consumer advocates raised concerns about the approach of relying on the responsible lending obligations, in preference to the original proposal of prohibiting multiple concurrent contracts, and took the view that 'responsible lending is ineffective at limiting harmful lending in the sector'.[52] In relation to industry concerns that there were not sufficient alternatives

44 Parliament of the Commonwealth of Australia, House of Representatives, *Parliamentary Debates* (Bill Shorten, Minister for Financial Services and Superannuation, 26 June 2012) 71.

45 See, for example, Ali, McRae and Ramsay (n 42) 430.

46 For example, Cash Doctors, 'Submission: Discussion Paper Reforms in Relation to Small Amount Credit Contracts; and Exposure Drafts of Consumer Credit and Corporations Legislation (Amendment) Bill 2011' (7 May 2012) 8; National Financial Services Federation Ltd, 'Submission to Consumer Credit Unit, Retail Investor Division – The Treasury, Consumer Credit and Corporations Legislation Amendment (Enhancements) Bill 2011' (8 May 2012) 9 (recommending that the cap be increased further), Appendix 2, 19.

47 National Financial Services Federation Ltd, 'Submission to Commonwealth Treasury – National Consumer Credit Protection Amendment (Enhancements) Bill 2011' (5 September 2011) 6.

48 Anna Ellison and Robert Foster, 'The Impact of Interest Rate Ceilings' (Policis) 86.

49 Australian Government, 'Regulation Impact Statement' (n 7) 60.

50 Consumer Action Law Centre, 'Government Reforms Offer a Branch to Consumers Stuck in High Cost Short Term Lending Quicksand' (Media Release, 25 August 2011).

51 For example, Consumer Action Law Centre, 'Credit Enhancements Bill a "Win" for Payday Lenders' (media release, 27 June 2012); see also Consumer Action Law Centre, Consumer Credit Legal Centre NSW and Financial Counselling Australia, 'Submission: Discussion Paper – Proposed Reforms relating to Small Amount Credit Contracts' (7 May 2012) 3. Note that this submission was also endorsed by 16 other consumer and community organisations.

52 Consumer Action Law Centre, Consumer Credit Legal Centre NSW and Financial Counselling Australia (n 51) 13. See also the discussion in Gillam and Consumer Action Law Centre (n 12) 211–212.

available to consumers seeking small loans if commercial businesses become unviable, consumer advocates argued that the evidence of high use of payday loans could not be equated with a demand for small loans, as, for many consumers, borrowing money would be very likely to reduce, rather than enhance, their welfare.[53]

In light of the concerns raised by industry and consumer groups, what has been the impact of the new laws? It is still early days, and there has not, to the author's knowledge at the time of writing, been published data or research on the impact of the new laws. However, it is possible to identify some data and other information that can shed some early light on the impact.

4.2 Changes in the availability of small loans

Given industry concerns about viability, measuring the change in the number of businesses offering small loans will be relevant to assessing the impact of the changes. However, this is difficult to do in the absence of reliable details of the size of the market before the changes. Estimates of the size of the small loan market varied in the period before the changes were introduced, and there has not been a more detailed assessment since then.

One possible measure of the impact of the changes on the viability of businesses offering small loans might be through Yellow Pages advertising. The number of businesses identified in the Yellow Pages online under the category of 'finance – short-term loans' shows a significant change since the implementation of the new laws – from 247 in April 2013 to 202 in September 2014, a decrease of 19 per cent.[54] This is close to the prediction of a 25 per cent reduction in the industry made in the 2011 Regulation Impact Statement, and it suggests that the changes have had some negative impact on viability of individual businesses, as was predicted by the industry.

However, there is no guarantee that the Yellow Pages listing is an accurate proxy for small loan businesses in Australia; or even an accurate proxy for the change in the number of businesses. This might be particularly the case if there has been an increase in lenders based entirely online, as lenders without a shopfront presence may see little benefit from advertising in the Yellow Pages. Reports suggest that the online market is booming; one recent estimate suggests that the online market is worth more than 300 million dollars,[55] and at least one large credit provider has converted to a fully online business since 2011.[56] A simple Google search also shows many different businesses purporting to offer or to provide assistance with small loans online, again giving some support to the suggestion of a significant online

53 See, for example, Gillam and Consumer Action Law Centre (n 12) 206–227; Care Inc Financial Counselling Service and the Consumer Law Centre, 'Submission: Strategies for Reducing Reliance on High Cost, Short Term, Small Amount Lending, Discussion Paper' (April 2012) 2–3.

54 Data from www.yellowpages.com.au on 8 April 2013 and 17 September 2014, using a search category of 'short-term finance', a pre-determined category on the website. The figures quoted include individual franchisees.

55 Tom Cowie, 'Rise of the Online Payday Lenders' *Sydney Morning Herald* (Sydney, 7 September 2014) www.smh.com.au/national/rise-of-the-online-payday-lenders-20140906-10c7lc.html accessed 10 November 2014.

56 In the Regulation Impact Statement, Cash Doctors was reported as having 79 branches. Since then, it has been renamed Nimble and now operates entirely online; see www.nimble.com.au.

market. An expansion of online providers can potentially increase competition and consumer choice. It also creates new challenges for regulators and concerns have been raised about unlicensed operators offering payday loans or loan services online.[57] However, these concerns are not necessarily unique to payday lending.

Some large shopfront lenders do not seem to have been significantly affected by the changes. The annual reports from Cash Converters International Pty Ltd show an increase in loan monies advanced, loan amounts and customer numbers between 2012 and 2013[58] and between 2013 and 2014 (although with an initial decrease in volume of cash advances in the first half of the financial year).[59] The company saw a positive outlook, with confidence that the improvement experienced in the second half of the financial year would continue into the 2015 financial year.[60] Similarly, the annual reports from Money3 show increased business in recent years. Its report of the 2012–2013 financial year (that is, before the price regulation amendments had come into effect) showed its loan book increasing by 88.1 per cent from the previous year: its branch written income increased by 40.6 per cent; its branch earned income increased by 26 per cent; and its branch network expanded.[61] Money3 also indicated a positive outlook for the 2013–2014 financial year,[62] noting that revenue from recently acquired branches had exceeded expectations, that revenue from existing branches had improved on the previous July and August[63] and that the new regulations have provided certainty and opportunity for the company.[64]

Despite some positive outlooks for some businesses offering SACCs, there is also anecdotal evidence of a trend towards consolidation, with one industry association representing payday lenders suggesting in late 2013 that smaller *mum and dad* operators had advised the association that they would not be renewing membership of the association (presumably reflecting a decision to exit the industry as well).[65] It has also been reported that by June 2013, only one-quarter of individuals licensed to provide unsecured loans under 3,000 dollars were running an actively operating business,[66] suggesting significant exit from the industry prior to the implementation of the 2013 changes. Consolidation has also occurred through the collapse of The Cash Store in 2013 (following changes to its business model to comply with the

57 For example, see National Financial Services Federation Ltd, 'Submission to Financial System Inquiry' (1 April 2014). See also Jonathon Pearlman and Jo Lennan, 'Life After Debt' *The Saturday Paper* (Melbourne, 26 July–1 August 2014).

58 For example, Cash Converters International Limited, 'Annual Report 2013' 21 (personal loans) and 22 (cash advance).

59 Ibid 7. In relation to cash advances, the report noted that 'the trend is upward'. For a discussion of Cash Converters' growth over the period 2002–2009, see Gillam and Consumer Action Law Centre (n 12) 102–116.

60 Cash Converters International Limited (n 58) 9.

61 Money3 Corporation Limited, 'Annual Report 2013' 1.

62 The 2014 Annual Report was not available at the timing of writing.

63 Money3 (n 61) 3.

64 Ibid 2.

65 Timothy Boreham, 'Payday D-day as Money3 Buys Rival Cash Store' *The Australian, Business Review* (Sydney, 30 September 2013) www.theaustralian.com.au/business/financial-services/payday-d-day-as-money3-buys-rival-cash-store/story-fn91wd6x-1226729552511 accessed 11 November 2014.

66 Timothy Boreham, 'Payday's Heyday Over as Lenders Consolidate' *The Australian, Business Section* (Sydney, 24 June 2013).

national laws),[67] with many of The Cash Store's branches and loan business having been acquired by Money3.[68]

However, even if there has been a reduction in the number of businesses offering small loan products in the period leading up to, and after, July 2013, it may not be possible to attribute the cause solely to the introduction of the changes discussed in this chapter. There were significant other amendments to the consumer credit legislation in the years immediately preceding the introduction of the small loan provisions. Prior to 2010, there were few regulatory barriers to entry for small businesses providing consumer credit. However, the national credit laws imposed licensing, compulsory External Dispute Resolution scheme membership and responsible lending obligations on all credit providers for the first time, and these earlier changes may have had as much, or more, of an influence on the viability of small credit businesses.

Thus, while there is no firm evidence to date, the indicators discussed above suggest that there may have been some consolation and/or exits in the sector since July 2013. However, many other businesses continue to operate and expand their market, both online and through traditional outlets. This may give some comfort that the Government's stated objective of 'allowing a viable and regulated credit industry to provide credit to consumers in need' is being achieved, even if not all businesses have survived the transition to the new regulatory environment.

4.3 The impact on price

Another measure of impact is whether there have been changes to the prices of SACCs offered since July 2013. To the extent that loans were previously offered at a cost above the price ceiling established in the National Consumer Credit Protection Act and National Credit Code, the new laws should have seen a reduction in the cost of small loans.

Again, it is not possible to provide a definitive analysis, given the lack of reliable industry data in the period before and after the change. However, a 2008 report included data on some loans offered in Queensland in 2006 (before the introduction of an interest rate cap in that state)[69] and it might be surmised that loans at similar costs were also available in other Australian jurisdictions that did not have an interest rate cap. Table 6.2 shows the costs of some of the small ($300) and large ($1,000) payday loans (defined in this survey as loans with a maximum duration of eight weeks)[70] available in Queensland in 2006, and compares them with the maximum charges that would now be permitted under the national law.[71] The lower cost is in bold.

67 Boreham (n 65).

68 Ibid.

69 Nicola Howell, Therese Wilson and James Davidson, 'Interest Rate Caps: Protection or Paternalism?' (Centre for Credit and Consumer Law, Griffith University, Brisbane, 2008). The report included product data from 40 lenders.

70 Ibid 38.

71 The one- and two-week loans in this report have been excluded from this analysis, since these short-term loans are no longer permitted.

Table 6.2 Comparison of costs of payday loans available in 2006 with current maximum permissible charges[72]

	Reference number (lender)	*Type of loan*	*Loan amount*	*Term*	*APR (all-inclusive) in 2006*	*Total payments in 2006*	*Maximum fees – NCCPA*	*Total maximum payments – NCCPA*
Most expensive	11	Small payday loan	$300	4 weeks	700%	$413.72	$60+$12	**$372**
Mid-range	7	Small payday loan	$300	4 weeks	493%	$377.32	$60+$12	**$372**
Least expensive	35	Small payday loan	$300	4 weeks	300%	**$350.68**	$60+$12	$372
Most expensive	22	Large payday loan	$1,000	4 weeks	487%	$1,254.52	$200+$40	**$1,240**
Least expensive	35	Large payday loan	$1,000	4 weeks	300%	**$1,151.64**	$200+$40	$1,240

72 Data sourced from Howell *et al.* (n 69) 42–43.

Table 6.3 Comparison of costs of payday loans available in 2009 with current maximum permissible charges[73]

Lender	*Loan amount*	*Term*	*APR (14-day loan) in 2009*	*APR (30-day loan) in 2009*	*Total payments in 2009*	*Maximum fees – NCCPA*	*Total maximum payments – NCCPA*
Cashdoctors (now operating as Nimble)	$250	Pay cycle	677.8%	316%	$315	$50 + $10	**$310**
Advancecash (now appears to be operating as a broker)	$300	Pay cycle	781.6%	364.7%	$389.94	$60 + $12	**$372**
Cash Today	$250	Pay cycle	797%	372.3%	$326.50	$50 + $10	**$310**

73 Data sourced from Gillam and Consumer Action Law Centre (n 12) 286–288 (appendix E).

Similarly, a 2010 report included some data on the cost of online payday loans from nine lenders in 2009;[74] Table 6.3 compares the costs in 2009 with the costs that would now be permitted under the national law for the lenders in this group that continue to operate.

If the prices of loans had remained relatively constant between 2006–2009 and 2013, the lower-priced loan products from these two samples would have needed little price change to be compliant with the new laws. However, the more expensive loans would need to have been reduced more significantly in price compared to their prices in 2006–2009.[75] This is consistent with the comment from one consumer organisation that the changes have 'removed the highest cost loans from the market'.[76]

As mentioned below, some lenders do not appear to disclose the costs of loans online before direct contact with the lender is made. However, other lenders do include price information on their websites and a brief review of a number of the major lenders' websites showed that, where price is disclosed, the price disclosed is the maximum permitted by the legislation.[77]

4.4 Repeat borrowing

A major concern about payday loans has been the extent to which consumers use them repeatedly; this repeated use is said to be the main cause of harm.[78] Despite the claims by industry that payday loans are intended to be used on a one-off basis to meet unexpected costs, it has been argued that repeat custom is the backbone of small loan businesses.[79] Qualitative interviews with lenders also confirm the importance of repeat business – for example, the *Caught Short* report stated that 'it was also clear that the core basis of most lenders' business was repeat borrowing, regardless of demographic'.[80] From the perspective of borrowers, too, there was evidence of high levels of repeat borrowing before the recent changes. For example, the *Caught Short* report found that 'two-thirds of participants in the study

74 Gillam and Consumer Action Law Centre (n 12).

75 A similar result is also observed for the small and large non-payday loans in the 2006 survey.

76 Consumer Credit Legal Centre NSW, 'Submission in Relation to the Financial System Inquiry' (April 2014) 22–23. Also, note that subsequent to the 2006 survey of Queensland lenders, an interest rate cap of 48 per cent was introduced in Queensland, which would have required price reductions in any event.

77 For example, as at 15 November 2014, the following websites disclose their loan price as 20 per cent establishment fee and 4 per cent monthly fee: www.nimble.com.au; ferratum.com.au/costs; www.cashstop.com.au/online-loans/rates-and-terms; www.iwantpayday.net; cashtoday.com.au; www.cashtrain.com.au (a trading name of Money3 Services); www.k24.com.au/content/fees (although the fees are disclosed as maximum fees). Another lender, offering loans up to $2,025, discloses the loan cost as $400 establishment fee and 48 per cent interest (i.e. the permitted maximum for a MACC): www.dollarsdirect.com.au/fee-schedule.

78 For example, Ali, McRae and Ramsay (n 42) 425.

79 For example, Banks *et al.*, 'Caught Short' (n 14) 66, reporting on comments from lenders. See also Ali, McRae and Ramsay (n 42) 430–431, where the authors discuss industry responses to the proposals to deal with rollovers. For a US perspective, see Natalie Martin, '1,000% Interest: Good While Supplies Last – A Study of Payday Loan Practices and Solutions' (2010) 52 Arizona Law Review 563, 573.

80 Banks *et al.*, 'Caught Short' (n 14) 65; one lender is quoted as having 98 per cent of customers as repeat business: 66.

were continuously indebted to one or more short-term, small-loan companies for considerable periods of time'.[81]

As noted above, the 2012 changes involved the introduction of a presumption of substantial hardship if the borrower was in default under a SACC, or had two or more SACCs in the last 90 days. There is limited information about the impact of these changes, in particular whether the use of the presumption is resulting in a decrease in the amount of loans being granted. However, a 2013–2014 survey of 49 borrowers (from an outer Melbourne region) found that almost three-quarters of the borrowers had only one loan at the time of the survey, while just over one-quarter reported having two or more loans,[82] thus raising the presumption of substantial hardship. However, it is worth noting that, in the absence of a real-time small loans database or universal and timely reporting of loans to credit-reporting agencies, it may be difficult for lenders to confirm the existence of other small loans.[83]

4.5 The availability of alternatives

A further issue is the availability of alternatives to commercial SACCs. At the time the proposed price regulation provisions were being considered, there were some encouraging signs about the potential for investment in alternatives. In April 2012, the then government released a discussion paper to 'canvass strategies to reduce the extent to which financially excluded consumers are dependent on these high cost small amount loans'.[84] The discussion paper flagged that potential areas for intervention could include: reducing the need for high-cost, short-term, small-amount credit; reducing the risks to individuals of using high-cost, short-term, small-amount credit; providing alternative products; and providing greater levels of assistance to individuals who are in a debt cycle.[85]

However, there has been no formal response to the submissions made to this discussion paper by either the current or former government.

The implementation of the new laws has potentially reduced somewhat the risk of using short-term, small-amount loans – both through the price regulation and through the additional responsible lending obligations. However, the response to other areas for intervention identified in the discussion paper has been patchy.

81 Ibid 43. Note, though, that an online survey (not representative) conducted in 2008 found a much lower level of repeat borrowing, with nearly three-quarters of respondents saying they had taken out either one or two loans in the preceding 18-month period: Gillam and Consumer Action Law Centre (n 12) 69. The authors note that the survey 'exhibits significant divergence from other research and warrants further investigation': 70.

82 Ely Lee, *Taking the Stress Out of Managing Money: A Report Examining the Use and Impact of Payday Lending on Low Income Families in the City of Greater Dandenong* (Hanover Welfare Services 2014) 29.

83 As noted in Banks *et al.*, 'without any central reporting system, lenders could only guess whether customers had loans with multiple lenders': Banks *et al.*, 'Caught Short' (n 14) 69. See also Ali, McRae and Ramsay (n 42) 441–442, where the authors note that, although a comprehensive credit reporting system has recently been introduced, it is not used by all lenders.

84 Australian Government, the Treasury, *Strategies for Reducing Reliance on High-Cost, Short-Term, Small Amount Lending: Discussion Paper* (April 2012) ix.

85 Ibid ix.

Commonly mentioned alternatives to payday loans include the No-Interest Loan Scheme (NILS) and Low-Interest Loan Scheme (LILS). These schemes are run by community organisations in partnership with financial institutions. A recent evaluation of the NILS reported that these schemes have been successful in diverting consumers from fringe credit, with 42 per cent of NILS recipients ceasing to borrow from fringe lenders as a result of a NILS loan.[86] There has been some increased investment in NILS by both state and federal governments in recent times.[87] However, there is still significant unmet need. Good Shepherd Microfinance recently suggested that the programme currently covers only 6 per cent of the market of financially excluded consumers, and argued for an injection of government funding of $75 million over five years to increase the reach of the programme to 14 per cent of the market.[88]

In terms of other programmes, one LILS scheme operating as a partnership between the Brotherhood of St. Laurence and Australia and New Zealand Banking Group Limited ceased providing new loans in February 2012.[89] Credit unions and community finance institutions do exist, but their reach with alternatives to payday loans is small.[90] The Australian Government has funded a pilot programme for Community Finance Development Institutions,[91] but this was due to cease in mid-2014.[92] The 2014 Financial System Inquiry supported 'continuing Government and industry efforts to increase financial inclusion', but made no specific recommendations on this point.[93]

One difficulty with reliance on community finance programmes to offer an alternative to payday loans is that these schemes in their current form, while they are important, may have impact only on the margins. Most community finance options are limited in the purposes for which they can be used, and may not be able to be used for regular living expenses,[94] despite the fact that the available evidence suggests that payday loans are predominantly used for these purposes, rather than

86 Centre for Social Impact, *Life Changing Loans at No Interest: An Outcomes Evaluation of Good Shepherd Microfinance's No Interest Loan Scheme* (Report prepared for Good Shepherd Microfinance, March 2014) 55.

87 See, for example, Good Shepherd Microfinance, 'Victoria Leads the Way in Microfinance' (media release, 7 May 2014); Good Shepherd Microfinance, 'No Interest Loans Program Expands into Remote and Regional Australia' (media release, 9 April 2013).

88 Good Shepherd Microfinance, 'Response to the Financial System Inquiry Interim Report' (August 2014) 21. See also Centre for Social Impact (n 86) 37.

89 Australia and New Zealand Banking Group Limited, 'ANZ Progress Loan' www.anz.com.au/personal/personal-loans-overview/progress-loan accessed 29 October 2014.

90 For example, see Ingrid Burkett and Genevieve Sheehan, *From the Margins to the Mainstream: The Challenges for Microfinance in Australia* (Brotherhood of St. Laurence, Foresters Community Finance 2009) 15, appendix 2 (directory of microfinance programs).

91 See discussion of this program in Wilson in this book.

92 Department of Social Services, 'Community Development Finance Institutions (CDFI) Pilot Project' www.dss.gov.au/our-responsibilities/communities-and-vulnerable-people/programs-services/financial-management-program/community-development-financial-institutions-cdfi-pilot-project accessed 11 November 2014.

93 Commonwealth of Australia, *Financial System Inquiry Final Report* (November 2014) 193.

94 For example, Marcus Banks, Gregory Marston, Roslyn Russell and Howard Karger, '"In a Perfect World it Would be Great if They Didn't Exist": How Australians Experience Payday Loans' (2015) 24 International Journal of Social Welfare 37, 44.

one-off expenses.[95] They are also often more time consuming in the application and payment processes in comparison to payday loans.[96] The size of the payday lending market in the commercial sector also vastly exceeds the size of the community finance sector, and the ability of community finance schemes to scale up to meet the unmet demand is likely to take some time, even with sufficient investment.[97]

Other alternatives to payday loans have also not been implemented. For example, a suggestion in the discussion paper that Centrelink advances be available more frequently does not appear to have been acted upon, as, at least for unemployment and student allowances, only one Centrelink advance is available in any 12-month period.[98]

More progress, however, has been made on mechanisms to reduce the need for payday (or other small loans) by establishing and improving policies for dealing with consumers in financial difficulty. Such hardship programmes have been introduced by credit providers, telecommunications providers and energy providers,[99] and some schemes have undergone significant improvement in recent times.[100] Given that a common reason for accessing a payday loan or other commercial small loan has been to pay bills,[101] ensuring that hardship programmes are promoted, accessible and effective can be an important mechanism for reducing the need for payday loans. Also relevant here is that Commonwealth Government support for financial counselling has been maintained following the change of government in 2013.[102]

As noted above, industry members had raised concerns that, if the form of the regulations made many businesses unviable, consumers would be left with limited options and some may resort to more harmful options, such as loan sharks. In practice, there is limited information about what consumers would actually do in the absence of commercial SACCs. In a small survey conducted by Hanover, the most

95 Banks *et al.*, 'Caught Short' (n 14) 32: 'the seven most commonly cited reasons borrowers gave when they took out their first loan were all to meet regular, weekly-type needs and expenses'.

96 For example, see a comparison of features (including time taken to process) of payday loans and alternatives to payday loans: Centre for Social Impact (n 86) 39.

97 In fact, in its submission to the Financial System Inquiry, Good Shepherd Microfinance only sought funding to increase the reach of NILS to 14 per cent of financially excluded consumers: Good Shepherd Microfinance, 'Response to the Financial System Inquiry Interim Report' (n 88) 21. See also discussion of the prospects of, and potential for, community finance schemes to be scaled up in Burkett and Sheehan (n 90); Centre for Social Impact (n 86).

98 Department of Human Services, 'Advance Payment Options' www.humanservices.gov.au/customer/enablers/advance-payment accessed 10 November 2014.

99 For a discussion of the legal framework for financial hardship in these sectors, see Paul Ali, Evgenia Bourova and Ian Ramsay, 'Financial Hardship: The Legal Frameworks' (Financial Hardship Project Research Report, Centre for Corporate Law and Securities Regulation 2014) http://law.unimelb.edu.au/cclsr/centre-activities/research/major-research-projects/financial-hardship-project accessed 30 October 2014.

100 The hardship variations in the National Credit Code were improved in 2013; see NCC s 72; see also more detailed obligations included in the 2013 Code of Banking Practice, cl 28.

101 See, for example, Gillam and Consumer Action Law Centre (n 12) 59, showing that bills were the second most common reason for borrowing. Also Connolly has reported that 'the most common need for credit was to meet every day living expenses such as food, rent and utility bills': Chris Connolly, 'Measuring Financial Exclusion in Australia' (Centre for Social Impact for National Australia Bank 2012) 7.

102 Financial Counselling Australia, 'More About Financial Counselling Funding' (media release, 16 May 2014).

common responses to a question about likely responses if payday loans did not exist were to borrow from family or friends, sell or pawn items or cut back on expenses.[103] No respondents mentioned they would seek out a loan from an illegal lender or loan shark.[104] However, this survey was limited in size and scope, and further research on the impact of the changes is needed.

Further, the alternatives identified in the discussion paper do not necessarily deal with what appears to be a key driver for using payday loans – insufficient income to meet daily living costs.[105] Many borrowers in the *Caught Short* study also explicitly identified increases in government income support payments or assistance, increases in the minimum wage or reduced taxation rates for low-income earners as measures that would assist them.[106] However, there appears little political appetite for increasing government pensions and benefits; in fact, it could be argued that the opposite is the case, at least for some categories of benefits.[107]

4.6 Compliance with the new laws

Also relevant to assessing the impact of the new laws is the level of compliance with those laws. A low level of compliance could suggest problems with the way in which the laws have been framed and/or a lessening of the intended protection for consumers.

Given the short time that the new laws have been in place, it is unsurprising that there have not yet been any court decisions that have considered the new laws.[108] The regulator, the Australian Securities and Investments Commission (ASIC) has, however, been involved in a number of matters where it has alleged a contravention of the new laws.

For example, ASIC has accepted an enforceable undertaking from a credit provider who was charging a subscription fee for a 'Membership Rewards Programme', in breach of the price regulations in the National Consumer Credit Protection Act 2009 (Cth). As part of the undertaking, Cash Stop refunded $14,000 to 650 affected

103 Lee (n 82) 36.

104 Ibid 36 (four borrowers reported that they would engage in illegal activity, but it is assumed that this referred to the borrower's illegal activity, rather than illegal activity of a lender (for example, unlicensed lending). Note also the critique of the substitution argument by Gillam and Consumer Action Law Centre (n 12) 186–191.

105 Banks and others suggest that 'The robust nature of the payday lending sector is largely attributable to inadequate social welfare payments': Banks *et al.*, 'In a Perfect World' (n 94) 45. See also discussion in Financial Counselling Australia, 'What Financial Counsellors Say About Payday Lending' (October 2011) 15–16.

106 Banks *et al.*, 'Caught Short' (n 14) 53.

107 Budget measures for the Australian Government proposed in May 2014 included a change to the indexation of aged, disability and carers pensions and parenting payments to a lower index, and limiting unemployment payments for people under 30 to six months each year; see Australian Council of Social Services, *A Budget That Divides a Nation: ACOSS 2014–15 Budget Analysis* (May 2014) 8.

108 Although the Australian Securities and Investments Commission has commenced litigation against a Queensland lender who has argued an exemption from the responsible lending and price regulation laws applies to its business: Australian Securities and Investments Commission, 'ASIC Takes Action Against Payday Lending Business' (media release 14-150, 3 July 2014).

customers.[109] ASIC has also issued an infringement notice to a payday lender for failing to comply with the obligation to obtain and consider consumers' account statements before granting loans.[110]

Other ASIC enforcement activity and litigation involving providers of SACCs has focused on alleged contraventions of the obligations in the national laws, or state laws, that existed before the price regulation and additional responsible lending obligations came into effect.[111]

Other preliminary information on the level of compliance with the new laws is provided by consumer and community organisations. In its submissions to the Financial System Inquiry, one organisation noted that the new laws have 'removed the highest cost loans from the market and importantly, limited the total amount that can be recovered in default charges'.[112] Another, however, suggests that the consumer harm caused by small-amount loans is repeat borrowing, and that the 2013 changes will not be sufficient to arrest 'problematic repeat lending'.[113]

Consumer organisations have also noted that there remains a significant problem of lenders seeking to circumvent the price regulation, and other credit regulation, by relying on exemptions in a way not originally intended and/or providing what is effectively consumer credit, but using mechanisms that are subject to less regulation

109 Australian Securities and Investments Commission, 'ASIC Investigation Leads to Cash Stop Financial Services Pty Ltd Refunding more than 650 consumers' (media release 14-035, 24 February 2014).

110 Australian Securities and Investments Commission, 'Payday Lender Penalised for Breaching New Responsible Lending Laws' (media release 14-313, 25 November 2014).

111 For example, *Re Laurence Sullivan and Same Day Money Pty Ltd and ASIC* [2013] AATA 591; Australian Securities and Investments Commission, 'Perth Lender Enters into Enforceable Undertaking and Pays Credit Infringement Notice Penalties' (media release 12-267, 7 November 2012); Australian Securities and Investments Commission, 'Small Amount Lender Pays $30,600 Penalty for Misleading Online Advertisements' (media release 14-065, 2 April 2014); Australian Securities and Investments Commission, 'Small Amount Lender Pays Infringement Notice Penalty for "Free" Loan Offer' (Media Release 13-284, 21 October 2013); Australian Securities and Investments Commission, 'ASIC Crackdown Stops Another Payday Lender from Overcharging Consumers' (Media Release 14-328, 9 December 2014); Australian Securities and Investments Commission, 'ASIC Commences Legal Action Against Fast Access Finance' (Media Release 13-205, 7 August 2013). There is also a class action on foot: www.mauriceblackburn.com.au/about/media-centre/media-statements/2013/cash-converters-to-face-pay-day-lending-class-action-claims; and some individual disputes have been considered by the External Dispute Schemes, for example, Credit Ombudsman Service Ltd, 'COSL Determination (Ms M) 13 January 2014'.

112 Consumer Credit Legal Centre (n 76) 22–23. Although this organisation has also noted that there remains high levels of non-compliance with the responsible lending obligations by payday lenders: Financial Rights Legal Centre (formerly Consumer Credit Legal Centre), 'Submission to the Financial System Inquiry Interim Report' (August 2014) 21–22. See also Foresters Community Finance, 'Submission to the Financial System Inquiry Interim Report' (2014): suggesting that reforms have put 'sensible caps on total repaid (twice loaned), caps on costs in the SACCS "20 + 4" and 48% actual real costs on medium amount loans' and that 'this has led to a much better regulated industry, with only few loopholes still being exploited'. See also Good Shepherd Microfinance, 'Response to the Financial System Inquiry Interim Report' (n 88) 14. Although some consumer advocates continue to argue for a more restricted cap, for example, Consumer Credit Legal Centre (n 76) 24; Legal Aid NSW, 'Submission to the Financial System Inquiry' (March 2014) 18; Legal Aid NSW, 'Submission to the Financial System Inquiry Interim Report' (August 2014) 11; Consumer Action Law Centre 'Submission to the Financial System Inquiry' (March 2014) 13.

113 Consumer Action Law Centre, 'Submission to the Financial System Inquiry' (n 112) 13. This organisation supports a price cap that would be low enough to make short-term loans unviable, and drive lenders to provide longer-term loans with smaller repayment amounts.

(for example, consumer lease contracts).[114] As discussed below, this issue of avoidance has been a perennial one in efforts to regulate small loans.

Thus, the evidence so far does not point to significant levels of non-compliance with the new laws, although there remain some concerns about compliance with the general responsible lending obligations and avoidance activities by providers of SACCs.

4.7 The need for further research

As discussed in this section, there is only limited information available about the impact of the new laws. Given the controversial nature of these laws, and the requirement for a review after July 2015, greater research efforts are needed. Unfortunately, there appears to be little appetite within governments to invest in a coordinated programme of consumer research. In 2008 the Productivity Commission recommended that 'the Australian Government … should take the lead role in developing arrangements to provide additional funding to … enable an expansion in policy-related consumer research'[115] and in 2009, the Treasury released an Issues Paper on options for funding consumer research (and consumer advocacy).[116] However, there has been no government response to this Issues Paper, and consumer and trade practices research is no longer included in either the strategic or operational priorities of the Consumer Affairs Forum (comprising the Commonwealth, State, Territory and New Zealand Ministers responsible for consumer protection).[117] A small loans database might also assist with monitoring the impact of the new laws on industry members.[118] However, there has not been any government response to a 2013 consultation paper on this issue,[119] and the question of whether or not to introduce a database is specifically to be considered in the review of some of the SACC provisions that is due 'as soon as practicable' after mid-2015.[120]

114 For example, Legal Aid NSW, 'Submission to the Financial System Inquiry' (n 112) 18–19. For a broader discussion of the regulatory framework for consumer leases, see Paul Ali Cosima McRae, Ian Ramsay and Tiong Tjin Saw, 'Consumer Leases and Consumer Protection: Regulatory Arbitrage and Consumer Harm' (2013) 41 Australian Business Law Review 240.

115 Productivity Commission (n 13) 49 (recommendation 11.3).

116 Australian Government, the Treasury, *Consumer Voices: Sustaining Advocacy and Research in Australia's New Consumer Policy Framework* (Issues Paper, May 2009).

117 Until December 2012, the principal strategies for the Consumer Affairs Forum (and its predecessor, the Ministerial Council on Consumer Affairs) included 'Research into consumer concerns and trade practices' – see 'MCCA Communiques' www.consumerlaw.gov.au/content/Content.aspx?doc=ministerial_council.htm accessed 17 November 2014. However, the Consumer Affairs Forum's Strategic Agenda 2013–2015 make no reference to research – see COAG Legislative and Governance Forum on Consumer Affairs, 'Strategic Agenda: An Integrated and Harmonised Approach to Consumer Protection' (1 July 2013) www.consumerlaw.gov.au/content/mcca/downloads/CAF_strategic_agenda_20130515.pdf accessed 17 November 2014.

118 For example, a database maintained by the regulator in the United States was used by researchers to track the payday lending activity of 11,000 borrowers over two years, giving insight into the market and use of these loans: Uriah King and Leslie Parrish, 'Payday Loans Inc: Short on Credit, Long on Debt' (Centre for Responsible Lending 2011) www.responsiblelending.org/payday-lending/research-analysis/payday-loan-inc.pdf accessed 12 September 2014.

119 Australian Securities and Investments Commission, *Review of the Effectiveness of an Online Database for Small Amount Lenders* (Consultation Paper 198, January 2013).

120 NCCPA, s 335A(1)(b).

Whether or not there will be any detailed empirical data on the impact of the new laws to inform this review remains to be seen.

5 Other remaining issues

5.1 Responding to avoidance activities

In Australia, attempts to regulate payday lending have regularly been met with industry resistance. Industry members have identified loopholes in the regulatory framework, and then structured products or business models to take advantage of such loopholes. In this way, lenders have been able to avoid (or accommodate) the application of consumer credit regulation (or some part of the regulation).[121] Specific techniques continued to be used unless or until they were challenged successfully in court proceedings[122] or addressed by legislative amendment.[123] A similar avoidance response of payday lenders to regulation has been observed in the United States.[124]

In developing the 2013 changes, the Australian Government explicitly acknowledged the issue of avoidance, and sought to draft the legislation so as to close down remaining loopholes, and to minimise the incentive and potential for avoidance.[125] For example, credit providers cannot exceed the price regulation by changing the amount of fees and charges after the contract has been entered into[126] or by splitting a SACC or MACC into two smaller loans.[127] The Government also had a wide-ranging power to implement regulations to 'enable the Government to quickly

121 For example, in the hearings before the Parliamentary Joint Committee, an industry representative referred to six models of 'accommodating' loopholes in New South Wales: Parliamentary Joint Committee on Corporations and Financial Services, 'Consumer Credit and Corporations Legislation Amendment (Enhancements) Bill 2011' (Proof Committee Hansard, 24 August 2011) 26–27. Note that these activities are not necessarily illegal, but can have the effect of subverting the clear objective of the legislation, and are often unintended consequences of the legislation. See also Sally Anderson, 'The Phenomenon of Payday Lending' (2013) 21 Australian Journal of Competition and Consumer Law 20, 33.

122 See, for example, *Carter v Fast Access Finance (Beaudesert Pty Ltd)* [2011] QCA, where the Tribunal rejected an argument that a transaction should be construed as a contract for the sale and purchase of diamonds, and ordered that the respondent pay to the applicants the payments that exceeded the principal sum lent. Note that ASIC is currently in litigation with Fast Access Finance on a similar point: Australian Securities and Investments Commission, 'ASIC Commences Legal Action Against Fast Access Finance' (n 111).

123 For a discussion of some of the changes made in New South Wales, see Stephen Corones, Denise McGill and Rebecca Durrant, 'Phase Two of the National Credit Reforms: Examining the Regulation of Payday Lenders' (Queensland University of Technology, 2011) 25–26. In the national context, the NCC was finally amended so that the bill facilities exemption could no longer be used to avoid the application of the Code, see NCC, s 6(7).

124 For example, Martin (n 79) 585–586.

125 See Parliament of the Commonwealth of Australia, 'Supplementary Explanatory Memorandum' (n 30) 14 [1.53]: 'The history of the sector in relation to State and Territory interest rate caps suggest that avoidance is common and anticipated to occur in relation to the cap on costs.' See also Parliament of the Commonwealth of Australia, 'Revised Explanatory Memorandum' (n 16) 63 [5.13].

126 NCC, s 32AA; see also NCCPR, reg 79AC.

127 NCCPR, reg 28XXF. If the price under the single loan would have been cheaper than the combined price of the two loans, the loan will be deemed unsuitable: NCCPR, reg 28XXF(2).

respond to attempts to circumvent the objective of these reforms'.[128] However, despite specific attention to avoidance in the drafting of the 2013 laws, further amendments were made to the National Consumer Credit Protection Regulations 2010 (Cth) in 2014 to address avoidance activity.[129]

The need for further amendments to address avoidance activities so early in the life of the small loans provisions perhaps highlights the need for a more pro-active mechanism for dealing with avoidance. In late 2012, the previous government released for consultation draft amendments to the National Consumer Credit Protection Act 2009 (Cth).[130] This exposure draft bill included a general anti-avoidance provision. The proposed amendments were 'intended to provide a systematic response to avoidance practices, rather than individual responses being developed that address a specific practice after it has come into use in the credit market'.[131]

However, this proposal appears to have stalled since the change of government in late 2013, and it is not known whether the new government intends to introduce amendments along these lines. The past experience of regulating in this sector suggests, however, that a pro-active approach is needed to discourage avoidance activities and the potential harm caused to consumers by those seeking to evade the application of the laws.[132]

5.2 Price disclosure and price comparisons

An interesting feature of the 2013 changes is that it also introduces different disclosure obligations for SACCs compared to other credit contracts. The National Consumer Credit Protection Act 2009 (Cth) imposes various obligations on credit providers to disclose the annual percentage rate (APR) and/or comparison rate[133]

128 Parliament of the Commonwealth of Australia, 'Revised Explanatory Memorandum' (n 16) 72 [5.56].

129 Parliament of the Commonwealth of Australia, 'Explanatory Statement, Select Legislative Instrument No 89, 2014, National Consumer Credit Protection Act 2009, National Consumer Credit Protection Amendment (Small Amount Credit Contracts) Regulation 2014'. Changes included clarifying the fees that are included in the short-term credit exemption for the application of the NCC (NCCPR, reg 50A), tightening the exemption for low-cost continuing credit contracts (NCCPR, reg 51) and making it clear that the persons prohibited from requiring or accepting fees from a borrower in relation to a SACC (other than the permitted fees) includes loan introducers (NCCPR, reg 79AE). NCC, s 31B(1) prohibits a credit provider or a prescribed person from requiring or accepting a fee or charge in relation to a SACC (other than a fee or charge permitted under s 31A or prescribed by the regulations).

130 Parliament of the Commonwealth of Australia, House of Representatives, 'Exposure Draft, National Consumer Credit Protection Amendment (Credit Reform Phase 2) Bill 2012' www.treasury.gov.au/ConsultationsandReviews/Consultations/2012/Credit-Reform-Phase-2-Bill-2012 accessed 14 January 2015.

131 The Parliament of the Commonwealth of Australia, House of Representatives, 'Exposure Draft, National Consumer Credit Protection Amendment (Credit Reform Phase 2) Bill 2012 with Questions and Commentary' 77 www.treasury.gov.au/ConsultationsandReviews/Consultations/2012/Credit-Reform-Phase-2-Bill-2012 accessed 14 January 2015.

132 Anderson seems to suggest that the black letter law approach to regulating payday lenders should be abandoned as it is not effective, and that instead new approaches (such as encouraging mainstream lenders into the market) should be considered: Anderson (n 121) 34.

133 The comparison rate is calculated by reference to the interest rate charged for the loan, as well as the ascertainable credit fees and charges: NCC, s 157(1); NCCPR, reg 100.

in the pre-contractual statement and the contract document.[134] Further, if an advertisement states the repayment amount, it must also include the APR for the loan.[135] If an APR is included in an advertisement, the relevant comparison rate must also be included, with the same prominence.[136] These obligations can help consumers to understand the costs of credit products and to compare the costs of different products.

However, these disclosure obligations do not apply to SACCs.[137] In fact, as no interest can be imposed for SACCs, the APR and comparison rate have little meaning for these loans.

This is likely a response to industry concerns about the use of an APR for short-term loans. The industry has long argued that an APR is not a relevant mechanism for indicating the cost of short-term loans.[138] It is argued that creating, and requiring disclosure of, an annual interest rate for a loan that is intended to last for only a few weeks, or perhaps months, is inappropriate. In addition, as the fixed costs of establishing and administering a loan can be similar whether the loan is for a small amount or a large amount, the costs can appear disproportionate in the case of small loans, and lead to very high APRs.[139] Arguably, these high APRs feed into public perceptions of payday loans as exploitative. There is also the difficulty that two products with the same total repayment, but different durations, can have very different APRs.[140]

However, these changes will make it more difficult for consumers to compare credit products. Credit fees and charges are still required to be disclosed in the pre-contractual statement of a SACC and this may give potential borrowers the opportunity to compare the price of a variety of small-amount credit contracts offered by different providers.[141] However, this comparison is made more difficult by the fact that the total fee information is not required to be disclosed in the Financial Information Table on the first page of the document.[142] The total fee information may therefore be buried in the contract document.

Further, in the absence of an APR, and therefore potential for a comparison rate, it will be almost impossible for potential borrowers to easily compare the costs of a

134 A credit provider must include the APR in the pre-contractual statement and contract document: NCC, ss 16(1)(a) (pre-contractual statement) and 17(1)(4) (contract document). The annual percentage rate is defined as 'a rate specified in the contract as an annual percentage rate': NCC, s 27(1).

135 NCC, s 150(3).

136 NCCPA, s 160(1).

137 NCC, ss 17(4), 17(5) and 17(6) do not apply to SACCs. See also Parliament of the Commonwealth of Australia, 'Revised Explanatory Memorandum' (n 16) 66 [5.20].

138 For example, Howell *et al.* (n 69) 86; see also Parliamentary Joint Committee on Corporations and Financial Services (n 17) 73 (industry views) and 116 (Committee views).

139 For example, the highest APR reported by Howell *et al.* was 3,380 per cent (for a $300 loan, with a term of one week). All payday loans surveyed in this report had an APR of at least 300 per cent: Howell *et al.* (n 69) 41–42.

140 Howell *et al.* note that 'many of the $300 products of two or four weeks duration have similar total repayments to the one week products listed, with much smaller APRs': ibid 42.

141 However, it is important not to be overconfident about the likelihood of consumers reading and understanding these disclosure documents. In the Gillam study, few borrowers had an understanding of the cost of their loan that was likely to be realistic: Gilliam and Consumer Action Law Centre (n 12) 65.

142 See NCC, s 16(4); NCCPR, reg 72(1) and (5).

small-amount credit contract with another type of credit contract.[143] This will also make it difficult for advisers, financial counsellors and others to provide comparisons to assist their customers and clients, or to increase consumer awareness of the relative costs of different types of loans.

Also limiting the potential for comparison is the fact that some large payday lending websites do not disclose the costs of loans before an application to borrow is made.[144] It may be that other features outweigh price in consumer decision making in this sector.[145] However, it is counter to a model of consumer empowerment to decrease the ability of borrowers to have an accurate understanding of the price differentials. The removal of the APR disclosure requirements for SACCs, and failing to introduce an alternative mechanism for comparisons, has this effect.[146]

It is acknowledged that disclosure is not always an effective regulatory tool[147] and that the APR and other interest-based calculations are not perfect measures. However, rather than abandoning disclosure, the challenge is to develop a regulatory framework that facilitates (and does not prevent) comparison shopping between all types of credit products.

6 A changing regulatory approach?

The changes to the regulation of consumer credit in Australia discussed in this chapter provide an example of a gradual change in regulatory approach in this market, which may ultimately flow through to the wider financial services market in the future. Consumer credit regulation originally focused on disclosure and truth in lending as the mechanism for facilitating effective consumer decision making and consumer empowerment.[148] Price regulation existed in some jurisdictions, but it was regularly avoided by lenders.[149]

More recently, however, regulation of product features has begun to play a greater role in consumer credit regulation. In addition to the price regulation discussed in this chapter, consumer credit product features are now restricted in the following ways:

143 Ali, McRae and Ramsay (n 99) 434.

144 As at 15 November 2014, the cost of loans did not appear to be disclosed on the websites for either Cash Converters or Money3. See also the discussion on the disclosure of price on payday lending websites in Gillam and Consumer Action Law Centre (n 12) 93–94.

145 For example, in the Gillam and Consumer Action Law Centre study, 'only 9.4% of consumers reported making a decision based on cost': Gillam and Consumer Action Law Centre (n 12) 66.

146 In any case, the argument that an APR is an inappropriate measure of cost for short-term loans has less weight if many loans have a practical life that extends considerably beyond the original term of the loan.

147 In its interim report, the Financial System Inquiry expressed the view that 'The current disclosure regime produces complex and lengthy documents that often do not enhance consumer understanding of financial products and services, and impose significant costs on industry participants': Commonwealth of Australia, *Financial System Inquiry Interim Report* (July 2014) 3–56.

148 Although some limited regulation of product features was imposed – for example, limitations on the permissible liability under related mortgages and guarantees: UCCC, ss 40, 44, 45 and 55.

149 See the discussion in Parliamentary Joint Committee on Corporations and Financial Services, 'Consumer Credit and Corporations Legislation Amendment (Enhancements) Bill 2011' (Proof Committee Hansard, 24 August 2011) 26–27.

- very short-term loans are banned;[150]
- certain termination fees on home loans are banned;[151]
- reverse mortgages must, among other things, offer a no negative equity guarantee, and provide protection for third-party occupants;[152] and
- unfair contract terms are prohibited.[153]

This suggests that there has begun to be an increasing acceptance in the consumer credit context of the validity of regulating product features. This is a challenge to the standard market orthodoxy of relying on consumers to make their own choices, largely unfettered by any third-party (such as a government) view on the safety or otherwise of particular products or services.

Such a shift in regulatory approach has not yet been significant in the wider financial services market. The 1997 Financial System Inquiry (the Wallis Inquiry) adopted a largely disclosure-focused approach to consumer protection in financial services. It argued that one of the primary reasons for regulation in the financial services sector is to deal with market failures arising from information asymmetry[154] and that there was a limited role for regulation designed for social purposes, including community services obligations.[155] The Wallis Inquiry expressed the view that 'Disclosure regulation is *at the core* of any scheme to protect consumers as it allows them to exercise informed choice'[156] and made a number of recommendations designed to improve the quality and effectiveness of disclosure.[157] The Wallis Inquiry did not argue for a role for product regulation; it did not make any recommendations that would restrict the design of products or that would restrict specific types of products from being marketed to retail clients or consumers.[158]

This emphasis on disclosure as the primary consumer protection mechanism, and a cautious approach to the prospect of regulating product features, continued in the Productivity Commission review of Australia's Consumer Policy Framework. In its final report, the Productivity Commission argued that 'a key goal of consumer policy is to overcome significant information failures that can hinder effective competition'.[159] Further, the Productivity Commission recommended that one of the operational objectives of consumer policy should be to 'ensure that consumers are sufficiently well-informed to benefit from and stimulate effective competition'.[160]

However, the Productivity Commission also acknowledged a potential role for regulation to address the social costs of consumer choices and to achieve social

150 NCCPA, ss 124CA and 133CA.

151 NCCPR, reg 79A.

152 NCC, ss 86A–86F; s 17(15A). See also the discussion in Burns, where the author notes 'The legislation proactively intervenes to change, redirect and standardise terms in reverse mortgages in order to redress concerns that features of terms of reverse mortgages may penalise vulnerable seniors': Fiona Burns, 'The Evolving Statutory Regulation of Reverse Mortgages in Australia's "Risk Society"' (2013) 39 Monash University Law Review 611, 648.

153 Australian Securities and Investments Commission Act 2001 (Cth), s 12BF.

154 Commonwealth of Australia, *Financial System Inquiry Final Report* (March 1997) 191.

155 Ibid 196.

156 Ibid 261 (emphasis added).

157 Ibid 264 (recommendation 8), 267–268 (recommendation 9) and 269 (recommendation 10).

158 Commonwealth of Australia, *Interim Report* (n 147) 3–54.

159 Productivity Commission (n 13) 28.

160 Ibid 41 (recommendation 3.1).

justice outcomes (as product regulation might be considered). In this regard, the operational objectives recommended by the Productivity Commission include to:

- ensure that goods and services are safe and fit for the purposes for which they are sold;
- prevent practices that are unfair or contrary to good faith; and
- meet the needs of those who, as consumers, are most vulnerable, or at greatest disadvantage.[161]

Most recently, the 2014 Financial System Inquiry (the Murray Inquiry) has considered the appropriate regulatory approach in financial services, including consumer protection regulation. The Inquiry's final report confirmed that product disclosure 'plays an important part in establishing the contract between issues and consumers'.[162] However, unlike the Wallis Inquiry, the Murray Inquiry emphasises the importance of *fairness* in the financial system, noting that this builds trust and confidence and avoids over-regulation.[163]

The Murray Inquiry's interim report had suggested that a more flexible regulatory toolkit might be needed, and that this could potentially include 'strategic targeted regulation of product features' in appropriate cases; mandated default product design; and providing ASIC with powers to ban products or product features.[164] In its final report, the Murray Inquiry did not take forward its original suggestion of product regulation; however, it has commenced on a similar path by recommending the introduction of a 'targeted and principles-based product design and distribution option'[165] and a 'proactive product intervention power that would enhance the regulatory toolkit available where there is risk of significant consumer detriment'.[166]

The Murray Inquiry has also made a specific recommendation in relation to default products in the retirement phase of superannuation, which would require regulations on the form of the default products.[167] Thus, if the Murray Inquiry recommendations are accepted by government, it is likely that product regulation will begin to have a greater role in the wider consumer financial services market.

7 Conclusion

In Australia, the community concerns about the high costs and potential risks of payday loans have now resulted in national regulation designed to address those concerns. Differentiated price regulation has been introduced, very short-term loans have been banned and more detailed responsible lending obligations have been introduced for small-amount loans. The Australian approach is a multi-faceted one

161 Ibid 41–42 (recommendation 3.1).
162 Commonwealth of Australia, *Final Report 2014* (n 93) 193.
163 Ibid 27.
164 Commonwealth of Australia, *Interim Report* (n 147) 3–60, 3–61. In relation to the suggestion of regulating product features, the Inquiry did suggest that 'any substantial shift in the regulatory regime would require compelling evidence to support it': 3–60.
165 Commonwealth of Australia, *Final Report 2014* (n 93) 198 (recommendation 21). Although note that this is not intended to apply to credit products: 98 (footnote 2).
166 Ibid 206 (recommendation 22).
167 Ibid 117 (recommendation 11), 127.

that seeks to acknowledge the different characteristics of small loans and small loan borrowers, rather than taking the one-size-fits-all approach of previous attempts in some parts of Australia to deal with payday loans.

Detailed information on the impact of the new provisions is not yet available. However, some initial indicators suggest that there remains a 'viable small loans market', even if consolidation in the market may have occurred.

The project of dealing with this issue of payday loans is, however, not yet complete. The extent to which the new responsible lending obligations have reduced the level of repeat borrowing and the extent to which the need for payday loans has been reduced or diverted to safer alternatives is not known and requires detailed examination and research. Further, the issues of addressing financial exclusion though promoting alternatives to payday loans, of minimising avoidance, and of facilitating (or at least not discouraging) price comparisons among credit products, including SACCs, need further substantive action.

Overall, however, the changes can be seen as demonstrating an increased acceptance of the limitations of a regulatory approach focused on disclosure and the legitimacy of regulating product features in consumer credit markets. This, in turn, perhaps reflects a greater acceptance that fairness and social justice are relevant considerations in the design of consumer credit regulation.

The recent Murray Inquiry into the financial system has also given support to fairness as a guiding principle for financial system regulation. While not explicitly endorsing the need for product regulation, the Murray Inquiry has acknowledged a 'broad shift in Australia's approach to consumer protection in the financial sector – away from primarily relying on disclosure and financial literacy'.[168] The Murray Inquiry has also made some recommendations that, if implemented, would begin to facilitate a focus on the importance of a link between product features and consumer needs. This in turn may, over time, lead to explicit recognition of the legitimacy of regulating product features in the broader financial services market. Then, the approaches to regulating financial services and regulating consumer credit may begin to merge, to the benefit of Australian consumers.

Addendum: Since this chapter was completed, the Review of the Small Amount Credit Contract Laws was announced. At least two empirical studies on post-July 2013 use of SACCs were referred to in submissions to the review. The final report of the review was released on 19 April 2016, and is available at http://consumercredit.treasury.gov.au/content/sacc_review.asp (accessed 27 July 2016). Among other things, the review recommended that the protected earnings amount regulation apply to all consumers; that the cap on the total amount of all SACC payments be reduced to 10 per cent of the consumer's net income; and that the rebuttable presumption in relation to loan suitability for SACC loans be removed. As of July 2016, the Australian Government had not provided a formal response to the SACC review's recommendations.

On 20 October 2015, the Australian Government released its response to the Financial System Inquiry report. Among other things, the Government accepted the report's recommendations to introduce a product design and distribution obligation and a product intervention power. The response is available at http://fsi.gov.au/.

168 Ibid 236.

7 High-cost credit in the UK

A philosophical justification for government intervention

Jodi Gardner[1]

1 Introduction

The regulation of high-cost credit in the UK has created significant media and academic attention, especially considering the reviews conducted by both the Competition & Markets Authority (CMA)[2] and the UK regulator of consumer credit, the Financial Conduct Authority (FCA).[3] Both of these bodies have undertaken significant empirical and statistical investigations of the current high-cost credit market, justifying government intervention on the basis of economic data and findings on the potential harm suffered by borrowers. While this is important research, it has resulted in a lack of philosophical analysis of the current problem.

Intervention into the consumer credit market to restrain borrowing inevitably means undermining the rights of those borrowers, namely, their right to freely enter into contracts of their choosing. This means, in addition to the economic rationalisations, philosophical justification is also needed; something which unfortunately is being overlooked in the current law reform process. This chapter aims to fill the current void by providing philosophical justifications for undermining the freedom of contract rights of high-cost credit users, and additionally highlighting the guidance this type of analysis can provide for how the law should respond.

There are three sections; Section 1 outlines the high-cost credit situation in the UK, including the borrower profile and the regulatory approach to these issues. Section 2 discusses the general philosophical issues raised by high-cost credit. Section 3 outlines how the law should respond in light of both the profile of high-cost credit borrowers provided by the FCA and CMA, and the philosophical justifications for intervention.

1 This research is funded by the generosity of The General Sir John Monash Foundation and the Arts & Humanities Research Council. I am eternally indebted to my indefatigable supervisor, Mindy Chen-Wishart, for her help and support in the development of these ideas, and to Karen Rowlingson and Lindsey Appleyard for their input and assistance.

2 Reference was made by the Office of Fair Trading on 27 June 2013 and the Statutory Deadline for the review is 26 June 2015.

3 The review commenced when the jurisdiction was transferred to the FCA in April 2014.

2 High-cost credit in the UK

2.1 What is high-cost credit?

High-cost credit is used in this chapter to refer to high-interest, short-term loans of money from profit-making institutions, including online and retail high-cost credit. While this type of financial product is frequently referred to as a 'payday loan', this term will not be used in the current chapter as it does not accurately define the product.[4] Payday loans are, strictly speaking, loans that are repaid at one time, usually shortly after the borrower has received their *pay* (hence the name). This term is therefore not a realistic description of the current regime, and only covers a small part of the short-term lending market. As outlined by the FCA, 'the common term for high-cost short-term products is "pay day loans"'.[5] While it is recognised that the colloquial term 'payday loan' is no longer limited to the narrow definition of loans that are repaid when the borrower next receives their income, the term 'high-cost credit' will instead be used in this chapter for accuracy and to avoid potential confusion.[6]

The definition of 'high-cost credit' and its relationship to other alternative financial products has created an unexpected level of controversy in the UK. The FCA has chosen its own terminology and definition for this type of credit product: 'high-cost short-term credit' (HCSTC). This is defined as unsecured loans of less than 12 months with an interest rate of over 100 per cent annual percentage rate (APR), but excluding home-collected credit, bills of sale or overdraft bank account fees.[7] The justifications for excluding these other alternative credit products, particularly home-collected credit, are far from clear,[8] especially as these products have similar potential for consumer detriment. For this reason, the FCA definition will not be used in this chapter. A number of parties have responded to the FCA consultation recommending that the definition be expanded,[9] but at the time of writing there had been no response to this and the FCA had continued to use the term HCSTC.

2.2 Who is using high-cost credit?

The recent economic and political conditions in the UK have created a *perfect storm* for the explosion of high-cost credit. Economically the country is only just recovering from the longest depression in over 100 years, which included a double-dip recession, stagnated wages and increased unemployment. This all happened while the cost of living increased dramatically, including costs for basic necessities such as

4 See, for example, discussion in Personal Finance Research Centre, *The Impact on Business and Consumers of a Cap on the Total Cost of Credit* (Department of Business and Innovation Skills 2013) 4–10.

5 Financial Conduct Authority, *Detailed Proposals for the FCA Regime for Consumer Credit* (Consultation Paper 13/10, 2013) paras 6.12–6.13.

6 Unfortunately the term 'payday loan' cannot be completely avoided as it is referred to in a number of publications and reviews. When a publication refers to a 'payday loan' or focuses only on this type of credit, for consistency this term is used in the chapter.

7 Loans from not-for-profit CDFIs are also excluded from this definition: Financial Conduct Authority, *Proposals for a Price Cap on High-Cost Short-Term Credit* (Consultation Paper 14/10, 2014) para 5.58.

8 See discussion in Financial Conduct Authority, *Detailed Proposals* (n 5) para 6.13.

9 Including the author, as part of the consultation response from the Centre on Household Assets and Savings Management, University of Birmingham.

food, fuel, heating and electricity. While the economy is slowly starting to show signs of improvement, the benefits of economic recovery are disproportionately being felt by those most advantaged in society. Millions of people and families around the UK continue to *do it tough*; 15 million people are falling behind on their bills, including six million people who use credit to make it through until payday and almost three million using further credit to keep up with their existing credit commitments.[10]

It is therefore no surprise that increasing numbers of people are turning to high-cost credit, both online and in person, for short-term injections of much-needed cash. The industry has grown exponentially since the global financial downturn. A UK newspaper report from 2013 described how nine out of the country's ten biggest high-cost credit companies have doubled their turnover in the last three years, with one company reporting a 32-fold increase in profits since the commencement of the recession.[11] The figures from the CMA highlight that the payday lending industry[12] currently issues around 10.2 million loans each year and the market is worth £2.8 billion.[13] The FCA has provided slightly different figures based on their definition of HCSTC[14] – 1.6 million people took out ten million loans worth £2.5 billion.[15] While the interest rates for these short-term loans vary dramatically, rates as high as 16,000 per cent APR are not unknown. The average payday loan is £260, but disturbingly one-quarter of loans are for £100 or less – indicating that many people may have a financial safety net of less than £100.[16]

During and after the recent period of international financial turbulence, growing numbers of UK consumers have accessed short-term finance to close the increasing gap between their income and the cost of living. There has been a consequent upsurge in the use of high-cost credit to *make ends meet*. New research highlights that when people are struggling, they take out 'distress' credit – which is higher cost, more damaging and more likely to tip them into problem debt.[17] It is also becoming increasingly evident that the majority of people who use high-cost credit are financially vulnerable in some way. The CMA recently conducted empirical research into the UK market, and its findings include:

10 These issues are discussed in-depth in StepChange Debt Charity, *Life on the Edge: Towards More Resilient Family Finances* (2014).

11 Meghna Mukerjee, 'It's Been a Good Year for Wonga: That's Never a Good Sign' (*NewStatesman*, 9 September 2013) www.newstatesman.com/business/2013/09/its-been-good-year-wonga-thats-never-good-sign accessed 9 September 2013. There is evidence that times are changing. The new regulatory regime (discussed below) and enforcement from the FCA has resulted in one of the major payday lenders, the Cheque Centre, exiting the market: Financial Conduct Authority, 'Cheque Centre Stops Selling Single Repayment Payday Loans and Agrees to Change Business Model to Meet FCA's Tougher Consumer Protection Requirements' (press release, 13 May 2014) www.fca.org.uk/news/cheque-centre-stops-selling-single-repayment-payday-loans-fca-tougher-consumer-protection accessed 19 June 2014.

12 This term is purposefully used here as the figures are related solely to the payday lending industry.

13 Competition & Markets Authority, *Payday Lending Market Investigation: Provisional Findings Report* (2014) para 2.76.

14 See discussion of the FCA definition above.

15 Financial Conduct Authority, *Detailed Proposals* (n 5) para 1.4.

16 Competition & Markets Authority, *Payday Lending Market Investigation: The Size and Concentration of the Payday Lending Sector Working Paper* (2014) para 4(a).

17 StepChange Debt Charity (n 10).

- 51 per cent of payday customers had not used any other form of credit during the previous 12 months (excluding other payday loans and overdrafts);[18]
- 56 per cent of borrowers had gone into overdraft on their accounts in the last 12 months, 27 per cent had gone into authorised overdraft, 52 per cent had a debt problem in the last five years and 38 per cent had a bad credit rating;[19]
- 53 per cent of borrowers used the funds from the loan in question for 'living expenses', although this is not further defined by the CMA. In addition, 7 per cent of borrowers used it on 'general shopping' and 10 per cent on their car or vehicle, meaning these three categories of 'general expenses' relate to 70 per cent of the market;[20]
- 56 per cent of people surveyed stated that they 'definitely' could not have gone without the credit, 32 per cent could have 'possibly' gone without and 7 per cent could have 'easily' gone without;[21]
- four out of ten borrowers had no access to alternative financial products, and the majority of these people took the loan as a 'last resort';[22] and
- six out of ten borrowers did not 'shop around' before entering into a loan,[23] indicating that some might have been able to find a better alternate source of credit.

When asked why they had used this type of credit, 45 per cent of borrowers stated that the alternatives were 'less convenient' and 31 per cent reported that the alternatives would not give them the money as quickly.[24] In addition, 74 per cent of people stated that the speed with which they would get access to the money is an 'extremely' or 'very' important factor in determining the appropriate financial product for their needs,[25] and 31 per cent of all borrowers stated it was the most important factor.[26] Therefore speed and convenience of payday loans and similar high-cost credit products are by far their most appealing characteristics.

It is also clear that society in general is becoming concerned about the problems associated with high-cost credit. Recent research shows that 93 per cent of the population believe further regulation is needed in the industry, with 68 per cent supporting stricter regulation of the advertising of high-cost credit and 65 per cent supporting a cap on the total cost of credit. This contrasts with only 7 per cent of people who believe that there is no problem with high-cost credit.[27] Fortunately the government has responded, and recently there has been increased regulatory attention on these important issues.

18 Competition & Markets Authority, *Research into the Payday Lending Market: Final Report* (2014) 29.
19 Ibid 30.
20 Ibid 68.
21 Ibid 68.
22 Ibid 80–81.
23 Ibid 96.
24 Ibid 84.
25 Ibid 74.
26 Ibid 92.
27 R3: The Association of Business Recovery Professionals, 'Rein in "Payday Lenders," Say 93 Percent of GB Population' (press release, 22 May 2012) www.r3.org.uk/index.cfm?page=1114&element=16322 accessed 9 May 2013.

2.3 How is high-cost credit being regulated?

Prior to April 2014, the Office of Fair Trading (OFT) oversaw the regulation of consumer credit, including high-cost credit. On 1 April 2014, the FCA took over jurisdiction for credit licences and providers of consumer credit. The FCA's approach to regulation differs from the OFT and includes an early intervention philosophy, a risk-based approach and greater regulatory powers/resources devoted to credit regulation. Under the FCA there are also new rules and additional regulatory burdens for providers of HCSTC. These include:

- rules requiring adequate affordability assessments, including a consideration of the borrowers' other financial commitments;
- allowing for a maximum of two rollovers of the loan amount;
- allowing for a maximum of two unsuccessful attempts at continuous payment authorities (CPAs) to pay off the loan in full;
- a prohibition on the use of CPAs for part payments;
- requiring a financial warning to be included in payday advertisements; and
- requiring lenders to provide borrowers who rollover a loan with an information sheet including information on how to access free debt advice.[28]

In November 2013, an amendment to the Banking Reform Bill was passed which required the FCA to implement a cap on the total cost of credit by early 2015. After a period of market analysis and international research, the FCA released its proposals for a price cap on HCSTC in July 2014. A detailed analysis of the proposals is beyond the scope of the current chapter; however, there are three key aspects. First, interest is capped at 0.8 per cent per day, which results in an APR of 1.270 per cent. Second, default fees and charges are limited to £15. Third, there is a total borrowing cap of 100 per cent, meaning that, at an absolute maximum, consumers will only ever have to pay back double the amount of money they borrowed. The FCA provided a short consultation period for these proposals, with a closing date of 1 September 2014. On 11 November 2014, the final rules related to the price cap were released, and they will come into force on 2 January 2015. The FCA did not make any significant variation to its original proposals. Small amendments were, however, made regarding: (1) how the cap is calculated for loans created before, but modified after, the enforcement date; (2) the calculation of the cap for refinanced loans; and (3) clarification on when an agreement is unenforceable. The major proposals, discussed above, remain unchanged and the cap will still only apply to HCSTC (as defined by the FCA).

It is clear from the regulatory reform process of the FCA and CMA that both organisations have engaged in detailed empirical research of the high-cost credit market. The CMA have analysed the competitive nature of the industry, highlighting that it is not working in a sufficiently competitive manner. This is largely due to the lack of transparency associated with these types of credit products and, as a result, price competition is exceptionally weak as borrowers generally do not *shop*

28 For full details, see Financial Conduct Authority, *Detailed Rules for the FCA Regime for Consumer Credit Including Feedback on FCA QCP 13/18 and 'Made Rules'* (policy statement 14/3, 2014). For more information on this issue, see Jodi Gardner, 'Payday Lending in the United Kingdom: Meeting the Needs of the Modern Borrower' (MPhil Thesis, University of Oxford 2013).

around before entering into a loan. On the basis of these findings, the CMA is in the process of suggesting a number of remedies to counter these issues. The FCA has engaged in economic modelling to determine the financial impact that regulatory limitations on access to credit would have on consumers, and used this as a basis for their proposals. While both of these processes are inherently valuable, they miss an important underlying issue: regulation in this manner impacts borrowers' rights and freedoms, namely the right to enter into contracts of their choosing. Therefore, in addition to the economic modelling being conducted, a philosophical evaluation is needed to justify the government intervention being undertaken.

3 The philosophical challenges of high-cost credit

In light of the analytical gap discussed in the previous section, the second part of this chapter provides an overview of the traditional liberal theory of contract law and the challenges that high-cost credit pose to this concept.

3.1 Libertarianism and high-cost credit

English law is strongly based on freedom of contract, with the attendant emphasis on respect for individual choice, negative liberty and limited government intervention into private affairs, all of which are strongly supported by many prominent libertarians including Fried,[29] Hayek,[30] Nozick[31] and Friedman.[32] This approach advocates that enforcement of an individual's promise is of highest importance, and in general means the predominance of negative autonomy above other societal values and individual rights, such as fairness, good faith and positive autonomy. John Stuart Mill's 'harm principle' dictates that the only legitimate reason the state can interfere with an individual's freedom is to prevent harm to others; protection of individuals from themselves, physically or morally, is not a sufficient premise.[33] From a contract law perspective, the government's role is merely to provide a sufficient framework for the creation and enforcement of contractual agreements between parties. The importance of contractual obligations is justified by the 'promise principle', the belief that all people are obligated to keep their promises. Fried explains traditional contract law as allowing autonomous individuals to impose obligations on themselves, as this is an exercise of individual free will.[34] Contract law is therefore fundamentally based on the notions of freedom, consent and choice, and the fact that obligations are freely chosen by parties.[35]

These liberal ideals have been the dominant voice in legal philosophy, common law and, until relatively recently, statute law.[36] As highlighted by Benson, 'the

29 Charles Fried, *Contract as Promise: A Theory of Contractual Obligation* (Harvard University Press 1981).

30 Friedrich Hayek, *The Constitution of Liberty* (University of Chicago Press 1960).

31 Robert Nozick, *Anarchy, State and Utopia* (Basic Books 1974).

32 Milton Friedman, *Capitalism and Freedom* (University of Chicago Press 1963).

33 John Stuart Mill, *On Liberty* (Longman, Roberts & Green 1859).

34 Fried (n 29).

35 Brian Bix, 'Contracts' in Franklin Miller and Alan Wertheimer (eds), *The Ethics of Consent: Theory and Practice* (Oxford University Press 2009) 251.

36 PS Atiyah, 'Contracts, Promises and the Law of Obligations' in PS Atiyah (ed), *Essays on Contract* (Oxford University Press 1990) 11.

common law conception of contract gives individuals an unfettered liberty to do as they please'.[37] The courts are therefore hesitant to intervene in an agreement between parties, or to impose any requirements of fairness of exchange. A contract will generally not be invalidated merely because of vague notions of justice, such as the fact that the terms were harsh, unreasonable or grossly unfair.[38] One important feature of contract theory is the desire to develop a body of law that applies to all types of contracts.[39] This focus on freedom of contract would therefore also cover consumer contracts, including those for the provision of credit. In the context of high-cost credit, this means that the relationship between lenders and borrowers is purely regulatory and contractual; there are no common law duties of care.[40] Thus, in the consumer credit setting, freedom of contract reigns regardless of the adequacy of consideration, the appropriateness of the loan, or the capacity to repay.[41] The liberal freedom of contract focus is also evident in the UK's regulation of individual affairs. Despite the fact that the Consumer Credit Act 1974 (UK) is consumer protection legislation, an OFT review of the legislation commented that 'the greatest strength of the act is that it does not seek to meet its objectives through interventionist action … rather it explicitly *endorses freedom of contract* within a framework of rules designed to ensure openness'.[42]

An important aspect of liberal theory is the concept of state neutrality, neutrality between competing notions of *the good* as well as neutrality between individuals.[43] On one view, when the law declares that certain types of contracts are illegal on the grounds of potential danger or harm, it is not acting in a neutral fashion and is determining what is *good* for society in general, and for the individuals in particular. When the courts intervene in a contractual dispute to protect a vulnerable individual, they appear to favour one party over the other and are therefore not remaining neutral.[44] However, if there are extreme inequalities between contracting parties, a strong adherence to neutrality will, in practice, support the status quo and thus favour the stronger party.[45] Neutrality is supported on the ground that it allows a *fair contest* between parties; however, as will be discussed below, lending to

37 Peter Benson, 'The Unity of Contract Law' in Peter Benson (ed), *The Theory of Contract Law* (Cambridge University Press 2001) 200.

38 Jack Beatson and Daniel Friedman, 'Introduction: From "Classical" to Modern Contract Law' in Jack Beatson and Daniel Friedman (eds), *Good Faith and Fault in Contract Law* (Oxford University Press 1997) 8–9.

39 Ibid 7.

40 Therese Wilson, 'The Bank and Customer Relationship, and *Australian Competition and Consumer Commission v Oceana Commercial Pty Ltd*' (2004) 25 Queensland Lawyer 2; *Foley v Hill* (1848) 2 HL Case 28, 9 ER 1002; Lee Aitken, 'A "Duty to Lend Responsibly": A New Terror for Lenders in a Consumer's World?' (2007) 18 Journal of Banking and Finance Law and Practice 18.

41 PS Atiyah, 'The Liberal Theory of Contract' in PS Atiyah (ed), *Essays on Contract* (Oxford University Press 1990); John Cartwright, *Unequal Bargaining: A Study of Vitiating Factors in the Formation of Contracts* (Oxford University Press 1991).

42 Office of Fair Trading, *Consumer Credit Deregulation: A Review by the Director General of Fair Trading of the Scope and Operation of the Consumer Credit Act 1974* (1994) (emphasis added).

43 John Rawls, *A Theory of Justice* (Harvard University Press 1971); see also Samuel Freeman, *Rawls* (Routledge 2007).

44 Dori Kimel, *From Promise to Contract: Towards a Liberal Theory of Contract* (Hart Publishing 2003) 121–122.

45 Ibid 122.

vulnerable individuals is far from a fair contest. The loans are often harmful and cause the borrower to go into financial hardship or a debt spiral.

Providers of high-cost credit are aware of this vulnerability and can exploit it to their own advantage. For example, in late 2014 the leading company in this area, Wonga, was found to have breached its responsible lending guidelines by providing loans to people who could not afford to repay without suffering financial hardship. The company has entered into an agreement with the FCA to provide remedial redress to over 350,000 customers, in excess of £220 million, as well as make significant changes to their lending guidelines and criteria. Earlier that year Wonga was also required to pay redress for unfair debt collection guidelines, including sending customers letters from fake law firms demanding repayment of their outstanding debt. The 2013 OFT Compliance Review highlighted that lenders in this industry make approximately 50 per cent of their revenue from the loans that are rolled over or refinanced at least once.[46] Therefore, lending in this exploitative manner is unfortunately often financially beneficial for the business. These extreme inequalities and the lack of a *fair contest* between lenders and borrowers show that for the state to be acting in a truly neutral fashion, it should intervene on behalf of the weaker party, the borrower.

The current inadequacies and limitations of the legal regime for high-cost credit clearly indicate that a libertarian approach does not adequately protect vulnerable borrowers, and often results in extreme consumer detriment. As outlined by Atiyah:

> No modern contract scholar would deny that respect for individual free choice remains an important value of Western societies, but I suspect most of these scholars would argue that the law must also accommodate countervailing values deriving from the pursuit of collective goals and from the paternalistic belief that collective judgments about the best interests of individuals are sometimes more likely to be correct than the individual's own judgment.... Judges and lawyers, in all countries, and for many years, faced with practical problems arising from human relationships, have concluded that pure autonomy, extreme liberal freedom of contract, is often unjust and ought not to be pursued at the expense of all other values.[47]

The high levels of interest being charged to people who can least afford to pay, the excessive profits that some lenders are currently earning and the media horror stories of individuals caught in a debt spiral, all justify a significant reconfiguration of the protection afforded to users of high-cost credit. Sandel stresses the need for society to have a richer and more morally engaged discourse about what is a 'good life' and how this should impact the products available on the market.[48] Increased public attention on this issue is therefore important, and government intervention should therefore be allowed, even required, to prevent harm to a borrower's ability

46 Office of Fair Trading, *Payday Lending: Final Compliance Review* (2013) 2.

47 Atiyah (n 41) 146.

48 Michael Sandel, 'What Shouldn't Be Sold' (Philosophy Bites) http://ec.libsyn.com/p/3/8/1/381482933460cb0c/Michael_Sandel_on_What_Shouldnt_Be_Sold.mp3?d13a76d516d9dec20c3d276ce028ed5089ab1ce3dae902ea1d01cf8e31d1cc5f696e&c_id=1779608 accessed 12 August 2013. See also Margaret Radin, 'Market-Inalienability' (1987) 100 Harvard Law Review 1849.

to live a 'good life'.[49] This discourse should also take into account the context in which the lending is occurring and therefore be influenced by social values, conventions and norms.[50] A 'good life' is multi-faceted, encompassing notions of success, happiness and, most importantly, meaningfulness.[51] Having a situation where many low-income individuals regularly have to resort to loans with thousands of per cent interest just to *get by* challenges society's norms about minimal living standards, negatively impacts on many people's ability to live a 'good life' and raises serious questions about the appropriateness of these types of financial products.

3.2 Challenges to libertarian perspectives

A number of aspects of high-cost credit challenge the suitability of the libertarian approach, including the dangerous nature of the product, the lack of choice and competition, the characteristics of borrowers and lender actions or omissions.

3.2.1 High-cost credit as a dangerous product

A strong analogy can be drawn between harmful credit and dangerous tangible products, creating the potential to use strict liability and tortious approaches to lender liability. High-cost credit can harm the personal autonomy of borrowers, and this is an appropriate and sufficient justification for state intervention.[52] Libertarianism is largely based on the notion of individual autonomy, and that respecting a person's autonomy means enforcing their agreements. However, on the basis of positive autonomy, the primary obligation of the state should be to promote and protect the real autonomy of all people.[53] The state should encourage self-authorship; all people should be able to pursue their own goals and relationships.[54] This is a much richer understanding of personal autonomy than the narrow focus on freedom to contract and, in fact, can often justify undermining contractual obligations.[55] In the context of high-cost credit, positive autonomy dictates that the law should move from a focus on negative liberty to the richer and more meaningful concept of autonomy, yielding a legal and social welfare system that allows all people to pursue the 'good life'. Instead, we have created an economic and social situation where people have to enter into these potentially harmful contracts just to *get by* in life. This does not accord with a 'good life' by any stretch of the imagination. As outlined by Chen-Wishart, 'voluntarily undertaking something repugnant is worse than undertaking it under coercion'.[56] Such contracts need not and should not be upheld.

49 Joseph Raz, *The Morality of Freedom* (Oxford University Press 1988) 417.
50 Michael Sandel, *Liberalism and the Limits of Justice* (2nd edn, Cambridge University Press 1998).
51 Susan Wolf, 'Happiness and Meaning: Two Aspects of the Good Life' (1997) 14 Social Philosophy and Policy 207.
52 Mindy Chen-Wishart, 'The Nature of Vitiating Factors in Contract' in Prince Saprai, George Letsas and Greg Klass (eds), *Philosophical Foundations of Contract Law* (Oxford University Press 2014).
53 Raz (n 49) 416.
54 Joseph Raz, 'Promises in Morality and Law' (1982) 95 Harvard Law Review 916; Mindy Chen-Wishart, 'In Defence of Consideration' (2013) 13 Oxford University Commonwealth Law Journal 209.
55 Chen-Wishart (n 54) 214.
56 Chen-Wishart (n 52) 26.

Raz highlights that personal autonomy can justify the restriction of a person's rights for the sake of providing them with greater autonomy or preventing harm to their future autonomy.[57] There are strong justifications for holding the manufacturers of dangerous products strictly liable for any harm caused, or for going a step further and completely preventing the product from entering the market.[58] States have generally actively intervened to ensure the safety of tangible products and it is arguable that this approach should be replicated with credit products. In the words of Warren:

> Consumers can enter the market to buy physical products confident that they won't be tricked into buying exploding toasters and other unreasonably dangerous products.... Consumers entering the market to buy financial products should enjoy the same protection.[59]

Consumers often use high-cost credit in a dangerous manner, resulting in financial hardship or a debt spiral.[60] Grossly unfair contracts are frequently considered unfair precisely because of their potential for adverse long-term impacts on the autonomy of the individual in question.[61] High-interest loans may deliver short-term relief to individuals but, due to the significant repayment burden, are likely to severely limit future autonomy and choices, and can result in extreme financial hardship. The negative impact that high-cost credit can have on borrowers and their future autonomy therefore justifies a movement away from the traditional libertarian focus on freedom of contract and towards a tortious approach to lender liability; one which recognises that harmful financial products can cause just as much damage as dangerous tangible products.[62]

3.2.2 Lack of competition and choice

There is a widely held belief that strong competition can correct existing market failings and therefore benefits consumers.[63] As a result, consumer protection regimes, particularly those related to the provision of consumer credit, have largely focused on increasing competition in the marketplace.[64] True competition, however, creates a choice of *suppliers* and a choice of *products*. The current high-cost credit market is lacking in both of these aspects, and this is a strong justification for

57 Raz (n 49) 419.

58 Roger Traynor, 'The Ways and Meanings of Defective Products and Strict Liability' (1965) 32 Tennessee Law Review 363.

59 Elizabeth Warren, 'Unsafe at Any Rate' (2007) Democracy: A Journal of Ideas 8.

60 See, for example, Gardner (n 28); StepChange Debt Charity (n 10); Carl Packman, *Loan Sharks: The Rise and Rise of Payday Lending* (Searching Finance 2012).

61 Chen-Wishart (n 52) 12.

62 Luke Nottage, 'Innovating for "Safe Consumer Credit": Drawing on Product Safety Regulation to Protect Consumers of Credit' in Therese Wilson (ed), *International Responses to Issues of Credit and Over-indebtedness in the Wake of Crisis* (Ashgate 2013).

63 Joshua Gans, 'Protecting Consumers by Protecting Competition: Does Behavioural Economics Support this Contention?' (2005) 13 Competition and Consumer Law Journal 1, 42; Department of Trade and Industry, *A Fair Deal for All: Extending Competitive Markets – Empowered Consumers, Successful Businesses* (2005).

64 Ian Manning and Alice de Jonge, *Regulating the Cost of Credit* (Consumer Affairs Victoria 2006) 13.

state intervention. As previously outlined, competition between suppliers is not working adequately, and in 2013 the industry was referred to the CMA for review.[65] The initial results have been released and, unsurprisingly, it was found that the high-cost credit market in the UK is not working sufficiently competitively, adding an average of £5 to £10 to each loan.[66] In addition, borrowers of high-cost credit generally have a severely limited choice of financial products. A significant percentage of consumers are using these high-cost products because they have an impaired credit history and therefore limited access to mainstream products.[67] Autonomy requires an adequate range of choices from which to pick. At the moment there is a lack of alternative financial products, which would include Community Development Financial Institutions (CDFIs), Credit Union products, or access to government loans such as the Social Fund. Because of this lack of choice and competition, users of high-cost credit have severely limited options and are more likely to accept a loan that may be detrimental to them in the long run, such as one with extremely high interest rates, financial repayments that they will be unable to meet without substantial hardship, or high default fees and charges.[68]

3.2.3 Borrower characteristics

The libertarian approach is based on unrealistic assumptions about individuals, and in particular the fiction that all parties are *rational* beings who have access to all required information and can look out for their own interests without state assistance.[69] A number of characteristics of borrowers of high-cost credit challenge the libertarian perspective of contractual relations, including consumer vulnerability, consumer need, unequal bargaining power and the poor quality of consent.

Many borrowers of high-cost credit have attributes that place them in a vulnerable position where they can be easily exploited by lenders, although determining when a consumer is sufficiently *vulnerable* can be difficult.[70] The common law doctrine of unconscionability generally requires a specifically identifiable characteristic or disadvantage, such as a disability, English as a second language or literacy problems.[71] The common law protection provided by this doctrine was stretched to include lower-income and less-educated parties in *Cresswell v Potter*, which may

65 Financial Conduct Authority (n 5) 53.

66 See discussion in Competitions & Markets Authority (n 13).

67 See, for example, Competition & Markets Authority (n 18); Department for Business Innovation & Skills, *Making Consumer Credit Fairer: BIS Report on Surveys of the Payday Lending Good Practice Charter and Codes of Practice* (2013); Keith Ernst, Debbie Bocian and Wei Li, *Steered Wrong: Brokers, Borrowers, and Subprime Loans* (Centre for Responsible Lending 2008).

68 See discussion in Lynden Griggs, 'The [Ir]rational Consumer and Why We Need National Legislation Governing Unfair Contract Terms' (2005) 13 Competition and Consumer Law Journal 1.

69 Daniel Farber, 'Contract Law and Modern Economic Theory' (1983) 78 Northwestern University Law Review 303.

70 Fred Morgan, Schuler Drue and Jeffrey Stoltman, 'A Framework for Examining the Legal Status of Vulnerable Consumers' (1995) 14 Journal of Public Policy & Marketing 267; Craig Smith and Elizabeth Cooper-Martin, 'Ethics and Target Marketing: The Role of Product Harm and Consumer Vulnerability' (1997) 61 Journal of Marketing 1.

71 *Boustany v Pigott* (1993) 69 P & CR 298 (PC); *Commercial Bank of Australia v Amadio* (1983) 151 CLR 447 (HCA).

benefit users of high-cost credit.[72] Despite these extensions to the notion of disadvantage, financial difficulties, in and of themselves, remain insufficient to warrant legal protection. In Lord Templeman's words, 'unequal bargaining power ... provide[s] no basis for equitable interference'.[73] Many people use high-cost credit not as an active choice but because it is, in fact, the only option for them to *get by* each month.[74] These borrowers may be unable to purchase mainstream products due to their previous interactions with the credit system.[75] This lack of choice means that consumers will continue to access these potentially dangerous products, justifying additional government protection.

There is also severely unequal bargaining power between the parties involved in high-cost credit.[76] Exchanges between parties with vast differences in wealth can include some form of advantage-taking due to the superior bargaining position of the wealthier party. For example, lenders are less likely to be in a position which forces them to make an agreement on unfavourable terms.[77] This can be compared with impecunious parties who are conversely almost always at some sort of disadvantage.[78] Consumer protection laws were created to address the distinct power disadvantage suffered by individual consumers.[79] Under a freedom of contract approach, this advantage-taking is irrelevant. The liberal version of contract law is generally associated with a particularly rigid conception of freedom of contract; it is a freedom to make contracts and have them enforced, even in circumstances where considerations of fairness and substantive equality may justify otherwise.[80]

The final characteristic to consider is the quality of consent provided by many people using high-cost credit. The ability for high-cost credit borrowers to provide true and informed consent is called into question by the lack of choice many of these people face. Consent in and of itself is a complex phenomenon. Hadfield highlights that behaviour is driven by various factors beyond an individual's control, including biological, psychological and sociological factors.[81] If an individual's voluntary and informed consent is limited, the mere notion of 'choice' is not sufficient to ground contractual obligations.[82] While this concept is based in feminist theory, the basic premise presents an inherent challenge to notions of rational choice that is highly applicable to high-cost credit contracts. It is therefore important to recognise that choice and consent are not as clear-cut as libertarians would have

72 [1978] 1 WLR 255 (Ch D).

73 *Boustany v Pigott* (1993) 69 P & CR 298 (PC), 303. See also Mindy Chen-Wishart, 'Undue Influence: Beyond Impaired Consent and Wrongdoing Towards a Relational Analysis' in Andrew Burrows and Alan Rodger (eds), *Mapping the Law: Essays in Memory of Peter Birks* (Oxford University Press 2006) 203.

74 Competition & Markets Authority (n 18) 80–81. See also discussion in Sendhil Mullainathan and Eldar Shafir, *Scarcity: Why Having Too Little Means So Much* (Allen Lane 2013).

75 Department for Business Innovation & Skills (n 67).

76 Justin Malbon, 'Predatory Lending' (2005) 33 Australian Business Law Review 224, 235.

77 Anthony Townsend Kronman, 'Contract Law and Distributive Justice' (1980) 89 Yale Law Journal 472, 496.

78 See comments by Justice Posner in *Selmer Co v Blakeslee-Midwest Co 704 F 2d 924* (7th Cir 1983) 928.

79 Iain Ramsay, 'Consumer Law, Regulatory Capitalism and the "New Learning" in Regulation' (2006) 28 Sydney Law Journal 9; Anthony Ogus, *Regulation: Legal Form and Economic Theory* (Clarendon Law Series 1994); Anthony Ogus, *Costs and Cautionary Tales: Economic Insights for the Law* (Hart Publishing 2006).

80 Kimel (n 44) 117.

81 Gillian Hadfield, 'An Expressive Theory of Contract: From Feminist Dilemmas to a Reconceptualisation of Rational Choice in Contract Law' (1998) 146 University of Pennsylvania Law Review 1235.

82 Ibid 1251.

them; consent and capacity are 'constitutive of who we are and how we develop as individuals and as communities'.[83] A number of common factors of consumer credit scenarios can undermine borrowers' ability to consent, including the use of legalistic and complex standard form contracts, provision of easy credit to vulnerable consumers and the inequality of bargaining power.

3.2.4 Lender actions or omissions

The final aspect to consider is the actions or omissions of lenders and how this may challenge the libertarian perspective of contractual relations. Reports from the OFT, Citizens Advice and the Department for Business, Innovation & Skills (BIS) have all outlined the unacceptable and exploitative way in which some lenders act towards borrowers, including advantage-taking and blatant abuses of power.[84] These actions clearly warrant additional consumer protection for borrowers where there is reprehensible conduct by the lender. It is, however, recognised that not all lenders act in this extreme manner. Further justification will therefore be required for intervention in contracts where lenders are not actively treating borrowers in an exploitative manner. Users of high-cost credit are often financially vulnerable and have limited choices. This additional justification can therefore arise on the basis of passive victimisation, drawing an analogy with the common law's protection of vulnerable third-party guarantors.

In *Royal Bank of Scotland Plc v Etridge (No 2)*,[85] legal intervention was warranted on the basis that even though the bank had not done anything actively wrong, it had notice that the guarantor was vulnerable and did not have a real choice when providing the bank guarantee. Despite this vulnerability, the bank protected its own interests and was a party to a grossly unequal bargain. The House of Lords held that these circumstances were unique and the bank's guilty knowledge justified common law intervention.[86] There is a remarkable parallel between this situation and high-cost credit transactions. Due to the obligation to undertake an affordability assessment, the lender will have actual knowledge of the precarious financial situation of the borrower, the fact that they are unlikely to have viable credit alternatives and the very realistic prospect that the borrower will be unable to repay without financial hardship. When providing a loan of thousands of per cent interest in these instances, the lender is making a grossly unequal bargain. By drawing an analogy to the common law treatment of bank guarantees, intervention in high-cost credit contracts can be justified without having to show evidence of actual lender wrongdoing; passive victimisation of the borrower is sufficient.

4 How should the law respond?

As there is clear justification for intervention into the contractual rights of users of high-cost credit, it must now be determined what intervention is appropriate.

83 Ibid 1260.
84 See discussion in Gardner (n 28).
85 [2001] UKHL 44; [2002] 2 AC 773 (HL).
86 See further, Mindy Chen-Wishart, *Contract Law* (4th edn, Oxford University Press 2012) ch 9; Malcolm Cope, *Duress, Undue Influence and Unconscientious Bargains* (The Law Book Company Limited 1985).

The complex and multi-faceted nature of the current problem highlights the need to approach it from two different perspectives. The *supply side* must be addressed by regulation of the consumer credit product and market. The *demand side* must be countered by creating an environment that decreases the need for consumers to access potentially harmful credit. This final part therefore discusses a number of potential steps forward on both sides of the high-cost credit transaction.

4.1 'Supply side'

4.1.1 Bankruptcy and related agreements

Bankruptcy can be considered the ultimate protection for indebted consumers; it gives them the opportunity to wipe the slate clean and be forgiven for existing debt while still being provided with a minimum standard of living. Bankruptcy is an instrument of distributive justice. It aims to achieve a 'fair division of wealth among members of society'[87] and has the effect of shifting wealth from one group of people to another.[88] Bankruptcy is not, however, an adequate response to the challenges posed by high-cost credit. There is no strong evidence of a link between the two in the UK, as ironically these borrowers cannot usually afford to go into bankruptcy. The cost of a bankruptcy application is currently £705,[89] putting it beyond the means of a vast majority of high-cost credit users. This means that a number of people who are paying off high-cost loans are living significantly below the bankruptcy minimum line, but cannot afford the one thing that would provide them with a financial lifeline. Bankruptcy therefore offers a certain level of protection for middle-income earners, but is virtually useless to low-income individuals struggling under the weight of problem debt.

There are other agreements that borrowers can enter into which are not as drastic as bankruptcy, but still allow the borrower to repay their debts. These are debt management plans (DMPs) and individual voluntary arrangements (IVAs). While both of these options are not as costly as bankruptcy, they are still not an adequate response to the issues associated with high-cost credit. Most providers of DMPs will charge the consumer fees to implement the agreement,[90] which is not binding on all creditors, so the borrower can continue to be contacted by organisations demanding repayment of existing debts. Consumers under an IVA will repay their loan over five or six years and at the end of the period the remaining debt is written off. IVAs are binding on all creditors[91] and therefore provide a greater level of coverage, but involve both a nominee and ongoing supervisor fee. In addition, similar to bankruptcy, the IVA will be recorded on the public register and the borrower's credit rating will be adversely impacted, as will their ability to access credit during the IVA period.

Each of these debt repayment options has its own positives and drawbacks; however, it is clear that they do not provide adequate protection for borrowers of

87 Kronman (n 77) 472.

88 Ibid 473.

89 'Guide to Bankruptcy' (*GOV.UK*, 2013) www.gov.uk/bankruptcy/overview accessed 2 October 2014.

90 A notable exception to this is StepChange Debt Charity.

91 Not including family court proceedings, student loans, court fines or debt relating to fraud, or any debts incurred after the IVA was in place.

high-cost credit. Bankruptcy and other debt repayment agreements are a drastic form of protection and are clearly at the far end of the outcome spectrum. They also have a number of detrimental impacts on society in general,[92] and are therefore not something that is appropriate to be regularly used for dealing with exploitative lending activity. High-cost credit borrowers need programmes in place that will prevent them from getting into significant financial difficulties in the first place, as opposed to financial *escape routes* when they become overburdened with problem debt.

4.1.2 Regulating the product

As outlined above, the FCA has recently announced its proposals for the regulation of HCSTC. The reforms aim to remove the most harmful aspects of the credit product while still ensuring a healthy market for high-cost credit. Yet, despite the numerous reports highlighting the dangerous and exploitative actions of lenders and the potential harm of these lending products, the regulator continues to focus on freedom of contract, stating that the proposals aim to 'best secure the appropriate degree of protection while minimising the impact on firms'.[93] Consumer groups have generally welcomed the move towards product regulation, but believe that this is not enough to counteract the harm caused by exploitative lending.[94]

Another way that high-cost credit could be regulated is through increased use of the court powers. The courts notionally have the right to amend credit contracts through the unfair relationship test, but this approach is under-utilised. Ramsay observes that: 'given its broad scope, the unfair relationship test could be used as a private law method of attacking irresponsible lending practices'.[95] This could be an effective approach to regulation of the market as it will allow the courts to set definite limits on what is acceptable and unacceptable lender behaviour. It does, however, involve borrowers or organisations taking individual matters to the court for clarification, and is therefore likely to be a piecemeal and expensive way for the law to develop. In addition, with the drastic legal aid cuts that have occurred in the UK, it is highly unlikely that borrowers would obtain legal assistance – therefore these cases would likely be run as litigants-in-person, creating another layer of difficulty.

4.1.3 Capping the cost of credit

As more parties became aware of the problems associated with these financial products, there were increasing calls for a restriction on the total cost of credit, meaning the imposition of a statutory limit on the interest, fees and charges for high-cost credit contracts. Despite the FCA's proposals for increased regulation of this area, the continued high levels of interest provided significant justification for a cap on

92 Michelle White, 'Personal Bankruptcy under the 1978 Bankruptcy Code: An Economic Analysis' (1988) 63 Indiana Law Journal 1.

93 Financial Conduct Authority (n 5) para 6.11.

94 Yvonne Roberts, 'As Even the Higher Paid Fall into Debt Trap, Charities Target Money Lenders' *The Observer* (6 October 2013) www.theguardian.com/society/2013/oct/06/broke-britain-doorstep-lending accessed 6 October 2013.

95 Iain Ramsay, *Consumer Law and Policy* (3rd edn, Hart Publishing 2012) 440.

the total cost of credit. The debate on whether the UK would benefit from some form of a cap also received unprecedented levels of media and academic interest and pressure was put on the government to respond.[96] This clearly worked and in November 2013 an amendment to the Financial Services (Banking Reform) Act 2013 (UK) was implemented which required the FCA to restrict the charges applicable to HCSTC by January 2015. After significant research on the impact of a cap on the total cost of credit, the FCA confirmed the structure of the total cost of credit cap on 14 November 2014.[97] The main aspects of the cap were discussed above. The response to the proposed approach was mixed, with a number of consumer organisations indicating that it did not go far enough to combat the potential harm associated with these credit products.[98] The continued limitation of the cap to credit products defined as HCSTC was also criticised, as this allows significant avoidance of the cap by other financial products, such as home-collected credit.[99]

The issues associated with capping the cost of credit are inherently complex, and in some instances an interest cap may not be in the best interests of consumers in the UK. A number of jurisdictions have interest rate caps, including Japan,[100] Germany, Greece, France, Ireland, Malta[101] and Australia.[102] A limitation on the cost of credit can be justified on the grounds of substantive fairness[103] or, as discussed above, distributive justice. The media *horror stories* citing interest repayments that quickly spiral out of control *prima facie* make an interest rate cap seem an appropriate response. There is also strong evidence that interest rate caps have had a positive impact in other jurisdictions, as they ensure loans can be provided only at a socially agreed maximum rate and force unscrupulous lenders out of the market.[104] Research from the Personal Finance Research Centre has, however, demonstrated the lack of empirical evidence about the impact of a cap in the UK.[105] It is clear that due to the high upfront costs and the short-term nature of the loans, any substantial

96 See, for example, Chris Deeming, Sharon Collard and David Hayes, *Affordable Credit: Lessons from Overseas* (Personal Finance Research Centre 2011); Damon Gibbons, *Taking on the Money Lenders: Lessons from Japan* (Centre for Responsible Credit 2012); Personal Finance Research Centre, *The Impact on Business and Consumers of a Cap on the Total Cost of Credit* (Department of Business and Innovation Skills 2013); Tim Wallace, 'Cap on Payday Loan Rates May Hurt Vulnerable' (City AM, 11 April 2013) www.cityam.com/article/cap-payday-loan-rates-may-hurt-vulnerable accessed 12 April 2013.

97 As at 28 October 2014. The FCA's consultation process had not finished at this stage, so further amendments could have been made after this occurred.

98 See, for example, the consultation responses from StepChange Debt Charity, the Centre for Responsible Credit and Leeds City Council.

99 For further discussion, see the consultation response from Centre on Household Assets and Savings Management, University of Birmingham.

100 See discussion in Gibbons (n 96).

101 Udo Reifner, Sebastien Clerc-Renaud and RA Michael Knobloch, *Study on Interest Rate Restrictions in the EU: Final Report for the EU Commission DG Internal Market and Services* (Institut für Finanzdienstleistungen eV 2010).

102 The Australian regime is discussed in detail in Chapter 5.

103 See discussion of substantive unfairness in Steven Smith, 'In Defence of Substantive Unfairness' (1996) Law Quarterly Review 138.

104 See analysis of Japan in Gibbons (n 96), and Australia in Marcus Banks, Greg Marston, Howard Karger and Roslyn Russell, *Caught Short: Exploring the Role of Small, Short-Term Loans in the Lives of Australians* (Social Policy Unit, the University of Queensland, Brisbane, 2012).

105 Deeming *et al.* (n 96).

cap on the cost of credit will price the vast majority of lenders out of the market.[106] A report produced by the Joseph Rowntree Foundation highlighted that, due to the significant costs involved in short-term lending, a not-for-profit home lending business would have to charge customers approximately 129 per cent APR merely to cover costs.[107] Any significant limitation on the cost of credit will therefore result in less access to high-cost credit products, particularly for low-income individuals, as few businesses will lend below the statutory threshold.

In response to loans of up to 16,000 per cent APR, an interest rate cap can quickly seem like the best option. Unfortunately it is not that straightforward, and banning high-cost credit will not stop people on low incomes experiencing financial difficulties.[108] As stated by the FCA:

> [M]any consumers use payday loans because, despite high APRs, that is the only source of credit available to high-risk borrowers in emergencies. They might be made worse off by caps on APRs or restrictions on how often they can borrow if they reduce availability to some consumers.[109]

Four out of every ten borrowers of high-cost credit have no access to alternative sources of credit. It is therefore possible that an interest rate cap in the UK will actually exacerbate existing financial difficulties, particularly for these consumers. Vulnerable borrowers desperate for cash will need to turn to other forms of credit, including unauthorised overdrafts. The unauthorised overdraft option may be even more expensive than a high-cost loan due to the crippling nature of some bank fees. *Money Mail* compared the cost of borrowing £200 for a period of ten days from different sources, and found that unauthorised overdrafts of even small amounts from high street banks were by far the most expensive. For example, one UK bank charges customers an £86 fee for an unauthorised overdraft. This can be compared with a *typical* payday lending fee of £25,[110] still disturbingly high but a better choice for a desperate consumer. The OFT has recently made it clear that further changes are needed to the fee structure for bank accounts, as well as proposals to increase competition and consumer confidence in the sector.[111] This will benefit consumers who, due to the excessively high cost of certain bank fees, may turn to high-cost credit when in desperate need of funds. There are strong justifications for a cap on the total cost of credit and the potential for this to provide borrowers with significant benefits, but it will need to occur in line with other banking reforms to ensure that it does not exacerbate pre-existing financial difficulties.

106 See discussion in Elaine Kempson, Anna Ellison, Claire Whyley and Paul Jones, *Is a Not-For-Profit Home Credit Business Feasible?* (Joseph Rowntree Foundation 2009).

107 Ibid.

108 Marie Burton, *Keeping the Plates Spinning: Perceptions of Payday Loans in Great Britain* (Consumer Focus 2010).

109 Cited in Wallace (n 96).

110 See discussion in Baines & Ernst, 'Extortionate Overdraft Bank Charges Make Payday Loans the Cheaper Option' (31 January 2013) www.bainesandernst.co.uk/news/extortionate-overdraft-bank-charges-payday-loans-cheaper-option accessed 15 February 2013.

111 Office of Fair Trading, 'OFT Says Major Change Still Needed in Personal Current Account Market' (press release 10/13, 25 January 2013) www.oft.gov.uk/news-and-updates/press/2013/10-13#.UY4pCsrsxn4 accessed 18 March 2013.

4.2 'Demand side'

4.2.1 Financial exclusion

The huge increase in demand for high-cost credit highlights ingrained problems in the fabric of UK society and provides evidence of the widespread issue of financial exclusion. There is no agreed definition of 'financial exclusion', although the European Commission defines it as 'a process whereby people encounter difficulties accessing and/or using financial services and products in the mainstream market that are appropriate to their needs and enable them to lead a normal social life in the society in which they belong'.[112] High-cost credit is generally marketed for discretionary purchases or one-off expenses. These products are an extremely expensive form of credit and are therefore not designed to be used on a regular or even semi-regular basis. If this type of lending is limited to a rare one-off occasion, there is some level of justification for the exceptionally high cost of the credit.[113] Nevertheless, the research into the market clearly shows that a large number of borrowers are using this type of credit frequently and for a variety of everyday expenses – some are then getting caught in a harmful debt spiral. Based on the above definition, the use of high-cost credit in this manner is clearly an indicator of financial exclusion. The consumers are not accessing or using financial services in the mainstream market in a way that is appropriate to their needs.[114]

Financial exclusion relates not only to the individual's financial situation but also to their general and social wellbeing. As highlighted by Ramsay:

> Differing patterns of credit use and access to credit may act as a potential multiplier of advantage and disadvantage in society potentially heightening social divisions.... Exclusion from access to credit may therefore mean both economic exclusion from markets ... and also exclusion from a central aspect of public expression in modern society.[115]

The financial exclusion experienced by these borrowers can exacerbate their pre-existing disadvantages. High-cost credit and subsequent debt spirals can result in

112 Social Affairs and Equal Opportunities Inclusion Directorate-General for Employment, Social Policy Aspects of Migration, Streamlining of Social Policies, *Financial Services Provision and the Prevention of Financial Exclusion* (European Commission 2008) 9; See also Social Affairs and Equal Opportunities Directorate-General for Employment, *Towards a Common Operational European Definition of Over-Indebtedness* (European Commission 2008).

113 Some consumer advocates, however, argue that the very nature of payday loans is exploitative and therefore the product is not justified under any circumstances; see Jeannie Paterson and Gerald Brodie, 'Targeting Business Models that Prey on Vulnerable Consumers: The Role of Prohibition on Unfair and Unconscionable Conduct' (International Association of Consumer Law Conference, Sydney, 4 July 2013).

114 Sharon Collard, Elaine Kempson and Claire Whyley, *Tackling Financial Exclusion: An Area-Based Approach* (Policy Press 2001); Nicola Howell and Therese Wilson, 'Access to Consumer Credit: The Problem of Financial Exclusion in Australia and the Current Regulatory Framework' (2005) 5 Macquarie Law Journal 127; Elaine Kempson and Sharon Collard, *Developing a Vision for Financial Inclusion* (Friends Provident Foundation 2012).

115 Iain Ramsay, 'Consumer Credit Law, Distributive Justice and the Welfare State' (1995) 15 Oxford Journal of Legal Studies 177, 181.

other types of exclusion, such as homelessness or rough housing;[116] children being kept from school as they cannot cover the cost of books, fees and uniforms; and adults being unable to hold down jobs as they cannot afford car repayments or public transportation. This type of situation severely limits people's long-term choices and their ability to pursue freely chosen goals and relationships. It is therefore critically important to address how and why such large numbers of people have become financially excluded from the mainstream credit system and need to use high-cost loans in an inappropriate and dangerous way.

4.2.2 Credit alternatives

The government is currently focusing on reforms to regulate HCSTC and to provide increased protection to borrowers. This is a step forward, but attention must also be paid to preventing the need for the loans in the first place. It should therefore be a priority of the current government to ensure that there are robust, efficient and widely available alternative credit products for low-income consumers. Steps have been taken in this direction, and the UK has recently invested £35.6 million into the credit union sector so that it can work as a viable alternative to commercial high-cost credit. It is estimated that this will save consumers almost £1 billion in interest repayments.[117] Unfortunately this is unlikely to be sufficient, and further reforms are required, such as an increased role for CDFIs[118] or the dismantled Social Fund.[119] The current government created the political conditions that led to an explosion in this type of financial product. It therefore must now take some responsibility for the consequences and ensure that there is access to sufficient affordable credit alternatives for low-income individuals.

4.2.3 Non-credit alternatives

As the CMA borrower profile has identified the main reasons why people need to access high-cost credit, processes can be put into play to respond to these underlying needs before consumers actually obtain the credit. Two common examples of underlying needs for high-cost loans are the payment of bills and existing financial obligations. These issues could be largely resolved by the implementation of financial hardship obligations, which legally require businesses to enter into penalty-free repayment plans when consumers suffer temporary financial difficulties preventing them from paying the money owed. Financial hardship obligations have been

116 See also Shelter, 'Know the Real Cost of Payday Loans' http://england.shelter.org.uk/get_advice/help_with_money/loans_debt_and_bankruptcy/payday_loans/cost_of_payday_loans accessed 11 September 2013.

117 Association of British Credit Unions, 'Credit Union Sector Set to Transform in Two Years' (8 May 2013) www.abcul.org/media-and-research/news/view/334 accessed 8 March 2013.

118 An example of this is the funding that the Australian Government has given to CDFIs. See Department of Families Housing Community Services and Indigenous Affairs, 'Community Development Financial Institutions (CDFI) Pilot Project' www.fahcsia.gov.au/our-responsibilities/communities-and-vulnerable-people/programs-services/financial-management-program/community-development-financial-institutions-cdfi-pilot-project accessed 7 August 2013.

119 Information about the April 2013 changes to the Social Fund is available at Citizens Advice Bureau, 'Changes to the Social Fund in England' www.adviceguide.org.uk/england/benefits_e/benefits_welfare_benefits_reform_e/changes_to_the_social_fund_in_england.htm accessed 8 August 2013.

implemented in Australia and a number of other countries,[120] and as a result consumers can deal directly with the issue causing the need for funds, as opposed to entering into expensive and potentially harmful loans.

Another common need for high-cost credit is one-off expenses or emergencies, highlighting that many consumers do not have sufficient savings to deal with these issues and therefore turn to credit. This is strongly linked with the shortage of consumer savings and lack of a *savings culture* in the UK. The figures paint a disturbing picture; *Now: Pensions* reports that 28 per cent of people have stopped saving since the recession, 32 per cent of people have less than £500 in savings, and as many as one in five have no savings at all. The need for promotion of savings, especially with low-income individuals, was identified by the previous Labour Government, and in response the Saving Gateway Accounts Act 2009 (UK) was drafted. Under this legislation the government would give people earning less than the threshold amount 50 pence for every £1 saved up to a total of £25 each month. Unfortunately, this legislation was cancelled when the Coalition Government came into power, and instead the amount allowed to be saved tax-free in an Individual Savings Account was increased.[121] The latter initiative is directed at middle-income consumers who are paying tax and therefore does little to help those who most need access to savings.

The borrower profile from the CMA also highlights that a large number of people are obtaining high-cost credit just to cover basic necessities, such as food and baby items (for example, nappies and formula). The UK is a developed welfare state and there is an expectation that the government will provide a minimal level of support for vulnerable and low-income citizens. Since the 2008 Global Financial Crisis and economic downturn, there has been a shift towards a more conservative approach to social security and away from the welfare state. This decreasing government support coincides with stagnated wages, increased unemployment and higher costs of living and, as such, comes at a time when people most need the support. The current explosion of demand for high-cost credit by low-income consumers to pay for life's necessities is calling into question whether mainstream society is failing these people. This clearly highlights disturbing flaws in the current system that need to be addressed. In a welfare state with a social security system,[122] it is unacceptable that such a large number of people are forced to turn to credit for everyday living expenses. These types of purchases are not something for which we should be relying on credit, and the state should ensure people have access to these basic essentials without resorting to expensive and potentially harmful credit.

120 See, for example, in Australia the National Credit Code (Cth), s 72 and Energy Legislation (Hardship, Metering and Other Matters) Act 2006 (Vic).

121 Jill Insley, 'Budget: Saving Scheme for Low Earners Scrapped' *Guardian* (25 June 2010) www.theguardian.com/money/2010/jun/24/budget-gateway-saving-scrapped accessed 6 October 2013.

122 For discussion of the causes of poverty and role of the government, see Tracy Shildrick and others, *Poverty and Insecurity: Life in 'Low-Pay, No-Pay' Britain* (Policy Press 2012); Jonathan Cribb, Andrew Hood, Robert Joyce, David Phillips, *Living Standards, Poverty and Inequality in the UK 2013* (Institute for Fiscal Studies 2013); Dalia Ben-Galim and Tess Lanning, *Strength Against Shocks: Low-income Families and Debt* (Institute for Public Policy Research 2010).

5 Conclusion

This chapter had two key aims. The first was to fill the current research gap by providing a philosophical justification for government intervention into high-cost credit contracts that can work as a complement to the current empirical approach of the FCA and CMA. The second was to use this philosophical justification to determine how this intervention should occur. It is clear that a multi-faceted approach is needed which addresses both the *supply* and *demand* aspects of the high-cost credit problem. The UK has recognised the urgent need for reform of the consumer credit industry, in particular high-cost loans. It has, however, responded by focusing solely on the *supply* aspects of the situation, increasing the regulation of the product and enhancing enforcement activities against those who do not comply with the legal regime. This is an excellent step forward, but is only part of a much broader, more complex picture of what is needed to protect users of high-cost credit. An analysis of the philosophical justifications for intervention illuminates the circumstances and motivations of high-cost credit users, thereby allowing the development of a holistic social and legal regime that responds to the underlying consumer needs. This approach will treat the cause of the situation and stop consumers from having to take out potentially harmful loans, as opposed to merely removing some of the most harmful aspects of an inherently dangerous product.

8 Apples and oranges?

Responsible mortgage lending in the UK and Australia

Karen Fairweather

1 Introduction

In 'From Truth in Lending to Responsible Lending', Iain Ramsay described the fundamental paradigm shift in consumer credit regulation that became apparent in the first decade of the new millennium.[1] The 'truth in lending' or 'information' paradigm is firmly rooted in neoclassical economic thinking. It posits that consumers will make rational, welfare-maximising borrowing decisions if provided with adequate information at appropriate times. While acknowledging that *some* intervention in the market is necessary to redress the information asymmetries that can lead to market failures, it expresses a fundamentally libertarian free-market philosophy. But the findings of behavioural economics research have exposed a whole range of cognitive biases that interfere with consumers' ability to efficiently process and act upon information, destroying confidence in the information paradigm of consumer law in general and consumer credit regulation in particular.[2] The 'responsible lending' paradigm, in contrast, is premised on the notion that consumers are not always capable of making appropriate borrowing choices and that the state is therefore justified in stepping in to limit that freedom of choice. It is indubitably a creature of paternalism.[3]

1 Iain Ramsay, 'From Truth in Lending to Responsible Lending' in Geraint Howells, Andre Janssen and Reiner Schulze (eds), *Information Rights and Obligations* (Ashgate 2005). On the development of responsible lending in the UK Consumer Credit regime, see Karen Fairweather, 'The Development of Responsible Lending in the UK Consumer Credit Regime' in James Devenney and Mel Kenny (eds), *Consumer Credit, Debt and Investment in Europe* (Cambridge University Press 2012).

2 The following is just a small selection of the vast literature on this subject: Melvin Eisenberg, 'The Limits of Cognition and the Limits of Contract' (1995) 47 Stanford Law Review 211; Christine Jolls, Cass Sunstein and Richard Thaler, 'A Behavioural Approach to Law and Economics' (1998) 50 Stanford Law Review 1471; Oren Bar-Gill, 'Seduction by Plastic' (2004) 98 Northwestern University Law Review 1373; Oren Bar-Gill, 'The Behavioural Economics of Consumer Contracts' (2008) 92 Minnesota Law Review 749; Susan Block Lieb and Edward Janger, 'The Myth of the Rational Borrower; Rationality, Behaviouralism and the Misguided "Reform" of Bankruptcy Law' (2006) 84 Texas Law Review 1481; Cass Sunstein, 'Homo Economicus, Homo Myopicus, and the Law and Economics of Consumer Choice: Boundedly Rational Borrowing' (2006) 73 University of Chicago Law Review 249; Peter Diamond and Hannu Vartianan (eds) *Behavioural Economics and its Applications* (Princeton University Press 2007); Iain Ramsay (n 1).

3 On the legitimacy of paternalism in the context of responsible lending laws, see Chapter 2.

Many of the world's developed economies have now incorporated responsible lending obligations into their consumer credit regimes.[4] Although the content, strength and means of enforcement of these obligations vary from country to country, they are, broadly speaking, concerned with ensuring that consumers do not enter into credit agreements that are unaffordable and, in some cases, inappropriate for their needs and circumstances. Central to these obligations are generally assessments of 'creditworthiness', 'affordability', 'suitability' or 'appropriateness'. Some of these examples were developed as instruments of consumer protection in the context of growing concerns about consumer over-indebtedness. But the Global Financial Crisis (the Crisis) soon made explicit, in the starkest possible terms, the link between irresponsible lending to consumers and global financial instability, prompting a number of international initiatives in the area.[5]

The UK has recently undergone a major overhaul of its mortgages regime. The new Mortgage Conduct of Business rules (MCOB), which came into effect on 26 April 2014 following a three-year review of the mortgage market, have brought about a significant strengthening of responsible lending standards. Further changes are on the horizon with the Mortgage Credit Directive (MCD)[6] due for transposition into UK law by March 2016. This chapter will present these recent and forthcoming changes using recent Australian developments and the responsible lending obligations in the National Consumer Credit Protection Act 2009 (Cth) (NCCPA) regime as a comparative backdrop.

2 An overview of the two regimes

2.1 The scope of the two regimes

To compare mortgage regulation in the UK and Australia is, in a sense, to compare apples with oranges. It is not possible to speak of an Australian 'mortgages regime' as such; mortgages are just one of the many products regulated by the Australian Securities and Investments Commission (ASIC) under the umbrella of 'consumer credit' under the NCCPA regime. Apart from some specific provisions on reverse mortgages, which are beyond the scope of this chapter, the NCCPA contains no

4 For example, responsible lending provisions have been introduced in the UK (by the Financial Services Authority's Mortgage Conduct of Business rules first made in 2004 under the Financial Services and Markets Act 2000 and also by the Consumer Credit Act 2006), South Africa (National Credit Act 2005), Australia (National Consumer Credit Protection Act 2009 (Cth)), the USA (Dodd–Frank Act 2010 – in the mortgages context) and New Zealand (Credit Contracts and Consumer Finance Amendment Act 2014). All EU Member States have been required to enact responsible lending requirements in relation to unsecured lending to consumers by virtue of the Consumer Credit Directive 2008. They will also be required to do so in relation to lending secured on residential immovable property by March 2016 as a result of the Mortgage Credit Directive 2014.

5 See, for example, Joint Forum (International Organization of Securities Commissions, Basel Committee and International Association of Insurance Supervisors), *Review of the Differentiated Nature and Scope of Financial Regulation: Key Issues and Recommendations* (2010) Recommendation 7; Financial Stability Board, *Thematic Review on Mortgage Origination Practices (Peer Review Report)* (March 2011); International Financial Consumer Protection Organisation, *FinCoNet Report on Responsible Lending: Review of Supervisory Tools for Suitable Consumer Lending Practices* (July 2014).

6 Directive 2014/17/EU of the European Parliament and of the Council of 4 February 2014 on credit agreements for consumers relating to residential immovable property and amending Directives 2008/48/EC and Regulation (EU) No 1093/2010 OJ L60/34.

targeted provisions on mortgage lending. Similarly, none of the regulatory guidance on responsible lending issued by ASIC is specifically targeted at mortgage lending. The UK, by way of contrast, has had a dedicated mortgages regime since October 2004, when the Financial Services Authority (FSA) began regulating first charge mortgage lending under the Financial Services and Markets Act 2000 (FSMA).[7] The MCOB rules were made by the FSA pursuant to its rule-making powers under section 138 of the FSMA. The new Financial Conduct Authority (FCA) assumed responsibility for this regime on 1 April 2013, when it took over the FSA's functions as a conduct of business regulator. The regime does not cover the entirety of mortgage lending to consumers in the UK. Second-charge lending, which represents a much smaller share of the overall mortgage market, has historically been regulated alongside other forms of consumer credit under the Consumer Credit Act 1974 (CCA) regime. On 1 April 2014, the FCA took over regulatory responsibility for consumer credit (including second-charge lending) from the OFT. Despite sharing a regulator since that date, the regulatory split between first- and second-charge lending has continued to exist, with second-charge lending subject to the conduct of business rules now located in the FCA's new specialist Consumer Credit Sourcebook (CONC) and those conduct-related provisions of the CCA that have been retained. This regulatory split will, however, be abolished in March 2016 when, to coincide with the UK's transposition of the MCD, second-charge lending will be brought within the scope of MCOB. 'Buy-to-let' or investor mortgages, which in Australia are regulated by ASIC under the NCCPA regime, have until now been largely unregulated in the UK.[8] However, consumer buy-to-let mortgages will be regulated for the first time by the FCA from 21 March 2016 under the Mortgage Credit Directive Order 2015.[9] The UK mortgages regime is wider than the Australian regime in that MCOB also covers certain loans for business purposes which are not regulated under the NCCPA regime.

2.2 The background to the current regimes

Australia and the UK share a deeply entrenched culture of home ownership and both have mature mortgage markets. In the decade leading up to the financial crisis the commonalities between these countries' housing and mortgage markets were apparent: housing booms fuelled by low interest rates and greater competition from non-deposit-taking institutions; a relaxation of lending standards, albeit to differing extents; the increasing role of intermediaries in the mortgage sales process; rising levels of mortgage debt causing exponential increases in the percentage of

7 Prior to this date, first-charge mortgages below a certain monetary threshold were, however, regulated under the Consumer Credit Act 1974 (CCA). From 21 March 2016, the CCA will no longer apply to these pre-2004 first charge mortgages, which will be brought within the scope of the FSMA regime and hence the MCOB rules. See Financial Conduct Authority, *Future Regulatory Treatment of CCA Regulated First Charge Mortgages* (Consultation Paper CP15/36 2015).

8 Buy-to-let *broking* has been regulated by the FCA since 1 April 2014.

9 SI 2015/910. The order establishes conduct standards based on the Mortgage Credit Directive which apply to a firm conducting broking, advisory or lending activity with a buy-to-let consumer. The legislation does not apply to buy-to-let mortgages entered into with those acting for business purposes. It gives the FCA power to register, supervise and take action against firms, but does not confer upon it general rule-making powers.

household debt to disposable household income, which in turn resulted in frequent expressions of public concern about over-indebtedness and its associated social and economic ills.[10] But the Crisis unwound very differently in the two countries. Although both responded to the Crisis by introducing or strengthening responsible lending requirements, they did so against the background of quite different experiences. If the Australian response was more of a pre-emptive strike, the new UK regime was a response to the exposure of real and relatively widespread problems in its mortgage market.

2.2.1 UK developments

The UK had been one of the first countries to introduce responsible lending obligations. The concept of responsible lending first found expression in 1997 in guidance issued by the Office of Fair Trading (OFT) on the subject of second-charge mortgage lending to credit-impaired borrowers. The guidelines were, however, of limited application and, as regulatory guidance, lacked the status of legal rules. It was not until the Financial Services Authority (FSA) became responsible for regulating first-charge mortgage lending[11] in October 2004 that there could be said to be any *legal* responsible lending obligation. The MCOB rules subjected lenders to what was, by pre-Crisis standards at least, a fairly rigorous lending regime.[12] On paper at least, this appeared to offer a high level of protection, certainly much higher than that offered by the Australian Uniform Consumer Credit Code (UCCC) and supplementary state and territory legislation. Moreover, intermediaries, who had played a significant role in the UK mortgage market for some time, were also regulated by the FSA. Where they sold mortgages on an ‘advised’ basis, they were subject to quite prescriptive responsible lending requirements in chapter 4 of MCOB.

The UK was badly affected by the Crisis, largely because of the heavy exposure of UK banks to US subprime mortgage instruments, their reliance on borrowing in financial markets rather than on deposits, and the large role securitisation had played in their funding of mortgages and other loans.[13] By the second quarter of 2008, the UK had entered recession and rapidly rising unemployment[14] and falling property prices[15] left an increasing number of households struggling to service their debt and/or in negative equity. With mortgage repossessions increasing by 58 per cent to

10 Certainly, the Australian and UK experiences were far from unusual. These features were present in a number of other advanced economies: see Bank for International Settlements, Committee on the Global Financial System, *Housing Finance in the Global Financial Market*, CGFS papers no 26 (January 2006).

11 The UK has historically operated a split system of regulation. First-charge lending has been regulated by the FSA under the Financial Services and Markets Act 2000 regime since October 2004. Other forms of consumer credit, including second-charge mortgage lending, were regulated by the OFT under the Consumer Credit Act 1974 regime.

12 See MCOB Sourcebook, chapter 11, entitled ‘Responsible Lending’. This has since been replaced by a new chapter 11.

13 For discussion of specific UK features of the financial crisis, see Financial Services Authority, *The Turner Review: A Regulatory Response to the Global Banking Crisis* (2009) para 1.2.

14 Unemployment also increased from 5.7 per cent in 2008 to 7.7 per cent in 2009, peaking at 8.1 per cent in 2011.

15 By March 2009, residential property prices had fallen 20 per cent from their 2007 peak.

40,000 in 2008,[16] it was becoming increasingly apparent just how risky some of the lending at the height of the boom had been. Startlingly, by the height of the mortgage market frenzy in 2007, nearly half of all mortgages were being sold on a 'non-income verified' (NIV) basis[17] and 'interest-only' loans accounted for nearly one-third of the market.[18] The proportion of high loan-to-income (high LTI) and high loan-to-value (high LTV) loans was also significant.[19]

It was against this background that the FSA embarked, in 2009, on its wholesale review of the mortgage market, the Mortgage Market Review (MMR). The FSA wasted no time in signalling a fundamental shift in its regulatory philosophy, announcing in October 2009 that:

> Our policy approach to date has been underpinned by a view that mortgage consumers will act rationally to protect their own interests. We believe that we need to change that approach, recognize the behavioural biases of consumers and be more interventionist to help protect consumers from themselves.[20]

Certainly, irresponsible lending had not occurred on anything like the scale that it had in the United States, but there was concern that historically low interest rates, government initiatives to protect homeowners in the wake of the Crisis and improved forbearance by lenders were masking the true extent of affordability problems among existing borrowers. The FSA concluded that substantial reform was necessary to ensure that the harmful lending practices that had occurred in the run-up to the Crisis could not re-emerge in a subsequent upswing.

2.2.2 Australian developments

In comparison with nearly every other advanced economy, Australia emerged largely unscathed from the Crisis. The reasons for this are complex,[21] but a significant factor was the very limited exposure of Australian banks to 'toxic' collateralised debt obligations and US subprime backed securities, and the far greater weighting of their balance sheets to domestic housing loans, which posed very low levels of risk.[22] Although mortgage arrears rates had steadily increased since around 2002, they remained low by historical and international standards. This was, in part, attributable to the relatively cautious lending culture that had persisted in Australia, despite some relaxation in lending standards resulting from competition from non-deposit-taking institutions. 'Non-conforming'[23] and 'low-doc' loans, for example, accounted for no more than 2 per cent and 10 per cent respectively of the market between

16 From 25,900 in 2007 to 40,000 in 2008: Council of Mortgage Lenders, table AP4.

17 Ibid exhibit 2.7.

18 Ibid.

19 Ibid. Mortgages with a loan-to-income ratio of 3.5 or more accounted for 28.4 per cent of the total market. Those with an LTV ratio of more than 90 per cent accounted for more than 13.6 per cent.

20 Financial Services Authority, *Mortgage Market Review* (Discussion Paper, DP 09/3, October 2009) para 1.41.

21 For in-depth analysis, see Jennifer Hill, 'Why Did Australia Fare So Well in the Global Financial Crisis?' in Eilís Ferran, Niamh Moloney, Jennifer Hill and John C Coffee, Jr. (eds), *The Regulatory Aftermath of the Global Financial Crisis* (Cambridge University Press 2012).

22 Reserve Bank of Australia, *Financial Stability Review* (March 2009) 17–19.

23 This terminology is used in Australia for 'subprime' or 'credit-impaired'.

2002 and 2007.[24] Although there was evidence of some stretching of LTV ratios, the evidence was that such ratios rarely exceeded 95 per cent,[25] and certainly never reached the 125 per cent mark seen in the now infamous Northern Rock 'Together' mortgage in the UK.

The Australian Prudential Regulation Authority (APRA) had undoubtedly played an important role in maintaining the cautious lending culture among banks and other authorised deposit-taking institutions, which were still responsible for originating over 80 per cent of Australia's mortgages.[26] There was, in fact, little in the way of conduct requirements to constrain irresponsible lending practices at the time. The UCCC, which had come into operation in November 1996, did allow for the reopening of a consumer credit contract where the lender knew or could reasonably have known that the debtor would not be able to repay or not without substantial hardship[27] and the licensing schemes that operated in some of the states and territories also allowed for disciplinary action against lenders who acted 'unfairly' or 'unjustly'.[28] In reality, banks' corporate memories of Australia's first post-deregulation banking crisis in the late 1980s and early 1990s were probably a more effective brake on lax lending practices. Such evidence as there was of irresponsible lending practices was, at least according to a 2007 House of Representatives Standing Committee report on home mortgage lending, largely confined to the very small 'non-conforming' sector of the market which was the domain of non-deposit-taking institutions.[29] After a short-lived contraction in the immediate aftermath of the Crisis, Australia's housing and mortgage markets resumed their upward trajectory.

Australia was on the eve of the birth of its national consumer credit regime when the Crisis reached its peak in 2008.[30] The regulation of consumer credit and finance brokers had been on the agenda for some time and responsible lending had been a recurrent theme in the many reports prepared around this time.[31] By 2007, finance brokers were involved in about 30 per cent of new mortgage transactions and concerns were expressed that the lowering of lending standards that had been observed was attributable, at least in part, to lenders' increasing reliance on the, then largely

24 Australian Government, The Treasury, *Financial Services and Credit Reform: Improving, Simplifying and Standardising Financial Services and Credit Regulation* (Green Paper, June 2008) table 2.

25 Senate Economics References Committee, *Consenting Adults Deficits and Household Debt Links between Australia's Current Account Deficit: The Demand for Imported Goods and Household Debt* (October 2005) para 5.16.

26 For example, in 2004, in response to the rising number of 'low-doc' mortgages, APRA increased the risk weight on such mortgages to 100 per cent: see Australian Prudential Regulation Authority, *Proposed Changes to the Risk-Weight of Residential Mortgage Lending* (Discussion Paper, November 2003).

27 Uniform Consumer Credit Code, s 70(2)(l).

28 For detailed discussion of the supervision and administration in the states and territories at this time, see Anthony Duggan and Elizabeth Lanyon, *Consumer Credit Law* (Butterworths 1999) ch. 12.

29 House of Representatives Standing Committee on Economics, Finance and Public Administration, *Home Loan Lending: Inquiry into Home Loan Lending Practices and the Processes Used to Deal with People in Financial Difficulty* (2007). Non-deposit-taking institutions were not subject to APRA regulation.

30 This involved a transfer of regulatory responsibility for consumer credit from the state and territory governments to the Commonwealth Government.

31 See, for example, Senate Economics References Committee (n 25); Consumer Affairs Victoria, *The Report of the Consumer Credit Review* (Merlino Report; 2006); House of Representatives (n 29); Productivity Commission, *Review of Australia's Consumer Policy Framework Final Report* (2008); Australian Government (n 24).

unregulated,[32] broking industry.[33] The Rudd Government, determined not to 'let a good crisis go to waste', resolved to make responsible lending a key plank in the new national regime. The NCCPA came into effect on 1 April 2010. It requires both lenders and intermediaries to hold a credit licence and subjects them to extensive responsible lending conduct requirements.

3 A comparison of the responsible lending obligations

3.1 The source of the regulation

The Australian regime is built upon two sources: the provisions of chapter 3 of the NCCPA and regulatory guidance issued by ASIC[34] (the Guidance). The UK MCOB regime is a set of rules made by the FCA[35] under the rule-making powers conferred upon it by the FSMA. The rules are supplemented by some guidance and evidential provisions contained within MCOB.[36] One consequence of these different regulatory sources is a difference in the degree of normativity of the two sets of rules. Many of the NCCPA responsible lending requirements are set out at a fairly high level of generality, with ASIC left to provide its interpretation of the law in detailed guidance. As the ultimate arbiter of compliance is the court rather than ASIC, it is obviously possible to comply with the Australian responsible lending requirements without following the regulatory guidance to the letter.[37] Thus far the legislative provisions have been subject to judicial consideration on only one occasion.[38] In contrast, the sole arbiter of compliance in the UK regime is the FCA. There is, consequently, very limited scope for UK firms to challenge the FCA's position on its rules and guidance.

3.2 The 'core' responsible lending requirements

At the heart of both countries' responsible lending regimes are the concepts of affordability, appropriateness and suitability, albeit couched in slightly different terms. The NCCPA requires those providing 'credit assistance'[39] and those providing credit to assess whether the mortgage contract will be 'not unsuitable' for the consumer. If it would be unsuitable, entering into the mortgage contract,[40] suggesting that the consumer apply for or assisting the consumer to apply for,[41] or

32 Finance brokers were not covered by the UCCC. Their regulation was a matter left to the states and territories to address on an individual basis. Only New South Wales, Victoria, the ACT and Western Australia had enacted broker-specific legislation. At the federal level, the only protections were the prohibitions on unconscionable conduct, misleading or deceptive conduct and the making of false or misleading misrepresentations and the implied warranties of due care and skill and fitness for purpose in the Australian Securities and Investments Commission Act 2001.

33 House of Representatives (n 29) paras 4.12–4.18.

34 Regulatory Guide 209, *Credit Licensing: Responsible Lending Conduct* (November 2014) (RG209).

35 The FSA prior to 1 April 2013.

36 The FCA has rule-making powers under FSMA, s 138.

37 Whether firms will risk departing from the letter of the Guidance is, of course, another matter.

38 In *ASIC v Cash Store Pty Ltd (in liq)* [2014] FCA 926.

39 As defined in NCCPA, s 8.

40 NCCPA, s 133(1)(a).

41 NCCPA, s 123 (1)(a).

suggesting that the consumer remain in,[42] the particular mortgage contract in question is prohibited. Increasing the credit limit[43] or suggesting or assisting the consumer to apply for an increase to the credit limit[44] is also prohibited if such increase would render the mortgage contract unsuitable. The 'unsuitability' assessment consists of two strands: a full assessment of affordability and an assessment of whether the mortgage meets 'the consumer's requirements or objectives'. There is no duty to assess a particular mortgage contract as unsuitable merely because another contract is more suitable, but if the credit provider or credit assistance provider cannot offer or suggest any contract that is 'not unsuitable' it must not enter into a contract or provide credit assistance.[45]

In the UK regime, those *providing advice* in relation to a regulated mortgage contract must 'take reasonable steps' to ensure that it is 'suitable' for the customer.[46] The contract will not be suitable unless it is 'appropriate to the needs and circumstances' of the customer.[47] However, the previous rule that the adviser had to recommend the most suitable product was not retained; given the large number of products that potentially meet a consumer's needs and circumstances, it was considered that it imposed too onerous a standard.[48] Subsumed within the assessment of the contract's appropriateness to the needs and circumstances of the customer is a limited assessment of affordability, restricted to considering whether the customer meets the lender's expected affordability requirements. Furthermore, consideration of whether the customer meets the lender's expected affordability requirements is not a minimum requirement applicable in all cases, but is merely mentioned as a potentially relevant consideration.[49] Lenders are not required to assess 'suitability' unless they also provide the customer with advice.[50] They are, however, required to undertake a full assessment of affordability in all cases[51] and must not enter into, or agree to vary, the contract unless they can demonstrate that the new or varied contract is affordable for the consumer.[52] In requiring an assessment of affordability *and* appropriateness in all cases, the Australian regime may appear, at first glance, to provide consumers with a higher level of protection. Given that the circumstances in which customers in the UK can be sold mortgages without receiving advice[53] have been so severely restricted by the new MCOB rules, that difference may, however, be negligible.

42 NCCPA, s 124(1).
43 NCCPA, s 133(1)(b).
44 NCCPA, s 123(1)(b).
45 There is, however, a defence available under NCCPA, s 124(7) to a credit assistance provider who suggests that the consumer remain in an unsuitable contract where, having made reasonable inquiries, the credit assistance provider reasonably believed that there was no other credit contract that was not unsuitable for the consumer and informed the consumer of the procedure for consumers in hardship under ss 72 and 94 of the National Credit Code.
46 MCOB 4.7A.2R.
47 MCOB 4.7A.5R(1).
48 Financial Services Authority, *Mortgage Market Review: Distribution and Disclosure* (Consultation Paper, CP 10/28, November 2010) para 2.28.
49 MCOB 4.7A.6R(1) and 4.7A.8G.
50 On the circumstances in which advice is now required see Section 3.3.
51 MCOB 11.6.2R1(a).
52 MCOB 11.6.2R(1)(b).
53 See discussion in Section 3.3 below.

3.3 The balance of responsibility between lenders and intermediaries

A striking feature of both mortgage markets in the run-up to the Crisis was the growth of the intermediated sales channel in the mortgage sales process, although the overall proportion of intermediated sales in the UK was significantly higher than in Australia. In 2000 intermediated sales in the UK accounted for 35 per cent of total mortgage lending.[54] By the height of the market in 2007/2008 that figure had reached 61.5 per cent.[55] Despite large numbers of intermediaries exiting the market as a result of the rapid contraction in mortgage lending since the Crisis, intermediated sales still account for over half of total mortgage lending.[56] In Australia, intermediated sales accounted for 25 per cent and 37 per cent of all mortgage sales in 2003 and 2007 respectively.[57] By September 2015, that figure had risen to 52.6 per cent.[58]

Given the extent to which both Australian and UK consumers rely on intermediaries in the mortgage sales process, it is clearly appropriate that they should bear some responsibility for the affordability and appropriateness of the mortgages they recommend or otherwise provide assistance with. But the two regimes differ in how they calibrate the balance of responsibility between lenders and intermediaries. The NCCPA regime imposes 'quasi-uniform' obligations in respect of assessments of 'unsuitability' across the different credit activities of providing credit and providing credit assistance. Providing 'credit assistance' includes: suggesting that a consumer apply for, or assisting a consumer to apply for, a particular credit contract with a particular credit provider; suggesting that a consumer apply for, or assisting the consumer to apply for, an increase in the credit limit of a particular credit contract with a particular credit provider; and suggesting that a consumer remains in a particular credit contract with a particular credit provider.[59] Thus, in an intermediated mortgage sale, both lender and intermediary must undertake independent and full 'unsuitability' assessments; the lender is not permitted to simply rely on the intermediary's 'preliminary' assessment.[60] The Explanatory Memorandum emphasised that the label 'preliminary':

> [D]oes not diminish the credit assistant's responsibilities with regard to making reasonable inquiries and undertaking reasonable verification of the information they can access. However, it recognises that the credit assistant does not have access to some information that is available to a credit provider (such as credit

54 Mintel (2002) cited in the *Mortgage Market Review: Distribution and Disclosure* (n 48) para 2.3.

55 Financial Conduct Authority, 'Mortgages Product Sales Data (PSD) Extended Tables 2005–2014' www.fca.org.uk/firms/systems-reporting/product-sales-data/interpreting-the-data#1 accessed 14 January 2015. The huge growth in product diversity that occurred around that time and the increasing number of products introduced by specialist and non-bank lenders with few or no branch networks have both been identified as drivers of the growth: *Mortgage Market Review* DP09/3 (n 20) para 5.5.

56 In the year 2013/2014, the figure was 55.5 per cent: FCA (n 55).

57 Australian Government, The Treasury, (n 24) 3–4, citing Fujitsu and JP Morgan, 'Australian Mortgage Industry – Volume 7' (March 2008).

58 Comparator 'Mortgage Quarterly Survey Report' (September Quarter 2015).

59 NCCPA, s 8.

60 Revised Explanatory Supplementary Memorandum, National Consumer Credit Protection Bill 2009 para 1.20.

bureau data and data arising from a banking relationship) and that a credit assistant is not making an assessment that takes into consideration the commercial risk of being the lender.[61]

ASIC has recognised that what may 'reasonably' be expected of a credit assistance provider in relation to inquiries into the consumer's requirements, objectives and financial situation and verifying the consumer's financial situation may well differ from what it is reasonable to expect of a credit provider.[62] These distinctions aside, the assessments required of lenders and intermediaries are the same. In summary, then, whenever the intermediated sales channel is used in Australia, regardless of whether the intermediary suggests the particular mortgage contract or merely assists the consumer to apply for that contract, both intermediary and lender must assess affordability and appropriateness.

Unfortunately, the position in the UK is less straightforward. Much of the difficulty is caused by the distinction that the previous MCOB rules had drawn between 'advised' and 'non-advised' sales. An 'advised' sale was one where a recommendation was made to a customer to take out a particular mortgage product. A 'non-advised' sale involved the customer being provided with information only and left to make their own choice.[63] At the height of the market, 70 per cent of all sales were advised.[64] Although both intermediated and direct sales could be 'advised' or 'non-advised', advice was far more common in intermediated sales. In 2007, 92 per cent of intermediated sales, as opposed to just 36 per cent of direct sales, were advised.[65] The distinction between advised and non-advised sales mattered. In an 'advised' sale (whether that advice was provided by the lender itself 'in branch' or by an intermediary) the firm advising was required to take reasonable steps not to recommend entry into, or a variation of, a mortgage contract unless it would be suitable for the customer.[66] This involved assessing both affordability and appropriateness 'to the needs and circumstances of the customer'.[67] Furthermore, in an advised sale, the firm had to recommend the 'most suitable' product from all those available to it. The rules were prescriptive, setting out in some detail what these assessments entailed.[68] In contrast, in a 'non-advised' sale no assessment of appropriateness was required. There was simply a 'high-level' obligation not to sell an inappropriate product.[69] The lack of any more detailed rules or guidance on this point meant that the obligation was, in reality, one not to sell an 'obviously' inappropriate product.[70]

The position under the old rules was that in the most common case of an intermediated, advised sale, the intermediary was required to assess both the affordability

61 Explanatory Memorandum, National Consumer Credit Protection Bill 2009 para 3.67.

62 ASIC, RG209.23–209.27.

63 Often referred to as an 'information-only' sale.

64 FSA, *Mortgage Market Review: Distribution and Disclosure* (Consultation Paper, CP10/28, November 2010) exhibit 2.9.

65 Ibid exhibits 2.5 and 2.6.

66 MCOB 4.7.2R (now deleted).

67 MCOB 4.7.4R(1) (now deleted).

68 See, for example, MCOB 4.7.7E (now deleted) and 4.7.8G (now deleted) on the affordability assessment and MCOB 4.7.11E (now deleted) on the appropriateness assessment.

69 MCOB 4.8.2G(2) (now deleted). That obligation fell on the lender in a direct sale and the intermediary in an intermediated sale.

70 FSA (n 64) para 2.11.

of the mortgage contract and its appropriateness to the needs and circumstances of the customer. The lender's only obligation was to undertake an assessment of affordability, which applied in all cases regardless of the sales channel and process used. This obligation was, in reality, less onerous than the intermediary's obligations in respect of affordability. Whereas the affordability assessment required of the intermediary was set out in some detail, the lender was simply required to show that it had taken account of the customer's ability to repay. With little in the way of detailed rules fleshing out what that entailed, lenders were left to adopt what they considered an appropriate affordability assessment, with the primary responsibility for assessing affordability being borne by the intermediary. In the case of a non-advised sale, the only protections were the lender's obligation to take account of the customer's ability to repay and the high-level obligation on either the lender or intermediary, depending on the sales channel, not to sell an inappropriate product.

In the MMR, the FSA took the view that the balance of responsibility between lenders and intermediaries required recalibration. As has been seen, lenders and intermediaries were subject to concurrent but unequally weighted obligations to assess affordability in intermediated advised sales. Although this 'double layer' of protection might have been expected to produce better outcomes for consumers, the opposite proved to be the case. Thematic work undertaken by the FSA suggested that these concurrent obligations were commonly a source of confusion or complacency, with the lender assuming that the intermediary had assessed affordability while the intermediary assumed that the lender had done so.[71] The new rules aim to put it beyond doubt that 'ultimate responsibility for affordability lies with the lender irrespective of the distribution channel chosen'.[72] With this in mind they limit advisers' obligations to considering whether the customer meets the lender's expected affordability criteria, where relevant,[73] at the same time as imposing more onerous and prescriptive affordability requirements on lenders.[74]

The absence of any meaningful obligation to assess the appropriateness of the mortgage contract in non-advised sales was a further shortcoming identified in the MMR. Given that around 30 per cent of mortgages had been sold on a 'non-advised' basis at the height of the market in 2007, this constituted a significant gap in consumer protection. The fact that a large proportion of these non-advised sales were to vulnerable 'high-risk' consumers only heightened the concern. Significantly, the vast majority of these non-advised mortgage sales were 'direct' sales by lenders. The FSA's initial proposal to extend the obligation to assess appropriateness to non-advised sales was ultimately abandoned. The evidence suggested that consumers already experienced great difficulty understanding and recognising the distinction between advised and non-advised sales.[75] The FSA was concerned that the proposal would only compound the confusion by further obscuring the distinction between

71 See FSA, *Mortgage Effectiveness Review: Stage 1 Report* (2006); FSA, *Mortgage Effectiveness Review: Stage 2 Report* (2008).

72 *Mortgage Market Review* DP09/3 (n 20) para 4.66.

73 MCOB 4.7A.6R(1) and 4.7A.8G. This obligation applies to both intermediary advisers and 'branch' (i.e. lender) advisers.

74 These requirements are discussed below in Section 3.4.

75 A significant proportion of customers appeared to believe they had received advice despite having been told repeatedly that the sales process was a 'non-advised' one.

the two processes.[76] A more uniform approach to assessments of appropriateness was instead achieved by removing the availability of the non-advised process outside of an extremely narrow range of circumstances.[77] The result is that mortgages must now nearly always be sold on an advised basis with a standardised affordability and appropriateness assessment applying to all sales.[78] 'Execution-only' sales are generally permitted only where a 'non-interactive' sales process is used.[79] They are also allowed in 'interactive' sales if the customer is a 'high net worth'[80] or 'professional'[81] customer, the loan is solely for a business purpose or the customer has rejected the advice given.[82] In all of these cases of permitted 'interactive' sales, the customer must identify the product he wishes to purchase and make a positive election in writing to proceed with the sale on an 'execution-only' basis.[83]

It was obvious that this change would have far-reaching consequences for many firms, both lenders and intermediaries. Firms previously utilising a purely non-advised sales process who wished to continue operating would, in reality, either have to move to a purely 'non-interactive' sales process or have their Part 4A permission[84] amended to include advising activities. They would also need to ensure they had sufficient staff with the necessary qualifications to provide advice, as well as ensuring appropriate systems, policies, procedures and controls were in place to operate and monitor an advised process. Since the majority of non-advised sales had been 'direct' sales by lenders, it is lenders who have been most affected by the change.

The position under the current rules can be summarised as follows. In the most common case of an intermediated advised sale, the intermediary must assess whether the mortgage contract is suitable. This means that it must be appropriate for the needs and circumstances of the customer. In making this assessment it may, depending on the circumstances, be necessary for the intermediary to consider whether the customer meets the lender's expected affordability criteria. It is then for the lender to undertake a full affordability assessment. In the case of a direct advised sale, the lender must undertake a full affordability assessment and an assessment of suitability, which encompasses both an assessment of appropriateness to the needs and circumstances of the customer and, depending on the circumstances, consideration of whether the

76 FSA, *Mortgage Market Review: Proposed Package of Reforms* (Consultation Paper, CP 11/31, December 2011) para 1.111–1.112.

77 The circumstances in which 'execution-only' sales are permitted are set out in MCOB 4.8A.2G.

78 With the exception of 'execution-only' sales.

79 MCOB 4.8A.2G(1). 'Interactive dialogue' between the customer and the firm includes SMS, mobile instant messaging, email and communication via social media sites: 4.8A.3G. Even where a non-interactive process is used, 'execution-only' sales will not be permitted where the customer is a 'right to buy' customer or consolidating debt: 4.8A.7R.

80 A 'high net worth mortgage customer' is one with an annual net income of no less than £300,000 or net assets of no less than £3,000,000, or whose obligations are guaranteed by a person with such income or assets: see Handbook Glossary.

81 A 'professional customer' is one who works or has recently worked in the home finance sector for at least one year in a professional position which requires knowledge of the home finance transactions or home finance services envisaged, and who the firm reasonably believe to be capable of understanding the risks involved in the transactions contemplated: see Handbook Glossary.

82 MCOB 4.8A.2G(2) and (3).

83 MCOB 4.8A.2G(2) and (3).

84 A Part 4A permission is a permission given by the FCA under Part 4A of the FSMA to carry on regulated activities: FSMA s 55A.

customer meets the lender's affordability criteria.[85] In the extremely narrow circumstances in which 'execution-only' sales are permitted, the lender must still undertake a full assessment of affordability but no suitability assessment is required.

3.4 Assessing affordability

3.4.1 The 'basics'

The UK regime requires lenders to assess whether the customer 'will be able to pay the sums due' under the mortgage contract.[86] In Australia, lenders and intermediaries must assess whether the consumer 'will be unable to comply with [its] financial obligations under the contract, or could only comply with substantial hardship'.[87] What is striking at first glance is the prescriptiveness of the UK rules in comparison with the Australian regime. The Australian assessment of affordability is proportionate or 'scalable', with the scope and intensity of the assessment varying according to the particular circumstances.[88] Given the wide range of consumer credit products to which the Australian regime applies, this non-prescriptive approach is only to be expected. In contrast, the new MCOB rules have introduced minimum requirements designed to ensure that all assessments of affordability are based on the customer's free disposable income. The lender must satisfy itself of the customer's ability to pay the sums as they fall due,[89] taking 'full account' of the customer's income[90] and, as a minimum, the customer's committed expenditure[91] and the basic essential expenditure[92] and basic quality-of-living costs[93] of the customer's household. The assessment must be made on the basis of repayment of both capital and interest over the term of the mortgage contract except in the, now limited, circumstances in which interest-only mortgages are permitted.[94]

85 The FSA confirmed that the lender's own sales staff would not be exonerated from the separate obligation to consider (where appropriate) whether the customer meets the lender's affordability requirements: *Mortgage Market Review: Proposed Package of Reforms* (n 76) paras 5.23 and 5.24.

86 MCOB 11.6.2R(1)(a).

87 NCCPA, ss 118(2), 119(2), 123(2), 124(2), 131(2), 133(2), 141(2), 142(2), 146(2), 147(2), 154(2), 156(2).

88 The assessment must be based on 'reasonable inquiries' about the consumer's financial situation and 'reasonable steps' to verify that situation: RG209.18. What is reasonable will depend on the circumstances: RG209.19. Factors relevant to scalability include the potential impact on the consumer of entering into the unsuitable credit contract; the complexity of the credit contract; the consumer's capacity to understand the credit contract; whether the consumer is an existing customer or a new customer: RG209.22.

89 MCOB 11.6.2R(1)(a) and 11.6.2R(2).

90 Net of income tax and national insurance: MCOB 11.6.5R(2)(a).

91 MCOB 11.6.5R(2)(b)(i). This is the customer's credit and other contractual commitments which will continue after the mortgage contract is entered into: MCOB 11.6.10R(1).

92 MCOB 11.6.5R(2)(b)(ii). This comprises expenditure for housekeeping (food and washing), gas, electricity and other heating, water, telephone, council tax, buildings insurance, ground rent and services charge for leasehold properties, and essential travel: 11.6.10R(2).

93 MCOB 11.6.5R(2)(b)(ii). These costs are the household expenditure which is hard to reduce and gives a basic quality of life beyond the absolute essential expenditure comprising 'basic essential expenditure': MCOB 11.6.10R(3).

94 MCOB 11.6.5R(3). On the circumstances in which interest-only mortgages are now permitted, see Section 3.4.5.

In practice, though, the affordability assessment demanded of Australian mortgage lenders may be no less rigorous. Given the potentially grave impact of entering into an unsuitable mortgage contract (loss of the consumer's home), such affordability assessments must surely lie at the top of the scale. Furthermore, the Federal Court has recently confirmed that the affordability assessment does import certain *minimum* requirements:

> Assessing whether there is a real chance of a person being able to comply with his or her financial obligations under the contract requires, at the very least, a sufficient understanding of the person's income and expenditure. It is axiomatic that 'reasonable inquiries' about a customer's financial situation must include inquiries about the customer's current income and living expenses. The extent to which further information and additional inquiries may be needed ... will be a matter of degree in each particular case.[95]

In light of the decision, ASIC amended the Guidance in November 2014 to distinguish between inquiries that are 'generally' required[96] and those that may, depending on the circumstances, be required.[97] The inquiries which are 'generally' required are those about the current amount and source of the consumer's income or benefits, the extent of the consumer's fixed expenses (such as rent, repayment of existing debts, child support and recurring expenses such as insurance) and the consumer's variable living expenses (such as food and utilities) and drivers of variable expenses, such as dependants and any particular or unusual circumstances. Despite the use of different terminology, there are broad similarities with the MCOB requirements. Like MCOB, ASIC's Guidance draws a distinction, albeit not perhaps quite so explicitly, between living expenditure which is absolutely essential or hard to reduce and other living expenditure. 'Discretionary expenditure',[98] is listed as a matter about which inquiries may, depending on the circumstances, be required, implying that only expenditure which can be characterised as 'non-discretionary', must 'generally' be taken into account.

The new MCOB rules recognise the practical difficulties of gathering accurate and comprehensive information from consumers about their expenditure. Lenders are therefore permitted to use statistical or modelled data[99] instead of information about the *actual* basic essential expenditure and basic quality-of-living costs of the customer's household.[100] In contrast, the Australian regime, while recognising the utility of 'benchmarks' in assessing affordability, particularly as a means of testing the reliability of the information the consumer has provided and identifying

95 *ASIC v Cash Store Pty Ltd (in liq)* [2014] FCA 926 per Davies J at [42].

96 RG209.32. These are inquiries as to the current amount and source of the consumer's income or benefits, the extent of the consumer's fixed expenses (such as rent, repayment of existing debts, child support and recurring expenses such as insurance) and the consumer's variable living expenses (such as food and utilities) and drivers of variable expenses, such as dependents and any particular or unusual circumstances.

97 RG209.33.

98 Take-away food, alcohol, tobacco and gambling are all listed as examples of 'discretionary expenditure': RG209.33(a).

99 Appropriate to the composition of the customer's household.

100 MCOB 11.6.12R(3).

situations where further inquiries may be warranted, does not allow consideration of the consumer's actual expenditure to be dispensed with.[101]

This raises a nice question about the situation in which the basic living expenditure is abnormally high but there is realistically significant scope to reduce that expenditure so as to render the mortgage affordable. In permitting the use of modelled or statistical data about expenditure, the UK approach clearly allows for the mortgage to be assessed as affordable in such a case. At first glance the Australian approach might appear to preclude consideration of the scope for reduction of expenditure. The Guidance, however, suggests that provided the assessment is not based purely on the 'benchmark' and inquiries are made as to whether the consumer is prepared and reasonably able to reduce their expenses in the future, the mortgage contract may be assessed as affordable.[102]

Central to the Australian affordability assessment is the notion of 'substantial hardship';[103] the contract is unaffordable if the consumer will only be able to comply with their financial obligations under it by reducing their expenditure to a point where they will suffer substantial hardship. The notion is not explicitly referred to in the MCOB rules, but it is implicit in the requirement that expenditure that is 'absolutely essential' or 'hard to reduce' must be taken into account.[104] The NCCPA leaves the concept of 'substantial hardship' undefined and ASIC has refused to provide any definitive formulation, preferring to leave it to the courts to develop and clarify the concept through case law.[105] Importantly, the Guidance provides that, generally, consumers should be able to make the repayments from income rather than equity in an asset.[106] Specifically, 'substantial hardship' is legislatively presumed where the consumer could only comply with their financial obligations by selling their principal place of residence.[107] In such situations, the onus is on the lender to show that the credit contract is nonetheless affordable. This position is broadly similar to that adopted by MCOB. Although MCOB does not require repayments to be made out of income, it does now expressly prohibit the formerly widespread practice of basing the affordability assessment on the equity in the property which is subject to the mortgage in question or expected rises in property prices.[108]

3.4.2 The impact of future changes

A factor identified in the MMR as contributing to the problem of unsustainable borrowing was a failure to take account of future changes of circumstances, particularly those relating to retirement. Given that just under one-fifth of all mortgages sold in

101 RG209.49; RG209.104.

102 RG 209.105.

103 NCCPA, ss 118(2), 119(2), 123(2), 124(2), 131(2), 133(2), 141(2), 142(2), 146(2), 147(2), 154(2), 156(2).

104 MCOB 11.6.5R(2)(b)(ii).

105 RG209.97. The Guidance does, however, provide a non-exhaustive list of potentially relevant factors to be taken into account in assessing whether the transaction is likely to result in substantial hardship: RG209.99–100.

106 RG209.107. Bridging loans and reverse mortgages are both given as examples of circumstances in which it might not be reasonable to expect payment out of income.

107 NCCPA, ss 118(3), 119(3), 123(3), 124(3), 131(3), 133(3), 141(3), 142(3), 146(2), 147(3), 154(3), 156(3).

108 MCOB 11.6.5R(1).

2007 would extend into retirement, this was a significant issue.[109] The new MCOB rules require lenders to take into account any actual or likely future changes to income or expenditure of which they are or should reasonably be aware from information obtained through the application process.[110] In particular, they are expected to take a 'prudent and proportionate' approach to assessing a customer's income beyond retirement. The closer the customer is to retirement the more robust must be the evidence of the level of post-retirement income, with lenders instructed to take a 'common sense view' when assessing information provided about the expected retirement date.[111] There is no statutory requirement in the Australian regime to take account of future changes, but the Guidance lists 'significant changes to the consumer's circumstances that are reasonably foreseeable' as a matter in respect of which inquiries might, depending on the circumstances, reasonably be required.[112] The changes which UK lenders are now required to factor in are not limited to changes in the *customer's* circumstances.[113] Significantly, the new rules have introduced an interest rate stress-test.[114] In all cases, lenders must take likely future interest rates over a minimum period of five years[115] into account.[116] If interest rates are likely to fall rather than rise or rise by less than 1 per cent during that period, the lender must nevertheless assume a minimum interest rate increase of 1 per cent.[117] The stress test will also be applied to second-charge mortgages from March 2016. This will involve stress-testing the second-charge mortgage itself as well as considering the effect of expected interest increases on mortgages secured by a higher priority charge over the property.[118] The Australian regime contains no such stress-testing requirement, but, again, foreseeable interest rate changes are a matter in respect of which it may be reasonable to require inquiries to be made.[119]

3.4.3 Credit-impaired consumers and debt consolidation

Although historically a relatively small part of both the Australian and UK markets, subprime mortgage lending poses particular regulatory challenges, as the US experience has shown. An impaired credit history has been identified as the strongest predictor of mortgage arrears and repossessions in the UK[120] and in both countries it is in the subprime sector that the lowest underwriting standards and poorest lending

109 Financial Services Authority, *Mortgage Market Review: Responsible Lending* (Consultation Paper, CP10/16, July 2010) exhibit 2.9.
110 MCOB 11.6.14R.
111 MCOB 11.6.15G(2).
112 RG209.33(f).
113 Account must be taken of known or likely future changes to the customer's income or expenditure of which the lender should reasonably be aware: MCOB 11.6.14R.
114 MCOB 11.6.5R(4).
115 Unless the interest rate is fixed for a period of five years or more or the duration of the mortgage contract is less than five years.
116 MCOB 11.6.18R(1).
117 MCOB 11.6.18R(3).
118 Financial Conduct Authority, *Implementation of the Mortgage Credit Directive and the New Regime for Second Charge Mortgages, Feedback to CP14/20 and Final Rules* (policy statement, PS15/9, March 2015) paras 41–45.
119 RG209.33(f).
120 Financial Services Authority, *Mortgage Market Review Data Pack, Supplement to PS12/16* (October 2012) exhibit 17.5.

practices have been found.[121] Borrowing for debt-consolidation purposes has also been recognised as a 'high-risk' characteristic. Although commonly marketed as a means of escaping a debt spiral, debt consolidation mortgages have the potential to lead the consumer further into the spiral when used inappropriately. Quite apart from the dangers inherent in transforming unsecured debts into debt secured against the consumer's home, the fact that the debts are now being repaid over a longer period will generally increase the total cost of the credit. Related to this is the problem that extending the period over which the debts are repaid normally results in a reduction in the consumer's monthly outgoings, which can lead to a newfound sense of prosperity and the temptation to take on more debt. Moreover, the consumer may not even use the mortgage advance for the stated debt-consolidation purpose, in which case the effect of the transaction is simply to facilitate the taking on of increased levels of debt, which may or may not be affordable, while increasing the overall cost of the original credit.

The Australian regime contains no targeted provisions on lending to credit-impaired consumers or for debt consolidation purposes; the Guidance simply lists the consumer's credit history[122] and the extent to which any debts are to be repaid from the credit advanced[123] as matters in respect of which inquiries may reasonably be required. In contrast, additional protection was considered necessary in the UK to mitigate the particularly high risks posed when these two characteristics are combined, that is when credit-impaired customers borrow for debt consolidation purposes. In such cases the lender is now required to do one of two things: take reasonable steps to ensure that, on completion of the transaction, the debts that were expected to be repaid out of the mortgage advance are in fact repaid where the loan would not be affordable if those debts were not repaid;[124] or assess affordability on the basis that the debts to be consolidated will not, in fact, be repaid out of the mortgage advance and factor their repayment in accordingly as 'committed expenditure'.[125] With the planned assimilation of second-charge lending into the wider mortgages regime in March 2016, the FCA has had to consider whether there are any features peculiar to second charges that might require a tailored approach. Second-charge lending is strongly associated with debt-consolidation, with around two-thirds of second-charge mortgage lending entered into for such purposes.[126] Given the particularly high incidence of payment problems in second-charge lending,[127] the FCA proposes extending this rule, which currently applies only to credit-impaired debt-consolidation mortgages, to all second-charge debt-consolidation mortgages, whether or not the customer is credit-impaired.[128]

121 Financial Services Authority, 'FSA Finds Poor Practice by Intermediaries and Lenders Within Sub-prime Market' (communication, July 2007) www.fsa.gov.uk/pages/Library/Communication/PR/2007/081.shtml accessed 15 January 2015; House of Representatives (n 29) para 3.27.

122 RG209.33(c).

123 RG209.33(b).

124 MCOB 11.6.16R(2). This can be done by the lender repaying the committed expenditure directly to the creditors concerned as a condition of granting the mortgage: MCOB 11.6.17G.

125 MCOB 11.6.16R(3).

126 Financial Conduct Authority, *Implementation of the Mortgage Credit Directive and the New Regime for Second Charge Mortgages* (Consultation Paper, CP 14/20, September 2014) para 3.12.

127 Around half of all second-charge mortgages went into arrears prior to the Crisis, with more than one-third going into arrears in the first year after origination: ibid annex 1, chart 7.

128 Ibid para 3.60–3.61. Financial Conduct Authority (n 118) paras 46–47.

3.4.4 Verifying income

A striking feature of the UK mortgage market leading up to the crisis was the growth in NIV mortgages. Between April 2005 and March 2010, income was not verified in 45 per cent of all new mortgages.[129] Only the United States and Ireland had a comparable proportion of NIV mortgages. In the so-called 'self-certification' mortgage, absence of any income verification was a product feature marketed by the lender, which charged a premium for the increased risk the arrangement posed. The self-certification mortgage had originated as a response to the problems faced by many self-employed customers in accessing mortgage credit, but over time it was routinely made available to employed customers. The obvious implication was that it was being used to facilitate unaffordable borrowing on the back of inflated statements of income. In contrast, the other type of NIV mortgage, the 'fast-tracked' mortgage, had originated as a *process* to be adopted in low-risk cases rather than as a *product*. If certain risk thresholds were met, such as a low LTV ratio or a high credit score, the lender might, at its discretion, process the application without requiring evidence of income. Although initially used only in low-risk cases, fast-tracking was increasingly applied to higher-risk categories of application. In 2007, 15 per cent of applications with an LTV of above 95 per cent and 40 per cent with an LTV of 85–90 per cent had not been income-verified.[130] According to FSA analysis, arrears rates can be 3–4 times higher for NIV mortgages than for income-verified mortgages.[131] In Australia, NIV mortgages never gained the foothold that they had in the UK market. Despite some evidence of an increase in 'low-doc' and 'no-doc' lending prior to the Crisis,[132] this remained a comparatively small proportion of the overall market.[133]

The previous MCOB rules had permitted self-certification where the lender considered it 'appropriate, having regard to the interests of the customer' and there were no reasonable grounds for doubting the information provided by the customer.[134] In reality, lenders began permitting self-certification whether or not the stated income and the reasons to self-certify were plausible.[135] Predictably, the industry argued that the proposal to ban NIV mortgages would have an adverse effect on the self-employed. The FSA insisted there was no reason why the self-employed or contract workers should not be able to verify their income, particularly bearing in mind the universal obligation to pay income tax; an irregular or fluctuating income flow did not equate to a 'non-verifiable' one.[136] It did, however, acknowledge that the self-employed would face delays in establishing a satisfactory track record of income and acquiring up-to-date evidence of income.[137]

129 *Mortgage Market Review: Responsible Lending* (n 109) exhibit 2.4.

130 Ibid exhibit 2.5. These figures include self-certification and fast-tracked mortgages.

131 *Mortgage Market Review* DP09/3 (n 20) para 4.53.

132 The Senate Economics References Committee (n 31) para 5.16; House of Representatives (n 29) paras 2.26–2.27.

133 'Low-doc' lending accounted for no more than 10 per cent of overall mortgage lending between 2004 and 2007: Australian Government, the Treasury (n 24) Table 2.

134 MCOB 11.3.2R (now deleted).

135 *Mortgage Market Review* DP 09/3 (n 20) para 4.52.

136 Ibid para 4.57.

137 *Mortgage Market Review: Proposed Package of Reforms* CP11/31 (n 77) para 3.103. For example, because of the time-lag that is common between the end of the trading year and the actual production of accounts.

The express prohibition on self-certification aside,[138] the new rules otherwise avoid a prescriptive approach to the issue of income verification with the type of evidence required being dependent on the particular circumstances.[139] Some attempt is made to address the concerns expressed in relation to self-employed customers, with MCOB suggesting that in such cases lenders may wish to consider using projections of future income where these form part of a credible business plan.[140] With the new rules in place for just over a year, it remains to be seen whether the income-verification requirement will really constitute the barrier to access for the self-employed that many in the industry have predicted. Turning to Australia, the NCCPA neither expressly permits nor prohibits NIV mortgages, but it is hard to imagine that relying solely on self-certification could ever constitute taking 'reasonable steps' to verify the consumer's financial situation. Certainly, this is the approach taken by the Financial Ombudsman Service, which has indicated that it considers verification of both employed and self-employed income as mandatory for the purposes of its jurisdiction in 'maladministration in lending' disputes.[141]

3.4.5 Interest-only mortgages

The MMR identified the interest-only mortgage as a particular source of concern. Interest-only mortgages became popular in the 1980s in the form of the endowment mortgage. This involved the customer making monthly interest payments as well as payments into an endowment policy over the life of the mortgage, which was assigned to the lender as security for repayment of the capital at the end of the mortgage term. Over time, lenders ceased to demand an assigned investment policy and began accepting a far wider range of strategies for repayment of the capital at the end of the mortgage term. With continuous appreciation in property prices from about 1998 onwards, sale of the mortgaged property itself came to be seen as an acceptable repayment strategy and lenders began assessing affordability on an interest-only basis. In a rising property market, interest-only mortgages thus became an increasingly popular means for consumers to extend their borrowing capacity. By 2007, such mortgages accounted for 33 per cent of the market. Significantly, only 25 per cent of those mortgages had a reported repayment vehicle in place.[142]

The problems associated with interest-only mortgage lending typically become apparent only at the end of the mortgage term. With an estimated 1.3 million interest-only mortgages in the UK worth £111 billion and due for repayment between 2012 and 2020,[143] the high proportion of those without an adequate repayment strategy in place is alarming. The new rules permit interest-only mortgages, where affordability may be assessed on an interest-only basis,[144] only where there is a

138 MCOB 11.6.8R(2).
139 MCOB 11.6.9G(2).
140 MCOB 11.6.9G(3).
141 Financial Ombudsman Service, 'Responsible Lending Conduct Obligations and Maladministration' (circular Issue 5, March 2011) www.fos.org.au/the-circular-5-home/responsible-lending-conduct-obligations-maladministration accessed 15 February 2015.
142 *Mortgage Market Review, Proposed Package of Reforms* CP 11/31 (n 76) exhibit 9.
143 *Mortgage Market Review Data Pack* (n 120) exhibit 11.25.
144 MCOB 11.6.48R.

clearly understood and credible repayment strategy in place.[145] Before entering into the mortgage, lenders are required to obtain evidence of the repayment strategy and satisfy themselves, as far as they are reasonably able at that point in time, that that strategy has the capacity to repay the capital.[146] If the repayment strategy requires the borrower to make regular payments out of income, those payments must be taken into account as 'committed expenditure' in the affordability assessment.[147]

Rather than defining an 'acceptable' repayment strategy, the rules leave it to lenders to assess the strategy on the basis of the individual circumstances of the consumer. The only express prohibition is on 'speculative' repayment strategies.[148] Regular deposits into a savings or investment product, periodic repayment of capital from irregular sources of income (such as bonuses or income from self-employment) and the sale of the customer's other assets are all listed as acceptable repayment strategies.[149] A particular focus of concern in interest-only lending was the widespread reliance on the sale of the mortgaged property as a repayment strategy. While not expressly prohibited, the rules do require lenders to proceed with particular caution where such a strategy is adopted. Where the property in question is the customer's main residence, the lender must consider whether the sale will realise sufficient funds for both repayment of capital (and, where applicable, any accrued interest) and the purchase of a cheaper property for the customer to reside in or the execution of any associated strategy.[150]

Obtaining evidence of an acceptable repayment strategy at the application stage of course provides no guarantee of its continued existence throughout the term of the mortgage. With this in mind, lenders must now also contact customers at least once during the term of the mortgage with a view to reviewing whether there is still a repayment strategy with the potential to repay the capital (and accrued interest, if applicable).[151] The rules recognise that customers cannot be forced to engage with the process and, in this situation, the lender discharges its obligations by making 'reasonable efforts' to contact the customer.[152] Concerns were expressed about the potential for mistreatment or exploitation of customers who are found not to have satisfactory repayment strategies in place, particularly in circumstances where they do not have the option of remortgaging to another lender. With this in mind, the FSA has reminded lenders of their continuing obligation to treat customers fairly.[153]

145 MCOB 11.6.41R(1)(a).
146 And any accrued interest where applicable: MCOB 11.6.41R(1)(b).
147 MCOB 11.6.48R. This is only the case if the lender chooses to assess affordability on an interest-only basis. If the lender assesses affordability on a capital-and-interest basis, then the cost of the repayment strategy obviously does not need to be included as 'committed expenditure'.
148 MCOB 11.6.41R(3). Although 'speculative' is not defined in MCOB, the FSA has explained that a speculative strategy is one 'where the borrower is reliant upon uncertain external events such as property price increases or an inheritance': FSA, *Mortgage Market Review: Feedback on CP11/31 and Final Rules* (position statement, PS12/16, October 2012) para 74. Both of these are listed in MCOB 11.6.46E as examples of repayment strategies that are unlikely to be acceptable.
149 MCOB 11.6.45G.
150 MCOB 11.6.46E(3).
151 MCOB 11.6.49R(2). This requirement does not apply where repayment is certain, such as in the case of a lifetime mortgage: MCOB 11.6.49R(1).
152 MCOB 11.6.49R(3).
153 MCOB 11.6.51G(2).

Although the requirement to review the repayment strategy applies only to mortgage contracts entered into on or after 26 April 2014, anxiety about the anticipated level of repayment problems in existing interest-only mortgages has brought into focus the potential conduct issues thrown up when interest-only mortgages reach maturity without satisfactory repayment strategies in place. After a period of consultation, the FCA issued Guidance on this subject in August 2013.[154]

While the NCCPA does not specifically address interest-only lending, the Explanatory Memorandum stressed that the assessment is concerned with the consumer's ability to meet '*all* the repayments, fees, charges and transaction costs of complying with the proposed credit contract'[155] 'over its entire term'.[156] It is implicit in this that the affordability assessment must involve consideration of the consumer's ability to make capital as well as interest repayments. Although the Guidance provides that repayments must *generally* be made out of income rather than equity in an asset, there is clearly some scope for lenders to accept alternative capital repayment strategies in interest-only mortgages.[157] Where an interest-only mortgage would otherwise be unaffordable, sale of the consumer's principal place of residence will effectively be presumed by sections 118(3) and 131(3) of the NCCPA to be an unacceptable repayment strategy.

As part of the wider concerns recently voiced by Australian regulators about higher-risk lending[158] and against a background of recent growth in interest-only mortgages,[159] ASIC announced a 'surveillance' into interest-only mortgages in December 2014 to ensure that consumers are not being provided with unsuitable loans that could leave them with unsustainable levels of debt.[160] Significantly, interest-only mortgages now account for a larger proportion of the market in Australia than at the height of the market in the UK, with the majority of interest-only mortgage lending extended to investors.[161] In August 2015, ASIC reported its findings of review of 11 lenders for the three-year period 2012–2014.[162] It uncovered a

154 See Financial Conduct Authority, *Finalised Guidance: Dealing Fairly with Interest-Only Mortgage Customers Who Risk Being Unable to Repay their Loan* (FG13/7, August 2013).

155 Revised Explanatory Memorandum (n 60) paras 3.69 and 3.139.

156 Ibid paras 3.74 and 3.149.

157 Puzzlingly, the statement in the Guidance that it may not always be a reasonable position to require repayment out of income applies only to preliminary assessments: RG209.107.

158 See Australian Prudential Authority, 'APRA Outlines Further Steps to Reinforce Sound Residential Mortgage Lending Practices' (media release, 9 December 2014) www.apra.gov.au/mediareleases/pages/14_30.aspx. The IMF has also expressed concerns about the risks posed by Australia's overheated property market. It has identified the growth of investor and interest-only loans focused on the Sydney market as a 'pocket of concern' and warned that, in the event of a sharp fall in house prices, bank capital levels are inadequate to prevent banks from making a very difficult macroeconomic situation worse: International Monetary Fund, *IMF Country Report* No 15/275 (September 2015).

159 Interest-only loans as a percentage of new housing loan approvals reached 42.5 per cent in the September quarter of 2014.

160 Australian Securities and Investments Commission, 'ASIC to Investigate Interest-Only Loans' (media release, 9 December 2014, 14-329MR) http://asic.gov.au/about-asic/media-centre/find-a-media-release/2014-releases/14–329mr-asic-to-investigate-interest-only-loans accessed 14 December 2014.

161 In the December 2014 quarter, 59 per cent of interest-only home loans were extended to investors and 41 per cent to owner-occupiers.

162 Australian Securities and Investments Commission, *Review of Interest-Only Home Loans* (REP 445, August 2015).

number of shortcomings in lenders' suitability assessments, both in terms of the affordability of the mortgage contract and the extent to which it meets consumers' requirements or objectives. In particular, in 40 per cent of the files reviewed, the affordability assessment had used payments that were artificially low because they were based on principal-and-interest repayments being made over the *full* term of the loan rather than the residual term of the loan remaining after the interest-only period.[163] Such a practice obviously poses particularly high risks to borrowers with longer interest-only periods. In 30 per cent of files, there was no evidence that the lender had considered whether the interest-only mortgage met the consumer's requirements and objectives, and in more than 20 per cent of cases lenders had relied on benchmarks rather than considering the consumer's actual living expenses.[164] In light of these findings, ASIC has indicated that it will be undertaking further surveillance, enforcement and other regulatory action in these areas.[165]

3.5 Assessing 'appropriateness'

A mortgage contract may be affordable but nonetheless unsuitable if it is inappropriate to the consumer's needs and circumstances or fails to meet their requirements and objectives. It may be that secured borrowing is not appropriate at all in the circumstances – for example where the borrower is advised to consolidate unsecured debt into mortgage debt in circumstances where reasonable rates of interest are available in respect of that unsecured debt. Alternatively, the particular features or terms of the mortgage contract may render it inappropriate in the circumstances. Common examples of inappropriate lending seen in the past include: lending more than the consumer wishes to borrow; selling a self-certification high-interest product to an employed consumer who can easily prove income and qualifies for a 'full-doc' lower-interest product; selling a consumer a mortgage product with an inappropriately long term, thereby increasing the overall interest charges paid; selling a consumer an interest-only mortgage to increase the total interest charges payable in circumstances where the consumer could easily manage a repayment mortgage; suggesting that the consumer re-mortgage with another lender in circumstances where they could have taken a further advance with their existing lender and avoided the fees and charges associated with re-mortgaging; and automatically rolling-up fees and charges into the loan where the customer could have afforded to pay those charges 'up-front'.

Both regimes recognise that the wide range of different consumers and products make a prescriptive approach to assessments of appropriateness unrealistic. In Australia the assessment must be based on 'reasonable' inquiries about the consumer's requirements and objectives. In *ASIC v Cash Store Pty Ltd (in liq)*, the failure to make reasonable inquiries about the consumer's requirements and objectives was found to have rendered the subsequent assessment inadequate.[166] ASIC suggests that the consumer's capacity to understand the credit contract is of particular relevance to the scalability of the obligation to make inquiries about the consumer's

163 Ibid para 20.
164 Ibid.
165 Ibid para 36.
166 [2014] FCA 926.

requirements and objectives.[167] More inquiries are likely to be necessary where it is evident that the consumer has limited capacity to understand the contract, has conflicting objectives, is confused about their objectives or has difficulty articulating them, or there is an apparent mismatch between the consumer's objectives and the product being considered by the consumer.[168] The Explanatory Memorandum indicates that generally the minimum requirement for satisfying reasonable inquiries about the consumer's requirements and objectives will be those necessary to understand the purpose for which the credit is sought, determine whether the type, length, rate, terms, special conditions, charges and other aspects of the proposed contract meet this purpose, or put forward credit products that do match the consumer's purpose.[169] ASIC has stressed the context-dependent nature of the assessment of appropriateness, providing a long but non-exhaustive list of potentially relevant factors.[170]

The MCOB rules set out a minimum set of factors to be considered, in so far as relevant, when assessing whether the contract is appropriate to the needs and circumstances of the customer.[171] Additional requirements are imposed in respect of particular trouble-spots identified in the MMR. Debt-consolidation is one example. In such cases, the assessment must also involve consideration of the costs associated with increasing the period over which a debt is to be repaid, whether it is appropriate for the customer to secure a previously unsecured loan and, where the customer is known to have payment difficulties, whether it would be appropriate for the customer to negotiate an arrangement with his creditors rather than enter into a mortgage contract.[172]

167 RG 209.22: other potentially relevant factors include the potential impact on the consumer of entering into an unsuitable credit contract, the complexity of the credit contract and whether the consumer is an existing customer.

168 Ibid.

169 Revised Explanatory Memorandum (n 60) 3.68 and 3.139.

170 RG 209.122. These include the nature of the credit requested by the consumer, and the consumer's stated objectives in obtaining the credit; where the consumer has more than one requirement or objective, the relative importance of each to the consumer; if the credit is to purchase a specific item, the term of the credit relative to the likely useful life of the asset; the interest rate, fees and charges applying to the contract; the consumer's understanding of the proposed contract; the complexity of the contract and whether a more basic product could meet the consumer's needs; if other expenses, such as premiums for insurance relating to the contract, are to be financed, whether the consumer is aware of this and accepts the additional costs of these expenses being financed; whether the consumer will need to finance a large final payment under the contract; and in relation to switching, the extent to which switching to the new contract will benefit the consumer.

171 These are the extent to which the customer's requirements fit within the lenders' eligibility requirements; whether an interest-only mortgage, repayment mortgage or a combination of the two is appropriate for the customer; the appropriateness of the particular term of the proposed mortgage contract for the customer; the appropriateness of the customer having stability in the amount of the required payments, especially having regard to the impact of significant future interest rate changes; the appropriateness of payments being minimised at the outset; whether it is appropriate for the customer to make early repayments; the appropriateness of any other features of the mortgage contract; whether the mortgage contract is appropriate based on the information provided by the customer about his credit history; the appropriateness of the customer paying any associated fees or charges up front rather than adding them to the sum advanced.

172 MCOB 4.7A.15R.

3.6 Buy-to-let mortgages

The Mortgage Credit Directive, which was adopted in February 2014, applies to all consumer mortgages. However, the UK has taken advantage of an exemption in the Directive which allows Members States not to apply its requirements to buy-to-let mortgage activity, provided they have an appropriate framework for this type of activity in place from 21 March 2016. Part 3 of the Mortgage Credit Directive Order 2015 lays down conduct standards based on the Directive which will apply to firms conducting broking, advisory or lending activity with buy-to-let consumers. The FCA will be responsible for authorising, supervising and, where necessary, taking action against such firms. These conduct standards include a requirement that prior to entering into a buy-to-let mortgage, firms undertake a thorough assessment of creditworthiness, taking appropriate account of factors relevant to verifying the prospect of the borrower meeting its obligations under that contract.[173] In particular, the assessment must not rely predominantly on the value of the property exceeding the amount of the credit or on the assumption that the property will increase in value.[174] It must be based on information that is 'necessary, sufficient and proportionate', including in particular: any values provided to the creditor as part of its assessment of the property; typical rental levels and rental demands within the property's locality; the impact of future interest rate rises, rental voids and rental arrears, and the ability of the borrower to meet payments should such pressure arise; and typical letting costs.[175]

3.7 Enforcing the responsible lending obligations

The primary means of enforcing the responsible lending obligations in both Australia and UK is, of course, action by the regulator, but both regimes recognise the value of private law redress as an enforcement mechanism. The Australian regime, in fact, prioritises the compensation of consumers over civil penalties.[176]

3.7.1 Public enforcement

Under the NCCPA, the 'most serious, "moral", economic and social harm'[177] of assisting with, suggesting or entering into an unsuitable contract constitute criminal offences,[178] although ASIC can instead opt for a civil penalty.[179] The maximum criminal penalty is 100 penalty units or two years' imprisonment or both. The maximum civil penalty is 2,000 penalty units. Breaches of the other responsible

173 Mortgage Credit Directive Order 2015, article 10(1).
174 Ibid article 10(3).
175 Ibid article 12(1).
176 NCCPA, s 181.
177 Revised Explanatory Memorandum (n 60) para 3.111.
178 Suggesting or assisting a consumer to enter into an unsuitable credit contract (s 123(6)); suggesting or assisting a consumer to apply for an increase to the credit limit under an unsuitable credit contract (s 123(6)); suggesting a consumer remain in an unsuitable credit contract (s 124(6)); entering into an unsuitable credit contract (s 133(6)); increasing the credit limit under an unsuitable credit contract (s 133(6)).
179 ss 123(1), 124(1) and 133(1).

lending obligations[180] attract civil penalties only.[181] Also available are administrative sanctions in the form of cancellation or suspension of a licence[182] or the imposition of licence conditions.[183] In extremely serious cases, banning orders are also available.[184] Another further option is an infringement notice.[185] This allows ASIC to impose penalties without going to court, making it a suitable response in cases of minor infringements.

In the UK context, the FCA has a wide range of disciplinary tools at its disposal, including the power to withdraw[186] or suspend a firm's authorisation,[187] censure firms through public statements,[188] impose financial penalties[189] and seek injunctions[190] and restitution orders.[191] Since 1 March 2014, section 234C of the FSMA has permitted designated consumer bodies to make a complaint to the FCA where a feature, or features, of the market is or appears to be significantly damaging or harming the interests of consumers. The Financial Ombudsman Service Ltd (FOS) is also authorised to make a reference to the FCA under section 234D where there has been a regular failure of firms to comply with applicable requirements to the detriment or possible detriment of consumers. In each case, the FCA has 90 days to decide how to respond[192] and it now has power to impose a consumer redress scheme[193] as well as sanctions.

3.7.2 Private law redress

In Australia, sections 177, 178 and 179 of the NCCPA provide private law remedies in respect of contraventions of civil penalty provisions or the commission of offences under the NCCPA.[194] Under section 177 the court can grant an injunction in respect of existing or future breaches. Section 178 gives the court power to award compensation to a person who suffers loss or damage as a result of the breach. Section 179 confers significant remedial discretion, allowing the court to make such order as it considers appropriate to compensate the plaintiff, either in whole or part, for loss or damage suffered or likely to be suffered, or to prevent or reduce that loss or damage suffered. The court can, among other things, vary the contract or declare it

180 For example, providing credit assistance without making the requisite inquiries and verification or preliminary assessment (s 115); failure on the part of the credit provider to make the requisite inquiries and verification or suitability assessment (s 149); failing to assess as unsuitable a credit contract which is unsuitable (credit assistance provider – s 118(1); credit provider – s 131(1)).

181 The standard of proof is, of course, lower in an action for a civil penalty than in criminal proceedings.

182 NCCPA, ss 55 and 56.

183 NCCPA, ss 45 and 46.

184 NCCPA, ss 79–85.

185 NCCPA, s 331.

186 FSMA, s 55J.

187 FSMA, s 206A.

188 FSMA, s 205.

189 FSMA, s 206.

190 FSMA, s 380.

191 FSMA, ss 382, 383, 384.

192 FSMA, s 234E.

193 FSMA, s 404.

194 ASIC can also apply for any of these remedies on behalf of consumers: NCCPA, ss 177, 178(2)(a) and 179(3)(a).

void or unenforceable in whole or part. The Explanatory Memorandum to the Bill proposed the following approach to providing a remedy for irresponsible lending under section 179:

> Samuel was an electrician who earned $1,200 a week. He spent $600 a week on expenses. He went to a lender to get a home loan of $200,000. Samuel needed a loan with an average interest rate that he could pay off over the medium term. Instead, he was offered a loan for $500,000 with a high fixed interest rate and therefore repayments that he could not readily afford.
>
> As he was experiencing hardship, Samuel sought an injunction against the lender collecting his mortgage repayments. Samuel then sought compensation for the loss and damage he had suffered for being put into an unsuitable loan. The court, under section 179, ordered the lender to reduce the overall debt Samuel owed to the lender commensurate with what he would have owed if he had been provided with a loan that was *not unsuitable* minus:
>
> - the amount he had already paid to the lender; and
> - the amount in compensation for any loss and damages he suffered as a result of getting the *unsuitable* product.
>
> This recognised that Samuel received a benefit from the initial credit provided, but that he experienced loss and damage from being put into the unsuitable loan.[195]

Puzzlingly, this appears to suggest, contrary to the established practice of the Australian Ombudsmen, FOS and Credit Ombudsman Service Ltd (COSL),[196] that the consumer will obtain a windfall to the extent that he is provided with unaffordable credit (here to the extent of $300,000). However, any compensation or order in relation to loss or damage can be mitigated (including limiting the amount of compensation) if the consumer has made a false or misleading representation in order to obtain the credit, to take into account what is 'practically just in the circumstances'.[197]

The UK regime places a much more limited remedial arsenal at the courts' disposal. Section 138D(2) of the FSMA gives private persons a right of action in damages where they can demonstrate loss as a result of a contravention of FCA rules, including those contained in the MCOB.[198] Section 138E(2) of the FSMA

195 Revised Explanatory Memorandum (n 60) para 4.91.

196 See Financial Ombudsman Service, 'Responsible Lending Conduct Obligations and Maladministration' (circular, Issue 5, March 2011) www.fos.org.au/the-circular-5-home/responsible-lending-conduct-obligations-maladministration/ accessed 14 January 2015; Credit Ombudsman Service, 'Responsible Lending', (position statement, Issue 5), paras 15.1–15.5 www.cio.org.au/cosl/assets/File/Position%20Statement%205%281%29.pdf accessed 14 January 2015.

197 Revised Explanatory Memorandum (n 60) para 4.92.

198 s 138D(2) FSMA. Where the mortgage is a second-charge mortgage, a remedy is currently available under s 140B of the Consumer Credit Act 1974 if the court is satisfied that the relationship between the creditor and the debtor arising out of the mortgage agreement is unfair to the debtor (s 140A). Section 140A is potentially broad enough to provide a remedy in respect of irresponsible lending. Section 140B gives the court broad remedial discretion. This avenue for redress will be lost when second-charge lending is subsumed within the MCOB regime in March 2016.

makes clear, however, that such a contravention does not make the transaction void or unenforceable. Private law claims for irresponsible lending throw up particular remedial difficulties. Causation may well pose problems in claims for damages and courts will need to be careful that the remedies they fashion are not seen to create a 'defaulter's charter' by absolving consumers of *all* responsibility for their borrowing choices.[199] In reality, in both countries the vast majority of complaints about unaffordable or unsuitable mortgage lending[200] will be dealt with by the Ombudsmen.[201] In *Thakker v Northern Rock (Asset Management) plc*[202] the English High Court had to consider the rather different question of whether a breach of the MCOB rules could defeat a lender's right to possession. The court accepted that the defendant may well have a good counter-claim for damages under the predecessor provision to section 138D(2) of the FSMA[203] for the bank's breaches of the MCOB rules, but held that this would not defeat the bank's right to possession.[204] Given that UK claims management companies are now focusing their attention on what they are keen to portray as 'the mortgage mis-selling scandal', judicial consideration of damages awards under section 138D(2) for contraventions of the MCOB's responsible lending obligations may not, however, be far off. It is already clear from case law applying the predecessor provision[205] in other contexts that causation may present a stumbling block for some mortgagors.[206] The FSA had, in fact (unsuccessfully), advocated amending the provision in 2011 so as to disapply the rules of causation and remoteness to ensure that consumers receive 'full redress'.

The UK's FOS undoubtedly has more latitude in dealing with mortgage mis-selling complaints. Complaints are to be determined on the basis of what is, in the opinion of the Ombudsman, fair and reasonable in all the circumstances of the case. Although the relevant law must be taken into account, it may also be departed from provided this is explained in the opinion and reasons given.[207] This extends to the principles of causation.[208] The approach of FOS in cases alleging unaffordable or unsuitable mortgage lending is already quite well established. FOS has made clear that where the consumer has contributed to the problem, any redress provided

199 John Pottow, 'Private Liability for Reckless Consumer Lending' (2007) University of Illinois Law Review 405, 441–476.

200 Or advice or assistance.

201 In Australia, all licensees are required to be a member of an approved external dispute resolution (EDR) scheme. Currently there are two approved schemes, the Financial Ombudsman Service Ltd and the Credit and Investments Ombudsman(formerly known as the Credit Ombudsman Service Limited). In the UK, the Financial Ombudsman Service was set up under Part XVI of FSMA to provide a quick, cheap and informal process for the resolution of disputes between consumers of financial services and financial services firms regulated by the FSA (now the FCA).

202 [2014] EWHC 2107.

203 s 150 FSMA.

204 Although the counter-claim could be relevant to the court's discretionary powers to adjourn proceedings or stay execution or postpone an order for possession under s 36 Administration of Justice Act 1970 and s 8 Administration of Justice Act 1973.

205 The previous s 150.

206 It was confirmed in *Rubenstein v HSBC Bank plc* [2012] EWCA Civ 1184 that the normal rules of causation and remoteness will apply.

207 *R (on the application of Heather Moor & Edgecomb Ltd) v Financial Ombudsman Service* [2008] EWCA Civ 642.

208 *R (on the application of IFG Financial Services) v Financial Ombudsman Service* [2005] EWHC 1153.

will reflect the contribution of *both* parties.[209] It has also acknowledged that realising the remedial objective of putting the consumer back in the position they would have been in had appropriate advice been given or appropriate lending practices followed will not always be straightforward, given the complexities of the individual circumstances of consumers.[210] For one thing, there is the problem of establishing the counterfactual, for another there is the problem of balancing any benefits that the consumer has received against the detriment suffered.

The FOS has been under an obligation to publish its determinations since 1 April 2013. A significant number of mortgage complaints that have been upheld have concerned the unsuitable provision of interest-only mortgages.[211] In the majority of these cases, the interest-only mortgage was unsuitable for the consumer because there was no credible capital repayment vehicle in place and the lender or intermediary had failed to take that consideration into account when assessing suitability. In most of the cases, the consumer had not requested an interest-only mortgage, could have afforded a repayment mortgage and there was no other basis for concluding that an interest-only mortgage was more suitable for the consumer than a repayment mortgage. The approach of the Ombudsman in providing relief in this type of case has therefore been to put the consumer in the position they would have been in had suitable advice been given; in other words, had the mortgage been set up on a repayment basis.[212] The starting point is therefore to calculate the difference between the current balance of the mortgage and what the balance of the mortgage would have been had it been set up on a repayment basis. Strictly speaking, of course, an award of compensation in this measure over-compensates the consumer as they have made a saving by virtue of having made lower monthly mortgage repayments. Nonetheless, in some cases the Ombudsman has applied something akin to a change-of-position defence, typically concluding that it would not be fair to take those savings into account as they are likely to have been swallowed up by the consumer's day-to-day living expenditure.[213] The award is, however, generally reduced to take into account any fault that can be attributed to the consumer for failing to appreciate that the mortgage had been set up on an interest-only basis or the implications of this. The degree of fault and the extent of the reduction will depend on the circumstances of the case. Of particular relevance are the adequateness and timing of explanations given by the lender or intermediary about the nature of an interest-only mortgage and the implications of not having a credible capital repayment vehicle in place and any other circumstances that should have alerted the consumer to the fact that the mortgage had been set up on an interest only basis.[214]

209 Financial Ombudsman Service, 'Speech by Tony Boorman, Decisions Director and Principal Ombudsman at the Council of Mortgage Lenders' Complaints-Handling Seminar' (12 March 2008) www.financial-ombudsman.org.uk/news/speech/CML_TB.html accessed 12 December 2014.

210 Ibid.

211 See, for example, Complaint Ref DRN9273265; Complaint Ref DRN6680014; Complaint Ref DRN6177248; Complaint Ref DRN0220473; Complaint Ref DRN1984867; Complaint Ref DRN7379010; Complaint Ref DRN8943586; Complaint Ref DRN2638654.

212 See, for example, Complaint Ref DRN0220473.

213 See, for example, Complaint Ref DRN7379010; Complaint Ref DRN0220473.

214 See, for example, Complaint Ref DRN1038406.

4 Apples and oranges?

While many of the same trends were observable in both mortgage markets in the run-up to the Crisis, the relaxation of lending standards that resulted from competition from non-deposit-taking institutions did not occur on the same scale in Australia as in the UK. The tail of poor lending practices in Australia was very much shorter than that identified in the UK and was confined largely to the very small 'non-conforming' sector of the market that was the preserve of non-deposit-taking institutions. In particular, neither the NIV mortgage (which accounted for nearly half of all UK mortgage sales at the height of the market in 2007) nor the exceptionally high LTV ratios witnessed in the UK ever became features of the Australian market. While poor lending practices were a particular problem in the very high volume of interest-only mortgage lending in the UK in the run-up to the Crisis, this is a much more recent phenomenon in Australia, with interest-only lending increasingly sharply since 2012. The introduction of the responsible lending obligations in the NCCPA 2009 was therefore more of a pre-emptive strike than a response to the type of real and relatively widespread problems uncovered in the UK by the FSA in its MMR.

As a regime tailored specifically to mortgage lending, the MCOB rules explicitly address those problems. The rules impose prescriptive minimum requirements in relation to assessments of affordability, and permit interest-only mortgages (where affordability may be assessed on an interest-only basis) only where there is a clearly understood and credible repayment strategy in place. Lenders are also required to contact interest-only mortgage customers at least once during the term of the mortgage for the purposes of reviewing the continued existence of a realistic repayment strategy. Execution-only sales are now permitted only in extremely narrow circumstances, with the result that full assessments of both affordability and appropriateness must be carried out in nearly every case. Non-income-verified mortgages are expressly prohibited. Additional protections apply where credit-impaired customers borrow for debt-consolidation purposes. With a view to preventing such borrowers being led deeper into a debt spiral, lenders are required to do one of two things: take reasonable steps to ensure that when the transaction is completed the debts that were expected to be repaid out of the mortgage advance are, in fact, repaid if the loan would not be affordable if those debts were not repaid, or assess affordability on the basis that the debts to be consolidated will not, in fact, be paid out of the mortgage advance.

The regulation of mortgage lending in Australia is subsumed within the more generic NCCPA regime. Most of the particular trouble-spots specifically targeted in the UK regime, such as interest-only mortgages, non-income verified mortgages and lending to credit-impaired borrowers for debt consolidation purposes, are not explicitly addressed by the NCCPA. The rather more abstract legal requirements of the NCCPA which impose duties on both lenders and intermediaries to undertake assessments of affordability and appropriateness as fleshed out in ASIC's Guidance may well provide as high a level of protection as the MCOB's more prescriptive requirements. Ultimately, though, the correct interpretation of the NCCPA's requirements is a question for the courts. One obvious question is the extent to which the provisions impose mandatory minimum requirements. The Federal Court has recently confirmed that the affordability assessment does, indeed, import some minimum requirements applicable in all cases.[215] One clear difference between the two regimes relates to the balance of responsibility between credit providers and intermediaries. As Pearson and Batten have observed, the Australian approach:

> [M]akes licensees responsible for each other as all are held to the same standard. This interlocking of responsibility of credit providers, credit assistants and intermediaries for each other is a fetter on any impulse towards dealing with those that are unlicensed and condoning practices not sanctioned by law.[216]

In contrast, the MCOB rules have put it beyond doubt that the ultimate responsibility, at least for assessments of affordability, rests with the lender.

215 *ASIC v Cash Store Pty Ltd (in liq)* [2014] FCA 926.
216 Gail Pearson and Richard Batten, *Understanding Australian Consumer Credit Law* (CCH 2010).

9 Sorting the sheep from the wolves in sheep's clothing

Defining Community Development Finance Institutions as distinct from fringe lenders in efforts to address financial exclusion

Therese Wilson[1]

1 Introduction

This chapter concerns one response to the problem of financial exclusion in Australia, namely support for the work of Community Development Finance Institutions (CDFIs). This support has included public funding, and it is therefore important that the criteria for eligibility for funding as a CDFI are well defined. Such clarity of definition, which has to date been lacking, will help to ensure that public expenditure is appropriately targeted to achieve the best outcomes in terms of addressing financial exclusion.

A report measuring the extent of financial exclusion in Australia defines financial exclusion as follows: 'Financial exclusion exists where individuals lack access to appropriate and affordable financial services and products; the key services and products are a transaction account, general insurance and a moderate amount of credit.'[2]

Implicit in this definition is recognition of the need to be able to access basic financial products in the Australian social context. This is supported by the use of the word *appropriate*, although I would suggest that the question of social context is crucial to any definition of financial exclusion and should be explicitly incorporated into it. By this I mean that what is regarded as appropriate, and in fact necessary, access to a financial service or product in one social context will be different in another. This has been recognised by the European Commission, which defines financial exclusion as involving people's difficulties in accessing 'financial services and products in the mainstream market that are appropriate to their needs and enable them to lead a normal social life in the society in which they belong'.[3]

1 This chapter is based on papers delivered at the International Association of Consumer Law conference at the University of Sydney and the Consumers Credit and the Law Symposium at the University of Queensland in June 2013; however, it was developed and completed during my visit at the European University Institute in Florence as a Visiting Fellow in November and December 2013. I would like to sincerely thank the Head of the Law Department at the EUI, Professor Hans-Wolfgang Micklitz, for the opportunity to visit at the EUI, and for his considerable support and encouragement.

2 Chris Connolly, 'Measuring Financial Exclusion in Australia' (Centre for Social Impact for National Australia Bank 2013).

3 European Commission, 'Financial Services Provision and the Prevention of Financial Exclusion' (Directorate-General for Employment, Social Affairs and Equal Opportunities, Inclusion, Social Policy Aspects of Migration, Streamlining of Social Policies, European Commission 2008).

When taking into account the social context in Australia, where it is expected that people will be able to access at least small amounts of credit from time to time in order to meet, for example, emergency bills or expenses that arise over and above *normal* expenses, then a lack of access to appropriate and affordable credit products is indicative of not only financial exclusion, but also social exclusion. Social exclusion might be manifest in such outcomes as an inability to purchase suitable clothing or pay for transportation to attend a job interview, an inability to purchase a computer on which a child can complete school homework tasks, an inability to replace a broken washing machine or refrigerator or an inability to generally participate in social activities.[4]

The latest research shows that 17.7 per cent of the Australian adult population (equating to 3,213,519 people) were either fully or severely excluded from access to appropriate financial products in 2012. The three financial products to which access is measured in these statistics are a transaction account, general insurance and a moderate amount of credit.[5] Fully excluded people had no access to any of these products and severely excluded people had access to only one, which in most cases would likely be a transaction account, given that a bank account is required for the receipt of welfare payments in Australia. Access to credit is measured in this study by reference to access to a mainstream credit card. This is clearly not a perfect measure; however, the authors of the study note that 'the rate of credit card ownership tracks the general rate of mainstream credit use in Australia very closely'.[6] Those most affected by financial exclusion in Australia are those on low incomes, described as the 'working poor', earning $25,000 or less per annum, and also those people born in non-English-speaking countries.[7] In this way, those who are most vulnerable and disadvantaged have that vulnerability and disadvantage entrenched by a lack of access to appropriate and affordable financial products.

CDFIs are a form of social enterprise which exist for the social purpose of addressing financial exclusion through the provision of credit and other financial products and services to financially excluded individuals, community sector organisations and social enterprises. They have been described as organisations that 'have a primary mission of improving economic conditions for low-income individuals and communities'.[8]

While seeking to achieve their social purpose, unlike more welfare-based models of credit and financial service delivery such as no-interest loans and low-interest loans,[9] CDFIs seek to achieve financial sustainability – that is, to fund their activities at least to some extent through generating their own income.

The quest for financial sustainability in the CDFI sector is driven by a concern regarding the unreliable nature of public funding, given that government funding is always dependent upon the will of the government of the day. This has particularly

4 Chant Link & Associates, 'A Report on Financial Exclusion in Australia' (Australia and New Zealand Banking Group Ltd 2004) 94; Valerie Ayres-Wearne and Janet Palafox, *NILS Small Loans: Big Changes – The Impacts of No Interest Loans on Households* (Good Shepherd Youth and Family Service 2005).

5 Connolly (n 2) 6.

6 Ibid 9.

7 Ibid 19.

8 Lehn Benjamin, Julia Sass Rubin and Sean Zielenbach, 'Community Development Financial Institutions: Current Issues and Future Prospects' (2004) 26(2) Journal of Urban Affairs 177, 178.

9 Good Shepherd Microfinance, *2014 Annual Report: A Life Changing Journey*, (Report, Good Shepherd Microfinance, 2014).

been felt recently by the CDFI sector in the UK, during a period of reduced public funding.[10]

Pursuing financial sustainability necessarily involves a focus on profitability, which arguably might lead to a failure to remain focused on social purpose. This has been described as 'mission drift' and can compromise the CDFI's ability to achieve its social purpose.[11] Any public funding should focus on organisations that have remained true to their social purpose, achieving the appropriate balance between sustainability and mission. Where mission drift has been too great, or an organisation never truly operationalised a social mission in the first place, then it is difficult to justify the expenditure of public funds to support such an organisation.

The question, then, is: what distinguishes CDFIs from organisations bearing more resemblance to the arguably exploitative fringe credit provider model?

Fringe credit providers, or fringe lenders, have been described as:

> Alternative credit providers in the business of providing personal credit, including to those people excluded from access to credit from mainstream financial institutions such as banks, but at high cost. Credit may take the form of payday loans defined as short term loans designed to tide the borrower over until payday, or may involve slightly longer term micro loans or non-payday loans.[12]

While both CDFIs and fringe credit providers seek to *fill a gap* left by mainstream financial service providers not meeting a market demand, having a clearly articulated social mission or purpose that directs the organisation's activities seems to be a crucial point of distinction as between the two types of organisations. Recent changes to consumer credit regulation in Australia, which will be canvassed below, should in theory reduce any of the harms previously associated with financial services provided by fringe lenders; however, the distinction between CDFIs and fringe lenders is still important. While not arguing that the pursuit of profit is in and of itself a bad thing, I will argue that receiving services from an entity that has a social purpose – that of addressing financial exclusion – as its very *raison d'être*, is likely to lead to better outcomes for financially excluded people and organisations than receiving those services from a purely profit-driven entity.

I acknowledge that there will not always be a clear distinction between types of organisations, as there will undoubtedly be a range of organisations sitting across the spectrum between social purpose-driven and purely profit-driven models. Most importantly, however, when considering eligibility for funding, organisations that are primarily social purpose-driven will make profit sacrifices and incur costs in undertaking certain activities seen as necessary to fulfil their social mission, which it will be argued give rise to a need for funding and justify making external funding available to them. An example of such an activity is gratis financial counselling and budgeting assistance as part of a lengthy and comprehensive interview and application process.

10 GHK Consultants, 'The National Evaluation of Community Development Finance Institutions (CDFIs): An Action-Orientated Summary for the Sector' (Department for Business Innovation and Skills and the Cabinet Office, GHK Consultants 2010) 25.

11 Julia Rubin, 'Adaptation or Extinction? Community Development Loan Funds at a Crossroads' (2008) 30(2) Journal of Urban Affairs 191, 192.

12 National Australia Bank, 'Do You Really Want to Hurt Me? Exploring the Costs of Fringe Lending – A Report on the NAB Small Loans Pilot' (2010) 9.

This chapter will define and explore the roles of CDFIs and fringe credit providers, and will argue that while fringe credit providers might serve a useful social purpose when properly regulated, government funding should only be available to fund the activities of CDFIs, not fringe credit providers, or entities that sit closer on the spectrum of organisations to the for-profit fringe credit model than the mission-driven CDFI model. This is largely because CDFIs are social purpose-driven and engage in profit-sacrificing activities in order to achieve their social purpose, in this way justifying their need for external government or industry funding. The chapter will culminate in suggesting criteria for assessing eligibility for government funding as a CDFI. While a social impact measurement would be an obvious criterion, it will be rejected as one which is too difficult and costly for CDFIs to provide on a regular basis in a bid for funding. It will be suggested that evidence of both a clearly articulated social purpose and its operationalisation as a guiding principle within the organisation is an appropriate criterion.

2 The role of CDFIs

In discussing the appropriate recipients of funding allocated to CDFI activity, it is important to first understand what CDFIs are, what role they play and therefore what social purpose they serve, in addressing financial exclusion.

2.1 The importance of definition

CDFIs are a form of social enterprise which exist for the social purpose of addressing financial exclusion. They are recognised in the United Kingdom and United States and more recently in Australia.[13]

What does it mean to say that CDFIs are a form of social enterprise? There have been numerous attempts to define what a social enterprise is, but in essence it is a business with a social mission. The social mission is described as 'the core of what distinguishes social entrepreneurs from business entrepreneurs even from socially responsible businesses. For a social entrepreneur, the social mission is fundamental'.[14]

A social enterprise is a *business* because it strives for financial sustainability in order to avoid being fully dependent upon external funding. However, it must focus on achieving its social mission and if it cannot, then it has no reason for existing. Profitability must always be secondary to social purpose for a social enterprise such as a CDFI. As Dees writes,

> making a profit, creating wealth, or serving the desires of customers may be part of the model, but these are means to a social end, not the end in itself. Profit is not the gauge of value creation; nor is customer satisfaction; social impact is the gauge.[15]

13 Alison Plant and Sue Warth, 'Community Development Financial Institutions Pilot Evaluation' (Westwood Spice on behalf of the Department of Families, Housing, Community Services and Indigenous Affairs 2013) www.fahcsia.gov.au/sites/default/files/documents/02_2013/cdfi_evaluation_report_0.pdf accessed 5 May 2013.

14 J Gregory Dees, 'The Meaning of "Social Entrepreneurship"' (31 October 1998, revised 30 May 2001) 4 www.caseatduke.org/documents/dees_sedef.pdf accessed 5 May 2013.

15 Ibid.

The need for a clear social mission is also reflected in industry documents that refer to best practices for CDFIs, requiring that 'the CDFI has a clear, realistic, and compelling mission to guide its activities'.[16] The articulated 'foundational principles' for CDFIs include having a social purpose, aiming to 'deliver wealth creation and asset building into communities that are most disadvantaged or underserved' and focusing on 'addressing financial exclusion of individuals, social enterprises/ businesses, and community sector organisations'.[17]

By way of contrast, a conventional business will focus on profitability, and if it cannot operate profitably it will or should cease to exist. These different foci will obviously impact significantly on the different activities which a social business may undertake as compared with a conventional for-profit business.

As stated above, there are no doubt a variety of businesses sitting along the spectrum between social enterprises and conventional profit-focused enterprises, giving different levels of priority to their social mission as compared with profit making.[18] There is said to be an increasing boundary blurring between for-profit and not-for-profit organisations.[19] This can make it difficult to clearly define a social enterprise, and might make it difficult to ascertain which organisations should be eligible for certain government funding. Where it has been determined that CDFIs should be the recipients of government funding, on the basis of their ability to have a positive social impact by addressing financial exclusion, there needs to be a model for identifying those organisations that should be classified as CDFIs and that should appropriately receive such government funding. Social impact itself can be difficult to assess, as will be discussed below, and so it will be argued that the identifying model needs to be built on the different, but related, criteria of social mission focus and consequential resource need.

2.2 Addressing financial exclusion

A CDFI's social purpose or mission is to address financial exclusion, primarily as it pertains to a lack of access to appropriate credit, but also to such other financial services as are necessary to enable people to lead a 'normal' life in their social context.[20]

Financial exclusion affects a significant number of Australian adults.[21] There is a recognised link between financial exclusion and social exclusion, which involves

16 Mark Pinsky, 'Taking Stock: CDFIs Look Ahead After 25 Years of Community Development Finance' (Brookings Institution Center on Urban and Metropolitan Policy and Harvard University Joint Center for Housing Studies 2001) 15 www.community-wealth.org/_pdfs/articles-publications/cdfis/paper-pinsky.pdf accessed 5 May 2013, citing Margaret Lehr, *Best Practices for CDFIs: Key Principles for Performance* (National Community Capital Association 1998).

17 Plant and Warth (n 12) 36, citing Foresters Community Finance Limited, 'Ten Foundational Principles for Community Development Finance Institutions (CDFIs) in Australia' www.foresters.org.au/images/stories/publications/Foresters_10_founding_Principles_of_CDFIs.pdf accessed 5 May 2013.

18 See discussion in Johanna Mair and Ignasi Marti, 'Social Entrepreneurship Research: A Source of Explanation, Prediction, and Delight' (2006) 41 Journal of World Business 36, 38–39.

19 J Gregory Dees and Beth Battle Anderson, 'For-Profit Social Ventures' in Marilyn Kourilsky and William Walstad (eds), *Social Entrepreneurship* (Senate Hall Academic Publishing 2003) www.caseatduke.org/news/documents/DeesAndersonCASE.pdf 1 accessed 5 May 2013.

20 European Commission (n 3) 9; Chant Link & Associates (n 4) 120.

21 See discussion above, citing Connolly (n 2).

being unable to participate fully in society as a result of financial exclusion.[22] Financially and socially excluded individuals are at a higher risk of over indebtedness (through having to access high-cost credit as a result of being excluded from more affordable mainstream credit options), sometimes leading to mental health problems, violence and crime.[23] This in turn can have significant social consequences, including burdening public health and legal aid systems.[24]

In seeking to address financial exclusion, CDFIs engage in personal microfinance and microenterprise lending to individuals, as well as providing credit and other financial services to financially excluded community sector organisations and social enterprises.

There is some doubt as to whether CDFIs can achieve their social purpose without some external support. That is, due to their social purpose-driven natures, it is unlikely that CDFIs can be fully financially self-sustaining. Certainly the demise of Shorebank Corporation in the United States suggests a need for some ongoing government and industry investment. Shorebank was a community development bank whose mission was 'to provide well-designed, responsible credit and other financial products and services to lower income communities, businesses and consumers'.[25] In August 2010, Shorebank was closed by regulators and has since been purchased by Urban Partnership Bank. Its demise has been attributed in part to it 'living its mission' and focusing on its social purpose.[26] This raises interesting questions about the ability of CDFIs to remain true to their social purpose while also remaining commercially viable in the absence of ongoing government and industry subsidisation, and strengthens the case for government funding to support the social mission of CDFIs.

3 The role of fringe credit providers

Alternative or fringe credit providers arguably play a valuable social role in addressing financial exclusion by *filling a gap* left by mainstream credit providers. This may be even more arguable in circumstances where recent regulation appears to prohibit the activities that have underpinned the harms associated with fringe credit. Even so, organisations carrying on for-profit businesses without regard to social mission should not normally be candidates for government funding.

3.1 Filling a gap in the market

While the market for consumer credit would in general be described as a competitive market, this is not the case when it comes to the provision of financial

22 Chant Link & Associates (n 4) 94.

23 Department of Trade and Industry UK, *Fair, Clear and Competitive: The Consumer Credit Market in the 21st Century* (White Paper, 2003) 76; Georges Gloukoviezoff, 'The Link Between Financial Exclusion and Over-indebtedness' (Directorate-General Employment, Social Affairs and Equal Opportunity, European Commission 2007).

24 Department of Trade and Industry UK (n 22) 77–78.

25 Ellen Seidman, 'Testimony of Ellen Seidman, Director, Financial Services and Education Project' (Committee on Financial Services, United States House of Representatives, Washington, DC, 13 February 2008).

26 Rick Cohen, 'Understanding Shorebank: A Community Development Bank Passes' (*3BL Media*, 30 August 2010) http://3blmedia.com/theCSRfeed/Understanding-Shorebank accessed 2 March 2013.

services to low-income Australians. A gap in financial service provision to those on low incomes seems to have arisen as a result of mainstream lenders pursuing the most profitable customers and perceiving the low-income market as a risky and unprofitable one.[27] This is a problem that has been recognised internationally, as have the serious social and economic consequences of the problem. The World Bank has referred to 'the lack of access to finance as a critical mechanism for generating persistent income inequality'.[28] In Europe, the Charter of Fundamental Rights of the European Union has recognised a right of access to 'services of general economic interest',[29] which commentators such as Wilhelmsson[30] and Micklitz[31] suggest should extend to access to appropriate financial services in order to address this financial exclusion gap. Wilhelmsson writes that:

> Many financial services and information society services are now central to the infrastructure of society, and the consumer cannot reasonably be expected to live without them. These aspects of those services can be treated as social rights in the same way that services provided by *traditional* public utilities are.[32]

I argue that CDFIs represent a market solution to the financial exclusion gap, as opposed to a purely welfare solution, notwithstanding the need for some government or industry funding to sustain CDFI activity. There should be a market, rather than welfare, solution to this market gap problem, not least because a lack of access to a financial product such as credit cannot be adequately addressed through increased welfare or charitable handouts. These do not offer the dignity or social benefits, including improved self-esteem, offered by financial inclusion.[33] Further, it is likely that the welfare state, at least in Australia, has reached its possible limits, at least with continued public support, and that other solutions need to be found. This accords with Pierson's prediction of a 'future in which welfare states focus on social investment rather than social costs' and where welfare states are 'enabling rather

27 Peter Cartwright, *Banks Consumers and Regulation* (Hart Publishing 2004) 212; Dean Wilson, 'Payday Lending in Victoria: A Research Report' (Consumer Law Centre Victoria 2002) 35; Elaine Kempson, Claire Whyley, Sharon Collard and John Caskey, 'In or Out? Financial Exclusion: A Literature and Research Review' (Financial Services Authority 2000) 20; Iain Ramsay, 'Access to Credit in the Alternative Consumer Credit Market' (Office of Consumer Affairs, Industry Canada and Ministry of the Attorney General British Columbia 2000) 5.

28 Asli Demirguc-Kunt, Thornston Beck and Patrick Honohan, 'Finance for All? Policies and Pitfalls in Expanding Access' (World Bank 2007) ix.

29 Charter of Fundamental Rights of the European Union 2010/C 83/02, article 36.

30 Thomas Wilhelmsson, 'Services of General Interest and European Private Law' in Charles Rickett and Thomas Telfer (eds), *International Perspectives on Consumers' Access to Justice* (Cambridge University Press 2003) 149.

31 Hans-W Micklitz, *Universal Services: Nucleus for a Social European Private Law* (European University Institute Working Paper 12, 2009).

32 Wilhelmsson (n 29) 154–155.

33 See, for example, discussion in Rosella Scutella and Genevieve Sheehan, *To Their Credit: Evaluating an Experiment with Personal Loans for People on Low Incomes* (Brotherhood of St Laurence 2006) and more recently Centre for Social Impact, 'StepUP Loan: A Little Help Goes a Long Way – Measuring the Impact of the StepUP Loan Program' (Good Shepherd Microfinance and National Australia Bank 2013).

than providing, customised rather than generic, smaller but smarter'.[34] It is likely to be more politically palatable in Australia's neoliberal context,[35] and therefore possible, to fund CDFIs to provide loans, rather than fund an increase in direct welfare payments. This is because the loan capital will be *recycled* and loan recipients will be assisted to *help themselves* and improve their positions through financial counselling and budgeting advice.

It must be acknowledged that the gap that has been left in the market in Australia has to some extent already been filled by alternative, micro or fringe credit providers. The size of the fringe credit market in Australia is estimated as being in the vicinity of $800 million per annum, with a growing number of providers.[36] The National Financial Services Federation is an industry body which represents fringe credit providers in Australia, and it divides the lending undertaken by its members into payday loans and micro loans. It has defined a 'payday loan' as:

> A small, short-term loan, they usually have a 2 to 4 week duration and are designed to meet unexpected expenses. They are not suited for long-term borrowing or continuing financial needs, and are best reserved for temporary cash flow problems.[37]

It has defined a 'micro loan' as:

> A loan with a duration of two months to two years. They are generally for amounts of $500 or more, with an industry average principal of $1000. These loans are generally used to meet larger expenses such as replacing whitegoods, car registration, rental bonds, dental expenses and unexpected travel.[38]

The interest rates on these loan products have traditionally been very high. A Queensland study found that an annual percentage interest rate, inclusive of fees and charges, of between 300 per cent and 3,380 per cent applied to the payday loan products; while an annual percentage interest rate, inclusive of fees and charges, of between 114 per cent and 580 per cent applied to the micro loan products.[39]

In addition to high costs, other harms associated with fringe credit products have been loan rollovers, and a failure to assess suitability and capacity to repay. Loan rollovers have been a particular problem with payday loans. The loan is *rolled over* where a borrower, who is unable to repay the loan at the end of the loan term, pays a further fee to renew the loan, thus extending the repayment period. The loan rollover can become inevitable due to the short-term nature of the loan coupled with

34 Christopher Pierson, *Beyond the Welfare State: The New Political Economy of Welfare* (3rd edn, Policy Press 2006) 184.

35 See discussion in Therese Wilson, 'The Responsible Lending Response' in Therese Wilson (ed), *International Responses to Issues of Credit and Over-indebtedness in the Wake of Crisis* (Ashgate 2013) 109, 110–113.

36 Plant and Warth (n 12) 26.

37 National Financial Services Federation, *Submission to Financial Services and Credit Reform Green Paper* (Green Paper 2008) 1.

38 Ibid 2.

39 Nicola Howell, Therese Wilson and James Davidson, 'Interest Rate Caps: Protection or Paternalism?' (Centre for Credit and Consumer Law 2008) 39.

the high cost.[40] The rollover has been described as 'the foundation of the payday lending business model', while at the same time being the feature most likely to lead a borrower into a 'debt trap' from which they will find it difficult to escape.[41]

Failure to assess suitability and capacity to repay has been identified in an Australian Securities Investment Commission (ASIC) report listing breaches of responsible lending obligations by micro lenders.[42] In particular, lenders' files were identified where: no purpose for the loan was recorded; there was limited documentation verifying the consumer's situation; lenders had not recorded verification of the consumer's expenses; or there was no record of how lenders had calculated a consumer's ability to meet repayment of the loan without substantial hardship.[43] The report did not suggest that any action would be taken with respect to these breaches. Rather, ASIC indicated that it would 'work with' the lenders to assist them in meeting the requirements of the legislation.[44]

3.2 Overcoming the harms

Fringe credit providers are in one sense performing a service by providing credit to people who would otherwise be denied access to it, and so may be regarded as having a positive social impact in addressing financial exclusion. However, people should still be regarded as financially excluded where the only credit products they can access are not appropriate to meet their needs. The harms of fringe credit, as outlined above, indicate that fringe credit products may not always be appropriate to meet people's needs, and that fringe credit providers may not be suitable organisations to address financial exclusion.

Recent regulation seeks to overcome these harms. To the extent that fringe credit providers can continue to operate profitably within the boundaries of this regulation, they may indeed come to perform a valuable social role. First, the very short-term payday loans with a term of less than 15 days for amounts of $2,000 or less have now been prohibited under section 133CA of the National Consumer Credit Protection Act 2009 (Cth) (NCCPA).

In relation to cost, the maximum charge for a small-amount credit contract for credit of $2,000 or less, for a term of between 16 days and one year, is now capped at an establishment fee of 20 per cent of the credit amount and a monthly fee of 4 per cent of the credit amount (effectively 68 per cent per annum for a 12-month loan, but a higher annual percentage rate for a shorter-term loan).[45] For all other consumer credit, the cap is 48 per cent per annum, subject to exemptions for authorised-deposit-taking institutions.[46]

40 Michael Berticsdoc, 'Fixing Payday Lending: The Potential of Greater Bank Involvement' (2005) 9 North Carolina Banking Institute 133, 138.

41 Uriah King, Leslie Parrish and Ozlem Tanik, 'Payday Lending Sinks Borrowers in Debt with $4.2 Billion in Predatory Fees Every Year' (Center for Responsible Lending 2006) 3.

42 Australian Securities and Investments Commission, 'Review of Microlenders' Responsible Lending Conduct and Disclosure Obligations' (November 2011).

43 Ibid 7–8.

44 Ibid 8.

45 National Credit Code (Schedule 1 to the NCCPA), s 31A.

46 Ibid s 32A.

Loan rollovers have effectively been curtailed as part of the responsible lending obligations under the NCCPA. Section 118(3A) of the NCCPA states that it is presumed that a consumer can only meet financial obligations with substantial hardship (and that therefore the loan is unsuitable and will be irresponsible) unless the contrary is proved, where a consumer is a debtor under another small-amount credit contract and is in default, or in the 90-day period beforehand, the consumer has been a debtor under two or more other small-amount credit contracts.

With regard to assessing suitability of a loan and a borrower's capacity to repay, under the NCCPA a credit provider must not enter into a credit contract with a consumer without first making a preliminary assessment as to suitability of the loan.[47] The preliminary assessment must be made within 90 days before the provision of credit. Prior to making the preliminary assessment, the credit provider must make reasonable enquiries about the consumer's requirements and objectives in relation to the credit contract and about the consumer's financial situation, and must take reasonable steps to verify the consumer's financial situation.[48]

The credit contract must be assessed by the credit provider as 'unsuitable' if the consumer will be unable to comply with the consumer's financial obligations under the contract or could only comply with those obligations with substantial hardship, or the contract will not meet the consumer's requirements or objectives.[49]

This regulatory regime should, in theory, be effective to eliminate the harms of fringe credit, and to the extent that fringe credit providers are able to operate profitably under this regime and comply with it, may result in positive outcomes for consumers otherwise facing financial exclusion. However, it will be argued below that fringe credit providers (or organisations closer on the spectrum to for-profit fringe credit providers than CDFIs) should still not qualify for government funding in support of their services, as they are not motivated by a social mission and do not incur the costs of being mission-driven. Further, the absence of a social mission makes it less likely that they will effectively address or impact upon financial exclusion in the way that a CDFI would.

It is also possible that regulation will not be effective in protecting consumers from the possible harms of fringe credit products, and so will not be sufficiently transformative on fringe credit providers. A potential limitation of the regulatory regime is the inability of the regulator, ASIC, to monitor and enforce the statutory obligations imposed upon lenders, largely due to a lack of resources. ASIC has been criticised by one commentator for its failure to take action with respect to unconscionable conduct by banks.[50] It is also notable that, notwithstanding the ASIC report referred to above, no action against the micro lenders in question appears to be contemplated.[51] A recent report into the effectiveness of state and federal regulators charged with consumer protection, including ASIC, has found that: 'in terms of the actual amount of reported enforcement work undertaken (the prosecutions, civil actions, enforceable undertakings obtained, substantiation notices issued

47 NCCPA, ss 128 and 129.

48 Ibid s 130.

49 Ibid s 131.

50 Evan Jones, 'The Crisis and the Australian Financial Sector' (2009–2010) 64 Journal of Australian Political Economy 91, 109–110.

51 Australian Securities and Investments Commission (n 41).

and infringement notices issued that agencies actually report) the results are disturbing'.[52]

Specifically with regard to ASIC, the report noted a 'downward trend' in criminal and civil proceedings, although this was offset by an increase in bans and Australian Financial Services Licence suspensions.[53] If Australian Credit Licence suspensions were also to become common in cases of breach of the obligations of the NCCPA and National Credit Code, this would probably be effective in preventing the provision of harmful credit products. There is no evidence as yet to demonstrate that this will be the approach taken by ASIC. It is therefore reasonable that there should still be concerns regarding the potential harms of fringe credit products.

4 Who should receive government funding?

The question of who should receive government funding to provide services as a CDFI arises because of the funding that has become available in Australia and that has been available in various forms in the United States and United Kingdom.[54] In Australia, funding became available for a CDFI pilot in 2009 as part of a programme to 'build financial resilience and wellbeing among those most at risk of financial and social exclusion'.[55] Five organisations received funding under the pilot, and an evaluation of their effectiveness in increasing the ability of disadvantaged individuals to gain access to appropriate credit has been undertaken.[56] The evaluation report raises some interesting issues about the types of organisations that should receive funding as part of a government programme to address financial exclusion.

4.1 Social impact to assess eligibility for funding?

One approach to determining eligibility for government funding as a CDFI is to assess the social impact of the organisation's activities. This is, in part, what the evaluation referred to above sought to do. This involved both surveys of borrowers and interviews with the pilot CDFIs to make the general claim that, 'Feedback from borrowers has underscored the positive difference which access to a small amount of affordable credit can make in the life of someone who is not included in the financial mainstream.'[57] The number of survey responses from borrowers was very low and it is difficult to glean any clear statistics or, as qualitative interviews with borrowers were not undertaken, any clear sense of the impact of the CDFI services upon the borrowers' status as financially excluded.[58]

52 Gordon Renouf, Teena Balgi and the Consumer Action Law Centre, *Regulator Watch: The Enforcement Performance of Australian Consumer Protection Regulators* (Consumer Action Law Centre 2013) 13.

53 Ibid 72.

54 See discussion in William Apgar and Mark Duda, 'The Twenty-Fifth Anniversary of the Community Reinvestment Act: Past Accomplishments and Future Regulatory Challenges' (2003) 9(2) Economic Policy Review – Federal Reserve Bank of New York 169; Ellen Seidman, 'The New Markets Tax Credit: A Valuable Tool for Economic Development' (Living Cities: The National Community Development Initiative 2008); Department for Work and Pensions, 'The Growth Fund: Modernising and Expanding the Third Sector' www.dwp.gov.uk/other-specialists/the-growth-fund accessed 2 March 2013.

55 Plant and Warth (n 12) 9.

56 Ibid.

57 Ibid 11.

58 Ibid 87–95. Forty-two borrowers responded to a first survey, and 16 to a second.

An example of a more comprehensive attempt to assess the social impact of a loans programme designed to address financial exclusion is a study recently undertaken in relation to a low-interest loan programme offered by a community sector organisation in partnership with a bank.[59] Five hundred borrowers participated in qualitative telephone interviews, and the published report that followed was able to identify, for example, a positive change in borrowers' financial inclusion status, reduced use of fringe credit providers, a reduction in anxiety and stress, an improvement in confidence and self-esteem and an improvement in living conditions.[60]

Clearly, however, it would not be possible for most organisations to undertake such extensive research on a regular basis in order to measure social impact and qualify for funding. It is well recognised that social impact is 'impossible to measure in an efficient, timely and reliable fashion'.[61] At most, in qualifying for funding, organisations could reasonably be required to provide case studies and data collected in the course of the lending process as linked to a clearly articulated social mission. This approach is, for example, reflected in the UK-based Community Development Finance Association Performance Framework for CDFIs in the UK, which is a mechanism through which CDFIs can put their case for funding. In assessing social performance, organisations are assessed on their ability to articulate their mission (for example, through a published mission statement), their ability to gather information and measure it against a benchmark and their ability to articulate a story of change.[62] The articulated social mission, shown to inform the organisation's activities through available evidence, should be central to a social performance assessment.

4.2 Social mission and consequential costs

As a social purpose-driven organisation, a CDFI is more likely to have an effective impact upon financial exclusion than is a profit-driven organisation because of the former's willingness to sacrifice profits and incur costs in achieving a social purpose. It is the cost of being true to a mission that in turn justifies government and industry funding and subsidisation for CDFIs. This cost was demonstrated in the evaluation of the CDFI pilot referred to above,[63] and arises in two key ways: a willingness to provide services such as financial counselling and budgeting advice to assist both those who receive and those who are denied loans, and a willingness to suspend payments without penalty and generally demonstrate flexibility in the event of borrower hardship.

The costs of being driven by a social purpose have been recognised in relation to social enterprises generally and CDFIs specifically. Dees and Anderson write in relation to social enterprises that

59 The StepUP Loan is offered by Good Shepherd Microfinance in partnership with the National Australia Bank; see Connolly (n 2).

60 Ibid 22–31.

61 Dees and Anderson (n 18) 7; see also Benjamin *et al.* (n 8) 191.

62 Community Development Finance Association, 'Change Matters 2: The Performance Framework for UK CDFIs' (2012) www.cdfa.org.uk/funding-and-development/change-matters-assessments accessed 17 April 2013.

63 Plant and Warth (n 12).

> any enterprise that is openly driven by a social purpose may also find itself under pressure to severely limit profits. A declared social mission creates internal pressure to do more social good even when it may not be prudent, from a business point of view, to do so.[64]

Plant and Warth write in the CDFI pilot evaluation that 'services for financially excluded populations are expensive to deliver', noting 'the challenge of balancing CDFIs' commitment to social purpose with the ability to remain sustainable as an organisation'.[65] The case of Shorebank, referred to above, is an example of the difficulties faced by social purpose-driven organisations seeking financial sustainability.

While CDFIs do need to focus on financial sustainability to some extent in order to avoid reliance on external funding, as stated above, a stronger focus on financial sustainability than mission can lead to 'mission drift', where CDFIs behave in a manner more like conventional for-profit businesses along the spectrum of organisations providing services to the financially excluded.[66] Other CDFIs may focus exclusively on social purpose to the detriment of financial sustainability and fail as a result.[67] The organisations involved in the CDFI pilot demonstrated different emphasises on social mission as compared to profitability, and provide useful examples of characteristics that CDFI recipients of government funding should be required to demonstrate. There needs to be an appropriate balance between focus on mission and focus on sustainability.

In terms of background and an articulated social mission, the pilot CDFI, which demonstrated adherence to social mission more or less to the exclusion of a focus on financial sustainability, was the Community Credit Foundation, which was established by Fitzroy and Carlton Community Credit Co-operative Ltd for the purpose of the pilot. The Co-operative has a long history, driven by its articulated social mission of providing savings and loans facilities to meet the needs of people on low incomes, informed by a commitment to social justice. Unlike the other CDFIs involved in the pilot, Community Credit Foundation declined to partner with a bank – banks having provided loan capital and therefore sustainability to the other pilot CDFIs – fearing that this might compromise its 'independence', for which one might read 'mission focus'. In the end, this focus on mission at the cost of sustainability meant that Community Credit Foundation was not in a position to deliver loans and had to withdraw from the pilot.[68]

Conversely, another of the pilot CDFIs was Fair Loans Foundation, which had its genesis as a for-profit organisation called Mobile Finance Pty Ltd trading as Money Fast. To the extent that it now purports to be mission driven, the evaluation report refers to its intent as being to 'offer a fair alternative to payday lending to people with poor credit history, defaults or other factors that would make them vulnerable to fringe lenders'. Unlike the remaining three pilot CDFIs, Fair Loans Foundation does not offer any financial counselling or budgeting service for customers who are

64 Dees and Anderson (n 18) 12.

65 Plant and Warth (n 12) 13.

66 See discussion in Lindsey Appleyard, 'Overcoming Financial Exclusion: Community Development Finance Institutions (CDFIs) and the Balancing of Financial and Social Objectives' (PhD thesis, School of Geography, Earth and Environmental Sciences, University of Birmingham 2007) 110.

67 Dees and Anderson (n 18) 22.

68 Plant and Warth (n 12) 83–86.

not successful in their loan application, and it focuses on achieving sustainability through scale by offering loans online. Towards the very end of the initial pilot period, it did introduce a Money Mentor who borrowers had to contact before funds were released. The Money Mentor had the role of providing assistance by phone and email to clients to explain the terms of the loan and other contract details and, if the clients wished, to help them with budgets and financial strategies. Only 20 per cent of those who contacted the Money Mentor chose to complete budgets and seek feedback.[69] The report notes that 'web-based products have the potential to achieve scale.... The Fair Loans model was good at solving short-term funding problems but phone and email contact with the money mentor may not be as effective in encouraging longer-term behaviour change'.[70]

Not offering financial counselling services to those who did not receive loans is one point of distinction between Fair Loans Foundation and the remaining three pilot CDFIs. Another point of distinction is that Fair Loans Foundation charges fees for deferral of payment, although the organisation does claim to take 'an understanding and socially responsible approach ... with each customer on a case by case basis, taking into account their personal circumstances and ability to repay'.[71]

The articulated social missions of the remaining three pilot CDFIs are clear. Many Rivers began in 2007 as a microfinance organisation, and is part of the Mission Australia group of companies. It exists to facilitate micro and small business loans in financially excluded indigenous communities and among refugees and ex-offenders.[72] Fair Finance Australia is a programme managed by Foresters Community Finance Limited, with a long history as a mutual organisation engaging in microfinance activities. Its stated aim in offering loans through Fair Finance is to 'increase individual financial inclusion by delivering affordable and accessible small consumer loans in an understanding and compassionate manner'.[73] In-roads is an initiative of Community Sector Banking which was established in 2007 as a joint venture between Bendigo Bank and Adelaide Bank. Community Sector Banking's vision is 'to be the financial institution that strengthens not-for-profits in delivering social change'. Through In-roads, Bendigo provides loan capital to community sector organisation partners who provide that loan capital to their clients.[74]

These three organisations undoubtedly incur costs and sacrifice profits in order to meet their social missions, through providing extensive financial counselling and budgeting assistance, not only to borrowers but also to those whose loan applications are declined; and through working with clients at no penalty to assist them when they cannot make payments that fall due.

In the case of Many Rivers, both pre- and post-loan support are extensive:

> Field Officers may work for several weeks or months with clients to support them in preparing their business plan, assist the client in applying for a business loan if required, and provide follow up as the business becomes established....

69 Ibid 76–82.
70 Ibid 11.
71 Ibid 78.
72 Ibid 47–54.
73 Ibid 55–60.
74 Ibid 61–71.

> Many Rivers policy is not to refuse access to a loan per se, but rather to work with people until they are ready to start their business or they determine it is not an option they wish to pursue.[75]

Additionally, in the case of defaults or potential defaults, Many Rivers Field Officers work with clients to negotiate deferrals or reductions in payments, and no fees are charged.[76]

Fair Finance typically spends 1.5 hours with clients in the loan application interview, and clients are taken through a budget process and given financial literacy information. Unsuccessful loan applicants are provided with support to assist them with their financial situation, including through financial education. If clients are having difficulties making payments, payments can be rescheduled or 'skipped' and added to the loan amount.[77]

In-roads' community sector partner organisations reported initial loan application meetings of between 30 minutes and three hours with potential clients, involving financial counselling and budgeting advice. Relationship Managers from those partner organisations work with clients if they experience difficulties in making payments, and report that they are usually able to find a solution to those difficulties.[78]

These activities have positive impacts on financial exclusion but come at a cost, as noted in the evaluation report:

> In addition to the provision of credit, a key component of the pilot was client support in the form of financial education, budgeting advice or money mentoring. This support proved to be of benefit to greater numbers of people than just those who secured loans.... For three of the organisations, Many Rivers, Fair Finance and In-roads, financial support took the form of intensive one-on-one work with, at times, very disadvantaged clients. For these CDFIs, a key outcome of the pilot was to provide individuals with a detailed understanding of their financial circumstances. This support proved to be a major strength of the pilot, but also its greatest cost.[79]

Government funding aimed at addressing financial exclusion should be provided to such organisations as are themselves primarily motivated by achieving the social purpose of addressing financial exclusion. This is demonstrated by those organisations undertaking such activities as extensive counselling and budgeting advice, not only for borrowers but also for declined applicants; and working constructively with borrowers at no cost to overcome financial difficulties and circumstances of hardship that lead to defaults or potential defaults. These are key indicators of a CDFI, as opposed to an alternative or fringe lender. These are also activities that involve profit sacrifice in the interest of achieving a social mission, which justifies the need for external funding.

75 Ibid 49–50.
76 Ibid 53.
77 Ibid 56–57.
78 Ibid 63, 66.
79 Ibid 10.

5 Conclusion

Financial exclusion, or lack of access to appropriate financial services or products, with its attendant problem of social exclusion, is a phenomenon that has attracted international attention in recent years, including in Australia. Commentators and governments have recognised the need for regulatory initiatives to improve access to appropriate financial services or products.[80]

Government funding of CDFIs as part of a strategy to address financial exclusion in Australia has been an appropriate government response, in the sense that CDFIs are in their true sense organisations that exist for the very purpose of addressing financial exclusion. This brings to mind one of the lessons of Teubner's system theory,[81] as developed by Dunsire,[82] which rings so intuitively true. It is that where systems or organisations are well placed to contribute to regulatory solutions, the role of regulation may simply be to enable them to survive. Dunsire refers to this as 'subsidization', likening government financial subsidy to energy inputs for biological organisms, feeding them with funding.[83] Dunsire explains subsidisation as follows: 'The key is to select a social actor or institution, often in the voluntary sector, which is already performing what the administrator regards as a public service, and simply ensure its metabolic survival.'[84]

The key, of course, is to select those organisations that are indeed performing the desirable public service. This undoubtedly requires some criteria to *cut through* the boundary blurring that can occur across the spectrum of organisations purportedly operating in the financial inclusion space. The boundary blurring that has been recognised between all forms of social enterprises and conventional for-profit enterprises[85] arises equally in the case of CDFIs and for-profit, alternative or fringe credit providers.

Measuring the social impact achieved by an organisation may be one way of ascertaining eligibility for funding. However, social impact can be difficult and costly to measure, making it a largely impractical criterion to apply.

In this chapter it has been suggested that an articulated social purpose or mission is an appropriate and practical criterion. Clearly, however, there would need to be evidence of that social purpose or mission being operationalised by the organisation, guiding its activities. This operationalisation of social mission will almost certainly involve some profit sacrifice. A CDFI should have no difficulty in providing evidence as to the existence of and operationalisation of a social mission. A purely profit-driven fringe credit provider will have difficulty in doing so and should not qualify for funding, not least because it should not require funding due to an absence of profit-sacrificing activities on its part.

80 See discussion regarding the centrality of the concept of 'access' in Micklitz (n 30) 25.

81 See Gunther Teubner, 'Substantive and Reflexive Elements in Modern Law' (1983) 17(2) Law and Society Review 239.

82 Andrew Dunsire, 'Tipping the Balance: Autopoiesis and Governance' (1996) 29(3) Administration and Society 299.

83 Ibid 309.

84 Ibid 320.

85 See, for example, discussion in Alan Curtis, 'Social Enterprise and the Effects of Isomorphism: The Blurring Boundaries Between the Not For Profit and For Profit Market' (EMES-SOCENT Conference Selected Papers no. LG13-66, 2013).

There may be a role for fringe credit providers in addressing financial exclusion where they can operate profitably while complying with regulation designed to overcome the harms of fringe credit. The NCCPA should in theory bring an end to very high cost loans, to loan rollovers and to any other irresponsible lending practices. How effectively the relevant provisions in the NCCPA will be enforced will determine how effective the provisions themselves are in this regard. Even assuming that fringe credit can be provided without involving the harms to borrowers canvassed above, I have argued that fringe credit providers, or organisations that sit closer on the spectrum to the for-profit fringe credit model than the CDFI model, should not be recipients of government funding designed to impact upon financial exclusion. Only CDFIs that are social mission or purpose driven, and that therefore sacrifice profits and incur costs in fulfilling that social mission, should be recipients of government funding for CDFI programmes.

It is suggested that the criteria which government should apply to eligibility for CDFI funding should be that:

1. the organisation has a clearly articulated social mission or purpose; and
2. the organisation can demonstrate its commitment to that social mission or purpose through profit-sacrificing activities such as:
    a. extensive financial counselling and budgeting advice to both successful loan applicants and those whose loan applications are declined; and
    b. flexible policies regarding hardship, for example, allowing loan repayments to be *deferred* at no charge where the borrower's circumstances require it.

While social impact itself can be difficult to measure, it would not be unreasonable to suggest that social impact in terms of addressing financial exclusion is likely to be higher in the case of services provided by CDFIs that meet these criteria.

Part IV

Unfair contract terms

10 Unfair contract terms legislation

Is it good consumer law?

Paul O'Shea

1 Introduction

Inequality of bargaining power is one of the structural features of consumer transactions. Standard form contracts are a prime example of this structural inequality. There is no clearer inequality between parties than when one can say *take it or leave it* to the other.[1] Little wonder, then, that this area has attracted so much attention from legislators.[2] Standard form contracts present such a challenge to classical notions of freely negotiated contracts that some authors have claimed that they are not contracts at all.[3] Yet, standard form contracts are the basis of the vast majority of consumer transactions. These written agreements, almost always in standard non-negotiable forms, help make consumer transactions special and help distinguish consumer law as an enclave or sub-system in which other norms interact with the black letter prescriptions of contract law.

Attempts to address inequality of bargaining power in consumer transactions through the common law, equity and statutory unjust contract provisions have met with limited success. This is not surprising. Consumer law is different. The parties are structurally unequal. It is the structural nature of the inequality which is the appropriate target of good consumer law. Regulatory interventions to address inequality of bargaining power would be better focused less on individual bargains, and their circumstances, than on the structural inequality evidenced in all consumer transactions. The mechanism by which such inequality is often realised is the standard form contract. The Australian Consumer Law 2010[4] (ACL) is the latest in a series of legislative attempts to regulate standard form contracts.

1 *Macaulay v Schroeder Publishing Co Ltd* [1976] 1 WLR 1308, 1316 (Lord Diplock); *George Mitchell (Chesterhall) Ltd v Finney Lock Seeds* [1982] 3 WLR 1036, 1943 (Lord Denning).

2 For example, Trade Practices Amendment (Australian Consumer Law) Act (No 1) 2010 (Cth); Fair Trading (Amendment) Act 2003 (Vic) and Unfair Contract Terms Act 1977 (UK) and Unfair Contract Terms in Consumer Contracts Regulations 1999 (UK).

3 W Slawson, 'Standard Form Contracts and Democratic Control of Lawmaking Power' (1975) 84 Harvard Law Review 529, 544.

4 Schedule 2 of the Competition and Consumer Act 2010 (Cth).

2 The interaction between information, freedom of contract and bargaining inequality in standard form contracts

Good consumer law should restore effective freedom of contract for consumers. As Hugh Collins said: 'what matters ... is consumer choice, not consumer rights'.[5] Standard form contracts limit consumer choice and are a manifestation of the structural inequality of bargaining power between consumers and suppliers. As Franz Kessler says:

> Standard contracts are typically used by enterprises with strong bargaining power. The weaker party, in need of the goods or services, is frequently not in a position to shop around for better terms, either because the author of the standard contract has a monopoly (natural or artificial) or because all competitors use the same clauses. His contractual intention is but a subjection more or less voluntary to terms dictated by the stronger party, terms whose consequences are often understood only in a vague way, if at all.[6]

Apart from the *take it or leave it* bargaining inequality, standard form contracts are also an acute example of the inequality of information power between consumers and suppliers. There are consequences to this for the efficiency and fairness of consumer markets.

In a famous 1970 article, George Akerlof pointed out that consumers pay less attention to so-called 'non-core' terms than to 'core' terms, such as price and product description. It is usually the non-core terms which make up the standard terms in standard form contracts. There is almost no effective competition for these standard terms. Consumers rarely read them. It is not surprising, then, that they are increasingly *one sided*, favouring suppliers over consumers and allocating all possible risks which may arise from the transaction to the consumer. In this 'race for the bottom' good products with more 'consumer friendly' standard terms are often driven out of the market.[7]

3 In defence of standard terms

Standard terms serve a constructive purpose in consumer markets. Kessler acknowledged that 'in so far as the reduction of cost of production and distribution achieved is reflected in reduced prices, society as a whole, ultimately, benefits from the use of standard contracts'.[8] The cost of individually negotiating each and every term, covering every foreseeable contingency, for each and every consumer, would add so much to each transaction as to render them hopelessly inefficient. As Korobokin points out, this has not and could not occur in any modern complex

5 H Collins, 'Good Faith in European Contract Law' (1994) Oxford Journal of Legal Studies 229.

6 F Kessler, 'Contracts of Adhesion: Some Thoughts About Freedom of Contract' (1943) 43 Columbia Law Review 629, 631–632.

7 G Akerlof, 'The Market for Lemons: Quality Uncertainty and the Market Mechanism' (1970) 84 Quarterly Journal of Economics 488, 500; J Burke, 'Contract as Commodity: a Nonfiction Approach' (2000) 24 Seton Hall Legal Journal 285, 293; Consumer Action Law Centre (R Smith), Submission No 100 to Productivity Commission, Inquiry into Australia's Consumer Policy Framework, 24 July 2007, 7.

8 Kessler (n 6).

economy: 'actual assent to each contract term in a transaction of any complexity simply is not possible; if terms are not imposed on one party by the other, some terms will almost certainly be imposed on both parties by the government'.[9]

To some extent, statutory implied terms reflect this necessity.[10] These rather basic consumer protections, however, rarely cover the more complex and more contingent situations addressed by the increasingly complex standard form contract terms common in modern consumer transactions. The non-core standard terms are usually left to the market and to the unequal bargaining power of the suppliers and their lawyers drafting the contracts proffered to consumers.

A few commentators suggest the banning of standard form contracts and their replacement with statutory forms. Scott and Black canvass as an option the mandatory approval in advance of standard forms by a government agency.[11] This would be a highly interventionist form of regulation if the approved form was the only form allowed. The contractual freedom of both consumers and suppliers would be substantially reduced and, of course, the potential arises for a growing and increasingly inefficient bureaucracy to process and monitor the use of the statutorily approved form. There would be many more opportunities for regulatory mistakes and biases.

Even consumer advocates accept the advantages of standard form contracts. In Australia, the Consumer Action Law Centre, in Victoria, conceded in its submission to the Productivity Commission Inquiry into Australia's Consumer Policy Framework, that 'standard form contracts, as a process, are efficient and may benefit consumers because in competitive markets reduced transaction costs will be reflected in lower prices or other improvements in sales terms'.[12] The Standing Committee of Officials of Consumer Affairs agreed.[13]

If standard form contract terms are an inevitable feature of modern society and consumer transactions, it remains then to analyse how they can be best regulated so as to protect consumers while preserving, where possible, freedom of contract.

4 Common law and equitable remedies

The common law has few, if any, remedies for inequality of bargaining power and almost none for harsh contract terms. This reflects the continued influence of classical contract theory.[14]

However, the exclusion, limitation and waiver clauses in standard form contracts have been the subject of many judicial attempts to ameliorate their inequitable effects on consumers. Many of these, however, rely not so much on the substance of

9 R Korobkin, 'Bounded Rationality, Standard Form Contracts and Unconscionability' (2003) 70 University of Chicago Law Review 1203, 1205.

10 For example, in Australia, there are implied terms for title, fitness for purposes and merchantable quality, as in ss 69–71 of the Trade Practices Act 1974 (Cth), now recast as 'consumer guarantees' in the Australian Consumer Law 2010 (Cth), ss 51–62.

11 C Scott and J Black, *Cranston's Consumers and the Law* (Butterworths, 2000) 80.

12 Consumer Action Law Centre, Melbourne, *Submission to Inquiry into Australia's Consumer Policy Framework* (Productivity Commission, 2008) 22.

13 Standing Committee of Officials of Consumer Affairs, *Unfair Contract Terms: A Discussion Paper* (Discussion Paper, January 2004) 16.

14 J Paterson, 'The Australian Unfair Contract Terms Law: The Rise of Substantive Unfairness as a Ground for Review of Standard Form Consumer Contracts' (2009) 33 Melbourne University Law Review 934, 935.

the clause but on how it was brought to the notice of the consumer.[15] This, of course, is easily overcome by suppliers providing the notice required by the courts.

Other 'lines of attack', as they are described by Scott and Black, on exclusion clauses are the *contra proferentum* rule, the doctrine of fundamental breach[16] and, in Australia, the 'four corners' rule.[17] Scott and Black describe 'the approach in Britain to objectionable features of standard form contracts and to exclusion clauses' as 'ad hoc' and 'rather limited'.[18] Until recently, the same could be said of Australia.

All of these common law approaches can be thwarted by clever drafting. Even in equity, there is no general principle in English or Australian law that allows a court to re-open or to provide relief simply because a bargain is harsh or unjust or because it was the result of inequality of bargaining.[19] For a consumer, or any other party, to obtain relief for an unjust or unfair contract in equity, there must be both these elements and more. There must also be an attempt by the more powerful party to take an unfair or unconscientious advantage of their superior position. The weaker party must suffer from more than the structural inequality shared by all consumers – they must have a special disadvantage.

Spiegelman CJ in *Attorney-General (NSW) v World Best Holdings Ltd*[20] made the position quite clear:

> Unconscionability is a well-established but narrow principle in equitable doctrine. It has been applied over the centuries with considerable restraint and in manner which is consistent with the maintenance of the basic principles of freedom of contract. It is not a principle of what *fairness* or *justice* or *good conscience* requires in the particular circumstances of the case.[21]

These approaches focus on 'situational unfairness', mostly of the 'procedural' kind, and they have had limited success for consumers. They are not, it is argued, an approach appropriate for consumer law. The application of these doctrines depends too much on the particular circumstances of the parties and the transaction and not enough on structural features which can be generalised for an entire category of transactions. Spiegelman's CJ words, however, do address the tension between freedom of contract and issues of fairness and justice in consumer contracts.

15 For example, *Thornton v Shoe Lane Parking Ltd* [1971] 2 QB 163; *Dillon v Baltic Shipping Co* (1989) 21 NSWLR 614; *Interfoto Picture Library Ltd v Stiletto Visual Programmes Ltd* [1989] QB 433; *Olley v Marlborough Court Ltd* [1949] 1 KB 532; *Causer v Browne* [1952] VLR 1; *Curtis v Chemical Cleaning & Dyeing Co Ltd* [1951] 1 KB 805. These cases relate to consumer transactions. There are many others of a less 'consumer law' nature on this point.

16 Scott and Black (n 11) 80.

17 *Council of the City of Sydney v West* (1965) 114 CLR 481 and *Darlington Futures Ltd v Delco Australia Pty Ltd* (1986) 161 CLR 500.

18 Scott and Black (n 11) 80.

19 *National Westminster Bank Plc v Morgan* [1985] AC 686, 708; *Commercial Bank of Australia Ltd v Amadio* (1983) 151 CLR 447, 459 (Gibbs CJ), 467 (Mason J).

20 (2005) 63 NSWLR 557, 566 [21].

21 *Attorney-General (NSW) v World Best Holdings Ltd* (2005) 63 NSWLR 557, 566 [21].

5 Great expectations: legislative attempts to address inequality of bargaining power

Scott and Black identify four ways in which legislation can address inequality of bargaining power particularly in the case of standard form contracts. First, a statute may declare specific contractual terms invalid.[22] Second, a broad standard of fairness could be imposed on all contracts or all consumer contracts. The Uniform Commercial Code of the United States contains such a provision,[23] as does the European Directive on Unfair Terms in Consumer Contracts.[24] Third, authorising a public agency to take action to have unfair terms declared void, which is the approach of the unfair contract terms (UCT) legislation being considered in this chapter. Fourth, mandatory approval in advance of standard form contracts by a government agency (or by regulation/legislation).

One approach, not directly covered by this typology, is the statutory granting of power to courts and tribunals to re-open contracts as unjust or unfair. Consumer credit has attracted such targeted legislative attention. Scott and Black examine such provisions when they discuss 'extortionate credit bargains' in the UK, which starts with the Moneylenders Act 1900 and was continued and expanded in the Consumer Credit Act 1974.[25] In Australia, this power was granted to courts in New South Wales by the Contracts Review Act 1980 (NSW) (CRA),[26] and in Australia generally under the National Consumer Credit Code 2010 (NCC).[27] While not a power to re-open contracts, the prohibition against 'unconscionable conduct' which is now contained in section 21 of the ACL[28] does require the court to consider issues around inequality of bargaining power.[29]

Like the CRA and the NCC, the 'unconscionable conduct' provision in the Australian Consumer Law and its Trade Practices Act predecessor uses a *shopping list* or *smorgasbord* of factors which the court must consider when determining whether a contract has been unfair, unjust or unconscionable. The success of these provisions as effective means of redressing structural imbalance between parties has been mixed. This is not surprising as this is regulation aimed at 'situational substantive' unfairness. It is not structural.

Andrew Robertson argues that the CRA does not redress 'the lack of meaningful choice in everyday consumer or business transactions' in that it may police

22 Scott and Black (n 11) 96. They give the example of clauses which excluded the implied terms in the Supply of Goods (Implied Terms) Act 1973 (UK) until the Unfair Contract Terms Act 1977 (UK) prevented this for consumer transactions. In Australia, the implied terms in the various state Sale of Goods Acts could be excluded by agreement but those in the later Fair Trading and Trade Practices Acts could not. The Australian *National* Consumer Credit Code, like its predecessor the Uniform Consumer Credit Code, contains several such provisions, e.g. sections 23–26 prohibiting up-front interest charges.

23 Uniform Commercial Code cl 2-302 (2001).

24 Council Directive 93/13/EC of 5 April 1993 on Unfair Terms in Consumer Contracts [1993] OJ L95/29.

25 Consumer Credit Act 1974 (UK), s 138.

26 Contracts Review Act 1980 (NSW), s 4.

27 NCCC s 76, which replicates Uniform Consumer Credit Code, s 70, effective in most states and territories in 1996.

28 Formerly Trade Practices Act 1974 (Cth), s 51AB.

29 For instance, one of the matters for the court to consider is 'the relative bargaining strengths of the parties'.

'procedurally unfair conduct resulting in unfair terms', but it does 'not address the lack of understanding or the lack of choice in day-to-day contracting' which is typical of standard form consumer contracts.[30] The reluctance of the courts to find unfairness solely on substantive grounds may reflect a hangover from classical contract theory.[31] It was noticeable in the cases on sections 51AA, 51AB and 51AC of the old Trade Practices Act 1974 (Cth) (TPA).[32] The terms of the bargain, no matter how inequitable, while evidence of such conduct are almost never themselves its proof.

The CRA, only ever adopted in New South Wales, allows for re-opening of contracts which are 'unjust', which is defined to include 'unconscionable, harsh or oppressive'. These inclusions could be interpreted as colouring 'unjust' to mean only contracts which are particularly harsh or oppressive and whose formation occurred in unconscionable circumstances, in the same sense as in equity or under the TPA. McHugh JA, when he was in the New South Wales Court of Appeal, seems to argue against this view when he says that it was 'a mistake to think that a contract, or one of its terms is only unjust when it is unconscionable, harsh or oppressive'.[33]

There are, however, relatively few cases under the CRA and this has been described as one of the 'notable failures' of the Act.[34] The inherent costs of litigation and the fear of adverse costs awards prevented most consumers from ever seeking CRA relief. Further, the judicial response to the CRA was to require both procedural and substantive injustice. Very few applications under the Act were successful and none of these were purely 'consumer' transactions.[35] In relation to consumer credit, the Australian states adopted largely uniform Credit Acts during the 1980s.[36] Like the CRA, it provided for a court re-opening of unjust credit contracts when they were 'unconscionable, harsh or oppressive' but also added an alternative ground – namely whether:

> The annual percentage rate is excessive, having regard to the risk, the value of any security, the amount of the consideration, the time for repayment, the amount financed and any other relevant circumstances.[37]

This raised the possibility that courts will consider the substantive terms of a credit contract alone as being grounds for re-opening. The unjust contracts provisions of

30 A Robertson, 'The Limits of Voluntariness in Contract' (2005) 29 Melbourne University Law Review 5, 9–10.

31 Paterson (n 14) 937. Others agree, see L Brown, 'The Impact of Section 51AC of the Trade Practices Act 1974 (Cth) on Commercial Certainty' (2004) 28 Melbourne University Law Review 589, 612–617; N Howell, 'Catching Up with Consumer Realities: The Need for Legislation Prohibiting Unfair Terms in Consumer Contracts' (2006) 34 Australian Business Law Review 447, 450–453.

32 *Hurley v MacDonalds Australia Ltd* [1999] FCA 1728; and *Australian Competition and Consumer Commission v Berbatis* (2003) 214 CLR 51.

33 *West v AGC (Advances) Ltd* (1986) 5 NSWLR 610, 620–621.

34 T Carlin, 'The Contracts Review Act 1980 (NSW): 20 Years On' (2001) 23 Sydney Law Review 125, 144.

35 A review by Tyrone Carlin in 2001 of the Act found only 60 cases in 20 years, of which 30 were successful for the applicant: ibid 137.

36 Credit Act 1984 (NSW); Credit Act 1984 (Vic); Credit Act 1984 (WA); Credit Act 1985 (ACT); Credit Act 1987 (Qld).

37 For example, NSW, s 145(1) and Qld, s 148(1).

the *Credit Acts* could have been a vehicle for courts to address directly the structural inequality between consumer and credit providers, one of the most profound and pervasive inequalities in consumer law.

The words of the statute, on its face, certainly provided this opportunity. However, the courts, again, rarely strayed from the requirement for both procedural and substantive injustice, thus confining the effect of the statute to individual facts and circumstances.[38]

The next incarnation of credit law in Australia, the Uniform Consumer Credit Code (UCCC), replaced the Credit Acts in 1996, as each state, under a 1993 agreement, adopted a template Code passed by the Queensland Parliament. Section 70 of the UCCC gave the court power to re-open unjust transactions. Section 70(2) lists the matters to be considered by a court, including the 'relative bargaining power of the parties'.[39] Of the other 13 specified matters, seven are clearly procedural in nature.[40] Of the other six, one concerns the 'form ... and intelligibility of the language in which' the contract is expressed.[41] The other five deal with matters of potentially substantive injustice.[42]

In the 14 years of its operation, the UCCC saw few successful applications for reopening of unjust contracts. The access to justice issues for consumers, discussed above in the context of the CRA, undoubtedly played a role despite the availability of cost-free forums in the states with specialist tribunals.[43] Early decisions on applications under the unjust contracts provisions of the Code were focused on its application and had little, if anything, to say about contractual injustice.[44]

In what is arguably the leading case on section 70 of the Code, *Permanent Mortgages v Cook*, the judge at first instance, Patten JA, lamented that no authorities on the section had been cited to him by counsel.[45] He did canvass cases on the CRA and concluded that whether he held the mortgage as unjust involved a 'balancing exercise' and that 'the beneficial nature of the Code indicates that it was intended to protect the unsophisticated and meagrely educated, such as the Defendants, from their own foolishness'.[46]

His Honour found that the lender and its agents were well aware of the improvidence of the loan and had actively encouraged it. This was 'something more' to use the phrase of Basten JA and brought relief to the Cooks as 'foolish' borrowers.[47]

The structural, as opposed to individual, inequality of bargaining power between consumers and suppliers does not of itself, even when it produces bad bargains and unjust contracts, lead to relief under these statutes. Focusing on individual

38 *Beneficial Finance Ltd v Adams* (1989) 217 ALR 60, *Moreland Finance Corp (Vic) Pty Ltd v Westendorp* [1993] 2 VR 284; *Custom Credit Corporation Ltd v Lupi* (1991) ASC 56-02; *Stateside Credit Corp Pty Ltd v Hudson* [1989] VR 519; *Hammon v Alliance Acceptance Co Ltd* (1989) ASC 55-517; *Tirant v LNS Autos Pty Ltd* (1986) ASC 55-470; *Custom Credit Corporation v Gray* (1991) ASC 56-096, 57,104 (McGarvie and Gobbo JJ) *West v AGC (Advances) Ltd* (1986) 5 NSWLR 610 at 612.

39 Consumer Credit Act Queensland 1994 (Qld) Appendix ('Consumer Credit Code'), s 70(2)(b).

40 Consumer Credit Code, ss 70(2)(c), (d), (f), (h), (i), (j), and (k).

41 Ibid s 70(2)(g).

42 Ibid ss 70(2)(a), (e), (l),(m) and (n).

43 NSW, Vict, WA but not Qld.

44 For example *McKenzie v Smith* (1998) ASC 155-025; *Rafiqi v Wacal Investments* (1998) ASC 155-024.

45 (2006) ASC 155-082 [87].

46 Ibid [88].

47 Ibid [95].

circumstances, as Wilson, Howell and Sheehan point out, 'reduces the potential development of precedent and widespread change in business practice'.[48]

Thus, common law remedies directed towards the 'situational procedural' and statutory provisions aimed at 'situational substantive' unfairness have had limited success. The best way to address inequality of bargaining power is by addressing the structural inequalities that arise through standard form contracts. Unfair contract terms legislation attempts this task.

6 Unfair contract terms legislation in the UK: a brief introduction

Apart from the general law and implied terms in sale of goods style legislation, similar to its Australian equivalents,[49] UCTs, as such, were first regulated in the UK by the Unfair Contract Terms Act 1977 (UK) (UCTA). This Act applies to exclusion and limitation of liability clauses.[50] Furthermore, in the case of consumer contracts, indemnity clauses and clauses which allow a supplier to evade liability for negligence or breach of contract by a secondary contract or a choice of law clause.[51] This Act has been criticised as being highly reactive and incapable of dealing with UCTs on a systemic basis. Scott and Collins argue that although

> the UCTA is intended to have wide effect ... the truth is that the title, Unfair Contract Terms Act 1977 was a misnomer because given its scope and the specific exemptions to it many unfair terms caught in other jurisdictions fall outside its ambit.[52]

Indeed, up until 1999, few cases had been brought under its terms.[53]

In 1999, the UK enacted the Unfair Terms in Consumer Contracts Regulations 1999 (UK) (UTCC Regs) in order to give effect to the European Union Directive on Unfair Terms in Consumer Contracts.[54] The regulations provide that unfair terms will not be binding on the consumer and that a term is unfair 'if, contrary to the requirement of good faith, it causes a significant imbalance in the parties' rights and obligations arising under the contract, to the detriment of the consumer'.[55] Examples of unfair terms are given in schedule two of the UTCC Regs and in bulletins published by the UK's Office of Fair Trading.[56] This is the so-called 'grey list'.

48 T Wilson, N Howell, and G Sheehan, 'Protecting the Most Vulnerable in Consumer Credit Transactions' (2009) 32 Journal of Consumer Policy 117, 128.

49 Supply of Goods (Implied Terms) Act 1973 (UK).

50 Ibid s 2.

51 Ibid ss 4,10 and 27(2).

52 Scott and Black (n 11) 86–88.

53 B St J Collins, 'Report on the Practical Implementation of Directive 93/13/EEC in the United Kingdom and the Republic of Ireland' in *The Integration of Directive 93/13 into the National Legal Systems* (1999) 317, as cited in Standing Committee of Officials of Consumer Affairs (n 13) 5.

54 Council Directive 93/13/EC of 5 April 1993 on Unfair Terms in Consumer Contracts [1993] OJ L95/29.

55 Unfair Terms in Consumer Contracts Regulations 1999 (UK), reg 5(1).

56 UK Office of Fair Trading, *Unfair Standard Terms* (2000) Annex B ('Terms that may be considered unfair').

The Regulations provide for two ways to deal with unfair terms. First, the Regulations can be raised by a consumer as a defence to any action by the supplier, trader or financier proffering the 'unfair term', as such terms are not binding on the consumer.[57] The balance of the contract is preserved if it is capable of enforcement without the 'unfair term'.[58] Second, the Director of Fair Trading can consider complaints in relation to unfair terms and can either accept undertakings regarding their continued use and/or seek injunctions from the court preventing such use by the firms proffering such terms in their standard contracts.[59] Interestingly, certain other bodies, including the UK Consumer Association, are 'qualified' to consider complaints and bring actions seeking injunctions.[60]

These provisions are all confined to standard form contracts where there has not been an opportunity for the consumer to 'influence the substance of the term' as it has been 'drafted in advance'.[61] Subject to legibility, they do not apply to the core provisions of a contract or to the adequacy of the price or consideration.[62] Scott and Black are very critical of this limitation, describing it as 'saying that this renders the title of the Directive, under which the Regulations were passed, a "misnomer" like that of the 1977 Act'.[63] Whether this is so, it is this exception or limitation which has been the subject of several important decisions on the UK UCTs provisions such as *OFT v Abbey National PLC (Abbey National)*[64] and *OFT v Ashbourne Management Services*[65] and an Issues Paper produced by the Law Commissions of England and Wales and Scotland in 2012.[66]

There are, however, arguments in support of this limitation, which will be canvassed later in this chapter.

7 Unfair contract terms legislation in the Australian State of Victoria

The Victorian parliament passed the Fair Trading (Amendment) Act 2003 (Vic) which amended the Fair Trading Act 1999 (Vic) to include, among other things, a legislative regime aimed squarely at unfair terms in consumer contracts. A panel set up by the Victorian Government in 2002 to review its Fair Trading Act examined the UK UCT Regulations and formed the view that they had a significant role in protecting UK consumers from unfair terms in contracts.[67]

Under the Victorian legislation, if a consumer believes a term to be unfair, he or she can take it to the court or the Victorian Civil and Administrative Tribunal and,

57 Unfair Terms in Consumer Contracts Regulations 1999 (UK), reg 8(1).
58 Ibid reg 8(2).
59 Ibid regs 10, 12.
60 Ibid sch 1.
61 Ibid reg 5.
62 Ibid reg 6.
63 Scott and Black (n 11) 91.
64 [2009] UKSC 6, [2010] 1 AC 696.
65 [2011] EWHC 1237.
66 The Law Commission and the Scottish Law Commission, *Unfair Terms in Consumer Contracts Issues: A New Approach?* (Issues Paper, 25 July 2012) http://lawcommission.justice.gov.uk/docs/unfair_terms_in_consumer_contracts_issues.pdf accessed 1 January 2014.
67 Consumer Affairs Victoria, *Preventing Unfair Terms in Consumer Credit Contracts* (2009).

if successful, the term is void, though the rest of the contract is enforceable.[68] Unlike the UTCC Regs, the Victorian Act does not only apply to standard form contracts, though whether the term has been the subject of negotiation is a factor in determining its fairness. Further, the Director of Fair Trading can apply to have certain standard form terms declared unfair by regulation and/or injunctions restraining persons from using such terms.[69]

The Victorian UCT legislation has been through two subtle but significant changes. Initially, the definition in section 32W included the phrase 'contrary to the requirements of good faith', a phrase which was the subject of some analysis in the Victorian Supreme Court in *Jetstar Airways Pty Ltd v Free*.[70] This was deleted by an amendment in 2009. Also, initially the Victorian UCT legislation did not apply to consumer credit contracts but in response to a Review of Consumer Credit the Victorian Government announced that it would bring vendor terms contracts within the ambit of the UCT provisions, and did so by regulation in August 2008. Then, as part of the June 2009 amendments, the UCT provisions were expanded to apply to consumer credit.[71]

8 Genesis of the Australian Consumer Law Unfair Contract Terms Provisions (ACL UCT)

At the same time as the Victorian Government established its panel to investigate UCTs, the Ministerial Council for Consumer Affairs (MCCA), made up of all the Australian state and territory fair trading or consumer affairs ministers, established its own working party to investigate ways of addressing unfair terms in consumer contracts and to consider the implementation of a 'more nationally consistent and effective regulatory regime'.[72] Law reform in federal systems is often slow and the execution of this resolution was no exception.[73]

Meanwhile, the Australian Productivity Commission was undertaking a massive review of Australia's Consumer Policy Framework, which commenced in December 2006. In its final report, produced in April 2008, it recommended the adoption by the Commonwealth of a generic ACL and including UCTs regulation. The newly elected Labour Federal Government accepted this and many other recommendations of this report, and put it to the Council of Australian Governments (COAG) in March 2008 and then to MCCA in May 2008. Matters proceeded swiftly, by comparison with the previous eight years, and by February 2009 the Commonwealth Minister for Consumer Affairs, Chris Bowen, produced a detailed consultation paper entitled *An Australian Consumer Law: Fair Markets – Confident Consumers*, which included the model adopted by COAG.[74] In March 2010, the first part of the ACL was passed as the Trade Practices Amendment (Australian Consumer Law) Act (No 1) 2010. The

68 Ibid s 32Y.
69 Ibid s 32ZA.
70 [2008] VSC 539.
71 Fair Trading and Other Acts Amendment Act 2009 (Vic), ss 5 and 6.
72 Standing Committee of Officials of Consumer Affairs (n 13), 5.
73 Evidence to Legislative Council Standing Committee on Law and Justice, Parliament of New South Wales, Sydney, 20 October 2006, 3 (L Baker).
74 Standing Committee of Officials of Consumer Affairs, 'An Australian Consumer Law: Fair Markets – Confident Consumers' (February 2009) 30.

UCT provisions became effective on 1 July 2010 as part of the Trade Practices and Australian Securities and Investment Commission Acts. On 1 January 2011, the Unfair Terms provisions were incorporated into the new ACL as schedule 2 of the Competition and Consumer Act 2010.

9 Analysis of the ACL UCT and comparisons with Victorian and UK models

9.1 Defining consumers

The UTCC Regs,[75] the Victorian legislation[76] and the ACL UCT[77] all adopted a functional rather than size-based definition of 'consumer' in order to confine the application of the legislation. Interestingly, the UTCC Regs definition defines 'consumer' as a natural person who is acting for purposes which are outside his or her business, which is defined to include their trade or profession.[78] Scott and Black speculate that 'it seems arguable that so long as one purpose is outside the person's business, he or she could still be a consumer despite there being a business purpose'.[79] They argue for a more restrictive interpretation that would be more consistent with other UK statute law, common law and European Union law. The issue does not arise under the Victorian legislation or the ACL UCT as they use the formula 'wholly or predominantly for personal, domestic or household use or consumption'.

Thus, the Australian approach was initially more restrictive, denying, as it did, small businesses the right to access protection from UCTs. Recently, UCT protection in Australia has been extended to small businesses defined as having 20 or fewer employees and for contracts with a value of $100,000, and up to $250,000 if the contract adheres for longer than 12 months.[80] Relative inequality has, in this instance, trumped function as the appropriate criteria for UCT protection.

9.2 Standard form contracts

Another common feature of all three UCT provisions is that they only apply to standard terms. The UTCC Regs apply to any term in a contract where the term has not been individually negotiated and the onus of establishing that a term was individually negotiated is on the business.[81] Indeed, a term is always regarded as not being individually negotiated when it has been drafted in advance 'and the consumer has not been able to influence the substance of the term'.[82]

75 Unfair Terms in Consumer Contracts Regulations 1999 (UK), reg 3 (1).
76 Fair Trading Act 1999 (Vic), s 32U (definition of 'consumer').
77 Australian Consumer Law, s 23(3).
78 Scott and Black (n 11) 90.
79 Ibid.
80 Treasury Legislation Amendment (Small Business and Unfair Contract Terms) Act 2015 (passed both houses on 20 October 2015).
81 Unfair Terms in Consumer Contracts Regulations 1999 (UK), reg 3(3).
82 Ibid reg 5(3).

The Victorian legislation defines 'standard form contracts' as one which has been drawn up for 'general use within a particular industry'.[83] The issue of individual negotiation does not arise except as a factor to be considered when determining whether the clause itself is unfair.[84] The Victorian legislation therefore covered any contract based on a standard form. Many of these may well be the subject of individual negotiation. Indeed, it is quite common in some industries, such as building and real estate, for standard form contracts to provide for the exclusion, often by the simple act of ruling through or *tick box* inclusion or deletion, of particular clauses and, further, for such contracts to be supplemented by so-called *special conditions.* The Victorian legislation, therefore, is much broader in application. However, when considering the unfairness of a term, the fact of its individual negotiation has been significant, at least for the Victorian Civil and Administration Tribunal, which hears applications at first instance under its UCTs legislation. Its Chair, Judge Harbison, stated:

> [T]erms of a consumer contract which have been the subject of genuine negotiation should not be lightly declared unfair. This legislation is designed to protect consumers from unfair contracts, not to allow a party to a contract who has genuinely reflected on its terms and negotiated them, to be released from a contract term from which he or she later wishes to be released.[85]

The Productivity Commission considered this point and recommended that negotiated contract terms should be exempt from any UCTs regime as 'parties to negotiated contracts, or their agents, are usually sufficiently sophisticated to ensure acceptable contract outcomes and can reasonably be expected to have their eyes wide open' and therefore, 'it would only be appropriate for a court or tribunal to void negotiated terms in highly special circumstances'.[86]

The ACL UCT, quite clearly, on this point, adopts the intent of the UTCC Regs but by very different legislative means. It uses a rebuttable presumption that the contract is standard form and that, therefore, the provisions apply. If a party to a proceeding under the ACL alleges that a contract is a standard form contract, unless the other party to the proceeding proves otherwise there is a rebuttable presumption to that effect.[87] Should the other party, the supplier, attempt to rebut the presumption, the court, in determining this question, may take into account such matters as it thinks relevant but must take into account certain prescribed matters such as which party had *all or most* of the bargaining power; how effective was the opportunity to negotiate; and whether one party presented a completed contract document to the other at the time of such negotiations.[88]

The burden of proof clearly lies with the supplier to establish that the relevant contract is not a standard contract. It is likely in most cases, therefore, that this burden will be difficult to satisfy. While the definition of 'standard form contracts' is

83 Fair Trading Act 1999 (Vic), s 32U (definition of 'standard form contract').

84 Fair Trading Act 1999 (Vic), s 32X.

85 *Director of Consumer Affairs Victoria v Craig Langley Pty Ltd & Matrix Pilates and Yoga Pty Ltd (Civil Claims)* [2008] VCAT 482, 66.

86 Productivity Commission, *Review of Australia's Consumer Policy Framework,* Inquiry Report No 45 (2008) Vol 2 161.

87 Australian Consumer Law, s 27(1).

88 Ibid s 27(2).

based on the circumstances of the contract as a whole, findings of 'unfairness' apply to individual terms and the contract continues to bind the parties if it is capable of operating without the unfair term.[89] This may frequently be the case, particularly as the ACL UCT, like its UK predecessor, expressly excludes application to 'terms that define the main subject matter of standard form contracts'.[90]

9.3 Excluding the main subject matter or the 'core terms'

In the ACL UCT, the 'core terms' are described as the 'terms that define the main subject matter of standard form contracts' and the heading to the relevant section says that they are 'unaffected'.[91] An 'unaffected' term is one which:

- defines the main subject matter of the contract; or
- sets the upfront price payable under the contract; or
- is a term required or expressly permitted by a law of the Commonwealth or a State or Territory.[92]

The 'upfront price' is defined so as to exclude those fees or charges that are contingent on the occurrence or non-occurrence of a particular event; in other words, those which are usually the subject matter of non-core standard terms. The UTCC Regs exclude from review those terms which relate to the 'definition of the main subject matter of the contract' or the 'adequacy of the price and remuneration'.[93] In *Director General of Fair Trading v First National Bank* (*First National Bank*), it was held by the Court of Appeal that provisions for default on a loan were not excluded terms even though they provided for a cost for such default and, in effect, established virtually a new loan on different terms. The court's reasoning was that the parties did not enter into the agreement on the assumption that the consumer would default and that such default was always contingent.[94]

On appeal, the House of Lords confirmed this point, if not the entirety of the earlier decision. Lord Bingham was clear about the approach to be taken:

> The object of the Act is to protect consumers against the inclusion of unfair and prejudicial terms in standard-form contracts into which they enter and that object would plainly be frustrated if the exemption provisions were so broadly interpreted as to cover any terms other than those falling squarely within it.[95]

However, in *Abbey National*[96] the newly constituted UK Supreme Court distinguished *First National*[97] and found that the relevant charges imposed by the *Abbey National* company on its customers, although technically contingent, were so prevalent (they

89 Ibid s 23(2).
90 Ibid s 26.
91 Ibid.
92 Ibid s 26(2).
93 Unfair Terms in Consumer Contracts Regulations 1999 (UK), reg 6(2).
94 [2000] 1 All ER (Comm) 371.
95 *Director General of Fair Trading v First National Bank plc* [2002] 1 AC 481 [12].
96 *Abbey National plc and Others v The Office of Fair Trading* [2009] EWCA 116.
97 [2000] 1 All ER (Comm) 371.

accounted for over 30 per cent of the revenue raised for the company from the products in question) and common that they were central to the bargain.[98] They were 'core' terms and, therefore, they fell within the exception and were not capable of review under the UCT provisions.[99] The resultant uncertainty has, in part, led to the reform proposals being considered in the Law Commissions' Issues Paper mentioned above.[100]

By contrast, the Victorian legislation does not expressly exclude core terms.

9.4 Defining fairness: principles-based approach

Professor Stephen Corones says that a 'significant feature of the ACL is that it adopts a principles based approach to drafting rather than a rules-based approach'.[101] The example he offers for this claim is the definition of 'unfair term' in section 24(1). Under the ACL, a term is unfair if:

- it would cause a significant imbalance in the parties' rights and obligations arising under the contract; and
- it is not reasonably necessary in order to protect the legitimate interests of the party who would be advantaged by the term; and
- it would cause detriment (whether financial or otherwise) to a party if it were to be applied or relied on.[102]

Other factors are (a) the extent to which the term is transparent and (b) the contract as a whole.[103]

Corones suggests that 'this leaves much work for the courts in deciding what constitutes a "legitimate interest"; what constitutes a "significant imbalance"; and whether the term at issue is "reasonably necessary" to protect the respondent's "legitimate interest"'.[104] Corones sees the *work* as being the province of the courts, though there is an opportunity here for alternative dispute resolution agencies.

9.5 Good faith or significant imbalance?

There is no mention of good faith in the ACL UCT provisions. This is in contrast to the approach of the UTCC Regs, where a term is unfair if it is in breach of good faith and causes significant imbalance in the rights and obligations of the parties:

> A contractual term which has not been individually negotiated shall be regarded as unfair if, contrary to the requirement of good faith, it causes a significant imbalance in the parties' rights and obligations arising under the contact to the detriment of the consumer.[105]

98 [2009] EWCA 116.
99 Ibid [51] *per* Lord Walker.
100 (n 66).
101 S Corones, *The Australian Consumer Law* (Lawbook Co 2011) 7.
102 Australian Consumer Law, s 24(1).
103 Ibid s 24(2).
104 Corones (n 101) 8.
105 Unfair Terms in Consumer Contracts Regulations 1999 (UK), reg 5(1).

The Victorian legislation started out with a reference to 'good faith' in 2001, but this was removed in 2009.

Of more primary importance, and indeed this is the first criteria mentioned in the ACL, is the 'significant imbalance'. Hugh Collins argues that the test 'of significant imbalance of the obligations obviously directs attention to the substantive unfairness of the contract'.[106] Thus, it is pivotal in focusing UCTs legislation on substantive as opposed to procedural unfairness. This formula is common to all three provisions. It is open to more than one interpretation.

As Scott and Black point out in the context of the UTCC Regs, 'significant' could be interpreted as requiring a 'really serious or exceptional' imbalance before the term could be avoided as being unfair. They say this accords with the 'traditional approach of English law to upholding bargains but enabling hard cases to be upset in a consumer context'.[107] Alternatively, the verb associated with the adjective 'significant' is 'signify', which can mean no more than to make something known or to identify it.[108] Thus, the imbalance in rights and obligations need only be capable of clear identification. This removes those which are merely trivial, but leaves many more than those which would be categorised as 'really serious'.

The ACL also requires that a term be considered in the light of the contract as a whole. As Paterson points out, the burden of a particular term must be considered in the light of other possible 'concessions elsewhere in the transaction'.[109] Unfortunately, when considering 'significant imbalance', judges in both the UK and Victoria have tended to conflate the concept with 'good faith'. Whether this will continue to be the case in the latter jurisdiction, after the removal of the good faith stipulation in 2009, remains to be seen. Good faith plays no expressed role in the ACL definition of an unfair term. In the leading case on the UTCC Regs, *First National Bank*, Lord Steyn said: 'it is, however, also right to say that there is a large area of overlap between the concepts of good faith and significant imbalance'.[110]

In the same case, Lord Bingham seemed to give hope to a more mechanical assessment of the balancing of rights and obligations between suppliers and consumers, free from the confusing conflation of 'good faith', by saying: 'The requirement of significant imbalance is met if a term is so weighted in favour of the supplier as to tilt the parties' rights and obligations under the contract in his favour'.[111] His Lordship does, however, muddy the waters by saying the test is 'composite', 'covering both the making and the substance of the contract'.[112]

Lord Steyn is clear, however, that 'any purely procedural or even predominantly procedural interpretation of the requirement of good faith must be rejected'.[113] In Victoria, in the pre-2009 decision of *Jetstar Airways Pty Ltd v Free*,[114] Cavanaugh J observes that 'the requirements of good faith have a procedural aspect and a

106 H Collins, 'Good Faith in European Contract Law' (1994) 14 Oxford Journal of Legal Studies 229, 249.

107 Scott and Black (n 11) 95.

108 A Delbridge and J Bernard, *The Macquarie Concise Dictionary* (The Macquarie Library Ltd 1988) 923.

109 Paterson (n 14) 940.

110 [2002] 1 AC 481, 500.

111 Ibid 494.

112 Ibid.

113 Ibid 500.

114 [2008] VSC 539.

substantive content' and that 'there is no separate requirement of "good faith" in consumer contracts; rather "good faith" is a touchstone which might be employed in determining whether a term in a consumer contract is an unfair term'.[115]

The ACL lacks this touchstone but this does not concern Paterson, who says that its absence from the ACL is 'largely due to continuing uncertainty over the function and meaning of the duty of good faith' under the UTCC regime and contract law generally.[116] In support of this proposition, Paterson cites criticism of the European Union Directive by Professor Hugh Beale[117] in a discussion of good faith in her own co-authored text on contract law[118] and the historical fact of its removal from the Victorian legislation. To this she could have added the clear statement of policy in the 2009 consultation paper on the ACL.[119] The absence of 'good faith' in the ACL UCTs legislation may be no more significant than its absence in consumer contracts themselves.

In the first decision on the ACL UCT, *ACCC v Bytecard Ltd*, the Federal Court found that a term in the standard form contract of an internet service provider which required the consumer to pay for any reconnection costs even if the provider and not the consumer caused the disconnection of services was 'unfair' and declared it void and unenforceable. The significant imbalance in the effect of the term was held sufficient.[120]

9.6 Detriment: actual or likely

The ACL UCT requires that a term cause detriment if relied on. The Bill merely required the 'substantial likelihood' of detriment. The consultation draft explained that:

> This is intended to clarify what is meant by 'detriment' and recognises the restrictions that an express requirement limiting the application of the provision to 'actual' detriment would have on the practical effectiveness of the provision. In requiring proof of a 'substantial likelihood of detriment' more than a hypothetical case of unfairness must be made out.[121]

Whether the shift away from this position to the more 'actual' detriment model finally adopted will have the limitation on the practical effectiveness of the provision foreshadowed in the consultation paper is yet to be seen. The relevant term does not have to be relied on, however, to be capable of being found unfair. Thus, the *actuality* of the detriment may still be, if not hypothetical, then certainly constructed.

115 Ibid [44].
116 Paterson (n 14) 41.
117 H Beale, 'Legislative Control of Fairness: The Directive on Unfair Terms in Consumer Contract' in J Beatson and D Friedman (eds), *Good Faith and Fault in Contract Law* (Clarendon Press 1995) 231, 242–246, which Cavanough J cites with approval in *Jetstar Airways Pty Ltd v Free* [2008] VSC 539.
118 J Paterson, A Robertson and A Duke, *Principles of Contract Law* (3rd edn, Lawbook Co 2009) 582–583.
119 (n 74) 4.
120 [2013] FCA 38.
121 C Bowen, 'The Australian Consumer Law: Consultation on Draft Unfair Contract Terms Provisions' (May 2009) 8.

Lord Steyn in *First National Bank*[122] said 'but the element of detriment to the consumer may not add much, it serves to make clear that the Directive is aimed at significant imbalance against the consumer, rather than the seller or supplier'.[123]

10 The ACL UCT and its predecessors: are they good consumer law?

10.1 Consumers

If good consumer law is less concerned with a functional definition of consumers and consumer law than it is with addressing inequality, then, it is argued small businesses, as a structurally weaker party in most transactions, should be able to claim its protection. Initially, the ACL UCT failed on this point in ways in which the TPA, CRA and indeed the Victorian legislation UCT did not. Small businesses frequently face inequality of bargaining power and standard form contracts. While they have some industry-specific protections, they are largely left to the vagaries of the general law of unconscionable conduct.[124] Interestingly, consumer credit law has been specifically expanded under the NCCP to include loans for personal investment some 13 years after the adoption of the UCCC. Twenty-four years after the passage of the original TPA, small business was given access to its unconscionable conduct provisions.[125] Only five years after the initial adoption of the UCT provisions in the ACL (and ASIC Act) small business can now access UCT protection for contracts up to a prescribed value.[126] Legislative recognition of the relative structural inequality of small business comes at an increasingly swifter pace.

10.2 Standard terms

I argue that it is the structural nature of the inequality of bargaining power which justifies regulatory intervention. The ACL, by creating a presumption in favour of a standard form contract, best achieves this outcome. By identifying the origin of the words themselves, in a contract or standard form term, as the trigger for the application of the relevant provisions, the Victorian legislation ignores the reality of a market where some standard terms can be incorporated after relatively free negotiations. It is an approach focused on form more than substance. Luckily, whether a term is freely negotiated, regardless of its drafting, is a factor in determining unfairness under the Victorian legislation, and the courts have regarded this as significant.

The UTCC Regs achieves a similar outcome on this point but does leave the proof of free negotiation, or its absence, to the consumer. Whether this has been too problematic in practice or not, the ACL approach is clearer and to be preferred.

122 [2000] 1 All ER (Comm) 371.

123 *Director General of Fair Trading v First National Bank plc* [2002] 1 AC 481, 499.

124 For example, the Franchising Code of Conduct in the CCA and the Retail Shop Leases Act 1994 (Qld).

125 Trade Practices (Fair Trading) Amendment Act 1998 (Cth).

126 (n 80).

10.3 Core terms

Scott and Black argue that the exclusion of 'core provisions' in a contract from the UTCC Regs is a 'very significant limit' on their reach and effectiveness. They go so far as to say that this results in the title of the Directive being a misnomer.[127] They also speculate on the possibility of suppliers seeking to define the core provisions as widely as possible.[128]

With respect, this critique seems unjustified. Faced with attempts by banks to exclude default terms and other contingent fees from the effect of the UTCC Regs, the House of Lords and the Court of Appeal, as discussed above, have found in favour of a narrow interpretation of the core terms exclusion in *First National Bank.*[129] On the other hand, in *Abbey National,*[130] as discussed above, more recent decisions did not. Just because a distinction has been applied, and the outcome favoured industry over consumers, does not mean it is unjustified.

The consultation draft for the ACL justifies this exclusion, saying that in the case of both the 'main subject matter' and the 'upfront price', that consumers have choices about whether to enter the contract or not. It is the effective reduction in that choice presented by the non-core standard terms which is the mischief to which the ACL is directed. The Productivity Commission took a similar approach:

> The argument for exclusion rests on the fact that prices are clearly visible to consumers and, unlike many other terms, cannot legitimately be seen as surprises veiled by a complex contract. Unless there are major barriers to effective competition, consumers can elect to avoid contracts with unfair prices. And where there are such barriers, competition policy is the more appropriate vehicle for achieving efficient prices rather than the discretionary use of unfair contracts law to impose de facto price controls.[131]

Paterson does point out, however, that the core terms exemption under the UTCC Regs only applies to the extent that a term has been expressed in plain and intelligible language and that the ACL makes no such provision.[132] Transparency is a factor in the ACL in determining unfairness, but it does not apply to 'main subject matter' and the 'up front price' as these are excluded altogether. Although the Victorian legislation does not expressly exclude core terms, there do not appear to be any relevant cases where such terms were avoided by application of the provisions.

It is the structural nature of the standard terms which serves to undermine the contractual freedom of consumers. By only addressing these and excluding the so-called 'core' terms, the ACL UCT provisions preserve the contractual freedom of both consumers and suppliers.

127 Scott and Black (n 11) 91.
128 Ibid 92.
129 (n 96).
130 [2009] EWCA 116.
131 Productivity Commission n 86, 162.
132 Paterson (n 14) 942.

10.4 Substantive vs procedural unfairness: has enough been done?

Given the approach by the courts in the UK and Victoria, there is no doubt that the ACL, to the extent that it is similar in its drafting to the UTCC Regs and the Victorian legislation, can relieve consumers from UCTs on the grounds of their substantive unfairness without the need to prove any procedural failure in the formation of the contract. Frank Zumbo says the two earlier regimes focus on 'the wording of a contract term and do so in an objective manner by reference to an established and universally applicable standard of unfairness'. By doing so, he asserts, they avoid the dependence of existing concepts of unconscionability on the 'inevitably unique circumstances of each individual case'.[133]

If there was any doubt, for instance, such as might arise by the inclusion of good faith in the definition of unfairness, this has been left out of the ACL and, thus, no requirement for a lack of good faith need be satisfied. This is more consistent, it is argued, with a focus on the substantive unfairness of contractual terms. Matters of good faith go more to the situational and procedural issues raised in particular consumer contracts rather than the more structural nature of unfair standard terms. Addressing these will remedy market failures for more consumers. It makes UCTs good consumer law. Good faith adds little to this.

Paterson expresses some concern that the transparency factor may lead some to argue that procedural fairness should still be 'the determinative consideration' in assessing whether the term is unfair. She makes a very strong argument, relying on recent developments in behavioural economics against such an approach, saying that consumers are unlikely to read the standard terms of the relevant contracts and that even if they did, they are not well placed to either assess their impact or the risks which they impose.[134]

With respect, these fears appear misplaced. The resilience of judicial resistance to the full impact of previous legislative attempts to address contractual unfairness has admittedly been, as discussed above, dogged. Yet, faced with the intent of the UTCC Regs and the Victorian legislation dealing with UCTs, the UK and Victorian courts respectively have grasped the nettle of substantive unfairness alone as a ground for avoiding contracts. The ACL appears drafted with even greater clarity. Its intent is clear. It is more likely to succeed as a means of addressing inequality of bargaining power for consumers faced with standard form contracts than anything that has gone before.

11 Conclusion

The ACL UCT addresses the structural, not circumstantial or incidental, inequality between consumers and suppliers by only applying to standard form contracts. Standard form contracts, as discussed above, present a challenge to traditional precepts of freedom of contract. The common law and other previous statutory attempts to address unfair or unjust contracts have largely failed as consumer law

133 F Zumbo, 'Promoting Fairer Consumer Contracts: Lessons from the United Kingdom and Victoria' (2007) 15 Trade Practices Law Journal 84, 85.

134 Paterson (n 14) 955.

because, I argue, they focus too much on individual and procedural circumstances and do not address the structural nature of standard form consumer contracts.

By excluding its application to core terms, the ACL UCT also maintains as much as possible the autonomy and freedom of both consumers and suppliers to negotiate their own transactions.

While more detailed examples of unfairness are provided in the ACL UCT, it is anchored largely by an open-textured and principles-based proscription against UCTs, allowing for its flexible application so as to achieve its goal of restoring effective consumer contractual freedom without undermining the general law of contract. The ACL UCT provides for a number of flexible responses by regulators short of enforcement by the courts. Alternative dispute resolution schemes will also play a role. The history of similar legislation in the UK[135] and Victoria[136] indicates that non-court forums and flexible regulatory responses will be the most likely way to resolve disputes arising from UCTs.[137]

By addressing non-negotiable unfair terms in standard form contracts, the ACL UCT, like its UK predecessor, without restricting the choices available in the market, enhances the effective freedom of contract for consumers. It is good consumer law.

135 The UK Office of Fair Trading reports that the vast majority of its enforcement actions have involved 'undertakings with no Admissions'. Office of Fair Trading, 'Regulation by Period: Community Infringements Specified UK Laws//Unfair Contract Terms 1999' (April 2012) www.oft.gov.uk/OFTwork/consumer-enforcement/traders/regulation-by-period accessed 1 January 2014.

136 Victorian government, Submission No 72 to Productivity Commission, Inquiry into Australia's Consumer Policy Framework, 22 May 2007, 57.

137 Zumbo (n 133).

11 The fragility of unfair terms law on bank charges

Towards a complex re-litigation in the UK?

Mel Kenny and James Devenney[1]

1 Introduction: interpreting *Abbey National*

At issue in *Abbey National*[2] was whether a contract term which allowed the imposition of supplementary bank charges was exempt from assessment for unfairness under the 1993 European Union (EU) Unfair Terms Directive (UTD), a measure of EU law implemented in the UK in the 1999 Unfair Terms in Consumer Contracts Regulations (UTCCR), because it was a 'core' or 'price' term, or whether it was assessable for fairness as a 'peripheral' and/or 'contingent' term? Was this, moreover, especially the case where the consumer was subsequently surprised by the extent of the charges imposed?

A complex knot of case law in both main UK jurisdictions (England and Wales on the one hand and Scotland on the other) culminated with the ruling in *Abbey National*, in which the Supreme Court held that terms relating to bank charges were, to a significant (if uncertain) extent, exempt from the assessment of unfairness. Yet *Abbey National* seems to amplify the inconsistencies within the domestic case law on unfairness and to be at variance with both the UTD and the central tenets of EU consumer policy. This exemplifies the uneven interface between EU and national consumer laws; an interface which increasingly demands clarification. Attempts at reconceptualisation have been initiated: the Department for Business, Innovation and Skills (BIS) promoted a new Consumer Rights Act,[3] passed on 26 March 2015,[4] while the Law Commissions were asked to clarify the law and address the issue of UTCCR exemption in the wake of *Abbey National*. The results of the Law

1 Our thanks to the conference organisers at the TC Beirne School of Law at the University of Queensland, in particular Karen Fairweather and Paul O'Shea and anonymous reviewers and the editors for their valuable observations. The usual disclaimer applies.

2 *OFT v Abbey National plc* [2009] UKSC 6, [2010] 1 AC 696. JP Devenney, 'Gordian Knots in Europeanised Private Law: Unfair Terms, Bank Charges and Political Compromises', (2011) 62 Northern Ireland Legal Quarterly 33; M Kenny 'Orchestrating Sub-prime Consumer Protection in Retail Banking: *Abbey National* in the Context of Europeanized Private Law' (2011) 19 European Review of Private Law 4.

3 BIS, *Enhancing Consumer Confidence by Clarifying Consumer Law* (Discussion Paper, July 2012): http://discuss.bis.gov.uk/consumer-bill-of-rights accessed 1 January 2015; www.bis.gov.uk/assets/biscore/consumer-issues/docs/e/12-937-enhancing-consumer-consultation-supply-of-goods-services-digital accessed 1 January 2015.

4 The legislation was enacted on 26 March 2015; see www.legislation.gov.uk/ukpga/2015/15/contents. The relevant provisions of the Consumer Rights Act 2015 came into force, after this paper was delivered, on 1 October 2015.

Commissions' deliberations emerged in the 2012 Issues Paper 'Unfair Terms in Consumer Contracts: A New Approach'.[5]

Clearly, *Abbey National* has clear and intriguing parallels to the subsequent Australian case of *Paciocco v ANZ Banking Group*,[6] a case decided on whether the relevant credit card and banking charges could be viewed as penalties. While the fragility of *Paciocco* and its juxtaposition with *Abbey National* will be the subject of elaboration elsewhere, this chapter evaluates the more specific fragility of *Abbey National*, a fragility elaborated in the Law Commissions' attempt at clarification, placing the unfairness exemption in its disjointed context (Section 2). Attention then turns to the dynamics of EU law: domestic UTD implementation and the Supreme Court's failure to refer interpretation of the UTD to the Court of Justice of the European Union (CJEU) (Section 3). The analysis proceeds with a brief consideration of the CJEU approach to unfairness and consumer protection (Section 4). The 2012 Issues Paper, championing the need to *correct* the reach of the UTCCR, is then analysed (Section 5). Finally, the chapter turns to the fragility of the resulting demarcation, the inadequacy of the approach subsequently taken in the 2015 Consumer Rights Act and the danger of a complex re-litigation of *Abbey National* (Section 6).

2 The disjointed 'Europeanised' and domestic context of *Abbey National*

UK consumer protection emerges from overlapping provisions: a 'wildly unsystematic' body of EU directives[7] – composed of measures dealing with *consumer contract formation and the relevant duties to inform*[8] and a couple of directives controlling the *content* of the bargain[9] – cutting across a body of national statute law, doctrine and implementing regulations.[10] Both sets of EU and national provisions have operated on the basis of different understandings of the role of consumer law. National

5 Law Commissions, *Unfair Terms in Consumer Contracts: A New Approach* (Issues Paper, July 2012) http://lawcommission.justice.gov.uk/docs/unfair_terms_in_consumer_contracts_issues.pdf accessed 1 January 2015.

6 *Paciocco v Australia and New Zealand Banking Group Ltd* [2014] FC 35.

7 S Weatherill, 'The Consumer Rights Directive: How and Why a Quest for "Coherence" has (Largely) Failed' (2012) 49 Common Market Law Review 1279, 1280.

8 Directive 85/577/EEC on Doorstep Sales (1985) OJ L372/31 and Directive 97/7/EC on Distance Sales (1997) OJ L144/19 both now repealed by: Directive 2011/83/EU on Consumer Rights (2011) OJ L304/64; Directive 90/314/EEC on Package Travel (1990) OJ L158/59; Directive 2008/122/EC on Timeshares (2009) OJ L33/10; Directive 2000/31/EC on E-Commerce (2000) OJ L178/1; Directive 2002/65/EC on the Distance Marketing of Consumer Financial Services (2002) OJ L271/16; Directive 2005/29/EC on Unfair Business-to-Consumer Commercial Practices (2005) OJ L149/22; Directive 2006/114/EC on Misleading and Comparative Advertising [2006] OJ L376/21; Directive 2007/64/EC on Payment Services (2007) OJ L319/1; Directive 2008/48/EC on Credit Agreements for Consumers (2008) OJ L133/66.

9 Directive 93/13/EEC on Unfair Terms in Consumer Contracts (1993) OJ L95/29; Directive 1999/44/EC on the Sale of Consumer Goods and Associated Guarantees (2000) OJ L160/1. Now both amended by Directive 2011/83/EU.

10 Sale of Goods Act 1979, Supply of Goods and Services Act 1982 and Supply of Goods (Implied Terms) Act 1973, Unfair Contract Terms Act 1977, Unfair Terms in Consumer Contract Regulations (UTCCR) 1999 (SI 1999/2083) (transposing Directive 93/13/EEC) and Consumer Protection from Unfair Trading Regulations 2008 (S.I./2008/1277) (transposing Directive 2005/29/EC on Unfair Commercial Practices).

consumer doctrine has aimed at protecting Lord Denning's 'little man', famously described in *George Mitchell v Finney Lock Seed.*[11] Meanwhile, at least two types of consumer emerged in the EU, depending on whether the context was free movement or consumer policy, and whether the intention was to deregulate national law or to re-regulate the internal market. In the context of the EU consumer directives, based almost exclusively on the 'internal market' legal basis of article 114 of the Treaty on the Functioning of the European Union (TFEU), a sensitive, sometimes even *nonchalant* consumer was deemed to require the highest levels of protection, a *nonchalant* consumer who could rely on national courts to review the fairness of transactions 'of their own motion'.[12] Meanwhile, in the free movement context a more robust consumer, '*reasonably well-informed, reasonably observant and circumspect*' emerged, a consumer in whose name the more idiosyncratic measures of national regulation were to be dismantled.[13] More recently, the importance of 'consumer confidence' to economic growth and market integration has reshaped this 'pluriform' definition of the European consumer.[14]

Predictably, tensions arose along the fault-lines between these regimes. In the case of unfair terms, tension grew between a domestic, privately enforced regime, instituted by the Unfair Contract Terms Act (UCTA) 1977, and targeting, in particular, exemption clauses; and the part-publicly enforced regime via the OFT, now the Competition and Markets Authority (CMA), of the 1993 UTD, a regime targeting *consumer* contracts and implemented in the UK first through the 1994, then the 1999 UTCCR.[15] Given that the UTD was a measure of 'minimum harmonisation', allowing member states to adopt or retain higher national standards, further fractures between the regimes were inevitable.[16]

Moreover, the judicial division of labour adopted to transmit *Europeanised* private law was prone to instability: the CJEU charged with the interpretation of EU law; the national courts with the *application* of that law and required to refer questions of interpretation, under article 267 TFEU, to the CJEU in a spirit of cooperation.[17] Thus, elaboration of the relevant standards was always vulnerable to ad hoc domestic litigation, the unpredictable and different approaches of national judiciaries to

11 *Per* Lord Denning MR, in *George Mitchell (Chesterhall) Ltd v Finney Lock Seeds Ltd* (1983) 2 QB 284 at 297: 'the freedom was all on the side of the big concern.... The big concern said, "Take it or leave it." The little man had no option but to take it. The big concern ... got away with it time after time.'

12 Protection of the 'nonchalant' consumer *inter alia* in Case C-168/05 *Elisa María Mostaza Claro v Centro Móvil Milenium SL* [2006] ECR I-10421 judgment, para 27.

13 V Mak, *Standards of Protection: In Search of the Average Consumer of EU Law in the Proposal for a Consumer Rights Directive* (TISCO Working Paper Finance and Services No.04/2010) http://ssrn.com/abstract=1626115 accessed 1 January 2015; robust consumer in free movement: Case C-210/96 *Gut Springenheide and Rudolf Tusky v Oberkreisdirektor des Kreises Steinfurt* [1998] ECR I-4657 para 37.

14 Mak (n 13). On the importance of consumer confidence, see the EU Commission's 2005 Communication: Healthier, Safer, More Confident Consumers (2005)COM 115 final para 4: 'The Internal Market cannot function properly without consumer confidence.'

15 1994 UTCCR (SI 1994/3159); 1999 UTCCR (n 10). Enforcement powers exercised as of 1 April 2014 by the CMA, replacing the OFT following the Enterprise and Regulatory Reform Act 2013. www.legislation.gov.uk/ukpga/2013/24/contents/enacted accessed 1 January 2015.

16 Article 8 UTD: 'Member States may adopt or retain the most stringent provisions ... in the area covered by this Directive.'

17 Case C-237/02 *Freiburger Kommunalbauten GmbH Baugesellschaft & Co. KG v Ludger Hofstetter and Ulrike Hofstetter* [2004] *ECR* I-3403 para 22. Cooperation of the national court elaborated *inter alia* in Case C-364/92 *SAT Fluggesellschaft v Eurocontrol* [1994] ECR I-43 para 9.

whether questions of interpretation had arisen, the variation in national remedies and the erratic approach taken to CJEU interpretation.[18] National procedural autonomy and the underdeveloped conceptual framework for state liability for failure to refer under article 267 TFEU further fuelled fragmentation.[19] Unsurprisingly, a disjointed regime emerged – a regime which, arguably, favoured the larger multinational enterprise. A welter of initiatives has aimed at reforming this regime.

First, at the EU level, re-alignment has occurred around the concept of 'maximum harmonisation'. This shift from 'minimum' to 'maximum' harmonisation,[20] and in this way seeking to preclude the adoption of national measures of 'upward derogation', has been seen in the EU Directives on Unfair Commercial Practices,[21] on Distance Marketing of Consumer Financial Services[22] and on Consumer Credit.[23] Yet despite this shift, the extent of harmonisation achieved by these measures has been questioned; the House of Lords EU Committee asking, *inter alia*, whether the now more limited scope of the new measures of 'maximum' harmonisation undermined those measures' overall comprehensiveness. Moreover, the Committee also challenged the proposition underlying 'maximum harmonisation', that legislative uniformity is the crucial factor in promoting market integration.[24]

In this vein, the 2011 Consumer Rights Directive (Directive 2011/83/EU), though a measure of 'maximum harmonisation', has emerged from the legislative process as a 'mouse of a directive'.[25] Rather than a comprehensive consolidation, the new Directive simply merged the Distance (Directive 97/7/EC) and doorstep selling (Directive 85/577/EEC) Directives and amended the UTD and the Directive on consumer sales and Guarantees (Directive 1999/44/EC) at the margins.[26] As national consent is needed for any 'maximum harmonisation' measures, a *quid pro quo* results: Member States react by reducing the scope of legislative intervention, realising that '(c)oherent EU law comes at a cost: incoherent national law'.[27]

18 Weatherill (n 7) 1304. M Kenny, 'Options Between Legislative Intervention and Judicial Collaboration: Improving the Effectiveness and Coherence of EU Law?' (2012) 63 Northern Ireland Legal Quarterly 435, 437–438.

19 F Snyder, 'The Effectiveness of European Community Law: Institutions, Processes and Techniques' (1993) 56 Modern Law Review 19, 51. M Broberg and N Fenger, *Preliminary References to the European Court of Justice* (Oxford University Press 2010) 39–46.

20 Consumer Policy Strategy 2002–2006, COM(2002) 208 final, (2002) OJ C137/2; Consumer Policy Strategy 2007–2013: Empowering Consumers, Enhancing Their Welfare, Effectively Protecting Them COM(2007) 99 final.

21 Directive 2005/29/EC (n 8).

22 Directive 2002/65/EC on the Distance Marketing of Consumer Financial Services (n 8). I Ramsay, *Consumer Law and Policy* (2nd edn, Hart 2007) 279–280.

23 Directive 2008/48/EC (n 8).

24 House of Lords' EU Committee, *Consumer Credit in the EU: Harmonisation and Consumer Protection* (2005–2006) www.publications.parliament.uk/pa/ld200506/ldselect/ldeucom/210/210i.pdf accessed 1 January 2015, paras 89 and 230.

25 Weatherill (n 7) 1290.

26 Directive 2011/83/EU on Consumer Rights (n 8) (implementing measures 13 June 2013, application 13 June 2014) http://register.consilium.europa.eu/pdf/en/11/pe00/pe00026.en11.pdf accessed 1 January 2015.

27 Weatherill (n 7) 1315.

Finally, yet broader proposals for a unifying 'consumer protection regulation' have been put forward, including[28] proposals for a common European sales law (CESL) for cross-border sales[29] (which was subsequently unexpectedly withdrawn),[30] a unified EU collective redress mechanism[31] and the introduction of EU alternative (and online) dispute resolution instruments.[32] Ongoing discussion of an EU Civil Code flank these initiatives.[33]

Aside from this, national initiatives have also been launched. These include: the Law Commissions' May 2012 recommendation on a private right of redress for misleading and aggressive practices[34] and, as previously alluded to, the Law Commissions' 2012 Issues Paper. Moreover, the Consumer Rights Act, which was designed to consolidate domestic and EU provisions on business-to-consumer (B2C) contracts, was enacted on 26 March 2015.[35] It specifies in section 62 that contract terms and notices must be fair, and supplies, in sections 64 and 63 respectively, the parameters as to when the assessment of fairness will be excluded and when contract terms may or must be regarded as unfair. Section 68 elaborates on the requirement of transparency, while schedule 2 to the Act seeks to provide guidance on when terms may be regarded as unfair. In determining when a price or subject matter

28 C Twigg-Flesner, 'Time To Do the Job Properly: The Case for a New Approach to EU Consumer Legislation' (2010) 33 Journal of Consumer Policy 355.

29 Proposal for a Regulation on a Common European Sales Law of 11 October 2011 (CESL) COM(2011) 635 final http://ec.europa.eu/justice/contract/files/common_sales_law/regulation_sales_law_en.pdf accessed 1 January 2015.

30 Subsequently see: A Digital Single Market Strategy for Europe (COM(2015) 192 final) and the proposal for a Directive of the European Parliament and of the Council on certain aspects concerning contracts for the online and other distance sales of goods (COM(2015) 0635 final).

31 European Parliament Report 'Towards a Coherent European Approach to Collective Redress' 12 January 2012. A7-0012-2012 www.europarl.europa.eu/sides/getDoc.do?type=REPORT&mode=XML&reference=A7-2012–12&language=EN accessed 1 January 2015.

32 Proposal for a Directive on Consumer ADR (amending Regulation (EC) No 2006/2004 and Directive 2009/22/EC) (COM(2011) 793 final) http://ec.europa.eu/consumers/redress_cons/docs/directive_adr_en.pdf accessed 1 January 2015. Proposal for a Regulation on Consumer ODR (COM(2011) 794 final) http://ec.europa.eu/consumers/redress_cons/docs/odr_regulation_en.pdf accessed 1 January 2015. Criticism: J Davies and E Szyszczak 'ADR: Effective Protection of Consumer Rights?' (2010) European Law Review 695,707; PH Lindblom, 'ADR: The Opiate of the Legal System? Perspectives on Alternative Dispute Resolution Generally and in Sweden' (2008) European Review of Private Law 63, 89.

33 *Policy Options for Progress Towards a European Contract Law for Consumers and Businesses* (Green Paper, COM(2010) 348 final). C Von Bar and E Clive, *Principles, Definitions and Model Rules of European Private Law: Draft Common Frame of Reference* (Oxford University Press, 2010); subsequently CFR initiative: Commission Decision 2010/233/EU; (2010) OJ L105/109.

34 Law Commissions, *Consumer Redress for Misleading and Aggressive Practices* (2012) http://lawcommission.justice.gov.uk/docs/lc332_consumer_redress.pdf accessed 1 January 2015.

35 The 2015 Consumer Rights Act replacing the B2C provisions in the Supply of Goods (Implied Terms) Act 1973, replacing certain B2C provisions in the Sale of Goods Act 1979, replacing B2C provisions in the Supply of Goods and Services Act 1982, superseding B2C provisions in the Sale and Supply of Goods Act 1994, replacing the provisions of the Sale and Supply of Goods to Consumers Regulations 2002 (implementing Directive 1999/44/EC of the European Parliament and of the Council of 25 May 1999 on certain aspects of the sale of consumer goods and associated guarantees (OJ L171/99, 12), replacing B2C provisions of the Unfair Contract Terms Act and replacing the Unfair Terms in Consumer Contract Regulations (implementing Directive 93/13/EEC on unfair terms in consumer contracts (OJ L95/93, 29)).

term is to be considered for fairness, the government has made clear that particular emphasis is placed in the Act on the *transparency* and *prominence* of terms.[36]

This chapter now turns to judgment in *Abbey National* to explore the problematic transposition, interpretation and application of the UTD.

3 *Abbey National*: dynamics of the UTD/UTCCR interplay

Abbey National arose pursuant to litigation and complaints to the Office of Fair Trading (OFT (now CMA))[37] on the excessive level of bank charges in respect of unauthorised overdrafts.[38] As a result of these charges, a small excess on a personal account could result in multiple and significant charges being levied.[39] The precedent of *Dunlop*, in which it had been held that penalties for breach of contract, sums 'extravagant and unconscionable in amount in comparison with the greatest loss that could conceivably … have followed from the breach',[40] were generally unenforceable, was, perhaps unsurprisingly, not followed.[41] *Abbey National* was to be resolved by reference to the interplay of the UTD and the implementing national measures found in the UTCCR.

3.1 Dynamics of the UTD/UTCCR interplay

The UTD provides that unfairness arises in pre-formulated contracts either where there is an imbalance of the parties' rights to the consumer's detriment[42] or where there has been little or no consumer input into the contract formation.[43] In this context contract terms must be written in 'plain, intelligible language' and the

36 *Consumer Rights Bill, Government Response to the Consultations on Consumer Rights* (2013) www.gov.uk/government/uploads/system/uploads/attachment_data/file/274787/bis-13-916-draft-consumer-rights-bill-governemnt-response-to-consultations-on-consumer-rights.pdf accessed 1 January 2015.

37 OFT, 'Personal Current Accounts in the UK' (April 2007) 2, followed by, *inter alia*, OFT 'Personal Current Accounts in the UK: A Market Study' (July 2008).

38 OFT's joint reply and defence to the counterclaims (11 November 2007) *OFT v Abbey National plc* [2008] EWHC 875 (Comm) at www.oft.gov.uk/shared_oft/personal-current-accounts/OFT's-joint-reply-and-def.pdf accessed 1 January 2015.

39 Lord Walker (n 2) para 24.

40 *Dunlop Pneumatic Tyre Co Ltd v Selfridge & Co Ltd* [1915] AC 79 (HL) *per* Lord Dunedin, paras 86–88.

41 *OFT v Abbey National plc* (EWHC) (n 38) *per* Andrew Smith J, para 2. See Kenny (n 2) 47. Unsurprisingly, in the field of *commercial* contracts, recalling Jackson J in *Alfred McAlpine Capital Projects Ltd v Tilebox Ltd* [2005] EWHC 281, para 48 (Pt 3): 'Because the rule about penalties is an anomaly within the law of contract, the courts are predisposed, where possible, to uphold contractual terms which fix the level of damages for breach.' Though continuing: 'This predisposition is even stronger in the case of commercial contracts freely entered into between parties of comparable bargaining power.' Further, para 48 (Pt 4):

> Looking at the bundle of authorities provided in this case, I note only four cases where the relevant clause has been struck down as a penalty. These are *Commissioner of Public Works v Hills* [1906] AC 368, *Bridge v Campbell Discount Co Ltd* [1962] AC 600, *Workers Trust and Merchant Bank Ltd v Dojap Investments Ltd* [1993] AC 573, and *Ariston SRL v Charly Records* (Court of Appeal 13th March 1990). In each of these four cases there was, in fact, a very wide gulf between (a) the level of damages likely to be suffered, and (b) the level of damages stipulated in the contract.

42 Directive 93/13/EEC on Unfair Terms in Consumer Contracts (n 9), article 3(1).

43 Ibid article 3(2).

interpretation most favourable to the consumer is to be adopted.[44] Furthermore, the UTD seeks to strike a balance between improving consumer protection, while ensuring contractual freedom, holding that the unfairness assessment shall not apply to 'the definition of the main subject matter of the contract or to the adequacy of the price and remuneration … as against the services or goods supplied in exchange'.[45] This recalls earlier debate in the UTD's legislative history on the balance to be struck between freedom of contract and consumer protection.[46]

The 1999 UTCCR adopted a copy-out approach to UTD implementation to 'reflect more closely the wording of the Directive'.[47] Regulation 6(2) UTCCR thus provided that the assessment of fairness should not relate: '(a) to the definition of the main subject matter of the contract, or (b) to the adequacy of the price or remuneration, as against the goods or services supplied in exchange'.[48] This was to be interpreted in the light of the general purpose of the UTD.[49] The question which therefore arose was whether the terms and charges at issue were peripheral and therefore subject to unfairness assessment, or whether they constituted 'main subject matter' terms (under Regulation 6(2)(a)) and/or conditions on the adequacy of price (under Regulation 6(2)(b)) and were thus exempted from unfairness assessment.[50]

DGFT v First National Bank (First National) had appeared to bind the national courts in this matter.[51] The case had elaborated UTCCR policy, a policy which, as Lord Bingham put it, aimed at: '(protecting) consumers against the inclusion of unfair and prejudicial terms in standard-form contracts' and requiring a narrow reading of the exemption as, otherwise, UTCCR policy 'would plainly be frustrated'.[52] A purposive interpretation was, as Lord Steyn observed, required; the UTD being the 'dominant text' the aim of which was: 'to improve the functioning of the European market place and the protection of consumers throughout the EC'.[53] However, while the High Court and Court of Appeal followed *First National*,[54] the Supreme Court in *Abbey National* distinguished the case.[55] Following Hugh Collins' highly contestable analysis of the legislative history of the UTD, the

44 Ibid article 5: 'Where there is doubt … the interpretation most favourable to the consumer shall prevail.'
45 Ibid article 4(2).
46 HE Brandner and P Ulmer, 'The Community Directive on Unfair Terms in Consumer Contracts: Some Critical Remarks on the Proposal Submitted by the EC Commission' (1991) 28 Common Market Law Review 647.
47 Explanatory Notes (1999 Unfair Terms in Consumer Contracts Regulations (UTCCR)) (n 10).
48 Ibid regulation 6(2) UTCCR.
49 Case 14/83 *Von Colson and Kamann v Land Nordrhein-Westfalen* [1984] ECR 1891, para 26; Case C-106/89 *Marleasing v La Comercial Internacional de Alimentacion SA*. [1990] ECR I-4135, para 8; *Office of Fair Trading v Foxtons* [2009] EWCA Civ 288, para 42 and *Director General of Fair Trading v First National Bank plc* [2001] UKHL 52, para 31.
50 *OFT v Abbey National plc and others* (2009) EWCA Civ 116.
51 *First National Bank* (n 49) cl 8, para 2. E Macdonald, 'Scope and Fairness of the Unfair Terms in Consumer Contracts Regulations: *Director General of Fair Trading v First National Bank*' (2002) 65 Modern Law Review 763.
52 Ibid *First National, per* Lord Bingham, para 12.
53 Ibid *per* Lord Steyn, para 31.
54 *OFT v Abbey National* (HC) (n 38) and *OFT v Abbey National* (CA) (n 50). E Macdonald, 'Bank Charges and the Core Exemption: *OFT v Abbey National plc*' (2008) 71 Modern Law Review 987.
55 *OFT* (n 2) *per* Lord Walker, para 43.

Supreme Court uncovered an intention in the UTD to enhance freedom of contract, rather than either consumer protection or contractual fairness.[56] More spectacularly, the extent of the charges, accounting for over 30 per cent of the banks' revenue streams, were held to prove that the terms went to the core of the bargain, rather than to refute that the terms could possibly be viewed as fair.[57] Nevertheless, the court did not represent that bank charges could never be challenged; as Lady Hale observed: 'I do not believe any challenge to the fairness of the relevant terms has been made on the basis that they cause the overall package of remuneration paid by those in debit to be excessive.'[58] Obviously, any challenge on these lines would fundamentally question the UK's model of banking services which has long adhered to the approach that banking services are 'free if in credit', an approach which depends on cross-subsidy from the vulnerable to the more affluent. As Devenney observes, it would be a brave court that would classify such an ingrained system as a whole as 'unfair'.[59]

3.2 Special protection for financial services?

But are *First National* and *Abbey National* so easily distinguishable? This author has suggested that one way of distinguishing the cases is to look to the *Europeanised* approach in *First National*, and the more 'formalistic' approach subsequently adopted in *Abbey National*.[60] This can be contrasted with other areas of private law where a more persuasive inverse shift can be observed: from the 'formalistic' approach (in the case of suretyships, in *Singh*)[61] to a more *Europeanised* approach (in *Kufner*).[62] A further counterpoint to suretyships is then seen in *Newham v Khatun* in the context of social housing.[63] Do these cases disclose the increasing prevalence of the *Europeanised* approach or is the explanation altogether simpler: the retrospective introduction of a formalistic special protection for the financial sector drawn up by the Supreme Court for the benefit of the City of London? Or was it always clear that *Abbey National* was to be a *sui generis* ruling, the more policy-oriented panel of Lords Philips, Walker, Mance, Neuberger and Lady Hale, simply lacking the overall private law background of Lords Bingham, Steyn, Hope, Millett and Rodger in *First National*?

56 H Collins, 'Good Faith in European Contract Law' (1994) Oxford Journal of Legal Studies 229. 'What matters … for EC contract law is consumer choice, not consumer rights.'

57 *OFT v Abbey National* (SC) (n 2) *per* Lord Walker, para 51:

> the bank charges levied … constitute part of the price or remuneration for the banking services provided and, in so far as the terms … are in plain intelligible language, no assessment … of the fairness of those terms may relate to their adequacy.

See also at para 41: 'I do not see how (the Court of Appeal) could have come to the conclusion that charges amounting to … 30 per cent of the revenue stream were "not part of the core or essential bargain."'

58 Ibid *per* Lady Hale, para 91.

59 Devenney (n 2) 54.

60 Kenny (n 2) 56–57.

61 *Bank of Scotland v Singh*, 2005 (unreported, 17 June 2005, HC). Held: suretyships outside UTCCR.

62 *Barclays Bank v Kufner* [2008] EWHC 2319; held: suretyships within UTCCR. J Devenney and M Kenny, 'Unfair Terms, Surety Transactions and European Harmonisation: A Crucible of Europeanised Private Law?' (2009) Conveyancer and Property Lawyer 295, 297.

63 *London Borough of Newham v Khatun* [2004] EWCA Civ 55.

3.3 Reference under article 267 TFEU to CJEU?

The confusion generated on the exemption from the unfairness assessment, based as it was on the interpretation of the UTD, begs the question of why reference was not made to the CJEU.[64] On this point the Supreme Court simply averred that, where a court of last resort was unanimous that an appeal should be allowed, the point should be treated as *Acte Clair*.[65] This is a more than a novel reading of *Acte Clair* and stands the *CILFIT* doctrine on its head.[66] Arguably, this is all the more problematic a position to take given the emerging doctrine of state liability for failure to refer a question of interpretation,[67] an unstable doctrine which underscores the need for circumspection in national courts when deciding not to refer to the CJEU.[68] Finally, the Supreme Court's conclusion that the Court of Appeal wrongly applied its interpretation of the exemption from the unfairness assessment was itself dependent on a particular view of the core–ancillary terms dichotomy and effectively concedes that the Supreme Court may also have been wrong on the interpretation.[69]

3.4 Provisional conclusions

While *Abbey National* did not go as far as shutting the door on challenges to bank charges, the chances of reversing the precedent, given the ingrained system of cross-subsidies at the heart of UK banking services, seem remote. Nevertheless, the precise demarcation of a sub-group of challengeable bank charges cases remains unresolved, and, more worryingly, may continue to influence commercial practice in other unprotected sectors of the economy. *Abbey National* thus underscores the problem of harmonising unfairness concepts across different, national legal traditions and patterns of consumer regulation.[70] More generally, *Abbey National* also highlights the weaknesses of the copy-out approach to transposition, whereby the national legislator effectively surrenders the opportunity to tailor national law to local conditions. Further points of criticism of the judgment include: the weight attached to the importance of the bank charges to the institutions' revenue streams;

64 2012 Issues Paper (n 5) paras 5.64–5.67. C Willett, 'General Clauses and the Competing Ethics of European Consumer Law in the UK' (2012) Cambridge Law Journal 412, 440: 'a reference might reveal whether general clauses should be understood by reference to an ethic of self-interest/reliance or an ethic of protection'.

65 *OFT* (n 2) *per* Lord Walker, para 49.

66 Case 283/81 *CILFIT v Ministero della Sanità* [1982] ECR 3415. Kenny (n 2) 55.

67 Case C-224/01 *Köbler v Austria* [2003] ECR I-10239, para 53: 'can be incurred only in the exceptional case where the court has manifestly infringed the applicable law'. Subsequently Case C-173/03 *Traghetti del Mediteranneo SpA v Italy* [2006] ECR I-5177.

68 PJ Wattel, '*Köbler, CILFIT and Welthgrove:* We Can't Go on Meeting Like This' (2004) 41 Common Market Law Review 177, 178–179: 'if a national highest court wants to avoid the real risk of making its government liable it had better ask for a preliminary ruling ... in ... every case involving a question of EC Law'. M Kenny, 'Options Between Legislative Intervention and Judicial Collaboration: Improving the Effectiveness and Coherence of EU Law?' (2012) 63 Northern Ireland Legal Quarterly 435.

69 Devenney (n 2) 51.

70 See M Kenny, J Devenney and L Fox O'Mahony, 'Conceptualising Unconscionability in Europe: In the Kaleidoscope of Private and Public Law' in M Kenny, J Devenney and L Fox O'Mahony, *Unconscionability in European Private Financial Transactions: Protecting the Vulnerable* (Cambridge University Press 2010) 377.

the lack of reference to the policy behind the UTD; and, finally, the Supreme Court's failure to protect the 'reasonable' or 'average' consumer against surprising contract terms.[71]

4 CJEU approach to unfairness and consumer protection

Yet the more convincing reason for the Supreme Court's non-referral to the CJEU in *Abbey National* can be seen in the pro-consumer tenor of the CJEU case law. CJEU case law has, *inter alia*, always insisted that national transposition must be clear and precise, reflecting: 'concern ... that the existing national legislation leaves no doubt as to the effects of the directive upon the legal position of individuals'.[72] Indeed, clarity has been held to be essential:

> It is essential that the legal situation resulting from national implementing measures be sufficiently precise and clear and that individuals be made fully aware of their rights so that ... they may rely on them before the national courts.[73]

Moreover, the CJEU has also insisted that the enforcement of consumer policy should not be simply about remedial action, but should be prospective, aiming to deter future resort to unfair terms: '[T]hat such actions may be brought even though the terms which it is sought to have prohibited have not been used in specific contracts, but have only been recommended.'[74]

Similarly, the CJEU has repeatedly called on national courts to raise the assessment of unfairness of their own motion[75] and has provided guidance on the types of clause, such as exclusive jurisdiction clauses, which 'must be regarded as unfair'.[76] Indeed, in such obvious cases, the CJEU has done more than simply provide the national court with an interpretation of EU law and has effectively determined the substance of the issue.[77] The CJEU has also embellished the rule in *Océano* with the ruling in *Pannon* that a court, where it considers a term unfair, must not apply it unless the consumer opposes that non-application:

> The national court is required to examine, of its own motion, the unfairness of a contractual term where it has available to it the legal and factual elements necessary.... Where it considers such a term to be unfair, it must not apply it, except if the consumer opposes that non-application.[78]

71 S Whittaker, 'Unfair Contract Terms, Unfair Prices and Bank Charges' (2011) 74 Modern Law Review 106, 115.

72 Case C-144/99 *Commission v Netherlands* [2001] ECR I-3541, para 17.

73 Case C-478/99 *Commission v Sweden* [2002] ECR I-4147, para 18.

74 Case C-372/99 *Commission v Italy* [2002] ECR I-819, para 15.

75 Joined Cases C-240-244/98 *Océano Grupo Editorial SA v Rocío Murciano Quintero and Salvat Editores SA v José M. Sanchez Alcón Prades and others*, [2000] ECR I-4941 para 26; Case C-473/00 *Cofidis v Fredout* [2002] ECR I-10875, para 33.

76 *Océano* (n 75) para 23. Casenote: T Corthaut (2002) 8 Columbia Journal of European Law 293.

77 S Whittaker, 'Judicial Interventionism and Consumer Contracts' (2001) 117 Law Quarterly Review 215.

78 Case C-243/08 *Pannon GSM Zrt. v Erzsébet Sustikné Győrfi* [2009] ECR I-4713, para 35.

The parameters to the own-motion review were further elaborated by the CJEU in *Asturcom*, in which it was held that the need for compliance 'cannot be stretched ... to mean that ... a national court is required ... to make up fully for the total inertia on the part of the consumer'.[79] In a similar vein, the CJEU has also outlined UTD policy to 'establish equality between consumers and traders',[80] 'though not ... (preventing) consumers entering into disadvantageous contracts'.[81] A subsidiary purpose of *Europeanised* consumer protection therefore emerges as that of ensuring 'fair competition'.[82]

These points emphasise a tenor in the CJEU case law which is fundamentally at odds with the judgment in *Abbey National*. The *Europeanised* approach promoted by the CJEU is further exemplified in cases such as *Mostaza Claro*, a case in which the purpose of UTD and the national court's duty to assist in the application of that policy was underscored.[83] Similarly, in *De Zotti* it was stressed that, notwithstanding any discretion enjoyed by the national court, minimum standards of protection must always be met.[84] This imperative of protecting the consumer was further bolstered in *Deutsche Tamoil*, in which the CJEU ruled that the parameters lent to national judicial discretion did not mean that compensation could only be reduced.[85]

Ausbanc and *Nemzeti* further developed the CJEU's understanding of the unfairness exemption. *Ausbanc* concerned a pre-formulated term rounding up a variable interest rate in a home loan agreement. In transposition the relevant Spanish legislation had not provided for implementation of article 4(2) UTD and, as article 8 UTD allows a 'more stringent' national approach in 'the area covered by this directive', this was held compatible with the UTD.[86] The court followed AG Trstenjak's analysis that article 4(2) did not 'set the scope' of the UTD, but instead charted a 'type of assessment' which was excluded from unfairness review. Terms describing the 'main subject matter' and 'price' are, by extension, not per se excluded from the scope of the UTD, but may be exempt from a *particular type* of assessment.[87] As AG Trstenjak observed, the UTD proceeded 'on the assumption that even contractual terms relating to the main subject matter or the price/quality ratio may sometimes certainly be unfair'.[88] Though the question of whether the relevant term fell within article 4(2) UTD was left for the national court to decide,[89] Spain was

79 Case C-40/08 *Asturcom Telecomunicaciones SL v Cristina Rodríguez Nogueira* [2009] ECR I-9579.

80 *Océano* (n 74) para 27. 'The system of protection laid down ... is based on the notion that the imbalance between the consumer and the seller or supplier may only be corrected by positive action unconnected with the actual parties to the contract.'

81 Case C-484/08 *Caja de Ahorros y Monte de Piedad de Madrid v Asociación de Usuarios de Servicios Bancarios (Ausbanc)* [2010] ECR I-4785, Opinion, AG Trstenjak, para 40. 'The consumer is not to be protected generally against entering into a disadvantageous transaction; he is deemed to be adequately protected, with regard to the main subject-matter.'

82 Case C-472/10 *Nemzeti Fogyasztóvédelmi Hatóság v Invitel Távközlési Zrt* (6 December 2011) Opinion, AG Trstenjak, para 41.

83 Case C-168/05 *Elisa María Mostaza Claro v Centro Móvil Milenium SL* [2006] ECR I-10421, paras 37–38.

84 Ibid para 36: '[W]ithin ... Art 17(2) ... Member States enjoy a margin of discretion.'

85 Ibid para 24.

86 UTD, article 8 (n 9).

87 *Ausbanc* (n 81) Opinion AG Trstenjak, para 64.

88 2012 Issues Paper (n 5) paras 7.22–7.30. AG Trstenjak, *Ausbanc* (n 81) para 65. E Kapnopoulou, *Das Recht der missbräuchlichen Klauseln in der Europäischen Union* (Tübingen 1997) 105.

89 2012 Issues Paper (n 5) para 7.30.

entitled to extend the level of protection.[90] Meanwhile, in *Nemzeti*, a price escalation clause in a fixed line telephone contract, allowing providers to charge additional unspecified costs for payment by money order, was held similarly assessable for fairness. As AG Trstenjak noted, not all price terms fell within the scope of the UTD exemption: 'the dispute hinges less on the amount of the cost ... than on the entitlement of the defendant ... unilaterally to amend the contract terms'.[91]

5 Response to *Abbey National:* the Law Commissions' 2012 Issues Paper

Unsurprisingly, following *Abbey National* the Law Commissions were asked to address the UTCCR exemption in their 2012 Issues Paper.

5.1 Comparative aspects

Some aspects of the 2012 Issues Paper will be of general interest to comparative private lawyers. First, though the differences between the English and Welsh and the Scottish legal systems are more pronounced in criminal law, differences still obtain in civil law, though unfairness in consumer transactions is not one of them. Nevertheless, there is a perception that *Europeanisation* presents less of a challenge for Scotland's 'mixed system' of law.[92] Second, the common law on unfairness of England and Wales is informed by the wider perspective provided by other common law jurisdictions, which, in turn, have been more or less susceptible to their own forms of subtle *Europeanisation*. This comparative dimension is reflected in Australia in particular in the introduction, in 2010, of the Australian Consumer Law, which was based in part on the UTD and expanded *inter alia* on the concept of the 'upfront price'.[93]

5.2 Domestic dissonance on the unfairness assessment

As to the issue of demarcation, the Law Commissions had the advantage of reflecting on the clash of *Abbey National* and *First National* in the context of subsequent cases, in particular *Ashbourne Management Services (Ashbourne)*,[94] in which Kitchin J held that a term requiring customers to remain as members of a gym for a minimum period of time was assessable for fairness under the UTCCR because the fairness assessment related not to the main subject matter but to the consequences for consumers:

90 *Ausbanc* (n 81), judgment, paras 43–44.

91 *Nemzeti* (n 82) Opinion AG Trstenjak, para 79. 2012 Issues Paper (n 5) paras 7.31–7.41.

92 *Inter alia*, H MacQueen, 'The Common Frame of Reference in Europe' (2010) *Tulane European and Civil Law Forum* 177.

93 2012 Issues Paper (n 5) paras 7.67–7.72: www.consumerlaw.gov.au accessed 1 January 2015. For a common law perspective on unfair terms in the context of insurance law: R Merkin, 'Unfair Terms in Insurance Contracts: A Solution in Search of a Problem' (2012) 23 Insurance Law Journal 272.

94 *OFT v Ashbourne Management Services* [2011] EWHC 1237 (Ch), [2011] ECC 31. 2012 Issues Paper (n 5), paras 5.74–5.83.

> The assessment ... relates to the obligation upon members to pay monthly subscriptions for the minimum period when they have overestimated the use they will make of their memberships and failed to appreciate that unforeseen circumstances may make their continued use of a gym impractical or their memberships unaffordable.... [I]t relates to the consequences to members of early termination in light of the minimum membership period. Accordingly I believe the assessment is not precluded by regulation 6(2).[95]

Ashbourne therefore adds to the kaleidoscope of approaches to unfairness in different private law contexts – *Abbey National, First National, Singh, Kufner* and *Khatun* (above) – and renders it difficult to identify which terms are exempted from the unfairness assessment.[96] Moreover, as the CJEU is the ultimate arbiter of interpretation, any future ruling may change the way the UTD has to be applied.[97] The current law, as the 2012 Issues Paper observes, may therefore 'lull traders into a false sense of security'.[98] Furthermore, any future interpretation is likely to be informed by the pro-consumer tenor of CJEU case law. The Law Commissions describe the shortcomings of *Abbey National* in graphic language: the scope of the exemption is 'unacceptably uncertain' and there is a need to render UTD implementation 'certain enough'.[99]

5.3 Demarcating Regulation 6(2) UTCCR

The 2012 Issues Paper highlights the conflicting propositions contained in *Abbey National:* that some parts of the judgment suggest that terms in plain, intelligible language are exempt and that any term requiring payment may constitute a price term. Similarly, those other parts of the judgment suggest that not all payments constitute the 'price or remuneration'; for example, terms on the grey list, including default payments and price escalation charges, are not exempt in the same way. Finally, that some parts of *Abbey National* suggest that price terms can be challenged as unfair provided the challenge is on grounds that do not relate to their appropriateness.

The Law Commissions conclude that, while *Abbey National* is currently binding, it does not equate to a blanket exemption from unfairness assessment for all possible patternings of contract terms or even those terms solely addressing bank charges. Furthermore, an interpretative decision from the CJEU may fundamentally change the way in which the UTD should be applied.[100] Clearly, any such interpretation is liable to be influenced by the consumer tenor found in the CJEU case law. Finally, the Commissions emphasise that, in terms of implementation, there is no common trend among Member States: while France and the UK have 'copied out' the provisions; Spain omitted transposition (*Ausbanc*) and thereby extended protection;[101]

95 *Ashbourne Management Services* (n 94), Kitchin J, para 175.
96 2012 Issues Paper (n 5) para 1.17.
97 Ibid para 7.73.
98 Ibid para 8.12.
99 Ibid para 8.13.
100 Ibid para 7.73.
101 Case 484/08 *Ausbanc* (n 81), judgment, para 32.

meanwhile, Germany integrated the test.[102] As a result, the Commissions conclude that the scope of the exemption is unacceptably uncertain and a new approach, affording a higher level of protection by narrowing the scope of the exemption, is needed.

5.4 2012 proposals: transparency and prominence

In common with the government's approach in the 2015 Consumer Rights Act (above), the 2012 Issues Paper focuses on the transparency and prominence of the relevant terms and the acknowledgement that exemption from the unfairness assessment does not apply to price escalation (*Nemzeti*), termination (*Ashbourne*) and default charges (*First National*).[103] However, the Law Commissions also recognise the constraints to reform: that any steps taken must be compatible with EU law and the grey list; must preserve the backstop provided by section 3 of the UCTA 1977,[104] while nevertheless ensuring the 'precise and clear' implementation of the UTD. Obviously, there is a tension in relying on *transparency* and *prominence* to deliver the appropriate level of consumer protection[105] while, at the same time, refraining from 'gold-plating' the UTD.[106] Nevertheless, as the Law Commissions note, given the clear danger of a reinterpretation of the UTD, the law as it stands may lull traders into a false sense of security.[107] Implementation must therefore be rendered 'certain enough'.[108]

5.5 2012 proposals: price terms

The Law Commissions therefore proposed that price terms should be excluded from review, but only where they are *transparent* and *prominent*.[109] Terms must therefore be legible, clearly presented, readily available[110] and prominent to the average consumer.[111] They also suggested that contingent fees should fall within the exemption, but again on the proviso that they are transparent and prominent.[112] As far as the grey list was concerned, the Commissions noted that it has assumed greater importance since *Abbey National*. In particular, terms granting traders price discretion need to be addressed in new legislation; is, for example, an explicit statement needed that the exemption does not apply to terms purporting to grant price

102 2012 Issues Paper (n 5) para 7.60.
103 Ibid para 8.16.
104 Section 3, UCTA 1977: 'Trader may not exempt liability for breach of contract, cannot render performance substantially different from that which was reasonably expected.'
105 C Willett and M Morgan-Taylor, 'Recognising the Limits of Transparency in EU Consumer Law' in J Devenney and M Kenny (eds) *European Consumer Protection: Theory and Practice* (Cambridge University Press 2012).
106 2012 Issues Paper (n 5) para 8.5.
107 Ibid para 8.12.
108 Ibid para 8.13.
109 Ibid paras 8.16–8.69.
110 Specified in s 14(3) 2005 Draft Bill reasserting *Thompson v LMS Railway* [1930] 1 KB 41. 2012 Issues Paper (n 5) paras 8.22–8.24.
111 2012 Issues Paper (n 5), paras 8.25–8.28.
112 Ibid para 8.42.

discretion after the consumer has become bound?[113] The Law Commissions acknowledged that price terms may be assessable, provided that any such assessment does not relate to the *appropriateness* of the price for the goods or services supplied. They recalled that once assessment is allowed, regard should be had to all the circumstances of the transaction, including the amount.[114] The Law Commissions considered whether legislation was necessary but concluded that the critical issue was whether any relevant term was part of the essential bargain. If it was not, then all aspects of the term, including the price, were assessable.[115]

5.6 2012 proposals: main subject matter terms

The Law Commissions also proposed the same approach for 'main subject matter' terms,[116] arguing that this followed the approach taken in the 2005 draft legislation. Again, they placed emphasis on the prominence of the relevant term rather than any reference to the parties' reasonable expectations.[117] As regards the 'subject matter' terms contained in the grey list, the Commissions observed that article 3(3) UTD allows unfairness assessment. Furthermore, they held that arbitration or exclusion clauses should always be assessable, however they were presented.[118] They considered the prominence of terms a useful guide to the demarcation of main and incidental terms. Furthermore, the Commissions argued that exclusion and arbitration clauses could not qualify as main terms.[119] They concluded that a new approach, affording a higher level of protection by narrowing the scope of the exemption, is needed.[120] Finally, they raised the issue of whether a statement is required that terms giving discretion on subject matter are to be subject to the unfairness test.[121]

6 Conclusions: *Abbey National* – subverting the system of EU law from within

Both the 'reformulation' now contained in the 2015 Consumer Rights Act and that found in the Law Commissions' 2012 Issues Paper, placed in the context of the realignment of *Europeanised* private law, emphasise the fragility of unfair terms law in the UK and sketches the prospect of a complex re-litigation of the exemption originally provided for in the UTD, *implemented* in the UTCCR and now superseded by the prominent and transparent exemption contained in the 2015 Consumer Rights Act. Re-litigation will inevitably lead to an important parallel readjustment of commercial practice. As *Ashbourne* indicates, this re-litigation could involve the unwinding of a range of cases originally falling within *Abbey National*, both within and outside the area of bank charges. Yet it is doubtful whether the government's response, the Law Commission's 2012 solution to the shortcomings in *Abbey National*

113 Ibid paras 8.54–8.58.
114 Ibid para 8.59–61, *OFT v Foxtons Ltd* [2009] EWHC 1681 (Ch), [2009] 3 EGLR 133.
115 Ibid para 8.64.
116 Ibid paras 8.70–8.83.
117 Ibid para 8.73.
118 Ibid para 8.74.
119 Ibid para 8.76.
120 Ibid para 7.75.
121 Ibid paras 8.79–8.80.

and the final approach adopted in the 2015 Act – reliance on enhancing the transparency and prominence of the relevant terms[122] – is adequate, given the limits of the information model in financial services.[123] Moreover, even if the guidance on the need to correct the scope of the UTCCR definition could somehow be suppressed, *Abbey National* appears implicitly overruled even within the more modest terms of the 2011 Consumer Rights Directive.[124] Meanwhile, the decision not to refer to the CJEU must be placed in the context of the CJEU's commitment to the protective function of the UTD. Moreover, even as a domestic and even common law proposition, dissonance is magnified with the Law Commissions' 'EU secondary law-compliant' reading of the exemption falling behind the scope given in *Ashbourne.* Yet it is equally clear that the Law Commissions were in a difficult position: left to triangulate the conundrum set by the Supreme Court of supporting the general proposition in *Abbey National*, yet, being apprised of the need to correct the reach of the UTCCR, seeking to ensure the clear and precise implementation of the UTD; while relying on transparency and prominence to subvert the role of regulation 6(2) in supplying anything more than a trivial level of consumer protection. Among this confusion the casualties are predictable: the vulnerable UK poor, the goal of effectively regulating the City of London and the cooperative application of EU law in the national higher court. The acid question to emerge from this is: if national instances fail to apply EU law, will the cause of top-down, more invasive EU law making be strengthened, or will national attention instead be reminded of the opportunities to subvert the EU legal system from within?

122 Ibid paras 8.2–8.3, 8.22–8.24, 8.25–8.28, 8.40–8.42, 8.70–8.73. *Government Response to the Consultations on Consumer Protection* (n 36).

123 P Rott. 'Effective Enforcement of Consumer Law: The Comeback of Public Law and Criminal Law' in J Devenney and M Kenny (eds) *European Consumer Protection: Theory and Practice* (Cambridge University Press 2012) 64–81. Willett and Morgan-Taylor (n 105).

124 Consumer Rights Directive, 2011/83/EU (n 8) articles 19 and 22.

12 The regulation of unfair terms in non-professional suretyship agreements

Lessons for the wider European Union harmonisation agenda

James Devenney and Mel Kenny

1 Introduction

This chapter is located in the context of European Union (EU) initiatives aimed at creating a single market in financial services[1] and the increasingly voluminous debate on the future of European private law.[2] The aim of the chapter is to reflect on wider EU regulation and harmonisation initiatives in this area[3] by using contracts of suretyship/guarantee as a case study. In so doing it will focus on situations where the surety/guarantor acts in a non-professional capacity (for example, a family member). The chapter will highlight the polycontextual nature of suretyship transactions and will explore the (largely procedural) protection afforded to a non-professional surety in England and Wales. It will note different approaches to suretyship protection across the EU (the 'uncommon' core)[4] and it will explore the desirability of applying the Unfair Terms in Consumer Contracts Directive[5] to such transactions. The chapter will argue that if EU harmonisation of the law relating to non-professional suretyships is deemed desirable, a dual-track EU harmonisation strategy – involving measures of legislative and non-legislative

1 See Mel Kenny, 'Standing Surety in Europe: Common Core or Tower of Babel' (2007) 70 Modern Law Review 175, 177–179.

2 See, for example, Basil S Markesinis, 'Why a Code is Not the Best Way to Advance the Cause of European Legal Unity' (1997) 5 European Review Private Law 519; Pierre Legrand, 'European Legal Systems are Not Converging' (1997) 45 International and Comparative Law Quarterly 52; Pierre Legrand, 'Against a European Civil Code' (1997) 60 Modern Law Review 44; Pierre Legrand, 'The Impossibility of Legal Transplants' (2003) 4 Maastricht Journal of European and Comparative Law 111; Pierre Legrand, 'Antivonbar' (2006) 1 Journal of Contract Law 1; Christian von Bar, 'From Principles to Codification: Prospects for European Private Law' (2002) 8 Columbia Journal of European Law 379; Ole Lando, 'Does the European Union Need a Civil Code' (2003) Recht der Internationalen Wirtschaft 49; Christian von Bar, Ole Lando and Stephen Swan, 'Communication on European Contract Law: Joint Response of the Commission on European Contract Law and the Study Group on a European Civil Code' (2002) 10 European Review of Private Law 183; Christian Twigg-Flesner, '"Good-Bye Harmonisation by Directives, Hello Cross-Border Only Regulation?" A Way Forward for EU Consumer Contract Law' (2011) European Review of Contract Law 235; Stephen Weatherill, 'The Consumer Rights Directive: How and Why a Quest for "Coherence" has (Largely) Failed' (2012) 49 Common Market Law Review 1279; James Devenney and Mel Kenny (eds), *The Transformation of Private Law: Harmonisation, Consolidation, Codification or Chaos?* (Cambridge University Press 2013).

3 See also James Devenney and Mel Kenny (eds), *Credit, Debt and Investment in Europe* (Cambridge University Press 2012).

4 See, generally, Aurelia Colombi Ciacchi and Stephen Weatherill (eds), *Regulating Unfair Banking Practices in Europe: The Case of Personal Suretyships* (Oxford University Press 2010).

5 Council Directive 93/13/EEC [1993] OJ L95/221.

harmonisation – recommends itself. It will also suggest that by focusing on *problematic* areas, such as non-professional suretyship agreements, it is possible to further illuminate the wider current debate on the future of aspects of European private law and, further, the challenges inherent in the harmonisation of any area of transnational commercial law.

2 The (contested) economic case

The backdrop to this debate is, of course, the view of *some*[6] that whatever the virtues of individual national systems, differences in the laws of Member States negatively impact on the development of the internal market. Thus the Green Paper 'On Policy Options for Progress Towards a European Contract Law for Consumers and Businesses'[7] stated:

> The internal market is built on a multitude of contracts governed by different national contract laws. Yet, differences between national contract laws may entail additional transaction costs and legal uncertainty for businesses and lead to a lack of consumer confidence in the internal market. Divergences in contract law rules may require businesses to adapt their contractual terms. Furthermore, national laws are rarely available in other European languages.... Partly for these reasons, consumers and businesses, in particular small and medium enterprises (SMEs) having limited resources, may be reluctant to engage in cross border transactions. This reluctance would in turn hinder cross border competition to the detriment of societal welfare. Consumers and businesses from small Member States might be particularly disadvantaged.[8]

Yet the economic case is, at best, disputed;[9] and there are issues about legal diversity, competition of legal orders and legal polycentricism in cross-border trade.[10]

3 The EU harmonisation agenda: the story so far

Existing EU interventions in the area of private law have led to fragmentation.[11] This has been, for example, the result of focusing on particular types of contract (such as consumer credit contracts or package travel contracts) or focusing on discrete areas of contract law (such as unfair terms). Fragmentation has also resulted from the way in which Member States have transposed directives, particularly minimum harmonisation directives:

6 Cf Roger Halson and David Campbell, 'Harmonisation and its Discontents: A Transaction Costs Critique of a European Contract Law' in Devenney and Kenny (eds), *The Transformation of Private Law: Harmonisation, Consolidation, Codification or Chaos?* (Cambridge University Press 2013).

7 COM (2010) 348 final.

8 Ibid 2.

9 See, for example, Law Commission, 'An Optional Common European Sales Law: Advantages and Problems Advice to the UK Government' (November 2010) S.51.

10 See Norbert Reich, 'Competition of Legal Orders: A New Paradigm of EC Law?' (1992) 29 Common Market Law Review 861.

11 See James Devenney and Mel Kenny, 'The Private Law Dimension to the "State of the Union" (D)CFR/CESL Initiatives and the Europeanisation of Private Law' in Devenney and Kenny (eds), *The Transformation of Private Law: Harmonisation, Consolidation, Codification or Chaos?* (Cambridge University Press 2013).

> The existing EU consumer protection rules are fragmented basically in two ways ... [including that] ... current directives allow Member States to adopt more stringent rules in their national laws (minimum harmonisation) and many Member States have made use of this possibility in order to ensure a higher level of consumer protection.[12]

The result has been a 'wildly unsystematic'[13] body of law. Some regard the foregoing as evidencing a need for greater EU intervention in this area.[14] One option is to move towards maximum harmonisation directives instead of minimum harmonisation directives. Thus, when the Consumer Rights Directive was first introduced it provided for wide-ranging maximum harmonisation:

> Council Directive 85/577/EEC ... to protect the consumer in respect of contracts negotiated away from business premises, Council Directive 93/13/EEC ... on unfair terms in consumer contracts, Directive 97/7/EC ... on the protection of consumers in respect of distance contracts, Directive 1999/44/EC ... on certain aspects of the sale of consumer goods and associated guarantees, lay down a number of contractual rights for consumers.... Those Directives have been reviewed in the light of experience with a view to simplifying and updating the applicable rules, removing inconsistencies and closing unwanted gaps in the rules. That review has shown that it is appropriate to replace those four Directives by this single Directive. This Directive should accordingly lay down standard rules for the common aspects and move away from the minimum harmonisation approach in the former Directives under which Member States could maintain or adopt stricter national rules.[15]

Yet wholesale use of maximum harmonisation directives ultimately proved too controversial.[16] However, an alternative emerged through one of the most significant initiatives in the search for more coherence in European private law: the publication of Christian von Bar and Eric Clive's, *Principles, Definitions and Model Rules of European Private Law: Draft Common Frame of Reference* ((D)CFR).[17] The magnitude of this work is immediately apparent:

> The following volumes contain the results of the work of the study group on a European Civil Code ... and the Research Group on Existing EU private law.... Nearly two hundred and fifty people of different generations collaborated in the research groups over a period of more than twenty five years. They have reflected important areas of private law.... The perspective is thoroughly European and ... model rules, with comments and notes, bring together rules derived largely from the legal systems of the Member States and the overarching Community law.[18]

12 Commission of the European Communities, *On the Review of the Consumer Acquis* (Green Paper) COM (2006) 744 final, 6.

13 Weatherill, 'The Consumer Rights Directive' (n 2) 1280. See also Twigg-Flesner (n 2).

14 Von Bar, 'From Principles to Codification' (n 2).

15 Original recitals (1)–(2).

16 Cf Weatherill, 'The Consumer Rights Directive' (n 2).

17 Christian von Bar and Eric Clive, *Principles, Definitions and Model Rules of European Private Law: Draft Common Frame of Reference* (Sellier 2009).

18 Ibid 1.

The (D)CFR was published in six volumes spanning ten books, and includes provisions on: general contract law (books II & III); specific contracts such as sales contracts (book IV, part A) and, importantly for present purposes, contracts relating to personal security (book IV, part G); non-contractual obligations (book VI); unjustified enrichment (book VII); and trusts (book X). One of the most controversial aspects of the (D)CFR was its ultimate purpose. Yet the authors of the (D)CFR were keen to stress that:

> The Study Group and the Acquis Group alone, however, bear responsibility for the content of these volumes. In particular, they do not contain a single rule or definition or principle which has been approved or mandated by a politically legitimated body at European or national level (save, of course, where it coincides with existing EU or national legislation). It may be that at a later point in time the DCFR will be carried over at least in part into a CFR, but that is a question for others to decide.[19]

Yet the debate raged:[20] Would the (D)CFR be the precursor to a European Civil Code or would it, for example, merely be used as a toolbox? The controversy was inflamed by the EU Commission's Green Paper 'On Policy Options for Progress Towards a European Contract Law for Consumers and Businesses'.[21] In that paper the Commission set out options for the future of European Contract Law, which included:

- a regulation establishing a European Contract Law (Option 6);
- a regulation establishing a European Civil Code (Option 7);
- a Directive on European Contract Law (Option 5); and
- an optional instrument (Option 4).

It became clear that an optional instrument was the favoured option.[22] The essential idea of an optional instrument was set out in the EU Commission's Green Paper 'On Policy Options for Progress Towards a European Contract Law for Consumers and Businesses':[23]

> A Regulation could set up an optional instrument, which would be conceived as a '2nd Regime' in each Member State, thus providing parties with an option between two regimes of domestic contract law. It would insert into the national

19 Ibid 3.

20 See, generally, Stefan Vogenauer, 'Common Frame of Reference and UNIDROIT Principles of International Commercial Contracts: Coexistence, Competition, or Overkill of Soft Law?' (2010) 6 European Review of Contract Law 143.

21 COM (2010) 348 final.

22
> I have come to the conclusion that as regards contract law, we need a new approach ... that on the one hand helps bring about the single market ... while on the other hand respects Europe's legal diversity and the principle of subsidiarity. For me, this can be achieved by proposing a legal instrument on European Contract Law that is voluntary and optional. That can be chosen by businesses and consumers and then serves as basis for their transactions. That does not replace existing national contract law, but that would exist alongside it.

Commissioner Reding, 'The Next Steps Towards a European Contract Law for Businesses and Consumers' (Speech/11/411) 3 June 2011.

23 COM (2010) 348 final.

> laws of the 27 Member States a comprehensive ... self-standing set of contract law rules which could be chosen by the parties.... It would provide parties, primarily those wishing to operate in the internal market, with an alternative set of rules. The instrument could be applicable in cross-border contracts only, or in both cross-border and domestic contracts.[24]

It also became clear that, at least initially, the scope of any political 'CFR' would be much narrower than the (D)CFR[25] and this was reflected in the Commission draft of 19 August 2011, which contained: provisions of general Contract Law (see parts II, III and VI) for use in relation to the contracts in part IV and V; provisions on the obligations and remedies of the parties to a sales contract or a contract for the supply of digital content (part IV); and provisions on the obligations and remedies of the parties to a related service contract (part V). Shortly thereafter, on 11 October 2011, a full proposal was published.[26] Article 3 of the 2011 proposal stated:

> The parties may agree that the Common European Sales Law governs their cross border contracts for the sale of goods, for the supply of digital content and for the provision of related services within the territorial, material and personal scope as set out in Articles 4 to 7.

Article 7 of the 2011 proposal stated:

> The Common European Sales Law may be used only if the seller of goods or the supplier of digital content is a trader. Where all the parties to a contract are traders, the Common European Sales Law may be used if at least one of those parties is a small or medium-sized enterprise (SME).[27]

24 Ibid 9.

25 See, generally, Vogenauer (n 20).

26

> On October 11th 2011, the European Commission proposed an optional Common European Sales Law will help break down these barriers and give consumers more choice and a high level of protection. It will facilitate trade by offering a single set of rules for cross-border contracts in all 27 EU countries. If traders offer their products on the basis of the Common European Sales law, consumers would have the option of choosing a user-friendly European contract with a high level of protection with just one click of a mouse. The Commission's proposal now needs approval from EU Member States and the European Parliament.

European Commission, 'European Commission Proposes an Optional Common European Sales Law to Boost Trade and Expand Consumer Choice' (Press Release IP/11/1175, 11 October 2011). European Commission, *Proposal for a Regulation of the European Parliament and of the Council on a Common European Sales Law* COM(2011) 635 Final.

27 However, the 2011 Proposed Art 13 stated:

> A Member State may decide to make the Common European Sales Law available for: (a) contracts where the habitual residence of the traders or, in the case of a contract between a trader and a consumer, the habitual residence of the trader, the address indicated by the consumer, the delivery address for goods and the billing address, are located in that Member State; and/or (b) contracts where all the parties are traders but none of them is an SME within the meaning of Art 7(2).

Significantly, a number of matters are outside of the optional instrument:

> All the matters … that are not addressed … are governed by the pre-existing rules of the national law … under Regulations (EC) No 593/2008 and (EC) No 864/2007 or any other relevant conflict of law rule. These issues include legal personality, the invalidity of a contract arising from lack of capacity, illegality … the language of the contract, matters of non-discrimination, representation, plurality of debtors and creditors, change of parties … set off and merger, property law including the transfer of ownership, intellectual property law and the law of torts.[28]

Similarly, the proposal stated that:

> The Common European Sales Law may not be used for contracts between a trader and a consumer where the trader grants or promises to grant to the consumer credit in the form of a deferred payment, loan or other similar financial accommodation. The Common European Sales Law may be used for contracts between a trader and a consumer where goods, digital content or related services of the same kind are supplied on a continuing basis and the consumer pays for such goods, digital content or related services for the duration of the supply by means of instalments.[29]

At that point the proposal for a Common European Sales Law seemed to have almost unstoppable momentum and was subsequently endorsed, in a slightly modified form, by the European Parliament's Committee for Legal Affairs (JURI)[30] and then the European Parliament itself.[31] However, on 16 December 2014 the EU Commission suddenly withdrew the proposed CESL from their 2015 work programme[32]

28 2011 Proposal Recital (27).

29 2011 Proposal, article 6.

30

> The proposal for an optional Common European Sales Law … was backed today by a large majority (19 votes for, 3 against and 2 abstentions) in the leading European Parliament committee on this proposal, the Committee for Legal Affairs (JURI)…. The European Parliament's Legal Affairs Committee is backing the adoption of an optional instrument limited to distance contracts, notably online contracts.

European Commission, 'Optional European Sales Law: Commission Proposal Backed by European Parliament committee' (MEMO/13/792, 17 September 2013).

31

> The proposal for an optional European Sales Law … was backed today by a majority (416 votes for, 159 against and 65 abstentions) in the European Parliament…. Today's plenary vote … follows a positive opinion on the initiative from the Legal Affairs (JURI) Committee (MEMO/13/792) limiting the European Sales Law to distance contracts, notably online contracts … the proposed Regulation will now have to be adopted by the Council of Ministers using the 'ordinary legislative procedure' (co-decision).

European Commission, 'Optional European Sales Law Receives Strong Backing by the European Parliament' (MEMO/14/137, 26 February 2014).

32 COM (2014) 910 final.

only for it to re-emerge in May 2015 in relation to the EU Commission's digital single market strategy.[33]

4 Contracts of suretyship

4.1 Introduction

Having outlined the broad harmonisation landscape, we switch our focus to contracts of suretyship. Here a party to a contract (A) seeks a measure of security in relation to the other party's (B's) performance of the contract by obtaining a guarantee from a third party (C). In essence, a contract of guarantee is a contract under which the guarantor (C) agrees to be answerable for the contractual default of B.[34] Such a contract may be illustrated by a simple example. B (often referred to as the 'principal debtor') wishes to borrow money from A (often referred to as the 'creditor'). A is unwilling to lend money to B unless the debt is guaranteed by C (a 'guarantor'). If C agrees to guarantee repayment of the loan by B, and the money is advanced to B, then if B defaults in repaying the loan C is *prima facie* answerable to A.

In many ways a contract of guarantee is an atypical contract. First, a guarantor undertakes secondary liability. In other words, the guarantor's liability is dependent on the default of the principal debtor.[35] Second, a contract of guarantee is an accessory contract; in general terms a contract of guarantee is dependent on the existence of a principal obligation between the creditor and principal debtor.[36] This leads to the principle that the liability of the guarantor is normally[37] co-extensive with the liability of the principal debtor.[38] Thus if the liability of the principal debtor is reduced, the liability of the guarantor is normally reduced *pro tanto*. Moreover, if the principal obligation is void or unenforceable, there will usually be no liability on the part of the guarantor.[39]

33 The Commission will propose: 1. rules to make cross-border e-commerce easier. This includes harmonised EU rules on contracts and consumer protection when you buy online: whether it is physical goods like shoes or furniture; or digital content like e-books or apps. Consumers are set to benefit from a wider range of rights and offers, while businesses will more easily sell to other EU countries.

European Commission, 'A Digital Single Market for Europe: Commission Sets out 16 Initiatives to Make it Happen' (Press Release IP/15/4919, 6 May 2015).

34 See Robert Bradgate, *Commercial Law* (3rd edn, Butterworths 2000) 538; Ewan McKendrick, *Goode on Commercial Law* (4th edn, Butterworths 2010) 878.

35 See McKendrick (n 34) 878. See also *Vossloh AG v Alpha Trains (UK) Ltd* [2010] EWHC 2443 (Ch).

36 See James Devenney, 'Aspects of Property, Security and Guarantees' in Michael Furmston and Jason Chuah (eds), *Commercial Law* (2nd edn, Pearson Publishing 2012) 2.4.1.2.

37 Ibid, although cf *Moschi v Lep Air Services Ltd* [1973] AC 331, 349 (Lord Diplock).

38 See *Moschi v Lep Air Services Ltd* [1973] AC 331.

39 See, for example, *Coutts & Co v Browne-Lecky* [1947] KB 104.

4.2 Vulnerability

A guarantor, particularly a non-professional guarantor, may occupy a vulnerable position[40] and indeed this is broadly recognised throughout the EU.[41] For example, a guarantor may be in a weak bargaining position with the creditor. Moreover, the guarantor may be in an unenviable position in relation to the principal debtor;[42] for example, in a number of cases which we shall mention below, the guarantor was subjected to considerable pressure from the principal debtor to execute the guarantee. These factors, and other factors,[43] may result in a situation where the guarantor is exposed to liability which is out of all proportion to the guarantor's resources and may result in the guarantor being subject to an indefinite obligation.[44]

Below we shall, briefly, explore the protection which the law of England and Wales affords to non-professional guarantors. In so doing, it is important not to lose sight of the following three general considerations. First, guarantee transactions are polycontextual in nature.[45] In other words, such agreements transcend traditional legal boundaries.[46] Therefore, the protection afforded to guarantors in a particular jurisdiction often involves a complex blend of various legal fields and concepts including (aspects of) specific guarantees law, contract law, property law, consumer law and family law.[47] Moreover, although a detailed consideration of such provisions is beyond the scope of this chapter, insolvency and social welfare provisions also impact on the overall level of guarantor protection in a particular jurisdiction.[48] Second, the level of guarantor protection in any particular jurisdiction often involves balancing the interests of the guarantor and the creditor.[49] Third, as we shall note below, the precise balance between the interests of the guarantor and the interests of the creditor may have wider social and economic consequences.

4.3 The protection afforded to non-professional sureties under the law of England and Wales

In England and Wales, as in other EU Member States, the protection afforded to non-professional sureties is polycontextual in nature.[50] For example, the formality requirements under the Statute of Frauds 1677 provide a measure of protection;

40 See James Devenney, Lorna Fox O'Mahony and Mel Kenny, 'Standing Surety in England and Wales: The Sphinx of Procedural Protection' (2008) Lloyd's Maritime and Commercial Law Quarterly 513, 514; Rebecca Parry, 'The Position of Family Sureties within the Framework of Protection for Consumer Debtors in European Member States' (2005) 13 European Review of Private Law 357.

41 See Parry (n 40).

42 See Devenney *et al.* (n 40) 514.

43 Ibid.

44 Ibid.

45 See Kenny (n 1) and Mel Kenny and James Devenney, 'The Fallacy of the Common Core: Polycontextualism in Surety Protection: A Hard Case in Harmonisation Discourse' in Mads Andenæs and Camilla Baasch Andersen (eds), *The Theory and Practice of Harmonisation* (Edward Elgar Publishing 2012).

46 Mel Kenny and James Devenney, 'The Fallacy of the Common Core'.

47 Ibid.

48 See Parry (n 40) 358. See further, Devenney *et al.* (n 40) and Lorna Fox O'Mahony, *Conceptualising Home: Theories, Laws and Policies* (Hart Publishing 2006) 220–228.

49 See, for example, *Royal Bank of Scotland v Etridge (No 2)* [2001] UKHL 44 [34]–[37].

50 See, further, Devenney *et al.* (n 40).

as Judge Pelling QC stated in *J. Pereira Fernandes SA v Mehta*,[51] the purpose of such provisions:

> [I]s to protect people from being held liable on informal communications because they may be made without sufficient consideration or expressed ambiguously or because such communication might be fraudulently alleged against the party to be charged.

Nevertheless, it is clear that general contractual vitiating factors are the mainstay of the protection afforded to non-professional sureties in England and Wales.[52] In particular, it is clear that much of the protection afforded to non-professional sureties in England and Wales stems from the concept of undue influence.[53] This raises two issues. First, what is the scope of the protection afforded to guarantors by the doctrine of undue influence? Second, what is the position where, as is more common, the contract of guarantee has been induced by the undue influence of the principal debtor rather than by the undue influence of the creditor?

In relation to the first issue, it is not easy to map the doctrine of undue influence for, as Lindley LJ famously noted in *Allcard v Skinner*,[54] 'no Court has ever attempted to define undue influence'.[55] Indeed, in recent years there has been much debate about the jurisprudential basis of the doctrine of undue influence.[56] Thus, Professors Birks and Chin argued that undue influence was essentially about the impairment of consent and that it was 'not necessary for the party claiming relief to point to fraud or unconscionable behaviour on the part of the other'.[57] Yet, while such a

51 [2006] EWHC 813.

52 See, generally, Belinda Fehlberg, *Sexually Transmitted Debt* (Clarendon 1997).

53 Ibid.

54 (1887) 36 Ch D 145.

55 Ibid 183. Lindley LJ did, however, also note (at 181) that undue influence involved 'some unfair and improper conduct, some coercion from outside, some overreaching, some form of cheating and generally, though not always, some personal advantage obtained by a donee placed in some close and confidential relation to the donor'. See further *Bank of Scotland v Bennett* [1997] 3 FCR 193, 216 (James Mumby QC, sitting as a Deputy Judge of the High Court).

56 See, for example, Rick Bigwood, 'Undue Influence: "Impaired Consent" or "Wicked Exploitation"' (1996) 16 Oxford Journal of Legal Studies 503; David Capper, 'Undue Influence and Unconscionability: A Rationalisation' (1998) 114 Law Quarterly Review 479; Mindy Chen-Wishart, 'The O'Brien Principle and Substantive Unfairness' [1997] Cambridge Law Journal 60; Fehlberg (n 52) 24–25; Lara McMurtry, 'Unconscionability and Undue Influence: An Interaction?' [2000] 64 The Conveyancer and Property Lawyer 573; Mike Oldham, '"Neither Borrower Nor Lender Be": The Life of O'Brien' (1995) Child and Family Law Quarterly 104, 108–109; Janet O'Sullivan, 'Undue Influence and Misrepresentation after O'Brien: Making Security Secure' in Francis Rose (ed), *Restitution and Banking Law* (Mansfield Press 1998) 42–69; Mark Pawlowski and James Brown, *Undue Influence and the Family Home* (Cavendish 2001) 7–17, 27–30, 205–212; NS Price, 'Undue Influence: *finis litium*' (1999) 115 Law Quarterly Review 8; Stephen Smith, *Atiyah's Introduction to the Law of Contract* (6th edn, Clarendon 2002) 288–291. This debate is reflected in the relevant case law: *Dunbar Bank plc v Nadeem* [1998] 3 All ER 376; *Credit Lyonnais Bank Nederland NV v Burch* [1997] 1 All ER 144; *Hammond v Osborn* [2002] EWCA Civ 885; *Portman Building Society v Dusangh* [2000] 2 All ER (Comm) 221, 233 (Ward LJ); *Royal Bank of Scotland v Etridge (No 2)* [2001] EWCA Civ 1466; *Irvani v Irvani* [2000] 1 Lloyd's Rep 412; *Barclays Bank plc v Goff* [2001] EWCA Civ 635.

57 Peter Birks and Chin Nyuk Yin, 'On the Nature of Undue Influence', in Jack Beatson and Daniel Friedmann (eds), *Good Faith and Fault in Contract Law* (Clarendon 1995) 61, although cf Peter Birks, 'Undue Influence as Wrongful Exploitation' (2004) 120 Law Quarterly Review 34.

view has gained some support in the case law,[58] Birks and Chin's overall thesis is not unproblematic.[59] For example, it may adopt a pathological view of 'trust',[60] as well as taking an unduly restrictive, capacity-driven view of undue influence.[61] Furthermore, their view does not sit easily with the language employed by the House of Lords in *National Westminster Bank plc v Morgan*,[62] *Barclays Bank plc v O'Brien*[63] and *Royal Bank of Scotland v Etridge (No 2)*,[64] nor with more recent opinions of the Judicial Committee of the Privy Council,[65] all of which adopt an unconscionability-based approach to undue influence.[66] Thus, in *Royal Bank of Scotland v Etridge (No 2)*, Lord Nicholls[67] stated:

> Undue influence is one of the grounds of relief developed by courts of equity as a court of conscience. The objective is to ensure that the influence of one person over another is not abused. In everyday life people constantly seek to influence the decisions of others … the law has set limits to the means properly employable for this purpose … equity extended the reach of the law to other unacceptable forms of persuasion.[68]

Yet, perhaps the most troublesome aspect of Birks and Chin's view of undue influence is their conceptualisation of unconscionability.[69] More specifically, Birks and Chin link the concept of unconscionability to a notion of 'wicked exploitation'. As has been argued elsewhere,[70] unconscionability can be a much more subtle and delicate concept and, accordingly, it can be argued that undue influence is based on a notion of unconscionability with clear parallels to the unconscionable bargain doctrine.[71] Whatever the true jurisprudential basis of undue influence, it is clear that an important dimension of the doctrine of undue influence is its ability to regulate

58 See, for example, *Hammond v Osborn* [2004] EWCA Civ 885, *Turkey v Awadh* [2005] EWCA Civ 382 and *Jennings v Cairns* [2003] EWCA 1935.

59 See Lorna Fox O'Mahony and James Devenney, 'The Elderly, Their Homes and the Unconscionable Bargain Doctrine' in Martin Dixon (ed), *Modern Studies in Property Law – Volume 5* (Hart Publishing 2009).

60 See Mindy Chen-Wishart, 'Undue Influence: Beyond Impaired Consent and Wrongdoing Towards a Relational Analysis' in Andrew Burrows and Alan Rodger (eds), *Mapping the Law: Essays in Memory of Peter Birks* (Oxford University Press 2006) 208.

61 Ibid.

62 [1985] AC 686.

63 [1994] AC 180.

64 [2001] UKHL 44.

65 See *R v Attorney-General for England and Wales* [2003] UKPC 22 and *National Commercial Bank (Jamaica) Ltd v Hew's Executors* [2003] UKPC 51. The late Professor Birks acknowledged the difficulties that these decisions created for his thesis: see Birks, 'Undue Influence as Wrongful Exploitation' (n 57).

66 See further, James Devenney and Adrian Chandler, 'Unconscionability and the Taxonomy of Undue Influence' (2007) Journal of Business Law 541, 541–542.

67 [2001] UKHL 44.

68 Ibid [6]–[7]. Lord Hobhouse added, at [103], that undue influence 'is an equitable wrong committed by the dominant party against the other which makes it unconscionable for the dominant party to enforce his legal rights against the other'. Lord Bingham agreed with Lord Nicholls.

69 See Devenney and Chandler (n 66) 541.

70 Ibid.

71 Ibid.

relational pressures.[72] Difficulties surrounding the application of the doctrine remain:

> The striking feature of this appeal is that fundamental misconceptions (relating to the doctrine of undue influence) persist, even though the doctrine is over 200 years old and its basis and scope were examined by the House of Lords in depth ... less than 3 years ago in the well-known case of *Royal Bank of Scotland Plc v Etridge (No 2)* [2002] 2 AC 773. The continuing confusions matter. Aspects of the instant case demonstrate the need for a wider understanding, both in and outside the legal profession, of the circumstances in which the court will intervene to protect the dependant and the vulnerable in dealings with their property.[73]

This uncertainty could, as we shall note below, affect the desirability of entering into such transactions by banks etc., which might result in a narrowing of access to credit. Here we are usually dealing with three-party situations where the complaint is that the contract of guarantee was procured not by the undue influence of the *creditor* (the bank) but by the undue influence of the *debtor*. In such cases it is more difficult to argue that the contract of guarantee should, automatically, be voidable. More specifically, in such cases the courts must balance both the interests of the guarantor and the creditor in the light of any public interest;[74] and in England and Wales the courts have, essentially, adopted a procedural framework which, if followed by the bank, will protect them.

In *Barclays Bank plc v O'Brien*[75] the House of Lords sought to balance these competing interests through an innovative use of the doctrine of notice. More specifically, where a contract of guarantee had been procured by the undue influence of the debtor, the guarantor would, subject to certain bars, only be entitled to have that transaction set aside if the creditor had notice of the debtor's misconduct. Significantly, notice could be either actual or constructive. Constructive notice, of course, refers to situations where a creditor is deemed to have notice by virtue of a failure to take certain steps, whether or not the creditor in fact has knowledge of the debtor's misconduct.[76] A creditor will, on pain of being fixed with constructive notice, be required to take certain steps in this context if they have been 'put on notice'. In *Barclays Bank plc v O'Brien*, Lord Browne-Wilkinson stated:

> [I]n my judgment a creditor is put on inquiry when a wife offers to stand surety for her husband's debts by the combination of two factors: (a) the transaction is on its face not to the financial advantage of the wife; and (b) there is a substantial risk in transactions of that kind that, in procuring the wife to act as surety,

72 See *Royal Bank of Scotland v Etridge (No 2)* [2001] UKHL 44 [8]. See also *Bainbridge v Browne* (1881) Ch D 188 (parent and child); *Allcard v Skinner* (1887) 36 Ch D 145 (spiritual advisor and advisee); *Avon Finance v Bridger* [1985] 2 All ER 281 (co-habiting couple); *Crédit Lyonnais Bank Nederland NV v Burch* [1997] 1 All ER 144 (employer and employee); *Barclays Bank plc v O'Brien* [1994] 1 AC 180 (husband and wife); *Grosvenor v Sherratt* (1860) 28 Beav 659 (uncle and niece).

73 See also *Niersmans v Pesticcio* [2004] EWCA Civ 372 [2] (Mummery LJ).

74 [2001] UKHL 44 [34]–[37]. See also Devenney *et al.* (n 40) 518.

75 [1994] 1 AC 180.

76 See Devenney *et al.* (n 40).

the husband has committed a legal or equitable wrong that entitles the wife to set aside the transaction.[77]

Subsequently there was some debate as to the correct application of these principles. In particular, in one line of authority there was some confusion as to whether or not a creditor was only put on notice where it knew that the relationship between the husband and wife was one of trust and confidence. Moreover, there was some uncertainty in relation to how these principles applied to other types of relationship. However, in *Royal Bank of Scotland v Etridge*,[78] Lord Nicholls stated that a creditor is always put on enquiry where the relationship between the principal debtor and the guarantor is non-commercial and this is known to the bank.

As noted above, once a creditor is put on enquiry it must, on pain of being fixed with constructive notice, take steps to minimise the risk of undue influence. So what steps must a creditor take in such circumstances? In *Royal Bank of Scotland v Etridge*[79] the House of Lords laid down a procedure for future surety transactions, requiring that creditors obtain from the surety's solicitor confirmation that the guarantor had understood the documentation.[80] In such situations a creditor would normally be obliged to supply the guarantor's solicitor with information on the underlying loan and the principal debtor's indebtedness to enable the solicitor to properly advise the guarantor.[81] Moreover, specific criteria applying to both creditors and their legal advisers in all non-business, third-party security cases have emerged from *Etridge* onward.[82]

5 European harmonisation and the applicability of the unfair terms in Consumer Contracts Regulations 1999 to Contracts of Suretyship

5.1 Introduction

The atypical, polycontextual nature of suretyship agreements has already contributed to difficulties in relation to a number of EU harmonisation initiatives. First, one can point to the debate over whether or not Council Directive 85/577/EEC on contracts negotiated away from business premises[83] covered suretyship transactions and the subsequent controversial, and somewhat ambiguous, decision of the European Court of Justice in *Bayerische Hypothekenbank v Edgar Dietzinger*[84] that some suretyship transactions were covered by that directive. Second, there was the potential

77 [1994] 1 AC 180, 196.
78 [2001] UKHL 44.
79 [2001] UKHL 44.
80 See Devenney *et al.* (n 40) 518.
81 [2001] UKHL 44 [79] (Lord Nicholls) cf also Debra Morris, 'Surety Wives in the House of Lords: Time for Solicitors to "Get Real"?' (2003) 11 Feminist Legal Studies 57.
82 See Devenney *et al.* (n 40) 518. See also *Kapoor v National Westminster Bank plc* [2011] EWHC 2986.
83 1985 OJ L372/31.
84 C-45/96 [1998] ECR 1-1199. See also Peter Rott, 'Consumer Guarantees in the Future Consumer Credit Directive: Mandatory Ban on Consumer Protection?' (2005) 13 European Review of Private Law 383, 384.

gap in consumer protection in relation to suretyship agreements and Council Directive 87/102/EEC[85] for the approximation of the laws, regulations and administrative provisions of the Member States concerning consumer credit, which was exposed by *Berliner Kindl Brauerei AG v Andreas Siepert*.[86] Finally, one can refer to the subsequent debates on a new consumer credit directive in relation to suretyship transactions.[87]

5.2 The unfair terms in Consumer Contracts Regulations 1999[88]

As is well known, the Unfair Terms in Consumer Contract Regulations 1999[89] attempt to implement the EC Council Directive on Unfair Terms in Consumer Contracts.[90] These Regulations are primarily concerned with 'unfair terms in contracts concluded between a *seller or a supplier* and a *consumer*'.[91] Regulation 5(1) defines an 'unfair term' as follows:

> A contractual term which has not been individually negotiated shall be regarded as unfair if, contrary to the requirement of good faith, it causes a significant imbalance in the parties' rights and obligations arising under the contract, to the detriment of the consumer.

Regulation 5(1) is supplemented by schedule 2 of the Regulations which contains a non-exhaustive list of terms which might be regarded as unfair. By virtue of regulation 8, a term which is found to be 'unfair' under the Regulations is not binding on the consumer.

If the Regulations apply to contracts of guarantee, a guarantor may be able to challenge a number of clauses which are common in guarantee transactions[92] provided, of course, that the guarantor is a consumer for the purposes of the

85 1987 OJ L372/31.

86 C208/98 [2000] ECR 1-1741.

87 See Kenny (n 1) 180.

88 Cf Consumer Rights Act 2015, s 2: '(2) "Trader" means a person acting for purposes relating to that person's trade, business, craft or profession, whether acting personally or through another person acting in the trader's name or on the trader's behalf. (3) "Consumer" means an individual acting for purposes that are wholly or mainly outside that individual's trade, business, craft or profession.' The relevant provisions of the Consumer Rights Act 2015 came into force, after delivery of this paper, on 1 October 2015 (subject to transitional provisions). The provisions do not apply to contracts entered into before that date and issues concerning the desirability of applying the unfair terms provisions in the Consumer Rights Act 2015 to contracts of suretyship remain (see pp. 254–256 below).

89 SI 1999/2083.

90 93/13/EEC, OJ L95/221. See further, Hugh Beale, 'Legislative Control of Fairness: The Directive on Unfair Terms in Consumer Contracts' in Jack Beatson and Daniel Friedmann (eds), *Good Faith and Fault in Contract Law* (Clarendon 1995).

91 Regulation 4 (emphasis added). The scope of the Regulations is curtailed by regulation 5(2). However, after some debate, it is now accepted that the Regulations may apply to contracts concerning land: see *London Borough of Newham v Khatun* [2004] EWCA Civ 55.

92 See Geraldine Andrews and Richard Millett, *The Law of Guarantees* (4th edn, Thompson 2005) who argued, at 85, that: 'If the regulations are applied to bank guarantees, it will be seen that there is considerable scope for an interventionist judiciary to redress the balance between creditor and surety significantly.'

Regulations.[93] For example, it has been argued that some clauses which exclude a guarantor's right to be discharged on the occurrence of certain events[94] may be vulnerable if the Regulations apply to such contracts.[95] Yet there is much uncertainty surrounding the issue of whether or not the Regulations apply to contracts of guarantee.[96] At the heart of the debate are the definitions of a 'consumer' and a 'seller/supplier' under the Regulations. A consumer is defined as 'any natural person who ... is acting for purposes which are outside his trade, business or profession', whereas a seller/supplier is defined as 'any natural or legal person who ... is acting for purposes relating to his trade, business or profession'.[97] The difficulty for a guarantor is that even if they are acting for purposes which are outside their trade, business or profession (a consumer), they supply the service. By contrast, the creditor, who is usually acting in the course of business (a seller or supplier), receives the service.[98] As such, this debate is part of the wider debate on whether or not, for the purposes of the Regulations, the consumer must be the recipient of goods or services.[99]

5.3 Case law

In *Bank of Scotland v Singh*[100] Judge Kershaw QC held that the Regulations were not applicable to contracts of guarantee and his view has subsequently been endorsed as both 'convincing'[101] and 'compelling'.[102] Nevertheless, in *Barclays Bank plc v Kufner*,[103] Field J expressly disagreed with these views and held that the Regulations were capable of applying to contracts of guarantee. *Barclays Bank plc v Kufner* centred around a bank loan made to a company (Kel) which was beneficially owned by the defendant. The loan – which was to assist with the purchase of a motor yacht – was secured by a mortgage over the yacht and the defendant provided a guarantee. Thereafter, Kel took steps to sell the yacht to another company (Paelten) and it

93 On the difficulties surrounding the definition of a consumer for the purpose of the Regulations, see, for example, *Standard Bank Ltd v Apostolakis* [2003] ILPr 766; *Heifer International Inc v Christiansen* [2007] EWHC 3015; *Evans v Cherry Tree Finance Ltd* [2008] EWCA Civ 331. For cases specifically dealing with this issue in areas related to the current context, see *Bank of Scotland v Singh* (QBD, unreported, 17 June 2005) and *Barclays Bank plc v Kufner* [2008] EWHC 2319 (Comm). See further Hans Schulte-Nölke, 'EC Consumer Law Compendium: Comparative Analysis' (2008) 730 http://ec.europa.eu/consumers/rights/docs/consumer_law_compendium_comparative_analysis_en_final.pdf accessed 1 December 2015.

94 Discussed further below at p. 255.

95 See Hugh Beale, *Chitty on Contracts* (30th edn, Sweet and Maxwell 2010) [44]–[134].

96 See Gerard McCormack, 'Protection of Surety Guarantors in England: Prophylactics and Procedure' in Aurelia Colombi Ciacchi (ed), *Protection of Non-Professional Sureties in Europe: Formal and Substantive Disparity* (Baden-Baden 2007) 172–173 and James Devenney and Mel Kenny, 'Unfair Terms, Surety Transactions and European Harmonisation: A Crucible of Europeanised Private Law?' (2009) The Conveyancer and Property Lawyer 295.

97 Regulation 3.

98 See also J O'Donovan and J Phillips, *The Modern Contract of Guarantee* (Sweet & Maxwell 2003) 223.

99 Cf Beale (n 95) [15]–[134] and Devenney and Kenny (n 96).

100 (QBD, unreported, 17 June 2005) discussed in Devenney and Kenny (n 96).

101 *Williamson v Governor of the Bank of Scotland* [2006] EWHC 1289 [46] *per* George Bompas QC, sitting as a Deputy Judge.

102 *Manches LLP v Carl Freer* [2006] EWHC 991 [25] *per* Judge Philip Price QC.

103 [2008] EWHC 2319 (Comm). Discussed in detail in Devenney and Kenny (n 96). See also *Royal Bank of Scotland plc v Chandra* [2010] EWHC 105, [2011] EWCA Civ 192.

was agreed that the bank would assist by making a loan to Paelten. The second loan would be secured by a mortgage over the yacht and would also be guaranteed by the defendant. Moreover, as a result, the loan to Kel, along with the defendant's liability under the first guarantee, would be discharged.

However, this plan encountered a technical difficulty: the Paelten mortgage (which was to be registered in Madeira) could not be registered until the Kel mortgage had been discharged. Accordingly the bank discharged the Kel mortgage. The bank then attempted to register the Paelten mortgage but the Madeira Shipping Registry declined to register this mortgage. Thereafter the facts become a little hazy, but it seems that the yacht was sold and its whereabouts became almost impossible to ascertain.

Subsequently the bank sought to enforce the defendant's Kel guarantee and the defendant sought to defend this claim on the ground, *inter alia*, that the bank was in breach of an 'equitable duty' not to release any security for the principal debt.[104] The difficulty for the defendant was that the contract of guarantee included, as is, it seems, commonplace,[105] a clause which purported to allow the bank to release securities for the principal debt. Accordingly the defendant sought to argue that such a clause was not binding on him as a result of the Regulations.[106]

As we have already noted, Field J accepted that the Regulations apply to contracts of guarantee. In so doing, he relied almost exclusively on the judgment of the European Court of Justice in *Bayerische Hypotheken und Wechselbank v Dietzinger*.[107] That case considered the applicability of Council Directive 85/577/EEC (on contracts negotiated away from business premises) to guarantees. Directive 85/577/EEC applies to certain situations where 'a trader supplies goods or services to a consumer'[108] and in a somewhat tentative judgment,[109] the European Court of Justice stated that:

> [I]t is apparent from the wording of Art. 1 of Directive 85/577 and from the ancillary nature of guarantees that the directive covers only a guarantee ancillary to a contract whereby, in the context of 'doorstep selling', a consumer assumes obligations towards the trader with a view to obtaining goods or services from him. Furthermore, since the directive is designed to protect only consumers, a guarantee comes within the scope of the directive only where, in accordance with the first indent of Art. 2, the guarantor has entered into a commitment for a purpose which can be regarded as unconnected with his trade or profession.[110]

In reaching this conclusion, the European Court of Justice held, not without controversy, that nothing in the Directive required 'the person concluding the contract

104 See *Skipton Building Ltd v Stott* [2001] QB 261.
105 See *Kufner* (n 93) [16].
106 See Devenney and Kenny (n 96).
107 Case C-45/96, [1998] ECR I-1199.
108 Article 1.
109 See Kenny (n 1) 180.
110 *Bayerische Hypotheken* (n 107) [20].

under which goods or services are to be supplied to be the person to whom they are supplied'[111] and that guarantees are merely ancillary to the main contract.[112]

5.4 The desirability of applying the unfair terms in Consumer Contracts Regulations 1999 to Contracts of Suretyship

Such an ingenious, if strained,[113] interpretation of the EC Council Directive on Unfair Terms in Consumer Contracts may be welcomed by some on the grounds of the (perceived) benefits of harmonisation in creating a single market in financial transactions.[114] Yet there are a number of counter arguments. First of all, as is demonstrated by the debates on the scope of the new Consumer Credit Directive, there has not been a rush for the harmonisation of this particular area of private law.[115]

Second, the harmonisation of this area of private law is fraught with danger.[116] As noted above, guarantee transactions are polycontextual. Thus the protection afforded to guarantors may be located in a number of different legal fields. Indeed, while most EU Member States have sought to increase the protection afforded to particular guarantors, there is much diversity in the nature of the protection so afforded.[117] Moreover, as has been argued elsewhere, the protection afforded to guarantors in individual EU Member States often involves different, complex, orchestrations of various legal fields, concepts and mechanisms.[118] Thus to tinker with just one aspect of these orchestrations – particularly one as fundamental as the policing of unfair terms – could be dangerous and could have unintended consequences.[119]

Indeed the application of the Regulations to contracts of guarantee may significantly alter the balance of interests between the guarantor and the creditor, and

111 Ibid [19].
112 Ibid [18]. See Devenney and Kenny (n 96).
113 Indeed it is arguable that such an interpretation is even more strained in the context of the EC Council Directive on Unfair Terms in Consumer Contracts than it is in the context of Directive 85/577/EEC on contracts negotiated away from business premises; the former directive provides a framework for addressing terms which cause a significant imbalance in the contract and such an interpretation opens that directive to contracts in which, almost by definition, the benefit flows one way (guarantees): see Devenney and Kenny (n 96) and *Manches LLP v Carl Freer* [2006] EWHC 991 [25] *per* Judge Philip Price QC. Cf also *Berliner Kindl Brauerei AG v Andreas Siepert* C-208/98 [2000] ECR 1-1741 [25]–[26] where the ECJ, in considering Council Directive 87/102/EEC for the approximation of the laws, regulations and administrative provisions of the Member States concerning consumer credit, stated:

> the scope of the Directive cannot be widened to cover contracts of guarantee solely on the ground that such agreements are ancillary to the principal agreement whose performance they underwrite, since there is no support for such an interpretation in the wording of the Directive ... or in its scheme and aims.

114 Cf Beale (n 95) [44]–[136].
115 See McCormack (n 96) 172–173 and Devenney and Kenny (n 96).
116 See Kenny and Devenney (n 45).
117 See Aurelia Colombi Ciacchi, 'Non-legislative Harmonisation of Private Law under the European Constitution: The Case of Unfair Suretyships' (2005) 13 European Review of Private Law 297 and Devenney and Kenny (n 96).
118 Kenny and Devenney (n 45).
119 See Devenney and Kenny (n 96).

this may result in such transactions becoming less attractive to banks, with the consequence that access to credit is narrowed: 'if the regulations are applied to bank guarantees, it will be seen that there is considerable scope for an interventionist judiciary to redress the balance between creditor and surety significantly'.[120] This would have significant social and economic consequences, given the role such transactions play in securing finance for householders:

> The problem ... raised by the present appeals is of comparatively recent origin. It arises out of the substantial growth in home ownership over the last 30 or 40 years. More than two-thirds of householders in the United Kingdom now own their own homes. For most home owning couples, their homes are their most valuable asset. They must surely be free, if they so wish, to use this asset as a means of raising money, whether for the purpose of the husband's business or for any other purpose. Bank finance is in fact by far the most important source of external capital for small businesses with fewer than ten employees. These businesses comprise about 95 per cent of all businesses in the country, responsible for nearly one-third of all employment. If the freedom of home owners to make economic use of their homes is not to be frustrated, a bank must be able to have confidence that a wife's signature of the necessary guarantee and charge will be as binding upon her as is the signature of anyone else on documents which he or she may sign. Otherwise banks will not be willing to lend money on the security of a jointly owned house or flat.[121]

Third, the extent to which such a strained interpretation actually contributes to the harmonisation of this area is debatable.[122] The EC Directive on Unfair Terms in Consumer Contracts is a minimum harmonisation directive which only sought 'to fix in a general way the criteria for assessing the unfair character of contract terms'.[123] The test for unfairness in Regulation 5 was explored in *Director General of Fair Trading v First National Bank plc*,[124] where Lord Bingham stated:

> Good faith in this context is not an artificial or technical concept; nor, since Lord Mansfield was its champion, is it a concept wholly unfamiliar to British lawyers. It looks to good standards of commercial morality and practice.[125]

Such an approach appears to be dependent on the normative assumptions operating in a particular jurisdiction[126] and, as has been argued elsewhere,[127] there are clear differences in such assumptions throughout the EU. Thus one might refer to, for example, the significant differences in the operation of the doctrine of undue

120 Andrews and Millett (n 92) 85.
121 *Royal Bank of Scotland v Etridge (No 2)* [2001] UKHL 44 [34]–[35] (Lord Nicholls).
122 See Devenney and Kenny (n 96).
123 Recital 15.
124 [2002] UKHL 52.
125 Ibid [17].
126 See Devenney and Kenny (n 96).
127 Kenny and Devenney (n 45).

influence in the Republic of Ireland when compared with England and Wales.[128] Thus it has been argued that different Member States use:

> Different benchmarks when reviewing contractual terms. Accordingly, traders cannot use a contractual clause which is valid across the EU, but must instead formulate different clauses for each member state. Hence, considerable obstacles to the functioning of the internal market exist. Providers can only perform pre-formulated contracts across borders with considerable transaction costs.[129]

Nor does it appear that such differences are being superseded by a real EU jurisprudence on unfair terms.[130]

5.5 Concluding remarks

This chapter has highlighted the polycontextual nature of suretyship transactions and the diverse treatment of suretyship transactions across the EU (the 'uncommon' core). The protection afforded to non-professional sureties in individual Member States often involves different complex, context-specific orchestrations of various legal fields, concepts and mechanisms. This diversity underlines the polycontextual, atypical nature of such agreements and can, in part, be explained by the fragmentation of the context in which such agreements operate. In each legal order sureties take a unique place in a subtle web of legal, social and behavioural standards. Thus, when comparing national levels of protection, one needs to consider a

128 See Patrick O'Callaghan, 'Protection from Unfair Suretyships in Ireland' in Aurelia Colombi Ciacchi (ed), *Protection of Non-Professional Sureties in Europe: Formal and Substantive Disparity* (Baden-Baden 2007); John Mee, 'Undue Influence and Bank Guarantees' (2002) 37 Irish Jurist 292.

129 Schulte-Nölke (n 93) 348.

130 See, for example, the European Commission's Report on Directive 93/13/EEC on Unfair Terms in Consumer Contracts (COM (2000) 248 final). At 32 it noted that:

> An analysis of CLAB shows that already 4.4% of the judgments handed down by national courts in the field covered by the Directive refer to the Community text. At the current stage of European construction this is a figure to be proud of and reflects the progressive impact of Community law on the national legal orders.

At 34 it noted that:

> National courts could have referred many cases to the Court of Justice for a preliminary ruling and it would have been very useful if the judgments of the Court of Justice had been able to cast light on the scope of some of the Directive's more obscure provisions. Indeed the doctrine reveals the reluctance of the national courts to refer cases to the Court of Justice in this legal field.

At 30 it noted:

> the application of the same general criterion in two Member States may give rise to very different decisions, as a result of the divergences between the rules of substantive law that apply to different contracts. Hence harmonisation under the Directive is more apparent than real.

See also *Freiburger Kommunalbauten GmbH Baugesellschaft and Co KG v Hofstetter* C-237/02 [2004] ECR-I 3403 [22], where the European Court of Justice noted that it 'may interpret general criteria used by the Community legislation in order to define the concept of unfair terms. However, it should not rule on the application of these general criteria to a particular term.'

number of norms and doctrines, social and economic factors and differences in banking practice. Accordingly, it would be dangerous for any harmonisation strategy in this area to lose sight of overall, context-specific, non-professional surety protection orchestrations in particular Member States. Indeed, such a strategy would risk further fragmentation.

Moreover, a harmonisation strategy in this area with a narrow focus may result in unintended consequences. For example, if additional obligations are placed on creditors it may be that suretyship transactions will tend to lose their appeal and resort will be made, instead, to other types of guarantees. Thus the perverse result of raising protection for sureties may be that the poorest are offered either worse terms on guarantees or refused access to prime credit altogether. The paradox of protection is that less can be more; promoting standards of weak 'constitutional' protection, as in Germany, may ensure broader and less costly access to credit. In effect there may be a double paradox: the 'lower' the effective level of protection, the more equitable the access to credit; the 'higher' the level of protection, the greater the problem of social exclusion. But we can go further: the treble paradox is that our concern with the social justice implications of the treatment of sureties works to obscure the reality of subprime lending in Europe – a paradox in which we can see the danger of charging private law with too many objectives. Furthermore, the problem of over-indebtedness does not disappear in those countries with higher standards of protection; they are simply transformed by the market into charges on mortgages and resort to demand guarantees. Inevitably there are associated implications for banking practice; 'low' protection levels can represent a moral hazard for creditors. Indeed a purely legislative harmonisation is unlikely to resolve all of the issues. It may be that, if harmonisation of the law relating to non-professional suretyships is deemed desirable, a dual-track harmonisation strategy – involving measures of legislative and non-legislative harmonisation – recommends itself.

Index

For Product Safety Concerns and Information please contact our
EU representative GPSR@taylorandfrancis.com Taylor & Francis
Verlag GmbH, Kaufingerstraße 24, 80331 München, Germany